THE GREAT FLOOD . . .
THE TROJAN WAR . . .
THE DESTRUCTION OF
SODOM AND GOMORRAH . . .

- Why is Earth's history a book whose chapters describe war after war?
- Was Man born to be a warrior, or was Mankind taught warfare by the gods?
- Were Aliens responsible for the most cataclysmic events in human history?
- Did the wars on Earth begin in the Heavens, and will celestial events determine Mankind's future on Earth?

THE WARS OF GODS AND MEN

"The Earth Chronicles is a series destined to be one of the most important and controversial additions to literature. Brilliant job . . . must reading!"

Critical Review

Avon Books by
Zecharia Sitchin

THE EARTH CHRONICLES

ZECHARIA SITCHIN

THE WARS OF GODS AND MEN

BOOK III OF THE EARTH CHRONICLES

HARPER

An Imprint of HarperCollinsPublishers

HARPER

An Imprint of HarperCollins*Publishers*
195 Broadway
New York, NY 10007

Copyright © 1985 by Zecharia Sitchin
Foreword copyright © 2007 by Zecharia Sitchin
Excerpt from *The End of Days* copyright © 2007 by Zecharia Sitchin
ISBN: 978-0-06-137927-7
ISBN-10: 0-06-137927-1

First Harper paperback printing: April 2007
First Avon Books paperback printing: June 1985

HarperCollins® and Harper® are trademarks of HarperCollins Publishers.

Printed in the United States of America

Visit Harper paperbacks on the World Wide Web
at www.harpercollins.com

20 19 18 17 16

TABLE OF CONTENTS

FOREWORD

Why is it that Mankind's history seems to be a book with chapter after chapter describing wars? Why is it that after two World Wars in the twentieth century, at least one of which was a war to end all wars, the twenty-first century began with acts of mass terrorism that defied precedent, followed by warfare and fear of a nuclear apocalypse?

Was Man born to be a warrior, doomed to fighting and bloodshed by his very nature—or was Man taught and trained to make war?

Setting out to assess the present by studying the past, *The Wars of Gods and Men* will show that long before men warred with men, the gods battled among themselves; that it was as the Wars of the Gods that the Wars of Man began. Moreover, it will show that the Wars of the Gods, for control of this Earth, had begun on their own planet. The tale of the *Anunnaki* who had come here from Nibiru is also a Book of Wars.

The sources for the reconstruction of events, on Earth as in the heavens, include written records by eyewitnesses—some of them actual reports dictated by the gods themselves. That portions of the tale are reflected in the Bible's book of Genesis is a rewarding bonus, with wider implications for accepting the veracity of the Bible.

More revealing—and unnerving—will be this book's step-by-step reporting of how antagonism, rivalry, and ambition among the gods got out of hand and led to the first use of nuclear weapons on Earth—4,000 years ago. The unintended consequences of the unleashed calamity was the collapse of Mankind's first civilization.

This is fact, not fiction; and it is gratifying that scientific researches subsequent to this book's initial publication have corroborated not only that event's circumstances, but also the precise date we gave it: 2024 B.C.

Will the current twenty-first century A.D. repeat the events of the twenty-first century B.C.? That chapter of the wars of gods and men is yet to be written.

Zecharia Sitchin
New York, October 2006

1

THE WARS OF MAN

In the spring of 1947, a shepherd boy searching for a lost sheep in the barren cliffs overlooking the Dead Sea, discovered a cave that contained Hebrew scrolls hidden inside earthenware jars. Those and other scrolls found in the area in subsequent years—collectively spoken of as the Dead Sea Scrolls—had lain undisturbed for nearly two thousand years, carefully wrapped and hidden away during the turbulent years when Judea challenged the might of the Roman empire.

Was this part of the official library of Jerusalem, carted away to safety before the city and its temple fell in A.D. 70, or—as most scholars assume—a library of the Essenes, a sect of hermits with messianic preoccupations? The opinions are divided, for the library contained both traditional biblical texts as well as writings dealing with the sect's customs, organization, and beliefs.

One of the longest and most complete scrolls, and perhaps the most dramatic, deals with a future war, a kind of Final War. Titled by scholars *The War of the Sons of Light Against the Sons of Darkness,* it envisages spreading warfare—local battles that will first involve Judea's immediate neighbors, which shall increase in ferocity and scope until the whole ancient world would be engulfed: "The first engagement of the Sons of Light against the Sons of Darkness, that is against the army of *Belial,* shall be an attack upon the troops of Edom, Moab, the Ammonites and the Philistine area; then upon that of the Kittians of Assyria; and upon those violators of the Covenant who give them aid. . . ." And after those battles, "they shall advance upon the Kittians of Egypt" and "in due time . . . against the kings of the north."

In this War of Men, the scroll prophesied, the God of Israel shall take an active role:

> On the day the Kittians fall, there shall be mighty combat and carnage, in the presence of the God of Israel;
> For that is the day which He appointed of old for the final battle against the Sons of Darkness.

The Prophet Ezekiel had already prophesied the Last Battle, "in the latter days," involving Gog and Magog, in which the Lord himself shall "smite thy bow out of thy left hand, and will cause thine arrows to fall out of thine right hand." But the Dead Sea scroll went further, foreseeing the actual participation of many gods in the battles, engaged in combat side by side with mortal men:

> On that day, the Company of the Divine and the Congregation of the Mortals shall engage side by side in combat and carnage.
> The Sons of Light shall battle against the Sons of Darkness with a show of godlike might, amid uproarious tumult, amid the war cries of gods and men.

Though Crusaders, Saracens, and countless others in historical times have gone to war "in the name of God," the belief that in a war to come the Lord himself shall be actually present on the battlefield, and that gods and men would fight side by side, sounds as fantasy, to be treated allegorically at best. Yet it is not as extraordinary a notion as it may appear to be, for in earlier times, it was indeed believed that the Wars of Men were not only decreed by the gods but were also fought with the gods' active participation.

One of the most romanticized wars, when "love had launched a thousand ships," was the War of Troy, between the Achaean Greeks and the Trojans. It was, know we not, launched by the Greeks to force the Trojans to return the beautiful Helen to her lawful spouse. Yet an epic Greek tale, the *Kypria,* represented the war as a premeditated scheme by the great god Zeus:

> There was a time when thousands upon thousands of men encumbered the broad bosom of the Earth. And having pity on them, Zeus in his great wisdom resolved to lighten Earth's burden.
> So he caused the strife at Ilion (Troy) to that end; that through death he might make a void in the race of men.

Homer, the Greek storyteller who related the war's events in the *Iliad,* blamed the whim of the gods for instigating the conflict and for turning and twisting it to its ultimate major proportions. Acting directly and indirectly, sometimes seen and sometimes unseen, the various gods nudged the principal actors of this human drama to their fates. And behind it all was Jove (Jupiter/Zeus): "While the other gods and the armed warriors on the plain slept soundly, Jove was wakeful, for he was thinking how to do honor to Achilles and destroy much people at the ships of the Achaeans.''

Even before the battle was joined, the god Apollo began the hostilities: ''He sat himself down away from the ships with a face as dark as night, and his silver bow rang death as he shot his arrow in the midst of them [the Achaeans] . . . For nine whole days he shot his arrows among the people. . . . And all day long, the pyres of the dead were burning.'' When the contending sides agreed to postpone hostilities so that their leaders might decide the issue in hand-to-hand combat, the unhappy gods instructed the goddess Minerva: ''Go at once into the Trojan and Achaean hosts, and contrive that the Trojans shall be the first to break their oaths and set upon the Achaeans.'' Eager for the mission, Minerva ''shot through the sky as some brilliant meteor . . . a fiery train of light followed in her wake.'' Later on, lest the raging warfare cease for the night, Minerva turned night into day by lighting up the battlefield: She ''lifted the thick veil of darkness from their eyes, and much light fell upon them, both on the side of the ships and on where the fight was raging; and the Achaeans could see Hector and all his men.''

As the battles raged on and on, sometimes pitching one hero against another, the gods, too, kept a watchful eye over individual warriors, swooping down to snatch away a beleaguered hero or to steady a driverless chariot. But when the gods and goddesses, finding themselves on opposing sides, began to hurt each other, Zeus called a halt, ordering them to keep out of the mortals' fighting.

The respite did not last long, for many of the leading combatants were sons of gods or goddesses (by human mates). Especially angered was Mars, when his son Ascalaphus was pierced to death by one of the Achaeans. ''Do not blame me, ye gods that dwell in heaven, if I go to the ships of the Achaeans and avenge the death of my son,'' Mars announced to the other Immortals, ''even if in the end I shall be struck by Jove's lightning and shall lie in blood and dust among the corpses.''

''So long as the gods held themselves aloof from the mortal warriors,'' wrote Homer, ''the Achaeans were triumphant, for Achilles who has long refused to fight was now with them.'' But in view of the mounting anger among the gods, and the help the Achaeans were now getting from the demigod Achilles, Jove changed his mind:

"For my own part, I shall stay here,
seated on Mount Olympus, and look on in peace.
But you others, do go among the Trojans and Achaeans,
and help either side as you might be disposed."
Thus spake Jove, and gave the word for war;
Whereon the gods took their several sides
and went into battle.

The Battle of Troy, indeed Troy itself, were long thought of as just part of the fascinating but incredible Greek legends, which scholars have tolerantly called mythology. Troy and the events pertaining to it were still considered to be purely mythological when Charles McLaren suggested, back in 1822, that a certain mound in eastern Turkey, called Hissarlik, was the site of the Homeric Troy. It was only when a businessman named Heinrich Schliemann, risking his own money, came up with spectacular discoveries as he dug up the mound in 1870, that scholars began to acknowledge the existence of Troy. It is now accepted that the Battle of Troy had actually taken place in the thirteenth century B.C. It was then, according to the Greek sources, that gods and men had fought side by side; in such beliefs the Greeks were not alone.

In those days, though the tip of Asia Minor facing Europe and the Aegean Sea were dotted with what were essentially Greek settlements, Asia Minor proper was dominated by the Hittites. Known at first to modern scholars only from biblical references, then from Egyptian inscriptions, the Hittites and their kingdom—Hatti—also came to life as archaeologists began to uncover their ancient cities.

The decipherment of the Hittite script and their Indo-European language made it possible to trace their origins to the second millennium B.C., when Aryan tribes began to migrate from the Caucasus area—some southeast to India, others southwest to Asia Minor. The Hittite kingdom flourished circa 1750 B.C. and began to decline five hundred years later. It was then that the Hittites were harassed by incursions from across the Aegean Sea. The Hittites spoke of the invaders as the people of Achiyawa; many scholars believe that they were the very same people whom Homer called Achioi—the Achaeans, whose attack upon the western tip of Asia Minor he immortalized in the *Iliad*.

For centuries prior to the war of Troy, the Hittites expanded their kingdom to imperial proportions, claiming to have done so upon the orders of their supreme god TESHUB ("The Stormer").

His olden title was "Storm God Whose Strength Makes Dead," and Hittite kings sometimes claimed that the god had actually taken a hand in the battle: "The mighty Stormgod, my Lord," [wrote the king Murshilis], "showed his divine power and shot a thunderbolt" at the enemy, helping to defeat it. Also aiding the Hittites in battle was the goddess ISHTAR, whose epithet was "Lady of the battlefield." It was to her "Divine Power" that many a victory was attributed, as she "came down [from the skies] to smite the hostile countries."

Hittite influence, as many references in the Old Testament indicate, extended south into Canaan; but they were there as settlers, not as conquerors. While they treated Canaan as a neutral zone, laying to it no claim, this was not the attitude of the Egyptians. Repeatedly the Pharaohs sought to extend their rule northward to Canaan and the Cedar Land (Lebanon); they succeeded in doing so, circa 1470 B.C., when they defeated a coalition of Canaanite kings at Megiddo.

The Old Testament, and inscriptions left by the Hittites' foes, pictured the Hittites as expert warriors who perfected the use of the chariot in the ancient Near East. But the Hittites' own inscriptions suggest that they went to war only when the gods gave the word, that the enemy was offered a chance to surrender peacefully before hostilities began, and that once a war was won, the Hittites were satisfied to receive tribute and take captives: the cities were not sacked; the populace was not massacred.

But Thothmes III, the Pharaoh who was victorious at the battle of Megiddo, was proud to say in his inscriptions: "Now his majesty went north, plundering towns and laying encampments waste." Of a vanquished king the Pharaoh wrote: "I desolated his towns, set fire to his encampments, made mounds of them; their resettlement can never take place. All the people I captured, I made prisoners; their countless cattle I carried off, and their goods as well. I took away every resource of life; I cut down their grain and felled all their groves and all their pleasant trees. I totally destroyed it." It was all done, the Pharaoh wrote, on the say-so of AMON-RA, his god.

The vicious nature of Egyptian warfare and the pitiless destructiveness they inflicted upon a vanquished foe were subjects of boastful inscriptions. The Pharaoh Pepi I, for example, commemorated his victory over the Asiatic "sand-dwellers" in a poem which hailed the army which "hacked up the land of the sand-dwellers . . . cut down its fig trees and vines . . . cast fire into all its dwellings, killed its people by many tens of thousands.'' The commemorative inscriptions were accompanied by vivid depictions of the battle scenes (Fig. 1).

Fig. 1

Adhering to this wanton tradition, the Pharaoh Pi-Ankhy, who sent troops from Upper Egypt to subdue the rebellious Lower Egypt, was enraged by his generals' suggestion that adversaries who survived the battle be spared. Vowing ''destruction forever,'' the Pharaoh announced that he would come to the captured city ''to ruin that which had remained.'' For this, he stated, ''My father Amon praises me.''

The god Amon, to whose battle orders the Egyptians attributed their viciousness, found his match in the God of Israel. In the words of the Prophet Jeremiah, ''Thus sayeth the Lord of Hosts, the God of Israel: 'I will punish Amon, god of Thebes, and those who trust in him, and shall bring retribution upon Egypt and its gods, its Pharaoh and its kings.' '' This, we learn from the Bible, was an ongoing confrontation; nearly a thousand years earlier, in the days of the Exodus, Yahweh, the God of Israel, smote Egypt with a series of afflictions intended not only to soften the heart of its ruler but also as ''judgments against all the gods of Egypt.''

The miraculous departure of the Israelites out of bondage in Egypt to the Promised Land was attributed in the biblical tale of Exodus to the direct intervention of Yahweh in those momentous events:

And they journeyed from Succoth
and encamped at Etham, at the edge of the desert.
And Yahweh went forth before them,
by day in a pillar of cloud to lead them the way,
and by night in a pillar of fire to give them light.

There then ensued a sea battle of which the Pharaoh preferred to
leave no inscriptions; we know of it from the Book of Exodus:

And the heart of the Pharaoh and his servants
was changed with respect to the people. . . .
And the Egyptians pursued after them,
and they overtook them encamped by the sea. . . .

And Yahweh drove back the sea with a strong east wind
all that night, and dried up the waters;
and the waters separated.
And the Children of Israel went into the midst of the sea
upon dry ground. . . .

At daybreak, when the Egyptians realized what had happened,
the Pharaoh ordered his chariots after the Israelites. But:

It came to pass at the time of the morning watch
that Yahweh surveyed the camp of the Egyptians
from the pillar of fire and cloud;
And he stunned the Egyptian camp
and loosened the wheels of their chariots,
making their driving difficult.
And the Egyptians said:
"Let us flee from the Israelites,
for Yahweh fighteth for them against Egypt."

But the Egyptian ruler pursuing the Israelites ordered his chariots
to press on with the attack. The result was calamitous for the Egyptians:

And the waters returned,
and covered the chariots and the horsemen
and all the host of the Pharaoh that was following them;
not one of them remained. . . .
And Israel beheld the great power
which Yahweh had shown upon the Egyptians.

The biblical language is almost identical to the words of a later Pharaoh, Ramses II, used by him to describe the miraculous appearance of Amon-Ra at his side during a decisive battle fought with the Hittites in 1286 B.C.

Taking place at the fortress of Kadesh in Lebanon, the battle pitted four divisions of the Pharaoh Ramses II against forces mobilized by the Hittite king Muwatallis from all parts of his empire. It ended with an Egyptian retreat, cutting short Egypt's northward thrust toward Syria and Mesopotamia. It also drained Hittite resources and left them weakened and exposed.

The Hittite victory might have been more decisive, for they had almost captured the Pharaoh himself. Only partial Hittite inscriptions dealing with the battle have been found; but Ramses, on his return to Egypt, saw fit to describe in detail the miracle of his escape.

Fig. 2

His inscriptions on temple walls, accompanied by detailed illustrations (Fig. 2), relate how the Egyptian armies had reached Kadesh and encamped south of it, readying themselves for the battle. Surprisingly the Hittite enemy did not step forward to do battle. Ramses then ordered two of his divisions to advance toward the fortress. It was then that the Hittite chariots appeared as if from nowhere, attacking the advancing divisions from behind and causing havoc in the encampments of the two others.

As the Egyptian troops began to flee in panic, Ramses suddenly realized that "His Majesty was all alone with his bodyguard"; and "when the king looked behind him, he saw that he was blocked off by 2,500 chariots"—not his own but of the Hittites. Abandoned by his officers, charioteers, and infantry, Ramses turned to his god, reminding him that he finds himself in this predicament only because he had followed the god's orders:

And His Majesty said:
"What now, my Father Amon?
Has a father forgotten his son?
Have I ever done anything without you?
Whatever I did or did not do,
was it not in accordance with your commands?"

Reminding the Egyptian god that the enemy was beholden to other gods, Ramses went on to ask: "What are these Asiatics to you, O Amon? These wretches who know nothing of thee, O God?"

As Ramses went on pleading with his god Amon to save him, for the god's powers were greater than those of "millions of foot soldiers, of hundreds of thousands of chariot-soldiers," a miracle happened: the god showed up on the battlefield!

Amon heard when I called him.
He held out his hand to me, and I rejoiced.
He stood behind me and called out:
"Forward! Forward!
Ramses, beloved of Amon, I am with thee!"

Following the command of his god, Ramses tore into the enemy troops. Under the influence of the god the Hittites were inexplicably enfeebled: "their hands dropped to their sides, they were unable to shoot their arrows nor raise their spears." And they called unto one another: "This is no mortal who is among us: this is a mighty god; his deeds are not the deeds of a man; a god is in his limbs." Thus unopposed, slaying the enemy left and right, Ramses managed to escape.

After the death of Muwatallis, Egypt and the Hittite kingdom signed a peace treaty, and the reigning Pharaoh took a Hittite princess to be his principal wife. The peace was needed because not only the Hittites but also the Egyptians were increasingly coming under attack by "Peoples of the Sea"—invaders from Crete and other Greek islands. They gained a foothold on the Mediterranean coast of Canaan to become the biblical Philistines; but their attacks on Egypt proper were beaten back by the Pharaoh Ramses III, who commemorated the battle scenes on temple walls (Fig. 3). He attributed his victories to his strict adherence to ''the plans of the All-Lord, my august divine father, the Lord of the Gods.'' It was to his god Amon-Ra, Ramses wrote, that the credit for the victories was due: for it was ''Amon-Ra who was after them, destroying them.''

Fig. 3

The bloody trail of man's war against his fellow men in behalf of the gods now takes us back to Mesopotamia—the Land Between the Rivers (Euphrates and Tigris)—the biblical Land of Shin'ar. There, as is related in Genesis 11, the first-ever cities arose, with buildings made with bricks and towers that scraped the skies. It was there that recorded history began; it was there that prehistory began with the settlements of the Olden Gods.

It is a tale of long ago, which we will soon unfold. But right now let us return to a thousand years before the dramatic times of Ramses II in Egypt. Then, in faraway Mesopotamia, kingship was taken over by an ambitious young man. He was called Sharru-Kin—''Righteous Ruler''; our textbooks call him Sargon the First. He built a new capital city, calling it Agade, and established the kingdom of Akkad. The Akkadian language, written in a wedge-like (cuneiform) script, was the mother tongue of all the Semitic languages, of which Hebrew and Arabic are still in use.

Reigning for the better part of the twenty-fourth century B.C., Sargon attributed his long reign (fifty-four years) to the special status granted him by the Great Gods, who made him ''Overseer of Ishtar, Anointed Priest of ANU, Great Righteous Shepherd of ENLIL.'' It was Enlil, Sargon wrote, ''who did not let anybody oppose Sargon'' and who gave Sargon ''the region from the Upper Sea to the Lower Sea'' (from the Mediterranean to the Persian

Gulf). It was therefore to "the gate of the House of Enlil" that Sargon brought the captive kings, ropes tied to the dog collars around their necks.

In one of his campaigns across the Zagros mountains, Sargon experienced the same godly feat that the combatants at Troy had witnessed. As he "was moving into the land of Warahshi . . . when he pressed forward in the darkness . . . Ishtar made a light to shine for him." Thus was Sargon able to "penetrate the gloom" of darkness as he led his troops through the mountain passes of today's Luristan.

The Akkadian dynasty begun by Sargon reached its peak under his grandson Naram-Sin ("Whom the god Sin loves"). His conquests, Naram-Sin wrote on his monuments, were possible because his god had armed him with a unique weapon, the "Weapon of the God," and because the other gods granted him their explicit consent—or even invited him—to enter their regions.

Naram-Sin's principal thrust was to the northwest, and his conquests included the city-state of Ebla, whose recently discovered archive of clay tablets has caused great scientific interest: "Although since the time of the separation of mankind none of the kings has ever destroyed Arman and Ibla, the god Nergal did open up the path for the mighty Naram-Sin and gave him Arman and Ibla. He also gave him as a present Amanus, the Cedar Mountain, to the Upper Sea."

Just as Naram-Sin could attribute his successful campaigns to his heeding the commands of his gods, so was his downfall attributed to his going to war against the word of the gods. Scholars have put together from fragments of several versions a text that has been titled *The Legend of Naram-Sin.* Speaking in the first person, Naram-Sin explains in this tale of woe that his troubles began when the goddess Ishtar "changed her plan" and the gods gave their blessing to "seven kings, brothers, glorious and noble; their troops numbered 360,000." Coming from what is now Iran, they invaded the mountain lands of Gutium and Elam to the east of Mesopotamia and were threatening Akkad itself. Naram-Sin asked the gods what to do and was told to put aside his weapons and, instead of going to battle, to go sleep with his wife (but, for some deep reason, avoid making love):

The gods reply to him:
"O Naram-Sin, this is our word:
This army against you . . .
Bind your weapons, in a corner place them!

> Hold back your boldness, stay at home!
> Together with your wife, in bed go sleep,
> but with her you must not . . .
> Out of your land, unto the enemy, you must not go."

But Naram-Sin, announcing that he would rely on his own weapons, decided to attack the enemy in spite of the gods' advice. "When the first year arrived, I sent out 120,000 troops, but none of them returned alive," Naram-Sin confessed in his inscription. More troops were annihilated in the second and third years, and Akkad was succumbing to death and hunger. On the fourth anniversary of the unauthorized war, Naram-Sin appealed to the great god Ea to overrule Ishtar and put his case before the other gods. They advised him to desist from further fighting, promising that "in days to come, Enlil will summon perdition upon the Sons of Evil," and Akkad would have respite.

The promised era of peace lasted about three centuries, during which the olden part of Mesopotamia, Sumer, reemerged as the center of kingship, and the oldest urban centers of the ancient world —Ur, Nippur, Lagash, Isin, Larsa—flourished again. Sumer, under the kings of Ur, was the center of an empire that encompassed the whole of the ancient Near East. But toward the end of the third millennium B.C., the land became the arena for contending loyalties and opposing armies; and then that great civilization—man's first known civilization—succumbed to a major catastrophe of unprecedented proportions.

It was a fateful event which, we believe, was echoed in biblical tales. It was an event whose memory lingered on for a long time, commemorated and bewailed in numerous lamentation poems; they gave a very graphic description of the havoc and desolation that befell that great heartland of ancient civilization. It was, those Mesopotamian texts stated, a catastrophe that befell Sumer as a result of a decision of the great gods sitting in council.

It took southern Mesopotamia almost a century to be resettled and another century to fully recover from the divine annihilation. By then, the center of Mesopotamian power had shifted northward, to Babylon. There, a new empire was to rise, proclaiming an ambitious god, MARDUK, as its supreme deity.

Circa 1800 B.C., Hammurabi, the king renowned for his law code, ascended the throne in Babylon and began to extend its boundaries. According to his inscriptions the gods not only told him if and when to launch his military campaigns but were literally leading his armies:

> Through the power of the great gods
> the king, beloved of the god Marduk,
> reestablished the foundations of Sumer and Akkad.
> Upon the command of Anu, and
> with Enlil advancing in front of his army,
> with the mighty powers which the great gods gave him,
> he was no match for the army of Emutbal
> and its king Rim-Sin. . . .

To defeat more enemies the god Marduk granted Hammurabi a "powerful weapon" called "Great Power of Marduk":

> With the Powerful Weapon
> with which Marduk proclaimed his triumphs,
> the hero [Hammurabi] overthrew in battle
> the armies of Eshnuna, Subartu and Gutium. . . .
> With the "Great Power of Marduk"
> he overthrew the armies of Sutium, Turukku, Kamu. . . .
> With the Mighty Power which Anu and Enlil had given him
> he defeated all his enemies
> as far as the country of Subartu.

But before long Babylon had to share its might with a new rival to its north—Assyria, where not Marduk but the bearded god ASHUR ("The All-Seeing") was proclaimed supreme. While Babylon tangled with the lands to its south and east, the Assyrians extended their rule northward and westward, as far as "the country of Lebanon, on the shores of the Great Sea." These were lands in the domains of the gods NINURTA and ADAD, and the Assyrian kings carefully noted that they launched their campaigns on the explicit commands of these great gods. Thus, Tiglat-Pileser I commemorated his wars, in the twelfth century B.C., in the following words:

> Tiglat-Pileser, the legitimate king, king of the world, king of Assyria, king of all the four regions of the earth;
> The courageous hero who is guided by the trust-inspiring commands given by Ashur and Ninurta, the great gods, his lords, thus overthrowing his enemies. . . .

At the command of my lord Ashur, my hand conquered from beyond the lower Zab River to the Upper Sea which is in the west. Three times I did march against the Nairi countries. . . . I made bow to my feet 30 kings of the Nairi countries. I took hostages from them, I received as their tribute horses broken to the yoke. . . .

Upon the command of Anu and Adad, the great gods, my lords, I went to the Lebanon mountains; I cut cedar beams for the temples of Anu and Adad.

In assuming the title "king of the world, king of the four regions of the Earth," the Assyrian kings directly challenged Babylon, for Babylon encompassed the ancient region of Sumer and Akkad. To legitimize their claim the Assyrian kings had to take control of those olden cities where the Great Gods had their homes in olden times; but the way to these sites was blocked by Babylon. The feat was achieved in the ninth century B.C. by Shalmaneser III; he said thus in his inscriptions:

I marched against Akkad to avenge . . . and inflicted defeat. . . . I entered Kutha, Babylon and Borsippa.

I offered sacrifices to the gods of the sacred cities of Akkad. I went further downstream to Chaldea, and received tribute from all the kings of Chaldea. . . .

At that time, Ashur, the great lord . . . gave me scepter, staff . . . all that was necessary to rule the people.

I was acting only upon the trustworthy commands given by Ashur, the great lord, my lord who loves me.

Describing his various military campaigns, Shalmaneser asserted that his victories were achieved with weapons provided by two gods: "I fought with the Mighty Force which Ashur, my lord, had given me; and with the strong weapons which Nergal, my leader, had presented to me." The weapon of Ashur was described as having a "terrifying brilliance." In a war with Adini the enemy fled on seeing "the terrifying Brilliance of Ashur; it overwhelmed them."

When Babylon, after several acts of defiance, was sacked by the Assyrian king Sennacherib (in 689 B.C.), its demise was made possible because its own god, Marduk, became angry with its king and people, and decreed that "seventy years shall be the measure of its desolation"—exactly as the God of Israel had later decreed for Jerusalem. With the subjugation of the whole of Mesopotamia, Sennacherib was able to assume the cherished title "King of Sumer and Akkad."

In his inscriptions, Sennacherib also described his military campaigns along the Mediterranean coast, leading to battles with the Egyptians at the gateway to the Sinai peninsula. His list of conquered cities reads like a chapter in the Old Testament—Sidon, Tyre, Byblos, Akko, Ashdod, Ashkalon—"strong cities" that Sennacherib "overwhelmed" with the aid of "the awe-inspiring Brilliance, the weapon of Ashur, my lord." Reliefs that illustrate his campaigns (as the one depicting the siege of Lachish, Fig. 4) show the attackers using rocketlike missiles against their enemy. In

Fig. 4

the conquered cities Sennacherib "killed their officials and patricians . . . and hung their bodies on poles surrounding the city; the common citizens I considered prisoners of war."

An artifact known as the Prism of Sennacherib preserved an historical inscription in which he made mention of the subjugation of Judea and his attack on Jerusalem. The quarrel Sennacherib had with its king, Hezekiah, was the fact that he held captive Padi, the king of the Philistine city of Ekron, "who was loyal to his solemn oath to his god Ashur."

"As to Hezekiah, the Judean," Sennacherib wrote, "who did not submit to my yoke, I laid siege to forty-six of his strong cities, walled forts, and to the countless small villages in their vicinity. . . . Hezekiah himself I made captive in Jerusalem, his royal residence; like a bird in a cage I surrounded him with earthworks. . . . His towns which I had plundered I cut off from his land and gave them over to Mitinti, king of Ashdod; Padi, king of Ekron; and Sillibel, king of Gaza. Thus I reduced his country."

The siege of Jerusalem offers several interesting aspects. It had no direct cause but only an indirect one: the forced holding there of the loyal king of Ekron. The "awe-inspiring Brilliance, the weapon of Ashur," which was employed to "overwhelm the strong cities" of Phoenicia and Philistia, was not used against Jerusalem. And the customary inscriptional ending—"I fought with them and inflicted defeat upon them"—is missing in the case of Jerusalem; Sennacherib merely reduced the size of Judea by giving its outlying areas to neighboring kings.

Moreover, the usual claim that a land or a city was attacked upon the "trustworthy orders" of the god Ashur was also absent in the case of Jerusalem; one wonders whether all this meant that the attack on the city was an unauthorized attack—a whim of Sennacherib himself but not the wish of his god?

This intriguing possibility becomes a convincing probability as we read the other side of the story—for such an other side does exist in the Old Testament.

While Sennacherib glossed over his failure to capture Jerusalem, the tale in II Kings, chapters 18 and 19, offers the full story. We learn from the biblical report that "in the fourteenth year of king Hezekiah Sennacherib, the king of Assyria, came upon all the walled cities of Judea and captured them." He then sent two of his generals with a large army to Jerusalem, the capital. But instead of storming the city, the Assyrian general Rab-Shakeh began a verbal exchange with the city's leaders—an exchange he insisted on conducting in Hebrew so that the whole populace might understand him.

What did he have to say that the populace ought to have known? As the biblical text makes clear, the verbal exchanges concerned the question of whether the Assyrian invasion of Judea was authorized by the Lord Yahweh!

"And Rab-Shakeh said unto them: Speak ye now to Hezekiah: Thus sayeth the great king, the king of Assyria: What confidence is it wherein thou trusteth?"

If ye say unto me:
"We trust in Yahweh, our God" . . .
Now then,
Am I come against this place to destroy it
without Yahweh?
Yahweh did say unto me:
"Go up against this land, and destroy it!"

The more the ministers of king Hezekiah, standing upon the city's walls, pleaded with Rab-Shakeh to cease saying these untrue things in Hebrew and to deliver his message in the then language of diplomacy, Aramaic, the more did Rab-Shakeh approach the walls to shout his words in Hebrew for all to hear. Soon he began to use foul language against Hezekiah's emissaries; then he started to degrade the king himself. Carried away by his own oratory, Rab-Shakeh abandoned his claim to have had Yahweh's permission to attack Jerusalem and went on to belittle the God himself.

When Hezekiah was told of the blasphemy, "he rent his clothes, and covered himself with sackcloth and went into the House of Yahweh. . . . And he sent word to the Prophet Isaiah, saying: 'This is a day of trouble, of rebuke, of blasphemy. . . . May Yahweh thy Lord hear all the words of Rab-Shakeh, whom his master the king of Assyria hath sent to scorn the Living God.' And the word of the Lord Yahweh came back through his Prophet Isaiah: 'Concerning the king of Assyria . . . the way that he came, he shall return; and unto this city he shall not come in . . . for I shall defend this city to save it.' "

And it came to pass that night,
that the angel of Yahweh went forth
and smote in the camp of the Assyrians
a hundred and eighty-five thousand;

and at sunrise, lo and behold,
they were all dead corpses.
So Sennacherib, the king of Assyria,
departed, and journeyed back and dwelt in Nineveh.

According to the Old Testament, after Sennacherib had returned
to Nineveh, "it came to pass, as he was worshiping in the temple
of his god Nisroch, that Adrammelech and Sharezzer his sons
smote him with a sword; and they escaped unto the land of Ararat.
And Esarhaddon, his son, reigned in his stead." Assyrian records
confirm the biblical statement: Sennacherib was indeed so assas-
sinated, and his younger son Esarhaddon did ascend the throne after him.

An inscription of Esarhaddon known as Prism B describes the
circumstances more fully. On the command of the great gods,
Sennacherib had publicly proclaimed his younger son as successor.
"He called together the people of Assyria, young and old, and he
made my brothers, the male offspring of my father, take a solemn
oath in the presence of the gods of Assyria . . . in order to secure
my succession." The brothers then broke their oath, killing
Sennacherib and seeking to kill Esarhaddon. But the gods snatched
him away "and made me stay in a hiding place . . . preserving me
for kingship."

After a period of turmoil Esarhaddon received "a trustworthy
command from the gods: 'Go, do not delay! We will march with
you!' "

The deity who was delegated to accompany Esarhaddon was
Ishtar. As his brothers' forces came out of Nineveh to beat off his
attack on the capital, "Ishtar, the Lady of Battle, who wished me
to be her high priest, stood at my side. She broke their bows, scattered their orderly battle array." Once the Ninevite troops were
disorganized, Ishtar addressed them in behalf of Esarhaddon.
"Upon her lofty command, they went over in masses to me and
rallied behind me," Esarhaddon wrote, "and recognized me as
their king."

Both Esarhaddon and his son and successor Ashurbanipal attempted to advance against Egypt, and both employed Weapons
of Brilliance in the battles. "The terror-inspiring Brilliance of
Ashur," Ashurbanipal wrote, "blinded the Pharaoh so that he became a madman."

Other inscriptions of Ashurbanipal suggest that this weapon,
which emitted an intense, blinding brightness, was worn by the

gods as part of their headgear. In one instance an enemy "was blinded by the brightness from the god-head." In another, "Ishtar, who dwells in Arbela, clad in Divine Fire and sporting the Radiant Headwear, rained flames upon Arabia."

The Old Testament, too, refers to such a Weapon of Brilliance that could blind. When the Angels (literally, emissaries) of the Lord came to Sodom prior to its destruction, the populace attempted to break down the door of the house in which they were resting. So the Angels "smote the people at the entrance of the house with blindness . . . and they were unable to find the doorway."

As Assyria rose to supremacy, even extending its rule over Lower Egypt, its kings, in the words of the Lord through his prophet Isaiah, forgot that they were only an instrument of the Lord: "Ho Assyria, the whip of mine anger! My wrath is the rod in their hands; against impious nations I send them; upon people who have crossed me I charge them." But the Assyrian kings went beyond mere punishment; "rather, it is in its heart to annihilate and wipe out nations not few." This went beyond the intention of the God; therefore, the Lord Yahweh announced, "I shall hold to account the king of Assyria, on account of the fruits of the growing haughtiness of his heart."

The biblical prophecies predicting the downfall of Assyria indeed came true: As invaders from the north and east were joined by rebellious Babylonians from the south, Ashur, the religious capital, fell in 614 B.C., and Nineveh, the royal capital, was captured and sacked two years later. The great Assyria was no more.

The disintegration of the Assyrian empire was seized by vassal kings in Egypt and Babylonia as an opportunity to attempt the restoration of their own hegemonies. The lands between them were once again the cherished prize, and the Egyptians, under the Pharaoh Necho, were quicker in invading these territories.

In Babylonia, Nebuchadnezzar II—as recorded in his inscriptions—was ordered by the god Marduk to march his army westward. The expedition was made possible because "another god," the one who held the original sovereignty over the area, "has not desired the cedar land" anymore; and now "a foreign enemy was ruling and robbing it."

In Jerusalem the word of the Lord Yahweh through his prophet Jeremiah was to side with Babylon, for the Lord Yahweh—calling

Nebuchadnezzar "my servant"—had decided to make the Babylonian king the instrument of His wrath against the gods of Egypt:

> Thus sayeth Yahweh, Lord of Hosts, the God of Israel:
> "Indeed will I send for and fetch Nebuchadnezzar, my servant. . . .
> And he shall smite the land of Egypt,
> and deliver such as are for death to death,
> and such as are for captivity to captivity,
> and such as are for the sword to the sword.
> And I will kindle a fire in the house of Egypt's gods,
> and he will burn them. . . .
> And he will break the obelisks of Heliopolis,
> the one which is in the land of Egypt;
> The houses of the gods of Egypt shall he burn with fire."

In the course of this campaign the Lord Yahweh announced that Jerusalem, too, shall be punished on account of its people's sins, having taken up the worship of the "Queen of Heaven" and of the gods of Egypt: "Mine anger and my fury shall be poured upon this place . . . and it shall burn and shall not be quenched. . . . In the city on which my name has been called, the doom will I begin." And so it was that in the year 586 B.C. "Nebuzaraddan, captain of the guard of the king of Babylon, came into Jerusalem; and he burned the House of Yahweh, and the king's house, and all the houses of Jerusalem . . . and all the walls around Jerusalem were torn down by the army of the Chaldeans." This desolation, Yahweh promised, however, would last only seventy years.

The king who was to fulfill this promise and enable the rebuilding of the Temple of Jerusalem was Cyrus. His ancestors, speaking an Indo-European language, are believed to have migrated south from the Caspian Sea area to the province of Anshan along the eastern coast of the Persian Gulf. There Hakham-Anish ("Wise Man"), the leader of the migrants, began a dynasty we call Achaemenid; his descendants—Cyrus, Darius, Xerxes—made history as rulers of what was to be the Persian empire.

When Cyrus ascended the throne of Anshan in 549 B.C., his land was a distant province of Elam and Media. In Babylon, then the center of power, the kingship was held by Nabunaid, who became king under most unusual circumstances: not by the customary choice by the god Marduk, but as a result of a unique pact between a High Priestess (the mother of Nabunaid) and the god

Sin. A partly damaged tablet contains the eventual indictment of Nabunaid: "He set an heretical statue upon a base . . . he called its name 'the god Sin'. . . . At the proper time of the New Year Festival, he advised that there be no celebrations. . . . He confounded the rites and upset the ordinances."

While Cyrus was busy fighting the Greeks of Asia Minor, Marduk—seeking to restore his position as the national god of Babylon—"scanned and looked throughout the countries, searching for a righteous ruler willing to be led. And he called out the name of Cyrus, King of Anshan, and pronounced his name to be ruler of all the lands."

After the first deeds of Cyrus proved to be in accord with the god's wishes, Marduk "ordered him to march against his own city Babylon. He made him [Cyrus] set out on the road to Babylon, going at his side like a real friend." Thus, literally accompanied by the Babylonian god, Cyrus was able to take Babylon without bloodshed. On a day equivalent to March 20, 538 B.C., Cyrus "held the hands of *Bel* [The Lord] Marduk" in Babylon's sacred precinct. On New Year's Day his son, Cambyses, officated at the restored festival honoring Marduk.

Cyrus left his successors an empire that encompassed all the earlier empires and kingdoms but one. Sumer, Akkad, Babylon, and Assyria in Mesopotamia; Elam and Media to the east; the lands to the north; the Hittite and Greek lands in Asia Minor; Phoenicia and Canaan and Philistia—all had now come under one sovereign king and one supreme god, Ahura-Mazda, God of Truth and Light. He was depicted in ancient Persia (Fig. 5a) as a bearded deity roaming the skies within a Winged Disc—very much in the manner in which the Assyrians had depicted their supreme god, Ashur (Fig. 5b).

When Cyrus died in 529 B.C., the only remaining independent land with its independent gods was Egypt. Four years later his son and successor, Cambyses, led his troops along the Mediterranean coast of the Sinai peninsula and defeated the Egyptians at Pelusium; a few months later he entered Memphis, the Egyptian royal capital, and proclaimed himself a Pharaoh.

Despite his victory, Cambyses carefully refrained from employing in his Egyptian inscriptions the usual opening formula "the great god, Ahura-Mazda, chose me." Egypt, he recognized, did not come within the domains of this god. In deference to the independent gods of Egypt, Cambyses prostrated himself before their statues, accepting their dominion. In return the Egyptian

a

b

Fig. 5

priests legitimized his rule over Egypt by granting him the title "Offspring of Ra."

The ancient world was now united under one king, chosen by the "great god of truth and light" and accepted by the gods of Egypt. Neither men nor gods had cause left to war with each other. Peace on Earth!

But peace failed to last. Across the Mediterranean Sea, the Greeks were increasing in wealth, power, and ambitions. Asia Minor, the Aegean Sea, and the eastern Mediterranean saw increasing clashes, both local and international. In 490 B.C., Darius I attempted to invade Greece and was defeated at Marathon; nine years later Xerxes I was defeated at Salamis. A century and a half later Alexander of Macedonia crossed over from Europe to launch a campaign of conquest that saw the blood of men flow in all the ancient lands as far as India.

Was he carrying out a "trustworthy command" of the gods? On

the contrary. Believing a legend that he was fathered by an Egyptian god, Alexander at first fought his way to Egypt to hear the god's oracle confirm his semidivine origins. But the oracle also predicted his early death, and Alexander's travels and conquests were thereafter motivated by a search for the Waters of Life, so that he might drink of them and evade his fate.

He died, in spite of all the carnage, young and in his prime. And ever since, the Wars of Men have been the wars of men alone.

2

THE CONTENDING OF HORUS AND SETH

Was it a sad commentary on the history of warfare that the messianic Essenes envisioned the Final War of Men as one in which the Company of the Divine would join the Congregation of the Mortals, and the "war cries of gods and men" would mingle on the battlefield?

Not at all. What *The War of the Sons of Light Against the Sons of Darkness* had envisioned was simply that human warfare shall end just as it had begun: with gods and men fighting side by side.

Incredible as it may sound, a document does exist that describes the first war in which the gods involved mortal men. It is an inscription on the walls of the great temple at Edfu, an ancient Egyptian holy city that was dedicated to the god Horus. It was there, Egyptian traditions held, that Horus established a foundry of "divine iron" and where, in a special enclosure, he maintained the great Winged Disk that could roam the skies. "When the doors of the foundry open," an Egyptian text declared, "the Disk riseth up":

The inscription (Fig. 6), remarkable for its geographical accuracy, begins with an exact date—a date not in the affairs of men but of the gods. It deals with events when the gods themselves, long before the Pharaohs, reigned over Egypt:

> In the year 363 His Majesty, Ra, the Holy One, the Falcon of the Horizon, the Immortal Who Forever Lives, was in the land of Khenn. He was accompanied by his warriors, for the enemies had conspired against their lord in the district which has been called Ua-Ua since that day.
>
> Ra went there in his boat, his companions with him. He landed in the district of the Throne Place of Horus, in the western part of this district, east of the House of Khennu, the one which has been called Royal Khennu from that time on.

Horus, the Winged Measurer, came to the boat of Ra. He said to his forefather: "O Falcon of the Horizon, I have seen the enemy conspire against thy Lordship, to take the Luminous Crown unto themselves."

Fig. 6

With a few words the ancient scribe succeeded in drawing the background as well as setting the stage for the unusual war that was about to unfold. We gather at once that the fighting was brought on by a conspiracy by certain "enemies" of the gods Ra and Horus, to take away the "Luminous Crown of Lordship" unto themselves. This, obviously, could have been done only by some other god or gods. To forestall the conspiracy Ra—"accompanied by his warriors"—went in his boat to a district where Horus had set up his headquarters.

The "boat" of Ra, as is known from many other texts, was a Celestial Boat in which Ra could soar to the farthest heavens. In this instance Ra used it to land far away from any waters, "in the western part" of the district of Ua-Ua. There he landed east of the "Throne Place" of Horus. And Horus came out to greet his forefather and reported to him that "the enemy" was gathering its forces.

> Then Ra, the Holy One, the Falcon of the Horizon, said unto Horus, the Winged Measurer: "Lofty issue of Ra, my begotten: Go quickly, knock down the enemy whom you have seen."

So instructed, Horus took off in the Winged Disk to search for the enemy from the skies:

> So Horus, the Winged Measurer, flew up toward the horizon in the Winged Disk of Ra; it is therefore that he has been called from that day on "Great God, Lord of the Skies."

From the skies, flying in the Winged Disk, Horus spotted the enemy forces and unleashed upon them a "storm" that could neither be seen nor heard, yet it brought instantaneous death:

> In the heights of the skies, from the Winged Disk, he saw the enemies, and came upon them from behind. From his forepart he let loose against them a Storm which they could neither see with their eyes, nor hear with their ears. It brought death to all of them in a single moment; not a being remained alive through this.

Horus then flew back to the boat of Ra in the Winged Disk, "which shined in many colors," and heard his victory made official by Thoth, the god of magical crafts:

> Then Horus, the Winged Measurer, reappeared in the Winged Disk, which shined in many colors; and he came back to the boat of Ra, the Falcon of the Horizon.
> And Thoth said: "O Lord of the gods! The Winged Measurer has returned in the great Winged Disk, shining with many colors". . . .

Therefore is he named from that day on "The Winged Measurer." And they named after Horus, the Winged Measurer, the city of Hut "Behutet," from that day on.

It was in Upper Egypt that the first battle, above reported, had taken place between Horus and "the enemies." Heinrich Brugsch, who first published the text of the inscription back in 1870 (*Die Sage von der geflügten Sonnenscheibe*), suggested that the "Land of Khenn" was Nubia, and that Horus had spotted the enemies at Syene (today's Aswan). More recent studies, such as *Egypt in Nubia* by Walter B. Emery, agree that Ta-Khenn was Nubia and that Ua-Ua was the name of its northern part, the area between the Nile's first and second cataracts. (The southern part of Nubia was called Kush.) These identifications seem valid, since the city of Behutet, which was granted to Horus as a prize for his first victory, was the very city of Edfu, which has been dedicated to Horus ever since.

Traditions held that Edfu was where Horus established a divine metal foundry, at which unique weapons made of "divine iron" were forged. It was there, too, that Horus trained an army of *mesniu*—"Metal People." They were depicted on the walls of the temple of Edfu as men with shaven heads, wearing a short tunic and a deep collar, carrying weapons in each hand. A depiction of an unidentified, harpoonlike weapon ⤙⤚ was included in the hieroglyphic words for "divine iron" and "metal people."

The *mesniu* were, according to Egyptian traditions, the first men ever to have been armed by the gods with weapons made of metal. They also were, as we shall soon gather from the unfolding tale, the first men to have been enlisted by a god to fight in the wars between the gods.

The area between Aswan and Edfu now firmly secured, and men-warriors armed and trained, the gods were ready to advance northward, toward the heartland of Egypt. The initial victories apparently also strengthened the alliance of the gods, for we are told that the Asiatic goddess Ishtar (the Egyptian text calls her by her Canaanite name, Ashtoreth) had joined the group. Hovering in the sky, Horus called on Ra to scout the land below:

And Horus said: "Advance, O Ra! Look for the enemies who are lying below, upon the land!"

Then Ra, the Holy One, travelled forth; and Ashtoreth was

with him. And they looked for the enemies upon the land; but each one of them was hidden.

Since the enemies on the land were hidden from sight, Ra had an idea: "And Ra said unto the gods accompanying him: 'Let us guide our vessel toward the water, for the enemy lies in the land.' And they called the waters 'The Travelled Waters' from that day on." While Ra could utilize the amphibious capabilities of his vehicle, Horus was in need of a waterborne vessel. So they gave him a boat, "and called it Mak-A (Great Protector) unto this day."

It was then that the first battle involving mortal men ensued:

But the enemies too went into the waters, making themselves as crocodiles and hippopotami, and they were striking at the boat of Ra, the Falcon of the Horizon. . . .

It was then that Horus, the Winged Measurer, came along with his helpers, those who served as warriors, each one called by name, with the Divine Iron and a chain in their hands, and they beat off the crocodiles and the hippopotami.

And they hauled up 651 enemies to that place; they were killed in sight of the city.

And Ra, the Falcon of the Horizon, said unto Horus, the Winged Measurer: "Let this place be known as the place where thine victory in the southlands has been established."

Having vanquished their enemies from the skies, on land, and in the waters, the victory of Horus seemed complete; and Thoth called for a celebration:

Then said Thoth unto the other gods: "O Gods of Heaven, let your hearts rejoice! O Gods of Earth, let your hearts rejoice! The young Horus has brought peace, having performed extraordinary feats in this campaign."

It was then that the Winged Disk was adopted as the emblem of Horus victorious:

It is from that day that the metal emblems of Horus have existed. It was Horus who had fashioned as his emblem the Winged Disk, placing it upon the forepart of the boat of Ra. The goddess of the north and the goddess of the south, represented as two serpents, he placed alongside.

And Horus stood behind the emblem, upon the boat of Ra, the Divine Iron and the chain in his hand.

In spite of the proclamation of Horus by Thoth as a bringer of peace, peace was not yet in hand. As the company of the gods kept advancing northward, ''they glimpsed two brightnesses on a plain southeast of Thebes. And Ra said to Thoth: 'This is the enemy; let Horus slaughter them. . . .' And Horus made a great massacre among them.''

Once again, with the aid of the army of men he had trained and armed, Horus was victorious; and Thoth kept naming the locations after the successful battles.

While the first aerial battle broke through the defenses separating Egypt from Nubia at Syene (Aswan), the ensuing battles on land and water secured for Horus the bend of the Nile, from Thebes to Dendera. There great temples and royal sites proliferated in days to come. Now the way was open into the heartland of Egypt.

For several days the gods advanced northward—Horus keeping watch from the skies in the Winged Disk, Ra and his companions sailing down the Nile, and the Metal People guarding the flanks on land. A series of brief, but fierce, encounters then ensued; the place names—well established in ancient Egyptian geography—indicate that the attacking gods reached the area of lakes that had stretched in antiquity from the Red Sea to the Mediterranean (some of which still remain):

> Then the enemies distanced themselves from him, toward the north. They placed themselves in the water district, facing the back-sea of the Mediterranean; and their hearts were stricken with fear of him.
> But Horus, the Winged Measurer, followed close behind them in the boat of Ra, the Divine Iron in his hand.
> And all his Helpers, armed with weapons of iron forged, were staged all around.

But the attempt to surround and entrap the enemies did not succeed: ''For four days and four nights he roamed the waters in pursuit of them, without seeing even one of the enemies.'' Ra then advised him to go up again in the Winged Disk, and this time Horus was able to see the fleeing enemies; ''he hurled his Divine Lance after them and he slew them, and performed a great overthrow of them. He also brought 142 enemy prisoners to the forepart of the boat of Ra,'' where they were quickly executed.

The Edfu temple inscription now shifts to a new panel, for indeed there began a new chapter in that War of the Gods. The enemies that had managed to escape "directed themselves by the Lake of the North, setting themselves toward the Mediterranean, which they desired to reach by sailing through the water district. But the god smote their hearts [with fear], and when they reached the middle of the waters as they fled, they directed themselves from the western lake to the waters which connect with the lakes of the district Mer, in order to join themselves there with the enemies who were the Land of Seth.''

These verses provide not only geographical information; they also identify "the enemies" for the first time. The conflict had shifted to the chain of lakes that in antiquity, much more than nowadays, physically separated Egypt proper from the Sinai peninsula. To the east, beyond this watery barrier, lay the domain of Seth—the erstwhile adversary and slayer of Osiris, the father of Horus. Seth, we now learn, was the enemy against whose forces Horus had been advancing from the south. And now Horus reached the line dividing Egypt from the Land of Seth.

For a while there was a lull in the fighting, during which Horus brought up to the front line his armed Metal People, and Ra reached the scene in his boat. The enemies, too, regrouped and crossed back the waters, and a major battle followed. This time, 381 of the enemy were captured and executed (no casualty figures on the side of Horus are ever given in the text); and Horus, in hot pursuit, crossed the waters into the territory of Seth.

It was then, according to the inscription in the great temple of Edfu, that Seth was so enraged that he faced Horus for a series of battles—on the ground and in the air—for god-to-god combat. Of this combat there have been found several versions, as we shall see. What is interesting at this point is the fact brought out by E. A. Wallis Budge in *The Gods of the Egyptians:* that in the first involvement of men in the Wars of the Gods, it was the arming of mankind with the Divine Iron that brought victory to Horus: "It is pretty clear that he owed his success chiefly to the superiority of the weapons with which he and his men were armed, and to the material of which they were made.''

Thus, according to Egyptian writings, did man learn to lift sword against man.

When all the fighting was over, Ra expressed satisfaction with the works of "these Metal People of Horus," and he decreed that henceforth they "shall dwell in sanctuaries" and shall be served with libations and offerings "as their reward, because they have slain the enemies of the god Horus." They were settled at Edfu, the Upper Egypt capital of Horus, and in This (Tanis in Greek, the biblical Zo'an), the Lower Egypt capital of the god. In time they outgrew their purely military role and attained the title Shamsu-Hor ("Attendants of Horus"), serving as his human aides and emissaries.

The inscription on the temple walls at Edfu, it has been established, was a copy of a text that was known to the Egyptian scribes from earlier sources; but when and by whom the original text had been composed, no one can really tell. Scholars who have studied the inscription have concluded that the accurate geographical and other data in the text indicate (in the words of E. A. Wallis Budge) "that we are not dealing entirely with mythological events; and it is nearly certain that the triumphant progress ascribed to *Hor-Behutet* (Horus of Edfu) is based upon the exploits of some victorious invader who established himself at Edfu in very early times."

As with all Egyptian historical texts, this one, too, begins with a date: "In the year 363." Such dates always indicate the year in the reign of the Pharaoh to whom the event pertains: each Pharaoh had his first year, second year, and so on. The text in question, however, deals not with the affairs of kings but with divine matters—a war among the gods. The text thus relates events that had happened in the "year 363" in the reign of certain gods and takes us back to the early times when gods, not men, ruled over Egypt.

That there indeed had been such a time, Egyptian traditions left no doubt. The Greek historian Herodotus (fifth century B.C.), on his extensive visit to Egypt, was given by the priests details of the Pharaonic dynasties and reigns. "The priests," he wrote, "said that Mên was the first king of Egypt, and that it was he who raised the dyke which protects Memphis from the inundations of the Nile," diverted the river, and proceeded to build Memphis on the reclaimed land. "Besides these works he also, the priests said, built the temple of Vulcan, which stands within the city, a vast edifice, very worthy of mention.

"Next they read me from a papyrus the names of 330 monarchs who were his successors upon the throne. In this number of successors there were eighteen Ethiopian kings, and one queen who was a native; all the rest were kings and Egyptians."

The priests then showed Herodotus rows of statues representing the successive Pharaohs and related to him various details pertaining to some of these kings and their claims to divine ancestry. "The beings represented by these images were very far indeed from being gods," Herodotus commented; "however," he went on to say:

> In times preceding them it was otherwise: Then Egypt had gods for its rulers, who dwelt upon the Earth with men, one of them being always supreme above the rest.
>
> The last of these was Horus, the son of Osiris, whom the Greeks called Apollo. He deposed Typhon, and ruled over Egypt as its last god-king.

In his book *Against Apion,* the first-century Jewish historian Flavius Josephus quoted as one of his sources on the history of Egypt the writings of an Egyptian priest named Manetho. Such writings were never found; but any doubt regarding the existence of such a historian was dispelled when it was realized that his writings formed the basis for several works by later Greek historians. It is now established with certainty that Manetho (his hieroglyphic name meant "Gift of Thoth"), indeed a high priest and great scholar, compiled the history of Egypt in several volumes at the command of king Ptolemy Philadelphus circa 270 B.C. The original manuscript was deposited in the great library of Alexandria, only to perish there together with numerous other invaluable documents when the building and its contents were set on fire by Muslim conquerors in A.D. 642.

Manetho was the first known historian to have divided the Egyptian rulers into dynasties—a practice continued to this day. His King List—names, lengths of reign, order of succession, and some other pertinent information—has been mainly preserved through the writings of Julius Africanus and Eusebius of Caesarea (in the third and fourth centuries A.D.). These and other versions based on Manetho agree that he listed as the first ruler of the first dynasty of Pharaohs the king Mên (Menes in Greek)—the very same king that Herodotus reported, based on his own investigations in Egypt.

This fact has since been confirmed by modern discoveries, such as the Tablet of Abydos (Fig. 7) in which the Pharaoh Seti I, accompanied by his son, Ramses II, listed the names of seventy-five of his predecessors. The first one to be named is Mena.

Fig. 7

If Herodotus was correct in regard to the dynasties of Egyptian Pharaohs, could he also have been right in regard to a "preceding time" when "Egypt had gods for its rulers"?

Manetho, we find, had agreed with Herodotus also on that matter. The dynasties of the Pharaohs, he wrote, were preceded by four other dynasties—two of gods, one of demigods, and a transitional dynasty. At first, he wrote, seven great gods reigned over Egypt for a total of 12,300 years:

Ptah	ruled	9,000 years
Ra	ruled	1,000 years
Shu	ruled	700 years
Geb	ruled	500 years
Osiris	ruled	450 years
Seth	ruled	350 years
Horus	ruled	300 years
Seven gods	ruled	12,300 years

The second dynasty of gods, Manetho wrote, consisted of twelve divine rulers, the first of whom was the god Thoth; they reigned for 1,570 years. In all, he said, nineteen gods ruled for 13,870 years. Then there followed a dynasty of thirty demigods, who reigned for 3,650 years; in all, there were forty-nine divine and semidivine rulers over Egypt, reigning a total of 17,520 years. Then, for 350 years, there was no ruler over the whole of Egypt; it was a chaotic time, during which ten human rulers continued the kingship at This. Only thereafter did Mên establish the first human dynasty of Pharaohs and built a new capital dedicated to the god Ptah—the "Vulcan" of Herodotus.

A century and a half of archaeological discoveries and the deciphering of the hieroglyphic writing have convinced scholars that the Pharaonic dynasties probably began in Egypt circa 3100 B.C.; indeed, under a ruler whose hieroglyph reads Mên. He united Upper and Lower Egypt and established his capital at a new city called Men-Nefer ("The Beauty of Mên")—Memphis in Greek. His accession to this throne of a united Egypt had indeed followed a chaotic period of a disunited Egypt, as Manetho had stated. An inscription on an artifact known as the Palermo Stone has preserved at least nine archaic names of kings who wore only the Red Crown of Lower Egypt and who ruled before Menes. Tombs and actual artifacts have been found belonging to archaic kings bearing such names as "Scorpion," Ka, Zeser, Narmer, and Sma. Sir Flinders Petrie, the noted Egyptologist, claimed in his *The Royal Tombs of the First Dynasty* and other writings that these names correspond to names given by Manetho in the list of ten human rulers who reigned at Tanis during the chaotic centuries. Petrie suggested that this group, which preceded the First Dynasty, be called "Dynasty O."

A major archaeological document dealing with Egyptian kingship, the so-called Turin Papyrus, begins with a dynasty of gods that lists Ra, Geb, Osiris, Seth, and Horus, then Thoth, Maat, and others, and assigns to Horus—just as Manetho did—a reign of 300 years. This papyrus, which dates from the time of Ramses II, lists after the divine rulers thirty-eight semidivine rulers: "Nineteen Chiefs of the White Wall and nineteen Venerables of the North." Between them and Menes, the Turin Papyrus states, there ruled human kings under the patronage of Horus; their epithet was Shamsu-Hor!

Addressing the Royal Society of Literature in London in 1843, the curator of Egyptian Antiquities at the British Museum, Dr. Samuel Birch, announced that he had counted on the papyrus and its fragments a total of 330 names—a number that "coincided with the 330 kings mentioned by Herodotus."

Even if they disagree among themselves on details, Egyptologists now agree that the archaeological discoveries sustain the information provided by the ancient historians concerning the dynasties begun by Menes, following a chaotic period of about ten rulers in a disunited Egypt; and that there had been a *prior period* when Egypt was united under rulers whose names could have been no other than Horus, Osiris, and so on. However, scholars who find it difficult to accept that these rulers were "gods" suggest that they were only "deified" human beings.

To throw more light on the subject, we can start with the very place chosen by Menes for the capital of the reunified Egypt. The location of Memphis, we find, was not a matter of chance; it was related to certain events pertaining to the gods. Nor was the manner in which Memphis was built unsymbolic: Menes built the city on an artificial mound, created through the diversion of the Nile at that spot and other extensive damming, dyking, and land-reclamation works. This he did in emulation of the manner in which Egypt itself had been created.

The Egyptians believed that "a very great god who came forth in the earliest times" arrived in the land and found it lying under water and mud. He undertook great works of dyking and land reclamation, literally raising Egypt out of the waters—thus explaining

Egypt's nickname "The Raised Land." This olden god was named Ptah—a "God of Heaven and Earth." He was considered to be a great engineer and master artificer.

The veracity of the legend of The Raised Land is enhanced by its technological aspects. The Nile is a peaceful and navigable river up to Syene (Aswan); beyond that, the river's southward course is treacherous and obstructed by several cataracts. Just as the level of the Nile is regulated today by the dams at Aswan, so apparently was it in prehistoric Egypt. Ptah, Egyptian legends held, established his base of operations on the island of Abu, the one called since Greek times Elephantine on account of its shape; it is located just above the first cataract of the Nile, at Aswan. In text and drawings (Fig. 8) Ptah, whose symbol was the serpent, was depicted as

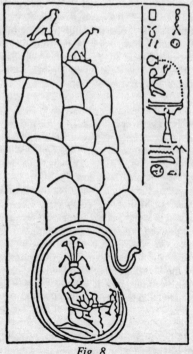

Fig. 8

controlling the Nile's waters from subterranean caverns. "It was he who kept the doors that held the inundations, who drew back the bolts at the proper time." In technical language we are being informed that at the most appropriate site from an engineering point of view, Ptah built "twin caverns" (two connected reservoirs) whose locks could be opened and closed, "bolted" and unbolted, thus regulating artificially the level and flow of the Nile's waters.

Ptah and the other gods were called, in Egyptian, *Ntr*—"Guardian, Watcher." They had come to Egypt, the Egyptians wrote, from *Ta-Ur*, the "Far/Foreign Land," whose name *Ur* meant "olden" but could have also been the actual place name—a place well known from Mesopotamian and biblical records: the ancient city of Ur in southern Mesopotamia. And the straits of the Red Sea, which connected Mesopotamia and Egypt, were called *Ta-Neter*, the "Place of the Gods," the passage by which they had come to Egypt. That the earliest gods did come from the biblical lands of Shem is additionally borne out by the puzzling fact that the names of these olden gods were of "Semitic" (Akkadian) derivation. Thus Ptah, which had no meaning in Egyptian, meant "he who fashioned things by carving and opening up" in the Semitic tongues.

In time—after 9,000 years, according to Manetho—Ra, a son of Ptah, became the ruler over Egypt. His name, too, had no meaning in Egyptian, but because Ra was associated with a bright celestial body, scholars assume that Ra meant "bright." We do know with greater certainty that one of his nicknames, *Tem,* had the Semitic connotation "the Complete, the Pure One."

It was believed by the Egyptians that Ra, too, had come to Earth from the "Planet of Millions of Years" in a Celestial Barge, the conical upper part of which, called *Ben-Ben* ("Pyramidion Bird"), was later on preserved in a specially built shrine in the sacred city *Anu* (the biblical *On,* which is better known by its Greek name Heliopolis). In dynastic times Egyptians made pilgrimages to this shrine to view the *Ben-Ben* and other relics associated with Ra and the celestial travels of the gods. It was to Ra as *Tem* that the Israelites were forced to build the city called in the Bible *Pi-Tom*—"The Gateway of Tem."

It was the Heliopolitan priests who first recorded the traditions of the gods of Egypt and who related that the first "company" of the gods headed by Ra consisted of nine "Guardians"—Ra and four divine couples who followed him. The first divine couple to rule when Ra tired of staying in Egypt were his own children, the male *Shu* ("Dryness") and the female *Tefnut* ("Moisture"); their main task, according to Egyptian tales, was to help Ra control the skies over the Earth.

Shu and Tefnut set the example for mortal Pharaohs in later times: the king selected his own half-sister as his royal spouse. They were followed on the divine throne—as both legends and Manetho inform us—by their children, again a brother-sister couple: *Geb* ("Who Piles Up the Earth") and *Nut* ("The Stretched-out Firmament").

The purely mythological approach to the Egyptian tales of the gods—that of primitive people watching Nature and seeing "gods" in its phenomena—has led scholars to assume that Geb represented the Earth deified, and Nut the Heavens; and that by calling Geb and Nut Father and Mother of the gods who thereafter reigned over Egypt, the Egyptians believed that the gods were born of the union of Earth and Heaven. But if the legends and verses in the *Pyramid Texts* and *The Book of the Dead* are to be taken more literally, it appears that Geb and Nut were so named on account of activities related to the periodic appearance of the *Bennu* bird, from which the Greeks obtained the legend of the Phoenix: an eagle whose feathers were red and gold, which died and reappeared at intervals lasting several millennia. It was for that bird—whose name was the same as that of the contraption in which Ra landed on Earth—that Geb engaged in great earthworks and Nut "stretched out the firmament of the sky." These feats, it appears, were carried out by the gods in the "Land of the Lions"; it was there that Geb "hath opened up the earth" for the great spherical object that came from the "stretched-out skies" and appeared on the horizon.

In the aftermath of the above-described feats, Geb and Nut turned over the direct rule of Egypt to their four children: *Asar* ("The All-Seeing"), whom the Greeks called Osiris, and his sister-wife *Ast*, better known as Isis; and Seth and his wife Nephtys (*Nebt-Hat*, "Lady of the House"), the sister of Isis. It was with these gods, who were truly gods of Egypt, that the Egyptian tales most concerned themselves; but in depicting them (Fig. 9) Seth was never shown without his animal disguise: his face was never seen, and the meaning of his name still defies Egyptologists, even if it is identical to the name given in the Bible to Adam and Eve's third son.

Fig. 9

With two brothers who married their own two sisters, the gods confronted a serious problem of succession. The only plausible solution was to divide the kingdom: Osiris was given the northern lowlands (Lower Egypt), and Seth was given the southern, mountainous part (Upper Egypt). How long this arrangement lasted we can only guess from Manetho's chronicles; but it is certain that Seth was not satisfied with the division of sovereignty and resorted to various schemes to gain control over the whole of Egypt.

Scholars have assumed that the sole motive of Seth was a craving for power. But once one grasps what the gods' rules of succession were, it becomes possible to understand the profound effect these rules had upon the affairs of the gods (and then of human kings). Since the gods (and then men) could have, in addition to the official spouse, one or more concubines, as well as beget children through illicit love affairs, the first rule of succession was this: the son first born to the official spouse was the heir to the throne. If the official spouse bore no son, the son first born to any of the concubines became the heir. However, if at any time, even after the birth of the Firstborn heir, a son was born to the ruler by his own half-sister, this son superseded the Firstborn and became the Legal Heir.

It was this custom that was the cause of much rivalry and strife among the Gods of Heaven and Earth and—we suggest—explains the basic motivation of Seth. Our source for this suggestion is the treatise *De Iside et Osiride (Of Isis and Osiris)* by Plutarch, a historian-biographer of the first century A.D., who wrote down for the Greeks and Romans of his time the legendary histories of the Near Eastern gods. The Egyptian sources on which he relied were believed at the time to have been writings of the god Thoth himself, who, as the Scribe of the Gods, recorded for all times their histories and deeds upon this Earth.

"Now the story of Isis and Osiris, its most significant [retained] and superfulous parts omitted, is thus briefly related," wrote Plutarch in his opening sentence and went on to tell that Nut (whom the Greeks compared with their goddess Rhea) had mothered three sons: the firstborn was Osiris, the last Seth. She also gave birth to two daughters, Isis and Nephtys. But not all of these children were really fathered by Geb: only Seth and Nephtys were. Osiris and his second brother were in truth fathered by the god Ra, who came unto his granddaughter Nut in stealth; and Isis was fathered by Thoth (the Greek god Hermes) who, "being likewise in love with the same goddess," reciprocated in various ways "in recompense for the favours which he had received from her."

The setting, then, was this: the firstborn was Osiris, and, though not by Geb, his claim to the succession was even greater, having been fathered by the great Ra himself. But the legitimate heir was Seth, having been born to the ruling Geb by his half-sister Nut. As if this were not enough, matters were further complicated by the race between the two brothers to assure that their son would be the next legitimate successor. To achieve that Seth could have fathered a son only by his half-sister Isis, whereas Osiris could achieve this by fathering a son by either Isis or Nephtys (both being only half-sisters to him). But Osiris deliberately blocked Seth's chances to have his descendants rule over Egypt by taking Isis as his spouse. Seth then married Nephtys; but as she was his full sister, none of their offspring could qualify.

So was the stage set for Seth's increasingly violent rage against Osiris, who deprived him both of the throne and of the succession.

The occasion for Seth's revenge, according to Plutarch, was the visit to Egypt of "a certain queen of Ethiopia named Aso." In conspiracy with his supporters Seth held a banquet in her honor, to which all the gods were invited. For his scheme Seth had a magnificent chest constructed, large enough to hold Osiris: "This chest he brought into the banqueting room; where, after it had been much admired by all who were present, Seth—as though in jest—promised to give it to any one of them whose body it would fit. Upon this the whole company, one after the other, went into the chest.

"Last of all, Osiris lay himself down in it, upon which the conspirators immediately ran together, clapped the cover upon it, and then fastened it down on the outside with nails, pouring likewise melted lead over it." They then carried the chest in which Osiris was imprisoned to the seashore, and where the Nile flows into the Mediterranean at Tanis sank the chest in the sea.

Dressed in mourning apparel and cutting off a lock of her hair as a sign of grief, Isis went in search of the chest. "At length she received more particular news of the chest, that it had been carried by the waves of the sea to the coast of Byblos" (in what is now Lebanon). Isis retrieved the chest holding the body of Osiris and hid it in a deserted place until she could figure out how to resurrect Osiris. But Seth somehow found all that out, seized the chest, and cut up the body of Osiris into fourteen pieces, which he dispersed all over Egypt.

Once again Isis went in search of the scattered limbs of her brother-husband. Some versions say that she buried the parts where she found them, starting the worship of Osiris at those places; others say she bound together the parts she found, starting the custom of mummification. All agree that she found all parts except one—the phallus of Osiris.

Nevertheless, before finally disposing of the body, she managed to extract from the body of Osiris its "essence," and self-inseminated herself with his seed, thus conceiving and giving birth to the boy Horus. She hid him from Seth in the papyrus swamps of the Nile delta.

Many legends have been found concerning the events that followed: legends copied and recopied on papyri, forming chapters of *The Book of the Dead,* or used as verses in the Pyramid texts. Put together they reveal a major drama that involved legal manuevering, kidnapping for purposes of state, a magical return from the dead, homosexuality, and finally a great war—a drama in which the stake was the Divine Throne of the gods.

Since all seemed to believe that Osiris had perished without leaving an heir, Seth saw this as his chance to obtain a legitimate heir by forcing Isis to espouse him. He kidnapped her and held her prisoner until she consented, but with the aid of the god Thoth, Isis managed to escape. A version recorded on the so-called Metternich Stela, composed as a tale by Isis in her own words, describes her escape in the night and her adventures until she reached the swamps where Horus was hidden. She found Horus dying from a scorpion's sting (Fig. 10). One can infer from the text that it was word of her son's dying that prompted her escape. The people who

Fig. 10

lived in the swamps came out at her cries but were helpless to be of any aid. Then help came from a spacecraft:

> Then Isis sent forth a cry to heaven and addressed her appeal to the Boat of Millions of Years.
>
> And the Celestial Disk stood still, and moved not from the place where it was.
>
> And Thoth came down, and he was provided with magical powers, and possessed the great power which made the word become indeed. And he said:
>
> "O Isis, thou goddess, thou glorious one, who has knowledge of the mouth; behold, no evil shall come upon the child Horus, for his protection cometh from the Boat of Ra.
>
> "I have come this day in the Boat of the Celestial Disk from the place where it was yesterday. When the night cometh, this Light shall drive away [the poison] for the healing of Horus. . . .
>
> "I have come from the skies to save the child for his mother."

Revived from death by the artful Thoth and, some texts say, immunized forever as a result of Thoth's treatment, Horus grew up as *Netch-atef,* "Avenger of his Father." Educated and trained in martial arts by goddesses and gods who sided with Osiris, he was groomed as a Divine Prince worthy of celestial association. Then, one day, he appeared before the Council of the Gods to claim the throne of Osiris.

Of the many gods who were surprised by his appearance, none was more so than Seth. All seemed to wonder: Did Osiris indeed father this son? As described in a text known as the *Chester Beatty Papyrus No. 1,* Seth suggested that the gods' deliberations be recessed so as to give him a chance to discuss the problem peacefully with his newly appeared nephew. He invited Horus to "come, let us pass a happy day in my house," and Horus agreed. But what Seth had in mind was not peacemaking; his mind was set on trickery:

> And when it was eventide, the bed was spread for them, and the twain lay thereon.
>
> And in the night Seth caused his member to become stiff, and he made it go between the loins of Horus.

When the gods next met in council, Seth demanded that the Office of Ruler be resolved as his, for Horus was disqualified: whether or not he was of the seed of Osiris, the seed of Seth was now in him, entitling him to succeed, not precede, Seth!

Now it was the turn of Horus to surprise the gods. When Seth poured out his semen, "I caught the seed between my hands," Horus said. In the morning he showed it to his mother, telling her what had happened. Isis then made Horus erect his member and pour his semen into a cup. Then she went to the garden of Seth and poured the semen of Horus on the lettuce that Seth then unknowingly ate. So, announced Horus, "Not only is Seth's seed not in me, but *my* seed is *in him!* It is Seth who has been disqualified!"

Baffled, the gods called upon Thoth to resolve the issue. He checked the semen that Horus had given his mother, which Isis kept in a pot; it was found to be indeed the semen of Seth. He then scanned the body of Seth and confirmed that it contained the semen of Horus. . . .

Enraged, Seth did not wait for the discussions to continue. Only a fight to the bitter end could now settle the issue, he shouted as he left.

Seth had by then, per Manetho, ruled 350 years. If we add to this the time—thirteen years, we believe—it had taken Isis to find the thirteen parts of the dismembered Osiris, it was indeed "in the year

363'' that Ra joined Horus in Nubia, from there to accompany Horus on his war against "the Enemy." In *Horus, Royal God of Egypt*, S. B. Mercer summed up the scholarly opinions on the subject with these emphatic words: "The story of the conflict between Horus and Seth represents a historical event."

According to the Edfu temple inscription, the first face-to-face battle between Horus and Seth took place at the "Lake of the Gods," thereafter known as the "Lake of Battle." Horus managed to hit Seth with his Divine Lance; when Seth fell down, Horus captured him and brought him before Ra. "His spear was in his [Seth's] neck, and the legs of the evil one were chained, and his mouth had been closed by a blow from the club of the god [Horus]." Ra decided that Isis and Horus could do with Seth and the other captured "conspirators" as they pleased.

But as Horus began to slay the captives by cutting off their heads, Isis had pity on her brother Seth, and set him free. There are several versions of what ensued, including one known as the *Fourth Sallier Papyrus;* and, according to most, the release of Seth so infuriated Horus that he beheaded his own mother, Isis; but the god Thoth put her severed head back in place and resurrected her. (This incident is also reported by Plutarch.)

After his escape Seth at first hid in a subterranean tunnel. After a lull of six days, a series of aerial battles ensued. Horus took to the air in a *Nar* (a "Fiery Pillar"), which was depicted as an elongated, cylindrical vessel equipped with fins or short wings. Its bulkhead contained two "eyes," which kept changing color from blue to red and back to blue; from the rear, jetlike trails were shown (Fig. 11); from the front, the contraption spewed out rays.

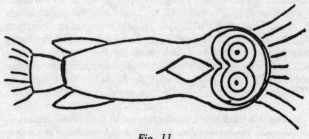

Fig. 11

(The Egyptian texts, all written by the followers of Horus, contain no description of Seth's aerial vehicle.)

The texts describe a battle that ranged far and wide, and the first to be hit was Horus—struck by a bolt of light from Seth's vehicle. The *Nar* lost one of its "eyes," and Horus continued the fight from the Winged Disk of Ra. From out of this he shot a "harpoon" at Seth; now Seth was hit, and lost his testicles. . . .

Dwelling on the nature of the weapon, W. Max Müller wrote in *Egyptian Mythology* that it had "a strange, practically impossible head" and was nicknamed in the hieroglyphic texts "the weapon of thirty." As ancient depictions reveal (Fig. 12a), the "harpoon" was indeed an ingenious three-in-one rocket: as the first, larger missile was fired, the way was opened for the two smaller missiles to be launched. The nickname ("Weapon of Thirty") suggests that the missiles were what we nowadays call Multiple Warhead Missiles, each missile holding ten warheads.

Through sheer coincidence, but probably because similar circumstances result in similar connotations, the McDonnell Douglas Corporation of St. Louis, Missouri, has named its newly developed naval guided missile "The Harpoon" (Fig. 12b).

The great gods called a truce and once again summoned the adversaries before the Council of the Gods. We glean details of the deliberations from a text inscribed on a stone column by the Pharaoh Shabako (eighth century B.C.), who stated that the text is a copy made from a very old leather scroll, "devoured by worms," which was found buried in the great temple of Ptah at Memphis. The Council, at first, redivided Egypt between Horus and Seth along the lines of the division at the time of Osiris, but Geb had second thoughts and upset the decision, for he was concerned with the question of continuity: Who would "open the body" to successive generations? Seth, having lost his testicles, could no longer have offspring. . . . And so Geb, "Lord Earth," gave as a heritage to Horus" the whole of Egypt. To Seth a dominion away from Egypt was to be given; henceforth, he was deemed by the Egyptians to have become an Asiatic deity.

The Council of the Gods adopted the recommendations unanimously. Its final action is thus described in the *Papyrus of Hunefer:*

> Horus is triumphant in the presence of the whole company of the gods. The sovereignty over the world hath been given unto him, and his dominion is in the uttermost parts of Earth.

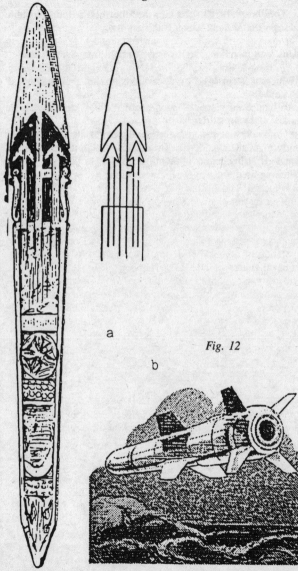

a

Fig. 12

b

The throne of the god Geb hath been adjudged unto him, along with the rank which hath been founded by the god Shu.

This legitimization, the Papyrus went on to say:

Hath been formalized by decrees [lodged] in the Chamber of Records;
    It hath been inscribed upon a metal tablet according to the commandments of thy father Ptah. . . .
    Gods celestial and gods terrestrial transfer themselves to the services of thy son Horus. They follow him to the Hall of Decrees. He shall lord over them.

3

THE MISSILES OF ZEUS
AND INDRA

After Herodotus had visited Egypt in the fifth century B.C., he was convinced that it was from the Egyptians that the Greeks had obtained their notions and beliefs of the gods; writing for his countrymen, he employed the names of Greek gods to describe the comparable Egyptian deities.

His conviction of the Egyptian origin of Greek theology stemmed not only from comparable attributes and meanings of the gods' names, but also (and mostly) from similarities in the tales concerning them. Of these, one uncanny parallel certainly must have struck him as no mere coincidence: it was the tale of the castration of one god by another in a struggle for supremacy.

The Greek sources from which Herodotus could have drawn are, fortunately, still available: various literary works, such as Homer's *Iliad;* the *Odes* of Pindar of Thebes, written and well known just before Herodotus' time; and first and foremost, the *Theogony* ("Divine Genealogy") by Hesiod, a native of Askara in central Greece who composed this work and another *(Works and Days)* in the eighth century B.C.

A poet, Hesiod chose to attribute the writing of the *Theogony* to the Muses, goddesses of music, literature, and art, who, he wrote, encouraged him "to celebrate in song" the histories "of the revered race of gods, from the beginning . . . and then to chant of the race of men and strong giants; and so gladden the heart of Zeus within Olympus." This all happened when he was "shepherding his lambs" one day near the Holy Mountain which was their abode.

In spite of this pastoral introduction, the tale of the gods as revealed to Hesiod was mostly one of passion, revolt, cunning, and mutilation; as well as of struggle and global wars. In spite of all the hymnal glorification of Zeus, there is no apparent attempt to cover up the chain of bloody violence that had led to his supremacy.

49

Whatever the Muses sang of, Hesiod wrote down; and "these things did sing the Muses, nine daughters begotten of Zeus":

> Verily, at first Chaos came to be,
> and next the wide-bosomed Gaea . . .
> And dim Tartarus, in the depths of wide-pathed Earth,
> and Eros, fairest among the deathless gods . . .
> From Chaos came forth Erebus and black Nyx;
> And of Nyx were born Aether and Hemera.

This first group of celestial gods was completed when *Gaea* ("Earth") brought forth *Uranus* ("Starry Heaven") and then espoused her own firstborn son so that he might be included in the First Dynasty of the gods. Besides Uranus, and soon after he was born, Gaea also gave birth to his graceful sister, Uraea, and to "Pontus, the fruitless Deep with his raging swell."

Then the next generation of gods were born—offspring of Gaea's mating with Uranus:

> Afterwards she lay with Uranus,
> and bare deep-swirling Oceanus;
> Coeus and Crius and Hyperion and Iapetus;
> Theia and Rhea, Themis and Mnemosyne;
> And gold-crowned Phoebe, and lovely Thetys.
> After them was born Cronos, the wily,
> youngest and most terrible of her children.

In spite of the fact that these twelve were offspring of the mating of a son with his own mother, the children—six males, six females—were worthy of their divine origins. But as Uranus got lustier and lustier, the offspring that followed—though formidable in might—displayed various deformities. First of the "monsters" to be born were the three Cyclopes, Brontes ("The Thunderer"), Steropes ("The Maker of Lightning"), and Arges ("Who Makes Radiation"); "in all else they were like the gods, but one eye only was set in the midst of their foreheads; and they were named 'Orb-eyed' (Cyclopes) because one orbed eye was set in their foreheads."

"And again three more sons were born of Gaea and Uranus, great and valiant beyond telling: Cottus and Briareos and Gyes, audacious children." Of giant size, the three were called Hekatoncheires ("The Hundred-Armed"): "From their shoulders sprang an hundred arms, not to be approached, and each had fifty heads upon his shoulders."

"And Cronos hated his lusty sire," Hesiod wrote; but "Uranus rejoiced in his evil doing."

It was then that Gaea "shaped a great sickle and told her plan to her dear sons," whereby their "sinful father" would be punished for his "vile outrages": to cut off the genitals of Uranus and put an end to his sexual drives. But "fear seized them all"; and only "great Cronos, the wily, took courage."

And so it was that Gaea gave Cronos the sickle she had made of gray flint and hid him "in an ambush" in her quarters, which were by the Mediterranean Sea.

> And Uranus came at nighttime, longing for love;
> and he lay about Gaea, spreading himself upon her.
> Then the son from his ambush
> stretched forth his left hand to grasp;
> and in his right hand he held
> the great long sickle with jagged teeth.
> Swiftly, he cut off his own father's genitals,
> and cast them away, to fall behind him . . .
> into the surging sea.

The deed was done, but the castration of Uranus did not completely terminate his line of offspring. As his blood gushed forth, some of the blood drops impregnated Gaea, and she conceived and bore "the strong Erinyes" (female Furies of vengeance) "and the great Gigantes with gleaming armor, holding long spears in their hands; and the Nymphs whom they call Meliae ['the Nymphs of the ash tree']." Of the castrated genitals, leaving a trail of foam as the surging sea carried them to the island of Cyprus, "there came forth an awful and lovely goddess . . . gods and men call her *Aphrodite* ['She of the Foam']."

The incapacitated Uranus called out to the monster-gods for vengeance. His own children, he cried out, had become *Titans*, Strainers who had "strained and did presumptuously the dreadful deed"; now the other gods had to make sure "that vengeance for it would afterwards come." The frightened Cronos then imprisoned the Cyclopes and the other monstrous giants far away, so that none would answer the call of Uranus.

All along, while Uranus was busy bringing forth his own offspring, the other gods were also proliferating; their children bore names indicating their attributes—by and large benevolent. Now, after the evil deed, the goddess Nyx responded to his call by bringing forth the deities of evil: "She bare the Destinies and the ruthless avenging Fates: Clotho ['The Spinner'] and Lachesis ['The Disposer of Lots'] and Atropos ['Inevitable']. . . . She bare Doom and Black Fate and Death . . . and Blame and Painful Woe . . . Famine and Sorrows." And she also brought into the world "Deceit and Strife . . . as also Fighting, Battles, Murders, Killings, Quarrels, Lying Words, Disputes, Lawlessness and Ruin." Lastly there was borne by Nyx *Nemesis* ("Retribution"). The call of Uranus has been answered: fighting, battles, and war came to be among the gods.

It was into this dangerous world that the Titans were bringing forth the third generation of the gods. Fearful of retribution, they kept closely to each other, five of the six brothers espousing five of their own six sisters. Of these divine brother-sister couples, most important was that of Cronos and Rhea, for it was Cronos, by reason of his bold deed, who had assumed the leadership among the gods. Of this union, Rhea gave birth to three daughters and three sons: Hestia, Demeter, and Hera; and Hades, Poseidon, and Zeus.

No sooner had one of these children been born than "the great Cronos swallowed each . . . intent that no other of the proud Sons of Heaven should hold kingly office among the deathless gods." The reason for eliminating his own offspring by swallowing them was a prophecy he had learned of, that "strong though he was, he was destined to be overcome by his own son": Fate was to repeat unto Cronos that which he had done unto his father.

But Fate could not be evaded. Wisened to the tricks of Cronos, Rhea hid her last-born son Zeus on the island of Crete. To Cronos she gave instead of the baby "a great stone wrapped in swaddling clothes." Not realizing the deception, Cronos swallowed the stone, thinking it was the baby Zeus. Soon thereafter he began vomiting, disgorging one by one all the children he had previously swallowed.

"As the years rolled on, the strength and glorious limbs of the prince [Zeus] increased quickly." For a while, as a worthy grandson of the lusty Uranus, Zeus chased lovely goddesses, often getting into trouble with their companion gods. But then he turned his mind to affairs of state. For ten years a war had been raging between the older Titans, "the lordly Titans from high Mount Othyres" (which was their abode), and the younger gods "whom rich-haired Rhea bare in union with Cronos" and who settled on the opposite Mount Olympus. "With bitter wrath they were fighting continually with one another at that time for ten full years, and the hard strife had no close or end for either side, and the issue of war hung evenly balanced.''

Was this fighting merely the culmination of deteriorating relations between neighboring godly colonies, an outbreak of rivalry between intermingled and unfaithful gods and goddesses (where mothers slept with their sons, and uncles impregnated their nieces), or the first instance of the everlasting rebellion of the young against the old regime? The *Theogony* does not provide a clear answer, but later Greek legends and plays suggest that all these motives combined to create a prolonged and ''stubborn war'' between the younger and the older gods.

It was this ongoing war that was seen by Zeus as his chance to seize the lordship over the gods and thereby—knowingly or unknowingly—fulfill the destiny to which his father Cronos had been fated, by deposing him.

As his first step Zeus ''set free from their deadly bonds the brothers of his father, sons of Uranus, whom his father in his foolishness had bound.'' In gratitude, the three Cyclopes gave him the divine weapons Gaea had hidden away from Uranus: ''The Thunder, and the Radiating Thunderbolt and the Lightning.'' They also gave Hades a magic helmet, which made its wearer invisible; and Poseidon received a magical trident, which could make the earth and sea shake.

To refresh the Hekatoncheires after their long captivity and return their vigor to them, Zeus provided the trio with ''nectar and ambrosia, the same that the gods eat''; then he addressed them and said:

> Hear me,
> O bright children of Uranus and Gaea,
>   that I may say what my heart within bids me.
> A long while now have we,
>   who are sprung from Cronos, and the Titan gods,
>   fought with each other every day,
>   to get victory and to prevail.
> Would you now show your great might and strength,
>   and face the Titans in the bitter strife?

And Cottus, one of the Hundred-Armed, answered him and said: ''Divine one, you speak that which we know well . . .

through your devising we are come back from the murky gloom
and from our merciless bonds. And so now, with fixed purpose and
deliberate counsel, we will aid your power in the dreadful strife,
and fight against the Titans in hard battle."

So "all that were born of Cronos, together with those dreaded
mighty ones of overwhelming strength whom Zeus brought up to
light . . . they all, both male and female, stirred up the hated battle
that day." Arrayed against these Olympians were the older Titans,
who also "eagerly strengthened their ranks."

As the battle was joined it ranged all over the Earth and in the
skies:

> The boundless sea rang terribly around,
>   and the earth crashed loudly;
> Wide heaven was shaken and groaned,
>   and high Olympus reeled from its foundations
>   under the charge of the undying gods.
> From the deep sound of the gods' feet,
>   and the fearful onset of their hard missiles,
>   the heavy quaking reached even far Tartarus.

In a verse reminiscent of the Dead Sea Scroll text, the *Theogony*
recalled the war cries of the battling gods:

> Thus, then, they launched their grievous
>   bolts at one another;
> And the cry of both armies as they shouted
>   reached to the starry heaven
>   as they clashed with a great battle-cry.

Zeus himself was fighting with all his might, using his Divine
Weapons to the utmost. "From the skies, opposite Mount
Olympus, he came forthwith, hurling his lightning. The bolts
flew thick and fast from his strong hand, Thunder and Lightning together, whirling as an awesome flame. The fertile earth
crashed around in burning, and the vast wood crackled aloud
with fire all about. All the land seethed, as did the sweetwater
streams and the salty sea."

Then Zeus hurled a Thunder-Stone (Fig. 13) against Mount
Othyres; it was, indeed, nothing short of an atomic explosion:

Fig. 13

The hot vapor lapped around the Titans,
  of Gaea born;
Flame unspeakable rose bright to the upper air.
The Flashing glare of the Thunder-Stone,
  its lightning, blinded their eyes—
  so strong it was.
Astounding heat seized Chaos . . .
It seemed as if Earth and wide Heaven above
  had come together;
A mighty crash, as though Earth was hurled to ruin.

"So great a crash was there while the gods clashed together in strife."

In addition to the awesome sound, the blinding flash, and the extreme heat, the hurling of the Thunder-Stone also created an immense wind storm:

> Also were the winds brought rumbling,
>   earthquake and duststorm,
>   thunder and lightning.

All this did the Thunder-Stone of great Zeus bring about. And when the two contending camps heard and saw what had happened, "an horrible uproar of terrible strife arose; mighty deeds were shown; and the battle inclined." The fighting was abating; for the gods had the upper hand over the Titans.

"Insatiated for war," the three Cyclopes set upon the Titans, overpowering them with hand-held missiles. "They bound them in bitter chains," and hurled them into captivity to far Tartarus. "There, by the counsel of Zeus who rides the clouds, the Titan gods are hidden under misty gloom, in a dank place at the ends of huge Earth." The three Cyclopes stayed there, too, as "trusty warders of Zeus," to watch over the imprisoned Titans.

As Zeus was about to claim "the aegis," the suzerainty over all the gods, a sudden challenger appeared on the scene. For, "when Zeus had driven the Titans from heaven, great Gaea bare her youngest child Typhoeus of the love of Tartarus, with the aid of golden Aphrodite." Typhoeus ("Typhon") was a real monster: "Strength was with his hands in all that he did, and the feet of the strong god were untiring. From his shoulders grew an hundred heads of a snake, a fearful dragon, with dark, flickering tongues. From under the brows of his eyes, in his marvellous heads, fire flashed; and fire burned from his heads as he glared. And there were voices in all his dreadful heads, which uttered incredible sounds": the sound of a man as he speaks, and the sound of a bull, and that of a lion, and the sound of a puppy. (According to Pindar and Aeschylus, Typhon was gigantic in height, "and his head reached to the stars.")

"Truly a thing past help would have happened on that day," the Muses revealed to Hesiod; it was almost inevitable that Typhoeus "would have come to reign over mortals and immortals." But Zeus was quick to perceive the danger and lost no time in attacking him.

The series of battles that ensued were no less awesome than the fighting between the gods and the Titans, for the Snake-God Typhon was equipped with wings and could fly about just as Zeus (Fig. 14). "Zeus thundered hard and mightily, and the earth around resounded terribly, as did the wide heaven above and the sea and the watery streams, even the nether parts of the Earth." Divine Weapons were again employed—by both combatants:

Fig. 14

Through the two of them,
   through the thunder and lightning,
   heat engulfed the dark-blue seas;
And through the fire from the Monster,
   and the scorching winds and blazing Thunderbolt,
   the whole Earth seethed, and sky and sea.
Great waves raged along the beaches . . .
And there arose an endless shaking.

In the Lower World, "Hades trembled where he ruled"; tremble did the Titans imprisoned at the ends of earth. Chasing each other in the skies and over land, Zeus managed to be the first to achieve a direct hit with his "lurid Thunderbolt." The bolt "burned all the marvelous heads of the monster, all that were around him"; and Typhoeus crashed down to earth in his marvelous contraption:

When Zeus had vanquished him
  and lashed him with his strokes,
    Typhoeus was hurled down a maimed wreck.
The huge earth groaned.
A flame shot forth from the stricken lord
  in the dim, rugged, secluded valley of the Mount,
    when he was smitten.
A great part of huge earth was scorched
  by the terrible vapor,
    melting as tin melts when heated by man's art . . .
In the glow of a blazing fire
  did the earth melt down.

In spite of the crash and the tremendous impact of Typhon's vehicle, the god himself remained alive. According to the *Theogony*, Zeus cast him, too, "into wide Tartarus." With this victory his reign was secure; and he turned to the important business of procreation, bringing forth progeny by wives and concubines alike.

Though the *Theogony* described only one battle between Zeus and Typhon, the other Greek writings assert that that was the final battle, preceded by several others in which Zeus was the first one to be hurt. Initally Zeus fought with Typhon at close quarters, using the special sickle his mother had given him for the "evil deed," for it was his purpose also to castrate Typhon. But Typhon enmeshed Zeus in his net, wrested his sickle away, and with it cut out the sinews of Zeus' hands and feet. He then deposited the helpless Zeus, his sinews, and his weapons in a cave.

But the gods Aegipan and Hermes found the cave, resurrected Zeus by restoring his sinews, and returned his weapons to him. Zeus then escaped and flew back "in a Winged Chariot" to Olympus, where he acquired a new supply of bolts for his Thunderer. With these Zeus renewed the attack on Typhon, driving him to Mount Nyssa, where the Fates tricked Typhon into eating the food of mortal men; whereupon he was weakened instead of being strengthened. The renewed fighting began in the skies over Mount Haemus in Thrace, continued over Mount Etna in Sicily, and ended over Mount Casius on the Asiatic coast of the eastern Mediterranean. There Zeus, using his Thunderbolt, shot Typhon down from the skies.

The similarity between the battles, the weapons used, the locations, as well as the tales of castration, mutilation, and resurrection—all in the course of a struggle for succession—convinced

Herodotus (and other Greek classical historians) that the Greeks had borrowed their theogony from the Egyptians. Aegipan stood for the African Ram God of Egypt, and Hermes paralleled the god Thoth. Hesiod himself reported that when Zeus came unto the mortal beauty Alcmena so that she might bear him the heroic Heracles, he slipped at night from Mount Olympus and went to the land of Typhaonion, resting there atop the *Phikion* (The Sphinx Mountain). "The deadly Sphinx that destroyed the *Cadmeans*" ("The Ancients"), which featured in the doings of Hera, the official spouse of Zeus, was also connected in these legends with Typhon and his domain. And Apollodorus reported that when Typhon was born and grew to an incredible size, the gods rushed to Egypt to take a look at the awesome monster.

Most scholars have held that Mount Casius, the site of the final battle between Zeus and Typhon, was located near the mouth of the Orontes river in today's Syria. But as Otto Eissfeldt has shown in a major study *(Baal Zaphon, Zeus Kasios und der Durchgang der Israeliten durches Meer)*, there was another mount called by that name in antiquity—a promontory on the Serbonic Sealet that juts out of the Sinai peninsula into the Mediterranean Sea. He suggested that that was the mount referred to in the legends.

Once again, all one had to do was to trust the information given to Herodotus in Egypt. Describing the land route from Phoenicia to Egypt via Philistia *(History,* Book III, 5), he wrote that the Asian lands "extend to Lake Serbonis, near the place where Mount Casius juts out into the sea. Egypt begins at Lake Serbonis, where the tale goes that Typhon hid himself."

Once again, Greek and Egyptian tales converged, with the Sinai peninsula as the climax.

Notwithstanding the many connecting threads the ancient Greeks had found between their theogony and that of Egypt, it was much farther away—in India—that nineteenth-century European scholars have found even more amazing parallels.

No sooner had Sanskrit, the language of ancient India, been mastered at the end of the eighteenth century than Europe began to be enchanted by translations of hitherto unknown writings. At first a field dominated by the British, the study of Sanskrit literature, philosophy, and mythology was by the mid-nineteenth century a favorite of German scholars, poets, and intellectuals, for Sanskrit turned out to be a mother tongue of the Indo-European languages (to which German belonged), and its bearers to India were migrants from the shores of the Caspian Sea—"Aryans," as the Germans believed their ancestors, too, to have been.

Central to this literature were the Vedas, sacred scriptures believed by Hindu tradition to be "not of human origin," having been composed by the gods themselves in a previous age. They were brought to the Indian subcontinent by the Aryan migrants sometime in the second millennium B.C., as oral traditions. But as time went on, more and more of the original 100,000 verses were lost; so, circa 200 B.C., a sage wrote down the remaining verses, dividing them into four parts: the Rig-Veda (the "Veda of Verses"), which is made up of ten books; the Sama-Veda (the "Chanted Vedas"); the Yajur-Veda (mostly sacrificial prayers); and the Atharva-Veda (spells and incantations).

In time, the various components of the Vedas and the auxiliary literature that stemmed from them (the Mantras, Brahmanas, Aranyakas, Upanishads) were augmented by the non-Vedic Puranas ("Ancient Writings"). Together with the great epic tales of the Mahabharata and the Ramayana, they make up the sources of the Aryan and Hindu tales of Heaven and Earth, gods and heroes.

Because of the long oral interval, the length and profusion of texts finally written down over many centuries, the many names, generic terms, and epithets employed for the deities interchangeably—and the fact that many of these original names and terms were non-Aryan after all—consistency and precision are not hallmarks of this Sanskrit literature. Yet some facts and events emerge as basic tenets of the Aryan-Hindu legacy.

In the beginning, these sources relate, there were only the celestial bodies, "The Primeval Ones Who Flow." There was an upheaval in the heavens, and "The Dragon" was split in two by the "Flowing One of Storms." Calling the two parts by names of non-Aryan origin, the tales assert that *Rehu,* the upper part of the destroyed planet, unceasingly traverses the heavens in search of vengeance; the lower part, *Ketu* ("The Cut-off One"), has joined the "Primeval Ones" in their "flowing" (orbits). Many Ages then passed, and a dynasty of Gods of Heaven and Earth made its appearance. The heavenly Mar-Ishi, who headed them, had seven (or ten) children by his consort *Prit-Hivi* ("The Broad One"), who personified the Earth. One of them, *Kas-Yapa* ("He of the Throne"), made himself chief of the *Devas* ("The Shiny Ones"), seizing the title *Dyaus-Pitar* ("Sky Father")—the undoubted source of the Greek title-name Zeus ("Dyaus") and its Roman parallel Jupiter ("Dyauspiter").

Quite prolific, Kasyapa begot many gods, giants, and monstrous offspring by diverse wives and concubines. Most prominent, and individually known and revered since Vedic times, were the Adityas—some born to Kasyapa by his consort Aditi ("Boundless"). Numbering seven at first, they were Vishnu, Varuna, Mitra, Rudra, Pushan, Tvashtri, and Indra. Then the Aditis were joined by Agni, a son of Kasyapa either by his spouse Aditi or (as some texts suggest) by his own mother Prithivi. As in the Greek Olympian circle, the number of the Aditis finally rose to twelve. Among them were Bhaga, who is believed by scholars to have become the supreme Slavic god Bogh. The last one to be born by Aditi—though whether he was fathered by Kasyapa was uncertain—was Surya.

Tvashtri ("Fashioner"), in his role as "All-Accomplishing," the artisan of the gods, provided them with aerial cars and magical weapons. From a blazing celestial metal he fashioned a discus for Vishnu, a trident for Rudra, a "fire weapon" for Agni, a "bolt-hurling Thunderer" for Indra, and a "flying mace" for Surya. In ancient Hindu depictions, all these weapons appeared as hand-held missiles of diverse shapes (Fig. 15). In addition, the gods acquired other weapons from Tvashtri's assistants; Indra, for example, obtained an "aerial net" with which he could snare his foes during sky battles.

Fig. 15

The celestial chariots or "aerial cars" were invariably described as bright and radiant, made of or plated with gold. Indra's *Vimana* (aerial car) had lights shining at its sides and moved "swifter than thought," traversing rapidly vast distances. Its unseen steeds were "Sun-eyed," emitting a reddish hue, but also changing colors. In other instances the aerial cars of the gods were described as multitiered; sometimes they could not only fly in the air, but also travel under water. In the epic tale of the Mahabharata, the arrival of the gods for a wedding feast in a fleet of aerial cars is described thus (we follow the translation of R. Dutt in *Mahabharata, The Epic of Ancient India*):

> The gods, in cloud-borne chariots,
>   came to view the scene so fair:
> Bright Adityas in their splendor,
>   Maruts in the moving air;
> Winged Suparnas, scaly Nagas,
>   Deva Rishies pure and high,
> For their music famed, Gandharvas;
>   (and) fair Apsaras of the sky. . . .
> Bright celestial cars in concourse
>   sailed upon the cloudless sky.

The texts also speak of the *Ashvins* ("Drivers"), gods who specialized in piloting aerial chariots. "Swift as young falcons," they were "the best of charioteers who reach the heavens," always piloting their craft in pairs, accompanied by a navigator. Their vehicles, which sometimes appeared in groups, were golden-made, "bright and radiant . . . with easy seat and lightly rolling." They were constructed on a triple principle, having three levels, three seats, three supporting poles, and three rotating wheels. "That chariot of yours," Hymn 22 of Book VIII of the Rig-Veda said in praise of the Ashvins, "hath a triple seat and reins of gold—the famous car that traverses Heaven and Earth." The rotating wheels, it appears, served diverse functions: one to raise the craft, another to give it direction, the third to speed it along: "One of your chariot's wheels is moving swiftly around; one speeds for you its onward course."

As in the Greek tales, so did the gods of the Vedas display little morality or restraint in sexual matters—sometimes getting away with it, sometimes not, as when the indignant Adityas selected Rudra ("The Three-Eyed") to kill their grandfather Dyaus for having violated their sister Ushas. (Dyaus, wounded, saved his life by fleeing to a distant celestial body.) Also as in the Greek tales, so did the gods according to Hindu lore mingle, in later times, in the loves and wars of mortal kings and heroes. In these instances the aerial vehicles of the gods played roles even greater than their weapons. Thus, when one hero drowned, the Ashvins appeared in a fleet of three aerial chariots, "self-activated watertight ships which traverse the air," dived into the ocean, retrieved the hero from the watery depths, and "conveyed him over land, beyond the liquid ocean." And then there was the tale of Yayati, a king who married the daughter of a god. When the couple bore children, the happy grandfather gave the king "a highly effulgent golden celestial chariot, which could go everywhere without interruption." Without losing time, "Yayati ascended the chariot and, irrepressible in battle, within six nights conquered the entire Earth."

As in the *Iliad*, so did Hindu traditions tell of wars of men and gods over beautiful heroines. Best known of these tales is the *Ramayana*, the long epic tale of Rama the prince whose beautiful wife was abducted by the king of Lanka (the island of Ceylon, off India). Among the gods who turned out to help Rama was Hanuman, the god with a monkey face, who conducted aerial battles with the winged Garuda (Fig. 16), one of the monstrous offspring of

Fig. 16

Kasyapa. In another instance, Sukra, a god "sullied by immorality," abducted Tara, the beautiful wife of Indra's charioteer. "The Illustrious Rudra" and other gods then came to the aid of the aggrieved husband. There ensued "a terrible battle, destructive of gods and demons, on account of Tara." In spite of their awesome weapons, the gods were bested and had to seek refuge with "the Prime Deity." Thereupon the grandfather of the gods himself came to Earth, and put an end to the fighting by returning Tara to her husband. Then Tara gave birth to a son "whose beauty overclouded the celestials . . . . Filled with suspicion, the gods demanded to know who the true father was: the lawful husband or the abductor-god." She proclaimed that the boy was the son of Soma, "Celestial Immortality"; and she named him Budah.

But all that was in times yet to come; in the olden days the gods battled among themselves for more important causes: supremacy and rule over the Earth and its resources. With so many offspring of Kasyapa by diverse wives and concubines, as well as the descendants of the other olden gods, conflict soon became inevitable. The dominance of the Adityas was especially resented by the *Asuras,* elder gods whose mothers bore them to Kasyapa before the Adityas were born. Bearing a non-Aryan name of a clear Near Eastern origin (being akin to names of the supreme gods of Assyria, Babylon, and Egypt—*Ashur, Asar, Osiris*), they eventually assumed in the Hindu traditions the role of the evil gods, the "demons."

Jealousy, rivalry, and other causes of friction finally led to war when the Earth, "which at first produced food without cultivation," succumbed to a global famine. The gods, the texts reveal, sustained their immortality by drinking Soma, an ambrosiac that was brought down to Earth from the Celestial Abode by an eagle and was drunk mixed with milk. The "kine" ("cow-cattle") of the gods also provided the gods' favored "sacrifices" of roasted meat. But a time came when all these necessities became scarcer and scarcer. The *Satapatha Brahmana* describes the events that followed:

> The gods and the Asuras, both sprung from the Father of Gods and Men, were contending for superiority. The gods vanquished the Asuras; yet afterwards, these once more harassed them. . . .
> The gods and the Asuras, both of them sprung from the Father of Gods and Men, were [again] contending for superiority. This

time, the gods were worsted. And the Asuras thought: "To us alone assuredly belongs this world!"

They thereupon said: "Well, then, let us divide this world between ourselves; and having divided it, let us subsist thereon." Accordingly, they set about dividing it from west to east.

Hearing this, the defeated Adityas went to plead for a share in Earth's resources:

When they heard this, the gods said: "The Asuras are actually dividing this Earth! Come, let us go where the Asuras are dividing it; for what would become of us if we were to get no share of Earth?"

Placing Vishnu at their head, they went to the Asuras.

Haughtily the Asuras offered to give the Adityas only as much of Earth as Vishnu could lie upon. . . . But the gods used a subterfuge and placed Vishnu in an "enclosure" that could "walk in three directions," thereby regaining three of the Earth's four regions.

The outsmarted Asuras then attacked from the south; and the gods asked Agni "how they could vanquish the Asuras forever." Agni suggested a pincer maneuver: while the gods attack from their regions, "I will go round to the northern side, and you will shut them in from here; and whilst shutting them in, we will put them down." Having so vanquished the Asuras, the *Satapatha Brahmana* records, "the gods were anxious as to how they might replenish the sacrifices"; accordingly, many of the battle segments of the ancient Hindu writings deal with the recapture of the kine and the resupply of the Soma beverage.

These wars were fought on land, in the air, and beneath the seas. The Asuras, according to the *Mahabharata*, made for themselves three metal fortresses in the skies, from which they attacked the three regions of the Earth. Their allies in the war with the gods could become invisible and used invisible weapons; and others fought from a city beneath the sea, which they had captured from the gods.

One who excelled in these battles was Indra ("Storm"). On land he smote ninety-nine strongholds of the Asuras, killing great numbers of their armed followers. In the skies he fought from his aerial car the Asuras, who were hiding in their "cloud fortresses."

Hymns in the Rig-Veda list groups of gods as well as individual deities defeated by Indra (we follow the translation by R. T. Griffith, *The Hymns of the Rig-Veda*):

> Thou slewest with thy bolt the Sasyu . . .
> Far from the floor of Heaven in all directions,
>   the ancient riteless ones fled to destruction . . .
> The Dasyu thou hast burned from the heavens.
>
> They met in fight the army of the blameless,
>   then the Navagvas put forth all their power.
> Like emasculates contending with men they fled,
>   by steep paths from Indra they scattered.
> Indra broke through Ilibsa's strong castles,
>   and Sushna with his horn he cut to pieces . . .
>
> Thou slewest thy fighting foe with thy Thunder . . .
> Fierce on his enemies fell Indra's weapon,
>   with his sharp rushing Thunderbolt
>   he rent their towns to pieces.
>
> Thou goest forth from fight to fight intrepidly,
>   destroying castle after castle with thy strength.
> Thou Indra, with thy friend who makes the foe bow down,
>   slewest from far away the guileful Namuchi.
> Thou hast struck down in death Karanja, Parnaya . . .
> Thou hast destroyed the hundred towns of Vangrida.
>
> The ridges of the lofty heaven thou madest shake
>   when thou, daring, by thyself smote Sambara.

Defeating the gods' enemies in groups as well as in single combat, and making them "flee to destruction," Indra turned his efforts to the freeing of the kine. The "demons" hid them inside a mountain, guarded by Vala ("Encircler"); Indra, aided by the Angirases, young gods who could emit divine flames, smashed into the fortified hideaway and freed the kine. (Some scholars, as J. Herbert in *Hindu Mythology,* hold that what Indra released or retrieved was a Divine Ray, not cows, for the Sanskrit word *go* has both meanings.)

When these wars of the gods began, the Adityas named Agni ("Agile") as Hotri, their "Chief of Office." As the wars progressed—some texts suggest for well over a thousand years—Vishnu ("Active") was made the Chief. But when the fighting was over, Indra, having contributed so much to the victory, claimed the supremacy. As in the Greek *Theogony,* one of his first acts to establish his claim was to slay his own father. The Rig-Veda (Book iv: 18, 12) asks Indra rhetorically: "Indra, who made thy mother a widow?" The answer follows also as a question: "What god was present in the fray, when thou didst slay thy father, seizing him by the foot?"

For this crime Indra was excluded by the gods from the drinking of the Soma, thereby endangering his continued immortality. They "ascended up to Heaven," leaving Indra with the kine he had retrieved. But "he went up after them, with the raised Thunder-weapon," ascending from the northern place of the gods. Fearing his weapon, the gods shouted: "Do not hurl!" and agreed to let Indra share once again in the divine nourishments.

Indra's seizing of the leadership of the gods, however, did not go unchallenged. The challenge came from Tvashtri, to whom oblique references are made in the Hymns as "the Firstborn"—a fact that may explain his own claim to the succession. Indra smote him quickly with the Thunder-Weapon, the very weapon that Tvashtri had fashioned for him. But then the struggle was taken over by Vritra ("The Obstructor"), whom some texts call the firstborn of Tvashtri but whom some scholars interpret as having been an artificial monster, because he quickly grew to an immense size. At first Indra was bested, and he fled to a far corner of Earth. When all the gods then abandoned him, only the twenty-one Maruts stood by his side. They were a group of gods who manned the fastest aerial cars, who "loud roaring as the winds make the mountains rock and reel" as they "lift themselves aloft":

> These verily wondrous, red of hue,
> Speed on their course with a roar
>   over the ridges of the sky . . .
> And spread themselves with beams of light . . .
> Bright, celestial, with lightning in their hands
>   and helmets of gold upon their heads.

With the aid of the Maruts, Indra returned to battle Vritra. The hymns which describe the fight in glowing terms have been translated by J. Muir *(Original Sanskirt Texts)* into rhyming poetic verses:

The valiant god his car ascends,
Swept by his fervid bounding speeds,
Athwart the sky the hero speeds.
The Marut-hosts his escort form,
Impetuous spirits of the storm.
On flashing lightning-cars they ride,
And gleam in warlike pomp and pride . . .
Like lions' roar their voice of doom;
With iron force their teeth consume.
The hills, the earth itself, they shake;
All creatures at their coming quake.

While earth quaked and all creatures ran for cover, only Vritra, the foe, calmly watched their approach:

Perched on a steep aerial height
Shone Vritra's stately fortress bright.
Upon the wall, in martial mood,
The bold gigantic demon stood,
Confiding in his magic arts,
And armed with store of fiery darts.

"Without alarm, defying the might of Indra's arm," unafraid of "the terrors of the deadly flight" rushing toward him, Vritra stood in wait.

And then was seen a dreadful sight,
When god and demon met in fight.
His sharpened missiles Vritra shot,
His thunderbolts and lightnings hot
    he hurled as thick as rain.
The god his fiercest rage defied;
His blunted weapons glanced aside,
    at Indra launched in vain.

When Vritra spent all his fiery missiles, Indra was able to take over the offensive:

The lightnings then began to flash,
The direful thunderbolts to crash,
    by Indra proudly hurled.

The gods themselves with awe were stilled
And stood aghast; and terror filled
   the universal world. . . .

The Thunderbolts hurled by Indra, "forged by the master hand of Tvashtri" of divine iron, were complex, blazing missiles:

Who the arrowy shower could stand,
Discharged by Indra's red right hand—
The thunderbolts with hundred joints,
The iron shafts with thousand points,
Which blaze and hiss athwart the sky,
Swift to their mark unerring fly,
And lay the proudest foeman low,
With sudden and resistless blow,
Whose very sound can put to flight
The fools who dare the Thunderer's might.

Unerringly the guided missiles hit their target:

And soon the knell of Vritra's doom
Was sounded by the clang and boom
   of Indra's iron shower;
Pierced, cloven, crushed, with horrid yell
The dying demon headlong fell
   down from his cloud-built tower.

Fallen to the ground "as trunks of trees that axe had felled," Vritra lay prostrate; but though "footless and handless, still he challenged Indra." Then Indra gave him the coup-de-grace, and "smote him with his bolt between the shoulders."

Indra's victory was complete; but as Fate would have it, the fruits of victory were not his alone. As he was claiming the throne of Kasyapa, his father, old doubts surfaced concerning his true parenthood. It was a fact that upon his birth his mother had hid him from Kasyapa's wrath. Why? Was there truth to the rumors that his true father was his own elder brother, Tvashtri?

The Vedas lift the veil of mystery only partly. They tell, however, that Indra, great god that he was, did not rule alone: he had to share powers with Agni and Surya his brothers—just as Zeus had to share dominions with his brothers Hades and Poseidon.

4

THE EARTH CHRONICLES

As if the similarities of the genealogies and warfare between the Greek and Hindu gods were not enough, tablets discovered in the Hittite royal archives (at a site nowadays called Boghazkoi) contained more tales of the same story: how, as one generation waned unto the other, one god fought another for supremacy.

The longest texts discovered dealt, as could be expected, with the Hittite supreme deity Teshub: his genealogy; his rightful assumption of dominion over Earth's upper regions; and the battles launched against him by the god KUMARBI and his offspring. As in the Greek and Egyptian tales, the Avenger of Kumarbi was hidden with the aid of allied gods until he grew up somewhere in a "dark-hued" part of Earth. The final battles raged in the skies and in the seas; in one battle Teshub was supported by seventy gods riding in their chariots. At first defeated and either hiding or exiled, Teshub finally faced his challenger in god-to-god combat. Armed with the "Thunder-stormer which scatters the rocks for ninety furlongs" and "the Lightning which flashes frightfully," he ascended skyward in his chariot, pulled by two gold-plated Bulls of Heaven, and "from the skies he set his face" toward his enemy. Though the fragmented tablets lack the tale's ending, it is evident that Teshub was finally victorious.

Who were these ancient gods, who fought each other for supremacy and sought dominion over Earth by pitting nation against nation?

Fittingly, perhaps, treaties that had ended some of the very wars launched by men for their gods provide important clues.

When the Egyptians and the Hittites made peace after more than two centuries of warfare, it was sealed by the marriage of the daughter of the Hittite king Hattusilish III to the Egyptian Pharaoh Ramses II. The Pharaoh recorded the event on commemorative stelas which he placed at Karnak, at Elephantine near Aswan, and at Abu Simbel.

Describing the journey and the arrival of the princess in Egypt, the inscription relates that when "His Majesty saw that she was as beautiful of face as a goddess," he at once fell in love with her and deemed her to be "something lovely granted him by the god Ptah" and a sign of Hittite acknowledgment of his "victory." What all this diplomatic maneuvering had entailed was clarified by other parts of the inscription: thirteen years earlier, Hattusilish had sent to the Pharaoh the text of a Peace Treaty; but Ramses II, still brooding over his near-fatal experience in the battle of Kadesh, ignored it. "The great Chief of Hatti then wrote appeasingly to His Majesty year after year; but the King Ramses paid no attention." Finally, the King of Hatti, instead of sending messages inscribed on tablets, "sent his eldest daughter, preceded by precious tribute" and accompanied by Hittite nobles. Wondering what all these gifts meant, Ramses sent an Egyptian escort to meet and accompany the Hittites. And, as related above, he succumbed to the beauty of the Hittite princess, made her a queen, and named her Maat-Neferu-Ra ("The Beauty Which Ra Sees").

Our knowledge of history and antiquity has also profited by that love at first sight, for the Pharaoh then accepted the lingering Peace Treaty, and proceeded to inscribe it, too, at Karnak, not far from where the tale of the Battle of Kadesh and the Tale of the Beautiful Hittite Princess had been commemorated. Two copies, one almost complete, the other fragmentary, have been discovered, deciphered, and translated by Egyptologists. As a result we not only have the full text of the Treaty but also know that the Hittite king wrote down the treaty in the Akkadian language, which was then (as French was a century and two ago) the common language of international relations.

To the Pharaoh he sent a copy of the Akkadian original written on a silver tablet, which the Egyptian inscription at Karnak described thus:

> What is in the middle of the tablet of silver, on the front side:
> Figures consisting of an image of Seth, embracing an image of the Great Prince of Hatti, surrounded by a border with the words "the seal of Seth, ruler of the sky; the seal of the regulation which Hattusilish made" . . .
> What is within that which surrounds the image of the seal of Seth on the other side:
> Figures consisting of a female image of the goddess of Hatti embracing a female image of the Princess of Hatti, surrounded by a border with the words "the seal of the Ra of the town of Arinna, the lord of the land" . . .
> What is within the [frame] surrounding the figures: the seal of Ra of Arinna, the lord of every land.

In the royal Hittie archives, archaeologists have in fact discovered royal seals depicting the chief Hittite deity embracing the Hittite king (Fig. 17), exactly as described in the Egyptian record, even including the inscription surrounding the border of the seal. Against all odds, the original treaty itself, inscribed on two tablets in the Akkadian language, was also found in these archives. But the Hittite texts called their chief deity Teshub, not "Seth of Hatti." Since *Teshub* meant "Windy Storm," and *Seth* (to judge by his Greek name Typhon) meant "Fierce Wind," it appeared that the Egyptians and Hittites were matching their pantheons according to the epithet-names of their gods. In line with that, Teshub's spouse HEBAT was called "Lady of the Skies" to parallel the goddess by that title in the Egyptian version of the treaty; Ra ("The Bright One") was paralleled by a Hittite "Lord of the Sky" whom the Akkadian version called SHAMASH ("The Bright One"), and so on.

The Egyptians and the Hittites, it became evident, were matching separate, but parallel, pantheons; and scholars began to wonder what other ancient treaties would reveal. One that provided surpris-

Fig. 17

ing information was the treaty made circa 1350 B.C. between the
Hittite king Shuppilulima and Mattiwaza, king of the Hurrian kingdom of Mitanni, which was situated on the Euphrates river midway
between the Land of the Hittites and the ancient lands of Sumer and
Akkad.

Executed as usual in two copies, the treaty's original was deposited in the shrine of the god Teshub in the Hurrian city Kahat—a
place and a tablet lost in the sands of time. But the duplicate tablet,
deposited in the Hittite holy city of Arinna "in front of the goddess
of the Rising Disc," was discovered by archaeologists some 3,300
years after it was written!

As all treaties in those days, the one between the Hittite and
Mitannian kings also ended with a call upon "the gods of the contracting parties to be present, to listen and to serve as witnesses,"
so that adherence to the treaty shall bring divine bliss, and its violation the wrath of the gods. These "gods of the contracting parties"
were then listed, beginning with Teshub and his consort Hebat as
the supreme reigning gods of both kingdoms, the gods "who regu-
late kingship and queenship" in Hatti and Mitanni and in whose
shrines the copies of the treaty were deposited. Then, a number of
younger deities, both male and female, offspring of the two
reigning gods, were listed by the provincial capitals where they
acted as governing deities, representing their parents.

Here, then, was a listing of the very same gods in the very same hi-
erarchical positions; unlike the Egyptian instance, when different
pantheons were being matched. As other discovered texts proved, the
Hittite pantheon was in fact borrowed from (or through) the Hurrians.
But this particular treaty held a special surprise: toward the end of the
tablet, among the divine witnesses, there were also listed *Mitra-ash,
Uruwana, Indar,* and the *Nashatiyanu* gods—the very Mitra, Varuna,
Indra, and the Nasatya gods of the Hindu pantheon!

Which of the three—Hittite, Hindu, Hurrian—was then the common source? The answer was provided in the same Hittite-
Mitannian treaty: none of them; for those so-called "Aryan" gods
were listed in the treaty together with their parents and grandpar-
ents, the "Olden Gods": the couples Anu and Antu, Enlil and his
spouse Ninlil, Ea and his wife Damkina; as well as "the divine
Sin, lord of the oath . . . Nergal of Kutha . . . the warrior god
Ninurta . . . the warlike Ishtar."

These are familiar names; they had been invoked in earlier days
by Sargon of Akkad, who had claimed that he was "Overseer of
Ishtar, anointed priest of Anu, great righteous shepherd of Enlil."

His grandson Naram-Sin ("Whom the god Sin loves") could attack the Cedar Mountain when the god Nergal "opened the path" for him. Hammurabi of Babylon marched against other lands "on the command of Anu, with Enlil advancing in front of the army." The Assyrian king Tiglat-Pileser went conquering on the command of Anu, Adad, and Ninurta; Shalmaneser fought with weapons provided by Nergal; Esarhaddon was accompanied by Ishtar on his march to Nineveh.

No less illuminating was the discovery that the Hittites and the Hurrians, though they pronounced the deities' names in their own language, wrote the names employing Sumerian script; even the "divine" determinative used was the Sumerian DIN.GIR, literally meaning "The Righteous Ones" (DIN) "Of the Rocketship" (GIR). Thus the name of Teshub was written DIN. GIR IM ("Divine Stormer"), which was the Sumerian name for the god ISHKUR, also known as Adad; or it was written DIN.GIR U, meaning "The god 10," which was the numerical rank of Ishkur/Adad—that of Anu being the highest (60), that of Enlil 50, that of Ea 40, and so on down the line. Also, like the Sumerian Ishkur/Adad, Teshub was depicted by the Hittites brandishing his lightning-emitting weapon, a "Weapon of Brilliance" (Fig. 18).

Fig. 18

By the time the Hittites and their writings were reclaimed from oblivion, scholars had already determined that before the Hittite and Egyptian civilizations, before Assyria and Babylon, even before Akkad, there arose in southern Mesopotamia the high civilization of Sumer. All the others were offshoots of that first-known civilization.

And it is by now established beyond doubt that it was in Sumer that the tales of gods and men were first recorded. It was there that numerous texts—more numerous than can be imagined, more detailed than could be expected—were first inscribed. It was there that the written records of history and prehistory on our planet Earth had originated. We call them THE EARTH CHRONICLES.

The discovery and understanding of the ancient civilizations has been a process of continuous astonishment, of incredible realizations. The monuments of antiquity—pyramids, ziggurats, vast platforms, columned ruins, carved stones—would have remained enigmas, mute evidence to bygone events, were it not for the Written Word. Were it not for that, the ancient monuments would have remained puzzles: their age uncertain; their creators obscure; their purpose unclear.

We owe what we know to the ancient scribes—a prolific and meticulous lot, who used monuments, artifacts, foundation stones, bricks, utensils, weapons of any conceivable material, as inviting slates on which to write down names and record events. Above all there were the clay tablets: flattened pieces of wet clay, some small enough to be held in the palm of the hand, on which the scribe deftly embossed with a stylus the symbols that formed syllables, words, and sentences. Then the tablet would be left to dry (or be kiln-dried), and a permanent record had been created—a record that has survived millennia of natural erosion and human destructiveness.

In place after place—in centers of commerce or of administration, in temples and palaces, in all parts of the ancient Near East— there were both state and private archives full of such tablets; and there were also actual libraries where the tablets, tens of thousands of them, were neatly arranged by subject, their contents entitled, their scribe named, their sequel numbered. Invariably, whenever they dealt with history or science or the gods, they were identified as copies of earlier tablets, tablets in the "olden language."

Astounded as the archaeologists were to uncover the grandeur of Assyria and Babylonia, they were even more puzzled to read in their inscriptions of "olden cities." And what was the meaning of the title "king of Sumer and Akkad" that the kings of these empires coveted so much?

It was only with the discovery of the records concerning Sargon of Agade that modern scholars were able to convince themselves that a great kingdom, the Kingdom of Akkad, had indeed arisen in Mesopotamia half a millennium before Assyria and Babylonia were to flourish. It was with the greatest amazement that scholars read in these records that Sargon "defeated Uruk and tore down its wall. . . . Sargon, king of Agade, was victorious over the inhabitants of Ur. . . . He defeated E-Nimmar and tore down its wall and defeated its territory from Lagash as far as the sea. His weapons he washed in the sea. In the battle with the inhabitants of Umma he was victorious. . . ."

The scholars were incredulous: Could there have been urban centers, walled cities, even before Sargon of Agade, even before 2500 B.C.?

As is now known, indeed there were. These were the cities and urban centers of Sumer, the "Sumer" in the title "king of Sumer and Akkad." It was, as a century of archaeological discoveries and scholarly research has established, the land where Civilization began nearly six thousand years ago; where suddenly and inexplicably, as though out of nowhere, there appeared a written language and literature; kings and priests; schools and temples; doctors and astronomers; high-rise buildings, canals, docks, and ships; an intensive agriculture; an advanced metallurgy; a textile industry; trade and commerce; laws and concepts of justice and morality; cosmological theories; and tales and records of history and prehistory.

In all these writings, be it long epic tales or two-line proverbs, in inscriptions mundane or divine, the same facts emerge as an unshakable tenet of the Sumerians and the peoples that followed them: in bygone days, the DIN.GIR—"The Righteous Ones of the Rocketships," the beings the Greeks began to call "gods"—had come to Earth from their own planet. They chose southern Mesopotamia to be their home away from home. They called the land KI.EN.GIR—"Land of the Lord of the Rockets" (the Akkadian name, *Shumer,* meant "Land of the Guardians"); and they established there the first settlements on Earth.

The statement that the first to establish settlements on Earth were astronauts from another planet was not lightly made by the Sumerians. In text after text, whenever the starting point was recalled, it was always this: 432,000 years before the Deluge, the DIN.GIR ("Righteous Ones of the Rocketships") came down to Earth from their own planet. The Sumerians considered it a twelfth member of our Solar System—a system made up of the Sun in the center, the Moon, all the nine planets we know of today, and one more large planet whose orbit lasts a *Sar,* 3,600 Earth-years. This orbit, they wrote, takes the planet to a "station" in the distant heavens, then brings it back to Earth's vicinity, crossing between Mars and Jupiter. It was in that position—as depicted in a 4,500-year-old Sumerian drawing (Fig. 19) that the planet obtained its name NIBIRU ("Crossing") and its symbol, the Cross.

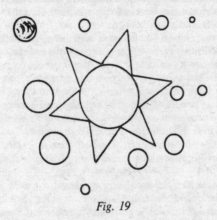

Fig. 19

The leader of the astronauts who had come to Earth from Nibiru, we know from numerous ancient texts, was called E. A ("Whose House Is Water"); after he had landed and established Eridu, the first Earth Station, he assumed the title EN.KI ("Lord of Earth"). A text that was discovered in the ruins of Sumer records his landing on Earth as a first-person report:

When I approached Earth
there was much flooding.
When I approached its green meadows,
heaps and mounds were piled up at my command.
I built my house in a pure place . . .
My house—its shade stretches over the Snake Marsh.

The text then proceeds to describe Ea's efforts to build extraordinary waterworks in the marshlands at the head of the Persian Gulf: He surveyed the marshlands, cut canals for drainage and water control, built dykes, dug ditches, and built structures of bricks molded from the local clays. He joined the Tigris and Euphrates rivers by canals; and at the edge of the marshlands he built his Water House, with a wharf and other facilities.

It all had a reason. On his planet gold was needed. Not for jewelry or another frivolous use, for at no time during the millennia that followed were these visitors to Earth ever shown wearing golden jewelry. Gold was, no doubt, required for the space programs of the Nibiruans, as is evident from the Hindu texts' references to the celestial chariots being covered with gold; indeed, gold is vital to many aspects of the space instruments and vehicles of our own times. But that alone could not have been the reason for the intensity of the Nibiruans' search for gold on Earth and their immense efforts to obtain it here and transfer it in large quantities to their own planet. The metal, with its unique properties, was needed back home for a vital need, affecting the very survival of life on that planet; as best as we can make out, this vital need could have been for suspending the gold particles in Nibiru's waning atmosphere and thus shield it from critical dissipation.

A son of Nibiru's ruler, Ea was well chosen for the mission. He was a brilliant scientist and engineer whose nickname was NU.DIM.MUD, "He Who Fashions Things." The plan, as his epithet-name E.A. indicated, was to extract the gold from the waters of the quiet Persian Gulf and the adjoining shallow marshlands that extended from the gulf into Mesopotamia. Sumerian depictions showed Ea as lord of the flowing waters, sitting in a laboratory and surrounded by interconnected flasks (Fig. 20).

But the unfolding tale suggests that all was not going well with this scheme. The gold production was far below expectations, and to speed it up, more astronauts—the rank and file were called *Anunnaki* ("Those Who From Heaven to Earth Came")—landed on Earth. They came in groups of fifty, and one of the texts reveals that one of these groups was led by Enki's firstborn son MAR.DUK. The text records Marduk's urgent message to his father describing a near-calamity on the flight to Earth, as the spaceship passed by one of the Solar System's large planets (probably Jupiter) and almost collided with one of that planet's satellites. Describing the "attack" on the spacecraft, the excited Marduk told his father:

Fig. 20

It has been created like a weapon;
It has charged forward like death . . .
The Anunnaki who are fifty it has smitten . . .
The flying, birdlike Supreme Orbiter
it has smitten on the breast.

A Sumerian engraving on a cylinder seal (Fig. 21) may well have illustrated the scene of Lord Earth (on the left) anxiously greeting his son, dressed as an astronaut (on the right), as the spaceship leaves Mars (the six-pointed star) and nears Earth (the seventh planet when counting from the outside in, symbolized by the seven dots and depicted together with the Moon).

Back on the home planet, where Enki's father AN (*Anu* in Akkadian) was the ruler, the progress of the landing parties was followed with anxiety and expectation. These must have turned to impatience at the slow progress, and then to disappointment. Evidently the scheme to extract gold from seawaters by laboratorylike processes did not work as expected.

But the gold was still badly needed; and the Anunnaki faced a

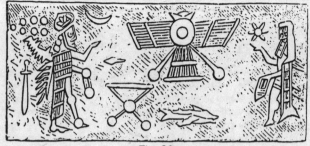

Fig. 21

tough decision: to abandon the project—which was out of the question—or to try to obtain the gold in a new way: mining. For gold, the Anunnaki knew by then, was naturally available in abundance in the AB.ZU ("The Primeval Source") on the continent of Africa. (In the Semitic languages that had evolved from the Sumerian, *Za-ab*—*Abzu* in reverse—has remained the word for gold to this very day).

There was, however, one major problem. The African gold had to be extracted from the depths of the earth through mining; and the far-reaching decision to change from the sophisticated water-treatment process to a backbreaking toil below the surface of the earth was not lightly taken. Clearly the new enterprise required more Anunnaki, a mining colony in "the place of the shining lodes," expanded facilities in Mesopotamia, and a fleet of ore vessels (MA.GUR UR.NU AB.ZU— "Ships for Ores of the Abzu") to connect the two. Could Enki handle it all by himself?

Anu felt that he could not; and eight Nibiru years after Enki's landing—28,800 Earth-years—he came to Earth to see things for himself. He came down accompanied by the Heir Apparent EN.LIL ("Lord of the Command")—a son who, Anu must have felt, could take charge of Earth mission and organize the gold deliveries to Nibiru.

The choice of Enlil for the mission might have been a necessary one, but it must have been an agonizing one as well; for it only sharpened the rivalry and jealousy between the two half-brothers. For Enki was the firstborn son of Anu by Id, one of his six concubines, and could have expected to follow Anu on Nibiru's throne.

But then—as in the biblical tale of Abraham, his concubine Hagar, and his half-sister wife Sarah—Anu's half-sister wife Antum bore him a son, Enlil. And by the Nibiruan rules of succession—so faithfully adopted by the biblical patriarch—Enlil became the legal heir instead of Enki. And now this rival, this robber of Enki's birthright, came to Earth to take over the command!

One cannot stress enough the importance of lineage and genealogy in the Wars of the Gods; the struggles for succession and supremacy, on Nibiru as on Earth later on.

Indeed, as we unravel the puzzling persistence and ferocity of the wars of the gods, trying to fit them into the framework of history and prehistory—a task never undertaken before—it becomes clear that they stemmed from a code of sexual behavior based not on morality but on considerations of genetic purity. At the core of these wars lay an intricate genealogy that determined hierarchy and succession; and sexual acts were judged not by their tenderness or violence but by their purpose and outcome.

There is a Sumerian tale of how Enlil, commander-in-chief of the Anunnaki, took a fancy to a young nurse whom he saw swimming naked in the river. He persuaded her to go sailing with him and made love to her against her protestations ("my vulva is small, it knows not intercourse"). In spite of his rank Enlil was arrested by the "fifty senior gods" as he returned to his city Nippur and was found by "the seven Anunnaki who judge" to have committed the crime of rape; they sentenced him to exile in the Abzu. (He was pardoned only when he married the young goddess, who had followed him into exile.)

Many songs celebrated the love affair between Inanna and a young god named Dumuzi, in which their "sleep-outs" were described with touching tenderness:

O that they put his hand in my hand for me.
O that they put his heart next to my heart for me.
Not only is it sweet to sleep hand in hand with him,
Sweetest of sweet is also the loveliness
of joining heart to heart with him.

We can understand the approving tone of the verse because Dumuzi was the intended bridegroom of Inanna, chosen by her with the approval of her brother Utu/Shamash. But how to explain a text in which Inanna describes passionate lovemaking with her own brother?

My beloved met me,
took his pleasure of me, rejoiced together with me.
The brother brought me to his house,
made me lie on its sweet bed . . .
In unison, the tongue-making in unison,
my brother of fairest face
made fifty times.

This can only be understood if we bear in mind that the code pro-
hibited marriage, but not lovemaking, between full brother and sister. On the other hand, marriage with a half-sister was allowed;
male progeny by a half-sister even had precedence in the hierarchical order. And while rape was condemned, sex—even irregular
and violent—was condoned if done for the sake of succession to the
throne. A long tale relates how Enki, seeking a male son by his
(and Enlil's) half-sister Sud, forced his attentions on her when she
was alone and "poured the semen in the womb." When she gave
birth to a daughter (rather than to a son), Enki lost no time making
love to the girl as soon as she became "young and fair . . . He
took his joy of her, he embraced her, lay in her lap; he touches the
thighs, he touches the . . . with the young one he cohabits." This
went on unabashedly with a succession of young daughters, until
Sud put a curse on Enki, which paralyzed him; only then did these
sexual antics in search of a male heir stop.

When Enki engaged in these sexual efforts, he was already espoused to Ninki, which illustrates that the same code which condemned rape did not prohibit extramarital affairs per se. We also
know that the gods were allowed any number of wives and concubines (a text catalogued as CT-24 listed six of Anu's concubines),
but, if married, they had to select one as their official spouse—
preferring, as we have mentioned, a half-sister for this role.

If the god, apart from his given name and many epithets, was
also bestowed with a title-name, his official consort was also honored with the feminine form of such title. Thus when AN received
his title-name ("The Heavenly"), his consort was called ANTU,
Anu and Antum in Akkadian. The nurse who had married Enlil
("Lord of Command") received the title-name Ninlil ("Lady of
Command"); Enki's spouse Damkina was called Ninki, and so on.

Because of the importance of the family relationships between
these great Anunnaki, many so-called God Lists prepared by ancient scribes were genealogical in nature. In one such major list,
titled by the ancient scribes the *"AN : ilu Anum"* series, there are

listed the "forty-two foreparents of Enlil," clearly arranged as twenty-one divine couples. This must have been a mark of great royal lineage, for two similar documents for Anu also list his twenty-one ancestral couples on Nibiru. We learn that the parents of Anu were AN.SHAR.GAL ("Great Prince of Heaven") and KI.SHAR.GAL ("Great Princess of Firm Ground"). As their names indicate, they were not the reigning couple on Nibiru: rather, the father was the Great Prince, meaning the heir apparent; and his spouse was a great princess, the firstborn daughter of the ruler (by a different wife) and thus a half-sister of Anshargal.

In these genealogical facts lies the key to the understanding of the events on Nibiru before the landing on Earth, and on Earth thereafter.

Sending Ea to Earth for gold implies that the Nibiruans had already been aware of the metal's availability on Earth well before the landing was launched. How?

One could offer several answers: They could have probed Earth with unmanned satellites, as we have been doing to other planets in our Solar System. They could have surveyed Earth by landing on it, as we have done on our Moon. Indeed, their landing on Mars cannot be ruled out as we read texts dealing with the space voyages from Nibiru to Earth.

Whether and when such manned *premeditated* landings on Earth had taken place, we do not know. But there does exist an ancient chronicle dealing with an earlier landing in dramatic circumstances: when the deposed ruler of Nibiru escaped to Earth in his spacecraft!

The event must have happened before Ea was sent to Earth by his father, for it was through that event that Anu became Nibiru's ruler. Indeed the event was the usurpation of the throne on Nibiru by Anu.

The information is contained in a text whose Hittite version has been titled by scholars *Kingship in Heaven*. It throws light on life at the royal court of Nibiru and tells a tale of betrayal and usurpation worthy of a Shakespearean plot. It reveals that when the time for succession arrived on Nibiru—through natural death or otherwise—it was not Anshargal, Anu's father and the heir apparent, who had ascended the throne. Instead a relative named Alalu (Alalush in the Hittite text) became the ruler.

As a gesture of reconciliation or by custom, Alalu appointed Anu to be his royal cup-bearer, an honored and trusted position also known to us from several Near Eastern texts and royal depictions (Fig. 22). But after nine Nibiruan years, Anu (Anush in the Hittite text) "gave battle to Alalu" and deposed him:

Fig. 22

Once in the olden days, Alalush was king in Heaven.
Alalush was seated on the throne;
The mighty Anush, first among the gods,
was standing before him:
He would bow to his feet,
set the drinking cup in his hand.
For nine counted periods, Alalush was king in Heaven.
In the ninth counted period,
Anush gave battle to Alalush.

It was then, the ancient text tells us, that the dramatic flight to Earth had occurred:

Alalush was defeated, he fled before Anush—
Down he descended to the dark-hued Earth.
Anush took his seat upon the throne.

While it is quite possible that much about Earth and its resources may have been known on Nibiru even before Alalu's flight, the fact is that we do have in this tale a record of the arrival on Earth of a spaceship bearing Nibiruans before Ea's mission to Earth. The *Sumerian King Lists* report that the first administrator of Eridu was called Alulim—a name that could have been yet another epithet for Ea/Enki, or the Sumerian rendering of Alalu's name; the possibility thus comes to mind that, though deposed, Alalu was sufficiently concerned about Nibiru's fate to advise his deposer that he had found gold in Earth's waters. That this is indeed what had happened might be indicated by the fact that a reconciliation between deposed and deposer did ensue; for Anu went ahead and appointed Kumarbi, a grandson of Alalu, to be his royal cup-bearer.

But the gesture of reconciliation only caused history on Nibiru to repeat itself. In spite of all the bestowed honors, the young Kumarbi could not forget that Anu had usurped the throne from his grandfather; and as time went on, Kumarbi's enmity toward Anu was becoming more and more obvious, and Anu "could not withstand the gaze of Kumarbi's eyes."

And so it was that, having decided to leave Nibiru for Earth and even take the Heir Apparent (Enlil) with him, Anu deemed it safer also to take along the young Kumarbi. Both decisions—to take Enlil with him and to take Kumarbi along—ended up making the visit one marred by strife and—for Anu—also filled with personal agony.

The decision to bring Enlil to Earth and put him in charge led to heated arguments with Enki—arguments echoed in the texts so far discovered. The angry Enki threatened to leave Earth and return to Nibiru; but could he be trusted not to usurp the throne there? If, as a compromise, Anu himself were to stay on Earth, appointing Enlil as surrogate ruler on Nibiru, could Enlil be trusted to step down when Anu returned? Finally it was decided to draw lots: let chance determine how it shall be. The division of authority that ensued is repeatedly mentioned in Sumerian and Akkadian texts. One of the longest of the Earth Chronicles, a text called *The Atra-Hasis Epic*, records the drawing of lots and its outcome:

> The gods clasped hands together,
> then cast lots and divided:
> Anu to heaven went up;
> To Enlil the Earth was made subject;
> That which the sea as a loop encloses,

they gave to the prince Enki.
To the Abzu Enki went down,
assumed the rulership of the Abzu.

Believing that he had managed to separate the rival brothers, "Anu to Heaven went up." But in the skies above Earth, an unexpected turn of events awaited him. Perhaps as a precaution, Kumarbi was left on the space platform orbiting Earth; when Anu returned to it, ready to take off on the long voyage back to Nibiru, he was confronted by an angry Kumarbi. Harsh words soon gave way to a scuffle: "Anu gave battle to Kumarbi, Kumarbi gave battle to Anu." As Kumarbi bested Anu in the wrestling, "Anu struggled free from the hands of Kumarbi." But Kumarbi managed to grab Anu by his feet, and "bit between his knees," hurting Anu in his "manhood." Ancient depictions were found of the event (Fig. 23a), as well as of the habit of wrestling Anunnaki (Fig. 23b) to hurt one another in the genitals.

a   b

Fig. 23

Disgraced and in pain, Anu took off on his way to Nibiru, leaving Kumarbi behind with the astronauts manning the space platforms and shuttlecraft. But before he departed, he put on Kumarbi a curse of "three monsters in his belly."

The similarity of this Hittite tale to the Greek tale of the castration of Uranus by Cronos, and the swallowing by Cronos of his sons, needs no elaboration. And, as in the Greek tales, this episode set the stage for the wars between the gods and the Titans.

After Anu had left, Earth Mission was launched in earnest.

As more Anunnaki landed on Earth—their mumber rose in time to 600—some were assigned to the Lower World to help Enki mine the gold; others manned the ore ships; and the rest stayed with Enlil in Mesopotamia. There, additional settlements were established in accordance with a master plan laid out by Enlil, as part of a complete organizational plan of action and clear-cut procedures:

> He perfected the procedures, the divine ordinances;
> Established five cities in perfect places,
> Called them by name,
> Laid them out as centers.
> The first of these cities, Eridu,
> He granted to Nudimmud, the pioneer.

Each of these pre-Diluvial settlements in Mesopotamia had a specific function, revealed by its name. First was E.RI.DU— "House in Faraway Built"—the gold-extracting facility by the waters' edge, which for all time remained Ea's Mesopotamian abode. Next came BAD.TIBIRA—"Bright Place Where the Ores Are Made Final"—the metallurgical center for smelting and refining. Next LA.RA.AK—"Seeing the Bright Glow"—was a beacon-city to guide the landing shuttlecraft. SIPPAR—"Bird City"—was the Landing Place; and SHU.RUP.PAK—"The Place of Utmost Well-Being"—was equipped as a medical center; it was put in the charge of SUD ("She Who Resuscitates"), a half-sister of both Enki and Enlil.

Another beacon-city, LA.AR.SA ("Seeing the Red Light"), was also built, for the complex operation depended on close coordination between the Anunnaki who had landed on Earth and 300 astronauts, called IGI.GI ("Those Who See and Observe"), who remained in constant Earth orbit. Acting as intermediaries between Earth and Nibiru, the Igigi stayed in Earth's skies on orbiting platforms, to which the processed ores were delivered from Earth by shuttlecraft, thereafter to be transferred to proper spaceships, which could ferry the gold to the Home Planet as it periodically neared Earth in its vast elliptical orbit. Astronauts and equipment were delivered to Earth by the same stages, in reverse.

All of that required a Mission Control Center, which Enlil proceeded to build and equip. It was named NIBRU.KI ("The Earth-Place of Nibiru")—Nippur in Akkadian. There, atop an artificially raised platform equipped with antennas—the prototype of the Mesopotamian "Towers of Babel" (Fig. 24)—was a secret chamber, the DIR.GA ("Dark, Glowing Chamber") where space charts ("the emblems of the stars") were displayed and where the DUR.AN.KI ("Bond Heaven-Earth") was maintained.

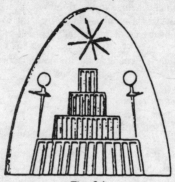

Fig. 24

The Chronicles have asserted that the first settlements of the Anunnaki on Earth were "laid out as centers." To this enigmatic statement was added the puzzle of the claim by post-Diluvial kings that in reestablishing in Sumer the cities wiped out by the Flood, they had followed

The everlasting ground plan,
that which for all time
the construction has determined.
It is the one which bears
the drawings from the Olden Times
and the writing of the Upper Heaven.

The puzzle will be solved if we mark out those first cities established by Enki and Enlil on the region's map and connect them with concentric circles. They were indeed "laid out as centers": all were equidistant from the Mission Control Center in Nippur. It was indeed a plan "from Upper Heaven," for it made sense only to those who could view the whole Near East from high above Earth: Choosing the twin-peaked Mount Ararat—the area's most conspicuous feature—as their landmark, they placed the spaceport where the north line based on Ararat crossed the visible Euphrates River. In this "everlasting ground plan," all the cities were arranged as an arrow, marking out the Landing Path to the Spaceport at Sippar (Fig. 25).

The periodic deliveries of gold to Nibiru mitigated the concerns,

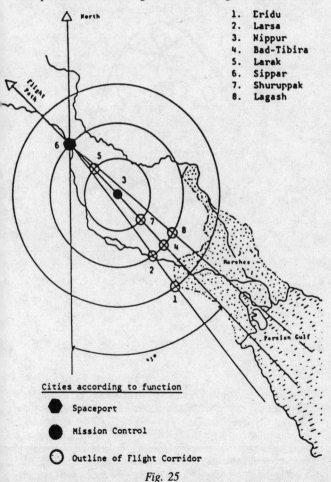

1. Eridu
2. Larsa
3. Nippur
4. Bad-Tibira
5. Larak
6. Sippar
7. Shuruppak
8. Lagash

Cities according to function

⬢ Spaceport

● Mission Control

◯ Outline of Flight Corridor

Fig. 25

even the rivalries, on that planet, for Anu stayed on as its ruler for a long time thereafter. But on Earth all the main actors were present on the "dark-hued" stage to give vent to every imaginable emotion and to incredible conflicts.

5

THE WARS OF
THE OLDEN GODS

Anu's first visit to Earth and the decisions then reached set the course of events on Earth for all the millennia that followed. In time they led to the creation of The Adam—Man as we know him, *Homo sapiens;* they also planted the seeds of future conflict on Earth between Enlil and Enki and their descendants.

But first there were the lingering and bitter struggles between the House of Anu and the House of Alalu, an enmity that burst out on Earth into the War of the Titans. It was a war that pitted "the gods who are in heaven" against the "gods who are upon dark-hued Earth"; it was, in its last climactic phase, an uprising of the Igigi!

That it had taken place in the early days of the settlement of the Nibiruans on Earth and in the aftermath of Anu's first visit to Earth, we know from the *Kingship in Heaven* text. Recalling the adversaries, it refers to them as "the mighty olden gods, the gods of the olden days." After naming five ancestors as "the fathers and mothers of the gods" who preceded Anu and Alalu, it begins the tale with the usurpations of the throne on Nibiru, the flight of Alalu, the visit of Anu to Earth, and the ensuing conflict with Kumarbi.

The story in the *Kingship in Heaven* text is augmented and continued in several other Hittite/Hurrian texts, which scholars call collectively *The Kumarbi Cycle.* Laboriously pieced together (and still badly fragmented), the texts have recently become more intelligible by the discovery of additional fragments and versions, reported and fitted into place by H. Güterbock *(Kumarbi Mythen von Churritischen Kronos)* and H. Otten *(Mythen vom Gotte Kumarbi—Neue Fragmente).*

How long Kumarbi remained aloft after the fight with Anu is not clear from these texts. We do learn that after the passage of some time, and after Kumarbi managed to spit out the "stones" that Anu caused to grow in his belly, Kumarbi came down to Earth. For reasons that may have been explained in missing parts of the texts, he went to Ea in the Abzu.

Mutilated verses then deal with the appearance on the scene of the Storm God Teshub, who, according to the Sumerians, was Enlil's youngest son Ishkur/Adad. The Storm God annoys Kumarbi by telling him of the wonderful attributes and objects that each god will grant him, Teshub; among these attributes shall be Wisdom, which shall be transferred away from Kumarbi. "Filled with fury Kumarbi went to Nippur." Breaks in the texts leave us ignorant as to what went on there, at Enlil's headquarters; but after a stay of seven months Kumarbi went back to consult with Ea.

Ea suggested that Kumarbi "ascend to heaven" and seek the help of Lama, who was "mother of the two gods" and thus, apparently, an ancestral matriarch of the two contesting dynasties. With some self-interest, Ea offered to transport Kumarbi to the Celestial Abode in his MAR.GID.DA (celestial chariot), which the Akkadians called *Ti-ia-ri-ta,* "the flying vehicle." But the goddess, having found out that Ea was coming without the permission of the Assembly of the Gods, sent "lightning winds" against Ea's spacecraft, forcing him and Kumarbi to return to Earth.

But rather than go down all the way, Kumarbi chose to stay with the orbiting gods whom the Hittite/Hurrian text calls Irsirra ("Those Who See and Orbit"), the Sumerian IGI.GI. With ample time on his hands, "Kumarbi was full with thoughts . . . thinking them out in his mind . . . he nurses thoughts of creating misfortune . . . he plots evil." The essence of his thoughts was that he should be proclaimed "the father of all the gods," the supreme deity!

Gaining the backing of the orbiting Irsirra gods, Kumarbi "put swift shoes on his feet" and flew down to Earth. There he sent his emissary to the other leading gods, demanding that they recognize his supremacy.

It was then that Anu decided that enough was enough. To vanquish once and for all the grandson of his adversary Alalu, Anu ordered his own grandson, the "Storm God" Teshub, to find Kumarbi and kill him. Ferocious battles then ensued between the terrestrial gods led by Teshub and the sky-borne gods led by Kumarbi; in one battle alone, no less than seventy gods participated, all riding in celestial chariots. Though most battle scenes are lost in the damaged text, we know that in the end Teshub had prevailed.

But the defeat of Kumarbi did not end the struggle. We learn from additional Hittite epic tales in the Kumarbi Cycle that before his demise, Kumarbi managed to impregnate a goddess of the mountain with his seed, leading to the birth of his Avenger, the "Stone God" Ullikummi. As he hid his marvelous (or monstrous) son among the Irsirra gods, he instructed him to grow and attack Teshub's "beautiful city Kummiya . . . Attack the Storm God and tear him to pieces . . . shoot down all the gods from the sky like birds!" Once he attained victory on Earth, Ullikummi was to "ascend to Heaven for Kingship" and seize by force the throne on Nibiru. Having issued these instructions, Kumarbi passed away from the scene.

For a long time the child was hidden. But as he grew up—assuming giant proportions—he was seen one day by Utu/Shamash as he was roaming the skies. Utu rushed to Teshub's abode, to inform him of the appearance of the Avenger. After giving Utu food and drink to becalm himself, Teshub urged him to "mount thy chariot and ascend to the skies," to keep an eye on the growing Ullikummi. Then he went up the Mountain of Viewing to see the Stone God for himself. "He looked at the awesome Stone God, and in wrath shook his fist."

Realizing there was no alternative to battle, Teshub readied his chariot for combat; the Hittite text calls it by its Sumerian name ID.DUG.GA, "The Flowing Leaden Rider." The instructions for outfitting the celestial chariot, for which the Hittite text heavily employed the original Sumerian terminology, merit quoting. They called for revving up the vehicle with the "Great Cracker"; attaching the "Bull" (power-plant) that "Lights Up" in front and the "Bull for Lofty Missile" in the back end; installing the radarlike or navigational device "That Which Shows The Way" in the forepart; activating the instruments with the powerful energy "Stones" (minerals); and then arming the vehicle with the "Storm Thunderer," loading it with no less than eight hundred "Fire Stones":

> The "Great Cracker" of the "Bright Lead Rider"
> let them lubricate with oil and stir up.
> The "Bull that Lights Up" let them put between the horns.
> The tail's "Bull that is Lofty Missile"
> let them plate with gold.
> The forepart's "That Which Shows The Way"
> let them put in and turn,
> provide it with powerful "Stones" inside.
> Let them bring out the "Storm Thunderer"
> which scatters rocks for 90 furlongs,

making sure the "Fire Stones" with 800 . . . to cover.
The "Lightning Which Flashes Frightfully"
let them bring out from its storage chamber.
Let them bring out the MAR.GID.DA and make it ready!

"From the skies, from among the clouds, the Storm God set his
face upon the Stone God." After the initial unsuccessful attacks,
Ninurta, the brother of Teshub/Adad, joined the battles. But the
Stone God remained unharmed and carried the battle to the very
gates of Kummiya, the Storm God's city.

In Kummiya, Teshub's spouse Hebat was following the battle
reports in an inner chamber of the god's house. But the missiles of
Ullikummi "forced Hebat to leave the house, and she could no
longer hear the messages of the gods . . . neither the messages of
Teshub, nor the messages of all the gods." She ordered her messenger to "put the Swift Shoes on his feet" and go to the place
where the gods were assembled, to bring back news of the battle;
for she feared that "the Stone God may have killed my husband,
the noble prince."

But Teshub was not killed. Advised by his attendant to hide at
some mountainous sites, he refused: If we do that, he said, "there
will be no king in Heaven!" The two then decided to go to Ea in
the Abzu, to seek there an oracle according to "the old tablets with
the words of fate."

Realizing that Kumarbi had brought forth a monster that was
getting out of hand, Ea went to Enlil to warn him of the danger:
"Ullikummi will block off the Heaven and the gods' holy
houses!" An assembly of the Great Anunnaki was called. With all
at a loss for a solution, Ea had one: From the sealed storehouse of
the "stone cutters," let them bring out a certain Olden Metal Cutter, and let them cut under the feet of Ullikummi the Stone God.

When this was achieved, the Stone God was crippled. When the
gods heard this, "they came to the place of assembly, and all the
gods began to bellow against Ullikummi." Teshub, encouraged,
jumped into his chariot; "he caught up with the Stone God
Ullikummi at the sea, and engaged him in battle." But Ullikummi
was still defiant, declaring: "Kummiya I shall destroy, the Sacred
House I shall take over, the gods I shall drive out . . . up to
Heaven I shall go to assume Kingship!"

The closing lines of the Hittite epic are completely damaged; but
can we doubt that they told us the Sanskrit tale of the final battle
between Indra and the "demon" Vritra?

And then was seen a dreadful sight,
when god and demon met in fight.
His sharpened missiles Vritra shot,
his thunderbolts and lightnings hot . . .
The lightnings then began to flash,
the direful thunderbolts to crash,
  by Indra proudly hurled . . .
And soon the knell of Vritra's doom
was sounded by the clang and boom
  of Indra's iron shower.
Pierced, cloven, crushed, with horrid yell
the dying demon headlong fell . . .
And Indra smote him with a bolt
between the shoulders.

These, we believe, were the battles of the "gods" and the Titans of the Greek tales. No one has yet found the meaning of "Titans"; but if the tales had a Sumerian origin, and if so did these gods' name, then TI.TA.AN in Sumerian would have literally meant "Those Who in Heaven Live"—precisely the designation of the Igigi led by Kumarbi; and their adversaries were the Anunnaki "Who are on Earth."

Sumerian texts indeed record an olden life-and-death battle between a grandson of Anu and a "demon" of a different clan; the tale is known as *The Myth of Zu*. Its hero is Ninurta, Enlil's son by his half-sister Sud; it could well have been the original tale from which the Hindu and Hittite tales were borrowed.

The setting for the events described in the Sumerian text is the time that had followed Anu's visit to Earth. Under the overall command of Enlil, the Anunnaki have settled to their tasks in the Abzu and in Mesopotamia: The ores are mined and transported, then smelted and refined. From a busy spaceport in Sippar, shuttlecraft take the precious metals aloft to the orbiting stations operated by the Igigi, thence on to the Home Planet by periodically visiting spaceships.

The complex system of space operations—the comings and goings by the space vehicles and communications between Earth and Nibiru, while both planets pursue their own destined orbits—is coordinated from Enlil's Mission Control Center in Nippur. There, atop a raised platform, was the DIR.GA room, the most restricted "holy of holies" where the vital celestial charts and orbital data panels—the "Tablets of Destinies"—were installed.

It was into this sacred chamber that a god named Zu gained access, seizing the vital tablets and thereby holding in his hands the fate of the Anunnaki on Earth and of Nibiru itself.

By combining portions of Old Babylonian and Assyrian versions of the Sumerian text, a good deal of the tale has been restored. But damaged portions still held the secret of Zu's true identity, as well as an explanation of how he had gained access to the Dirga. Only in 1979 did two scholars (W. W. Hallo and W. L. Moran) come up with the answer by using a tablet found in the Babylonian Collection of Yale University to reconstruct the beginning of the ancient tale.

In Sumerian the name ZU meant "He Who Knows," one expert in certain knowledge. Several references to the evil hero of this tale as AN.ZU—"He Who Knows the Heavens"—suggest a connection with the space program that had linked Earth with Nibiru; and the now-restored beginning of the chronicle indeed relates how Zu, an orphan, was adopted by the astronauts who manned the shuttlecraft and orbiting platforms, the Igigi—learning from them the secrets of the heavens and of space travel.

The action begins as the Igigi, "being gathered from all parts," decided to make an appeal to Enlil. Their complaint was that "until that time for the Igigi a break-taking place had not yet been built." In other words, there simply was no facility on Earth for the rest and recreation of the Igigi, where they could relax from the rigors of space and its weightlessness. To voice their complaint they selected Zu to be their spokesman, sending him to Enlil's center in Nippur.

Enlil, "the father of the gods, in the Dur-An-Ki, saw him, and thought of what they [the Igigi] said." As "in his mind he pondered" the request, "he studied the heavenly Zu closely." Who, after all, was this emissary, not one of the astronauts and yet wearing their uniform? As his suspicions grew, Ea—aware of Zu's true ancestry—spoke up; he suggested to Enlil that a decision on the request of the Igigi could be postponed if Zu were delayed at Enlil's headquarters. "Your service let him enter," Ea said to Enlil; "in the sanctuary, to the innermost seat, let him be the one to block the way."

> To the words that Ea spoke to him
> the god [Enlil] consented.
> At the sanctuary Zu took up his position . . .
> At the entrance to the chamber
> Enlil had assigned him.

And so it was, with Ea's connivance, that an adversary god—a secret descendant of Alalu—was admitted to Enlil's innermost and most sensitive chamber. We read that there Zu "constantly views Enlil, the father of the gods, the god of the Bond-Heaven-Earth . . . his celestial Tablet of Destines Zu constantly views." And soon a scheme took shape: "The removal of the Enlilship he conceives in his heart":

> I will take the celestial Tablet of Destinies;
> The decrees of the gods I will govern;
> I will establish my throne,
> be master of the Heavenly Decrees;
> The Igigi in their space I will command!

"His heart having thus plotted aggression," Zu saw his chance one day as Enlil went to take a cooling swim. "He seized the Tablet of Destinies in his hands" and in his Bird "took off and flew to safety in the HUR.SAG.MU" ("Mountain of the Sky-Chambers"). No sooner had this happened than everything came to a standstill:

> Suspended were the divine formulas;
> The lighted brightness petered out;
> Silence prevailed.
> In space, the Igigi were confounded;
> The sanctuary's brilliance was taken off.

At first "father Enlil was speechless." As the communications were restored, "the gods on Earth gathered one by one at the news." Anu, on Nibiru, was also informed. It was clear that Zu must be captured and the Tablet of Destinies restored to the Dir-Ga. But who will do it? Several of the younger gods known for their valor were approached. But none dared track Zu to the distant mountain, for he was now as powerful as Enlil, having also stolen the "Brilliance" of Enlil; "and he who opposes him shall become as clay . . . at his Brilliance the gods waste away."

It was then that Ninurta, Enlil's legal heir, stepped forth to undertake the task, for—as his mother Sud had pointed out—Zu deprived not only Enlil but also Ninurta of the "Enlilship." She advised him to attack Zu in his hideaway mountain also with a weapon of "Brilliance," but to do so only after he was able to approach Zu behind a dust screen. To achieve the latter she lent Ninurta her own "seven whirlwinds that stir up the dust."

With "his battle courage grown firmer," Ninurta repaired to

Mount Hazzi—the mountain encountered in the Kumarbi tales—
where he hitched to his chariot his seven weapons, attached the
whirlwinds that stir up the dust, and set out against Zu "to launch a
terrifying war, a fierce battle":

> Zu and Ninurta met at the mountainside.
> When Zu perceived him, he broke out in rage.
> With his Brilliance, he made the mountain
> bright as daylight;
> He let loose rays in a rage.

Unable to identify his challenger because of the dust storm, Zu
shouted to Ninurta: "I have carried off all Authority, the decrees of
the gods I [now] direct! Who are thou to come fight with me? Explain thyself!"

But Ninurta continued to "advance aggressively" against Zu,
announcing that he was designated by Anu himself to seize Zu and
restore the Tablet of Destinies. Hearing this, Zu cut off his Brilliance, and "the face of the mountain was covered with darkness."
Unafraid, Ninurta "entered the gloom." From the "breast" of his
vehicle, he let loose a Lightning at Zu, "but the shot could not approach Zu; it turned back." With the powers Zu had obtained, no
lightning bolt could "approach his body."

So "the battle was stilled, the conflict ceased; the weapons were
stopped in the midst of the mountain; they vanquished not Zu."

Stalemated, Ninurta asked his younger brother Ishkur/Adad to
obtain the advice of Enlil. "Ishkur, the prince, took the report; the
news of the battle he reported to Enlil."

Enlil instructed Ishkur to go back and tell Ninurta: "In the battle do
not tire; prove thy strength!" More practically, he sent Ninurta a
tillu—a missile (pictographically written ▷——▶)—to attach to
the Stormer that shoots the projectiles. Ninurta in his "Whirlwind
Bird," he said, should then come as close as possible to the Bird of
Zu, until they are "wing to wing." Then he should aim the missile at
the "pinions" of Zu's Whirlbird, and "let the missile fly like a lightning; when the Fiery Brilliance will engulf the pinions, his wings will
vibrate like butterflies; then will Zu be vanquished."

The final battle scenes are missing from all the tablets, but we
know that more than one "Whirlbird" participated in the combat.
Fragments of duplicates, found in the ruins of a Hittite archive at a
site now called Sultan-Tepe, tell us that Ninurta arrayed "seven
whirlwinds which stir up the dust," armed his chariot with the

"Ill Winds" weapons, and attacked Zu as suggested by his father. "The earth shook . . . the [illegible] became dark, the skies became black . . . the pinions of Zu were overcome." Zu was captured and brought back before Enlil in Nippur; the Tablet of Destinies was reinstalled where it belonged; "Lordship again entered the Ekur; the Divine Formulas were returned."

The captured Zu was put on trial before a court-martial consisting of the Seven Great Anunnaki; he was found guilty and sentenced to death; Ninurta, his vanquisher, "cut his throat." Many depictions were found showing the trial scene, in which Zu, on account of his association with the Igigi astronauts, was dressed up as a bird. An archaic relief found in central Mesopotamia illustrated the actual execution of Zu. This one shows Zu—who belonged to those "Who Observe and See"—as a demonic cock with an extra eye in the forehead (Fig. 26).

Fig. 26

* * *

The defeat of Zu lingered in the memory of the Anunnaki as a great deliverance. Perhaps because of the assumption that the spirit of Zu—representing betrayal, duplicity, and all evil in general— persists in causing ill and suffering, the trial and execution of Zu were transmitted to mankind's generations in the form of an elaborate ritual. In this annual commemoration a bull was chosen to stand for Zu and atone for his evil deed.

Long instructions for the ritual have been found in both Babylonian and Assyrian versions, all indicating their earlier Sumerian source. After extensive preparations, a "great bull, strong bull who treads upon clean pastures" was brought into the temple and purified on the first day of a certain month. It was then whispered into the bull's left ear through a reed tube: "Bull, the guilty Zu are you"; and into the right ear: "Bull, you have been chosen for the rite and the ceremonies." On the fifteenth day the bull was brought before the images of "the Seven Gods Who Judge" and the symbols of the twelve celestial bodies of the Solar System.

The trial of Zu was then reenacted. The bull was put down before Enlil, "the Great Shepherd." The accusing priest recited rhetorical accusational questions, as though addressed to Enlil: How could you have given "the stored treasure" to the enemy? How could you have let him to come and dwell in the "pure place"? How could he gain access to your quarters? Then the playacting called for Ea and other gods to beseech Enlil to calm himself, for Ninurta had stepped forward and asked his father: "Point my hands in the right direction! Give me the right words of command!"

Following this recital of the evidence given at the trial, judgment was passed. As the bull was being slaughtered in accordance with detailed instructions, the priests recited the bull's verdict: His liver was to be boiled in a sacrifical kettle; his skin and muscles were to be burned inside the temple; but his "evil tongue shall remain outside."

Then the priests, playing the roles of the other gods, broke out in a hymn of praise to Ninurta:

> Wash your hands, wash your hands!
> You are now as Enlil, wash your hands!
> You are as Enlil [upon] the Earth;
> May all the gods rejoice in you!

When the gods looked for a volunteer to fight Zu, they promised the vanquisher of Zu:

Thy name shall be the greatest
in the Assembly of the Great Gods;
Among the gods, thy brothers,
thou shall have no equal;
Glorified before the gods
and potent shall be thy name!

After Ninurta's victory the promise had to be kept. But therein was the rub and the seed of future fights among the gods: Ninurta was indeed Enlil's Legal Heir but on Nibiru, not on Earth. Now, as the commemorative temple ritual makes clear, he was made "as Enlil—upon Earth." We know from other texts dealing with the gods of Sumer and Akkad that their hierarchical order was also expressed numerically. Anu was given the highest number of the Sumerian sexagesimal system, 60. His Legal Heir, Enlil, had the rank of 50; the firstborn son (and heir in the event of Enlil's demise), Ea, was 40. Now, as the enigmatic statement that Ninurta has become "as Enlil" attests, he, too, was given the rank of 50.

The partly mutilated ending of the temple ritual text contains the following legible verses: "O Marduk, for your king speak the words: 'I release!' O Adad, for your king speak the words: 'I release!' " We can safely guess that the mutilated lines also included a similar release by Sin of his claim to kingship among the gods and recognition of Ninurta's Enlilship. We know that thereafter, Sin —Enlil's firstborn on Earth—held the rank of 30, his son Shamash 20, and his daughter Ishtar 15, and Ishkur (*Adad* in Akkadian) the rank of 10. (There is no record of Marduk's numerical rank.)

The conspiracy of Zu and his evil plotting remained also in mankind's memory, evolving into a fear of birdlike demons who can cause affliction and pestilence (Fig. 27). Some of these demons were called *Lillu*, a term that played on the double meaning "to howl" and "of the night"; their female leader, *Lillitu*—Lilith— was depicted as a naked, winged goddess with birdlike feet (Fig. 28). The many *shurpu* ("purification by burning") texts that have been found were formulas for incantations against these evil spirits—forerunners of the sorcery and witchcraft that had lasted throughout the millennia.

In spite of the solemn vows taken after the defeat of Zu to honor and respect Enlil's supremacy and Ninurta's position as second-in-command, the basic factors causing rivalry and contention had remained—breaking into the open from time to time in the ensuing

Fig. 27

millennia. Realizing that this would be so, Anu and Enlil provided Ninurta with new, marvelous weapons. Anu gave him the SHAR.UR ("Supreme Hunter") and the SHAR.GAZ ("Supreme Smiter"); Enlil gave him several weapons, of which the unique IB—a weapon with "fifty killing heads"—was the most awesome, leading to references in the chronicles to Ninurta as "The Lord of the Ib." Thus armed, Ninurta became the "Foremost Warrior of Enlil," ready to fight off all challenges to the Enlilship.

The next such challenge came in the shape of a mutiny of the Anunnaki who were working in the gold mines of the Abzu. The mutiny, and the events that had led to it and followed it, are fully described in a text called by scholars *The Atra-Hasis Epic*—a full-fledged Earth Chronicle which, inter alia, records the events that had led to the creation of *Homo sapiens*—Man as we know him.

The text informs us that after Anu had gone back to Nibiru and Earth was divided between Enlil and Enki, the Anunnaki toiled in the mines of the Abzu for "forty counted periods"—forty orbits of their planet, or 144,000 Earth-years. But the work was diffi-

Fig. 28

cult and backbreaking: "inside the mountains . . . in the deeply cut shafts . . . the Anunnaki suffered the toil; excessive was their toil, for forty counted periods."

The mining operations, deep inside the earth, were never interrupted: the Anunnaki "suffered the toil day and night." But as the shafts grew deeper and the toil harsher, dissatisfaction grew: "They were complaining, backbiting, grumbling in the excavations."

To help maintain discipline Enlil sent Ninurta to the Abzu, but this strained relations with Enki even more. It was then that Enlil decided to go to the Abzu and personally evaluate the situation. The discontended Anunnaki seized the opportunity to mutiny!

The *Atra-Hasis* chronicle, in language as vivid as that of a modern reporter, in more than 150 lines of text, unambiguously describes the events that followed: How the rebellious Anunnaki put their tools on fire and, in the middle of the night, marched on Enlil's dwelling; how some shouted "Let us kill him . . . Let us break the yoke!"; how an unnamed leader reminded them that Enlil was the "Chief Officer of Old Time," and advised negotiations; and how Enlil, enraged, took up his weapons, but he, too, was reminded by his chamberlain: "My lord, these are your sons. . . ."

As Enlil remained a prisoner in his own quarters, he sent a message to Anu and asked that he come to Earth. When Anu arrived, the Great Anunnaki assembled for a court-martial. "Enki, Ruler of the Abzu, was also present." Enlil demanded to know who the instigator of the mutiny was, calling for a death penalty. Not getting the support of Anu, Enlil offered his resignation: "Noble one," he said to Anu, "take away the office, take away the power; to Heaven will I ascend with you." But Anu, calming Enlil, also expressed understanding of the miners' hardships.

Encouraged, Enki "opened his mouth and addressed the gods." Repeating Anu's summation, he had a solution to offer: While the Chief Medical Officer, their sister Sud, was here in the Abzu with them:

> Let her create a Primitive Worker;
> And let him bear the yoke . . .
> Let the Worker carry the toil of the gods,
> Let him bear the yoke!

In the following one hundred lines of the *Atra-Hasis* text, and in several other "Creation of Man" texts that have been discovered in various states of preservation, the tale of the genetic engineering of *Homo sapiens* has been told in amazing detail. To achieve the feat Enki suggested that a "Being that already exists"—Apewoman—be used to create the *Lulu Amelu* ("The Mixed Worker") by "binding" upon the less evolved beings "the mold of the gods." The goddess

Sud purified the "essence" of a young male Anunnaki; she mixed it into the egg of an Apewoman. The fertilized egg was then implanted in the womb of a female Anunnaki, for the required period of pregnancy. When the "mixed creature" was born, Sud lifted him up and shouted: "I have created! My hands have made it!"

The "Primitive Worker"—*Homo sapiens*—had come into being. It happened some 300,000 years ago; it came about through a feat of genetic engineering and embryo-implant techniques which mankind itself is beginning to employ. There has undoubtedly been a long process of evolution; but then the Anunnaki had taken a hand in the process and jumped the gun on evolution, "creating" us sooner than we might have evolved on our own. Scholars have been searching for a long time for the "missing link" in man's evolution. The Sumerian texts reveal that the "missing link" was a feat of genetic manipulation performed in a laboratory. . . . It was not a feat over and done with in an instant. The texts make clear that it had taken the Anunnaki considerable trial and error to achieve the desired "perfect model" of the Primitive Worker, but once achieved, a mass-production process was launched: fourteen "birth goddesses" at a time were implanted with the genetically manipulated Apewomen eggs: seven to bear male and seven to bear female Workers. As soon as they grew up, the Workers were put to work in the mines; and as their numbers grew, they assumed more and more of the physical chores in the Abzu.

The armed clash between Enlil and Enki that was soon to take place, however, was over these same slave laborers. . . .

The more the production of ores improved in the Abzu, the greater was the work load on the Anunnaki that had remained to operate the facilities in Mesopotamia. The climate was milder, rains were more plentiful, and the rivers of Mesopotamia were constantly overflowing. Increasingly the Mesopotamian Anunnaki "were digging the river," raising dikes and deepening the canals. Soon they too began to clamor for the slave workers, the "creatures of bright countenance" but with thick black hair:

> The Anunnaki stepped up to Enlil . . .
> Black-headed Ones they were requesting of him.
> To the Black-headed people
> to give the pickax to hold.

We read of these events in a text named by Samuel N. Kramer *The Myth of the Pickax.* Though portions are missing, it is understood that Enki refused Enlil's request for the transfer of Primitive Workers to Mesopotamia. Deciding to take matters into his own hands, Enlil took the extreme step of disconnecting the communications with the home planet: "In the 'Bond Heaven-Earth' he made a gash . . . verily did he speed to disconnect Heaven from Earth." Then he launched an armed attack against the Land of the Mines.

The Anunnaki in the Abzu assembled the Primitive Workers in a central compound, strengthening its walls against the coming attack. But Enlil fashioned a marvelous weapon, the AL.A.NI ("Ax That Produces Power") equipped with a "horn" and an "earth splitter" that could drill through walls and earthworks. With these weapons Enlil drove a hole through the fortifications. As the hole widened "Primitive Workers were breaking out toward Enlil. He eyed the Black-headed Ones in fascination."

Thereafter the Primitive Workers performed the manual tasks in both Lands: In the Land of the Mines they "bore the work and suffered the toil"; in Mesopotamia, "with picks and spades they built gods' houses, they built the big canal banks; food they grew for the sustenance of the gods."

Many ancient drawings engraved on cylinder seals depicted these Primitive Workers performing their tasks, naked as the animals of the field (Fig. 29). Various Sumerian texts recorded this animallike stage in human development:

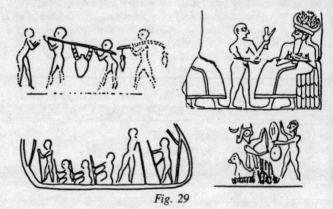

Fig. 29

When Mankind was first created,
They knew not the eating of bread,
Knew not the dressing of garments,
Ate plants with their mouth like sheep,
Drank water from the ditch . . .

How long, however, could young female Anunnaki be asked (or forced) to perform the roles of "birth goddesses"? Unbeknownst to Enlil, and with the connivance of Sud, Enki contrived to give the new creature one more genetic twist: granting to the hybrid beings—incapable of procreating, as all hybrids are—the ability to have offspring, the sexual "Knowing" for having children. The event is echoed in the biblical tale of Adam and Eve in the Garden of Eden, and although the original Sumerian text of the tale has not yet been found, a number of Sumerian depictions of the event were indeed discovered. They show different aspects of the tale: the Tree of Life; the offering of the forbidden fruit; the angry encounter that ensued between the "Lord God" and the "Serpent." Yet another shows Eve girdled in a garment around her loins while Adam is still naked (Fig. 30), another detail related in the Bible.

Fig. 30

While the Serpent God features in all these ancient depictions, the illustration reproduced here is of particular significance as it writes out, in archaic Sumerian the god's epithet/name as ✳—➤. The "star" spells "god" and the triangular symbol reads BUR, BURU, or BUZUR—all terms that make the epithet/name mean "God Who Solves Secrets," "God of the Deep Mines," and variations thereof. The Bible (in the original Hebrew) calls the god who tempted Eve *Nahash,* translated "Serpent," but literally meaning "He Who Solves Secrets" and "He Who Knows Metals," the exact parallels of the god's name in the Sumerian depiction. This depiction is of further interest because it shows the Serpent God with his hands and feet in tethers, suggesting that Enki was arrested after his unauthorized deed.

In his anger Enlil ordered the expulsion of The Adam—the *Homo sapiens* Earthling—from the E.DIN ("The Abode of the Righteous Ones"). No longer confined to the settlements of the Anunnaki, Man began to roam the Earth.

> "And Adam *knew* Eve his wife, and she conceived and bore Cain . . . and she bore again his brother Abel." The gods were no longer alone on Earth.

Little did the Anunnaki then know the role that the Primitive Worker would play in the wars between them.

6

MANKIND EMERGES

Ever since George Smith found and reported in 1876 *(The Chaldean Account of Genesis)* detailed Mesopotamian tales of Creation, followed by L. W. King's *The Seven Tablets of Creation*, scholars and theologians alike have come to recognize that the Creation Tales of the Old Testamant (Genesis Chapters 1 through 3) are condensed and edited versions of original Sumerian texts. A century later, in our work, *The 12th Planet* (1976), we have shown that these texts were no primitive myths, but depositories of advanced scientific knowledge with which modern scholars are only now beginning to catch up.

The unmanned space probes of Jupiter and Saturn confirmed many "incredible" facets of the Sumerian knowledge regarding our Solar System, such as that the outer planets have numerous satellites and that water is present on some of them. Those distant planets, and some of their principal satellites, were found to have active cores that generate internal heat; some radiate out more heat than they can ever receive from the distant Sun. Volcanic activity provided those celestial bodies with their own atmospheres. All the basic requirements for the development of life exist out there, just as the Sumerians had said 6,000 years ago.

What, then, of the existence of a twelfth member of our Solar System—a tenth planet beyond Pluto, the Sumerian Nibiru (and Babylonian Marduk)—a planet whose existence was a basic and far-reaching conclusion in *The 12th Planet?*

In 1978, astronomers at the U.S. Naval Observatory in Washington determined that Pluto—being smaller than formerly believed—could not by itself account for perturbations in the orbits of Uranus and Neptune; they postulated the existence of yet another celestial body beyond Pluto. In 1982 the U.S. National Aeronautics and Space Administration (NASA) announced its conclusion that there indeed exists such a body; whether or not it is another large planet, it planned to determine by deploying in a certain manner its two *Pioneer* spacecraft that had been hurtling into space beyond Saturn.

109

And at the close of 1983, astronomers at the Jet Propulsion Laboratory in California announced that IRAS—the infrared telescope mounted on a spacecraft and launched under NASA's auspices with the cooperation of other nations—had discovered beyond Pluto a very distant "mystery celestial body" about four times the size of Earth and *moving toward Earth*. They have not yet called it a planet; but our Earth Chronicles leave the ultimate finding in no doubt.

In 1983, rocks were found in Antarctica and elsewhere which are undoubtedly fragments of the Moon and Mars; and the scientists are totally baffled as to how that could have happened. The Sumerian tale of the Creation of the Solar System, the collision between Nibiru's satellites and Tiamat, and the rest of the cosmogony in the celebrated *Epic of Creation* offer a comprehensive explanation.

And what about the texts describing how Man was created through genetic manipulation: in vitro fertilization and reimplantation?

Recent advances in genetic sciences and technologies have affirmed the Sumerian concept of gradual evolution on the one hand, and on the other hand, the (otherwise inexplicable) appearance of the biologically advanced *Homo sapiens* through genetic engineering by the Anunnaki. Even the very recent method of test tube procreation—extracting a female egg, impregnating it with purified male semen, and reimplanting the fertilized egg in a woman's womb—is the very same procedure described in the Sumerian texts from millennia ago.

If the two principal events—the creation of Earth and the creation of Man—are correctly reported in the Bible, ought we not to accept the veracity of the biblical tale regarding the emergence of mankind on Earth?

And if the biblical tales are but a condensed version of more detailed, earlier Sumerian chronicles, could not the latter be used to enhance and complete the biblical record of those earliest times?

Since one is the reflection of the other, let us hold up a mirror to that ancient flame of memories. . . . Let us continue the unraveling of the wondrous tale.

After relating how "*The* Adam" (literally, "the Earthling") was granted the ability to procreate, the Book of Genesis moves from recounting the general events on Earth to the saga of a specific branch of mankind: the person named Adam and his descendants.

"This is the Book of the Generations of Adam," the Old Testament informs us. Such a book, we can safely assume, had surely existed. The evidence strongly suggests that the person whom the Bible called Adam was the one whom the Sumerians called *Adapa*, an Earthling "perfected" by Enki and deemed to have been genetically related to him. "Wide understanding Enki perfected for him, to disclose the designs of the Earth; to him he gave Knowing; but immortality he did not give him."

Portions of the "Tale of Adapa" have been found; the complete text might well have been the "Book of the Generations of Adam" to which the Old Testament refers. Assyrian kings probably had access to such a record, for many of them claimed to have retained one or another of Adapa's virtues. Sargon and Sennacherib held that they had inherited the wisdom that Enki had granted Adapa; Sinsharishkun and Esarhaddon boasted that they were born "in the image of the wise Adapa"; according to an inscription of Esarhaddon, he had erected in the temple of Ashur a statue with the image of Adapa; and Ashurbanipal asserted that he had learned "the secret of tablet-writing from before the Deluge" as Adapa had known.

The Sumerian sources hold that there had been both rural cultures—cultivation and shepherding—as well as urban settlements before the Deluge had swept all off the face of the Earth. The Book of Genesis relates that the first son of Adam and Eve, Cain, "was a tiller of the earth," and his brother Abel "was a herder of sheep." Then, after Cain was exiled "away from the presence of the Lord" for having killed Abel, urban settlements—Cities of Man—were established: in the land of Nud, east of Eden, Cain had a son whom he named Enoch and built a city called likewise, the name meaning "Foundation." The Old Testament, having no particular interest in the line of Cain, skips quickly to the fourth generation after Enoch, when Lamech was born:

And Lamech took unto himself two wives:
The name of one was Adah,
and the name of the other Zillah.
And Adah bore Jabal; he was the father of
    such as dwell in tents and have cattle.
And his brother's name was Jubal; he was the
    father of all such as play lyre and pipe.
And Zillah also bore Tubal-Cain,
    an artificer of gold and copper and iron.

The pseudepigraphical *Book of Jubilees*, believed to have been composed in the second century B.C. from earlier material, adds the information that Cain espoused his own sister Awan and she bore him Enoch "at the close of the fourth Jubilee. And in the first year of the first week of the fifth Jubilee, houses were built on the earth, and Cain built a city and called its name Foundation, after the name of his son." Where did this additional information come from?

It has long been held that this part of the Genesis tale stands alone, without corroboration or parallel in the Mesopotamian texts. But we have found that it is just not so.

First, we have come upon a Babylonian tablet in the British Museum (No. 74329, Fig. 31), catalogued as "containing an otherwise unknown myth." Yet it may in fact be a Babylonian/Assyrian version from circa 2000 B.C. of *a missing Sumerian record of the Line of Cain!*

As copied by A. R. Millard and translated by W. G. Lambert (*Kadmos*, vol. VI), it speaks of the beginnings of a group of people who were ploughmen, which corresponds to the biblical "tiller of the land." They are called *Amakandu*—"People Who In Sorrow Roam"; it parallels the condemnation of Cain: "Banned be thou from the soil which hath received thy brother's blood . . . a restless nomad shalt thou be upon the earth." And, most remarkably, the Mesopotamian chief of these exiled people was called *Ka'in!* Also, just as in the biblical tale:

> He built in Dunnu
> a city with twin towers.
> Ka'in dedicated to himself
> the lordship over the city.

The name of this place is intriguing. Because the order of syllables could be reversed in Sumerian without changing the meaning, the name could also be spelled NU.DUN, paralleling the biblical name Nud as the place of Cain's exile. The Sumerian name meant "the excavated resting place"—very much similar to the biblical interpretation of the name as meaning "Foundation."

After the death (or murder) of Ka'in, "he was laid to rest in the city of Dunnu, which he loved." As in the biblical tale, the Mesopotamian text records the history of four following generations: brothers married their sisters and murdered their parents, taking over the rulership in Dunnu as well as settling in new places, the last of which was named *Shupat* ("Judgment").

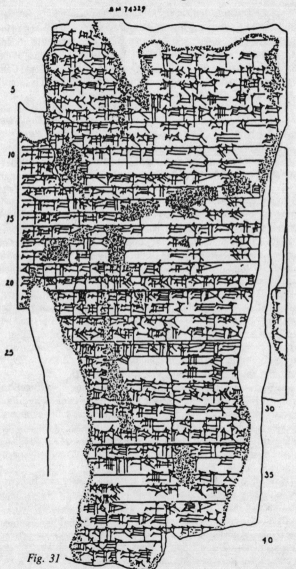

Fig. 31

A second source indicating Mesopotamian chronicles for the biblical tale of Adam and his son Cain are Assyrian texts. We find, for example, that an archaic Assyrian King List states that in the earliest times, when their forefathers were tent-dwellers—a term duplicated in the Bible regarding the line of Cain—the patriarch of their people was named Adamu, the biblical Adam.

We also find among traditional Assyrian eponyms of royal names the combination Ashur-bel-Ka'ini ("Ashur, lord of the Ka'-inites"); and the Assyrian scribes paralleled this with the Sumerian ASHUR-EN.DUNI ("Ashur is lord of *Duni*"), implying that the Ka'ini ("The people of Kain") and the Duni ("The people of Dun") were one and the same; and thus reaffirming the biblical Cain and Land of Nud or Dun.

Having dealt briefly with the line of Cain, the Old Testament turned its full attention to a new line descended of Adam: "And Adam knew his wife again, and she bore a son, and called his name Seth, for [she said] the Lord hath granted me another offspring instead of Abel, whom Cain had slain." The Book of Genesis then adds: "One hundred and thirty years did Adam live when he begot a son in his likeness and after his image, and called his name Seth.

"And the days of Adam after he had begotten Seth were eight hundred years, and he begot [other] sons and daughters; and all the days that Adam lived were nine hundred and thirty years, and he died. And Seth lived a hundred and five years and begot Enosh; and after he begot Enosh Seth lived eight hundred and seven years, and he begot [other] sons and daughters; and all the days of Seth were nine hundred and twelve years, and he died."

The name of Seth's son and the next pre-Diluvial patriarch in which the Bible was interested was *Enosh;* it has come to mean in Hebrew "Human, Mortal," and it is clear that the Old Testament considered him the progenitor of the human lineage at the core of the ancient chronicles. It states in respect to him, that "It was then that the name of Yahweh began to be called," that worship and priesthood began.

There are a number of Sumerian texts that shed more light on this intriguing aspect. The available portions of the *Adapa* text state that he was "perfected" and treated as a son by Enki in Enki's city Eridu. It is likely then, as William Hallo (*Antediluvian Cities*) had suggested, that the great-grandson of Enosh was named *Yared* to mean "He of Eridu." Here, then, is the answer: While the Bible loses interest in the banished descendants of Adam, it focuses its attention on the patriarchs from Adam's line who had stayed in Eden—southern Mesopotamia—and were the first to be called to priesthood.

In the fourth generation after Enosh the firstborn son was named Enoch; scholars believe that here the name's meaning stemmed from a variant of the Hebrew root, connoting "to train, to educate." Of him the Old Testament briefly states that he "had walked with the Deity" and did not die on Earth, "for the Deity had taken him." The sole verse in Genesis 5:24 is substantially enlarged upon in the extra-biblical *Books of Enoch*. They detail his first visit with the Angels of God to be instructed in various sciences and ethics. Then, after returning to Earth to pass the knowledge and the requisites of priesthood to his sons, he was taken aloft once more, to permanently join the *Nefilim* (the biblical term meaning "Those Who Had Dropped Down") in their celestial abode.

The Sumerian King List records the priestly reign of Enmeduranki in Sippar, then the location of the Spaceport under the command of Utu/Shamash. His name, "Priestly lord of the Dur-an-ki," indicates that he had been trained in Nippur. A little-known tablet, reported by W. G. Lambert ("Enmeduranki and Related Material"), reads as follows:

Enmeduranki [was] a prince in Sippar,
Beloved of Anu, Enlil and Ea.
Shamash in the Bright Temple appointed him.
Shamash and Adad [took him] to the assembly [of the gods] . . .
They showed him how to observe oil on water,
a secret of Anu, Enlil and Ea.
They gave him the Divine Tablet,
the *kibdu* secret of Heaven and Earth . . .
They taught him how to make calculations with numbers.

When the instruction of Enmeduranki in the secret knowledge of the gods was accomplished, he was returned to Sumer. The "men of Nippur, Sippar and Babylon were called into his presence." He informed them of his experiences and of the establishment of priesthood. It shall be passed, the gods commanded, from father to son: "The learned savant, who guards the secrets of the gods, will bind his favored son with an oath before Shamash and Adad . . . and will instruct him in the secrets of the gods."

The tablet concludes with a postscript: "Thus was the line of priests created—those who are allowed to approach Shamash and Adad.''

By the time of the seventh generation after Enosh, on the eve of the Deluge, the Earth and its inhabitants were gripped by a new Ice Age. The Mesopotamian texts detail the sufferings by mankind, the shortages of food, even cannibalism. The Book of Genesis only hints at the situation by stating that when Noah (''Respite'') was born, he was so named by his father in the hope that his birth shall signal a respite ''from the work and toil that cometh from the Earth which the Lord hath cursed.'' The biblical version tells us little about Noah, apart from the fact that he was ''righteous and of pure genealogy.'' The Mesopotamian texts inform us that the hero of the Deluge lived in Shuruppak, the medical center run by Sud.

The Sumerian texts relate that as mankind's hardships were increasing, Enki suggested, and Enlil vehemently opposed, the taking of measures to alleviate the suffering. What upset Enlil no end was the increasing sexual relationships between the young male Anunnaki and the Daughters of Man. The Book of Genesis describes the ''taking of wives'' by the Nefilim in the following words:

> And it came to pass,
> When the Earthlings began to increase in number
> upon the face of the Earth,
> and daughters were born unto them—
> That the sons of the gods
> saw the daughters of the Earthlings
> that they were compatible;
> And they took unto themselves wives
> of whichever they chose.

A ''mythical tablet'' (CBS-14061) reported by E. Chiera *(Sumerian Religious Texts)* tells the story of those early days and of a young god named Martu, who complained that he, too, should be permitted to espouse a human wife. It happened, the text begins, when

> The city of Nin-ab existed, Shid-tab did not exist;
> The holy tiara existed, the holy crown did not exist . . .
> Cohabitation there was . . .
> Bringing forth [of children] there was.

"Nin-ab," the text continues, "was a city in the settled Great Land." Its high priest, an accomplished musician, had a wife and a daughter. As the people gathered to offer the gods the roasted meat of the sacrifices, Martu, who was single, saw the priest's daughter. Desiring her, he went to his mother and complained:

> In my city I have friends, they have taken wives.
> I have companions, they have taken wives.
> In my city, unlike my friends, I have not taken a wife;
> I have no wife, I have no children.

Asking whether the maiden whom he desired "appreciated his gaze," the goddess gave her consent. The other young gods then prepared a feast; as the marriage was announced, "in the city of Nin-ab, the people by the sound of the copper drum were called; the seven tambourines were sounded."

This growing togetherness between the young astronauts and the descendants of the Primitive Worker was not to Enlil's liking. The Sumerian texts tell us that "as the Land extended and the people multiplied," Enlil became increasingly "disturbed by Mankind's pronouncements" and its infatuation with sex and lust. The get-togethers between the Anunnaki and the daughters of Man caused him to lose sleep. "And the Lord said: 'I will destroy the Earthling whom I have created off the face of the Earth.' "

The texts inform us that when it was decided to develop the deep mines in the Abzu, the Anunnaki also proceeded to establish a scientific monitoring station at the tip of Africa. It was put in charge of Ereshkigal, a granddaughter of Enlil. A Sumerian epic tale recorded the hazardous voyage of Enki and Ereshkigal from Mesopotamia to that far-off mountainland (Kur)—a text that implies that Ereshkigal was either abducted or in some other manner coerced by Enki on that voyage, having been "carried off to Kur as a prize."

(Ereshkigal, we know from other epics, was later on attacked at her station by Nergal, one of Enki's sons, as a result of an insult involving Ereshkigal's emissary. At the last moment, Ereshkigal saved her life by offering Nergal to marry her and control together with her the station's "Tablets of Wisdom.")

Enlil now saw his chance to get rid of the Earthlings when this scientific station at the tip of Africa began to report a dangerous situation: the growing ice cap over Antarctica had become unstable, resting upon a layer of slippery slush. The problem was that this instability had developed just as Nibiru was about to make its approach to Earth's vicinity; and Nibiru's gravitational pull could upset the ice cap's balance and cause it to slip into the Antarctic Ocean. The immense tidal waves that this would cause could engulf the whole globe.

When the Igigi orbiting Earth confirmed the certainty of such a catastrophe, the Anunnaki began to assemble in Sippar, the spaceport. Enlil, however, insisted that mankind be kept unaware of the coming Deluge; and at a special session of the Assembly of the Gods, he made all of them, and especially Enki, swear to keep the secret.

The last part of the *Atra-Hasis* text, a major part of the *Epic of Gilgamesh,* and other Mesopotamian texts describe at length the events that followed—how the catastrophe of the Deluge was used by Enlil to achieve the annihilation of mankind; and how Enki, opposed to the decision which Enlil forced upon the Assembly of the Gods, contrived to save his faithful follower Ziusudra (''Noah'') by designing for him a submersible vessel that could withstand the avalanche of water.

The Anunnaki themselves, on a signal, ''lifted up'' in their *Rukub ilani* (''chariots of the gods''), the fired-up rocket ships ''setting the land ablaze with their glare.'' Orbiting the Earth in their shuttlecraft, they watched in horror the onslaught of the tidal waves below. All that was upon the Earth was swept off in one colossal avalanche of water: A.MA.RU BA.UR RA.TA—''The Flood swept thereover.'' Sud, who had created Man with Enki, ''saw and wept. . . . Ishtar cried out like a woman in travail . . . the gods, the Anunnaki, weep with her.'' Rolling back and forth, the tidal waves swept the soil away, leaving behind vast deposits of mud: ''All that had been created, turned back to clay.''

In *The 12th Planet* we have presented the evidence for our conclusion that the Deluge, bringing about an abrupt end to the last Ice Age, had occurred some 13,000 years ago.

As the waters of the Deluge ''went back from off the land'' and started to subside, the Anunnaki began to land on Mount Nisir (''Mount of Salvation'')—Mount Ararat. There Ziusudra/Noah also arrived, his vessel guided by a navigator provided by Enki. Enlil was outraged to discover that the ''seed of Mankind'' was saved; but Enki persuaded him to relent: The gods, he argued, could no longer exist on Earth without the help of man. ''And the Lord blessed Noah and his sons, and said unto them: 'Be fruitful and multiply, and replenish the Earth.' ''

The Old Testament, focusing its interest on the line of Noah alone, lists no other passengers in the rescue ship. But the more detailed Mesopotamian Deluge texts also mention the Ark's navigator and disclose that at the last moment friends or helpers of Ziusudra (and their families) also came on board. Greek versions of the account by Berossus state that after the Deluge, Ziusudra, his family, and the pilot were taken by the gods to stay with them; the other people were given directions to find their way back to Mesopotamia by themselves.

The immediate problem facing all that were rescued was food. To Noah and his sons the Lord said: "All the animals that are upon the earth, and all that flies in the skies, and all that creepeth on the ground, and all the fishes of the sea, into your hands are given; all that teemeth and that liveth, shall be yours for food." And then came a significant addition: "As grassy vegetation all manner of grain have I given you."

This little-noticed statement (Genesis 9:3), which touches on the origins of agriculture, is substantially enlarged upon in the Sumerian texts. Scholars are agreed that agriculture began in the Mesopotamia-Syria-Israel crescent but are at a loss to explain why it did not begin in the plains (where cultivation is easy) but rather in the highlands. They are agreed that it began with the harvesting of "wild ancestors" of wheat and barley some 12,000 years ago but are baffled by the genetic uniformity of those early grain grasses; and they are totally at a loss to explain the botano-genetic feat whereby—within a mere 2,000 years—such wild emmers doubled, trebled, and quadrupled their chromosome pairs to become the cultivable wheat and barley of outstanding nutritional value with the incredible ability to grow almost anywhere and with the unusual twice-a-year crops.

Coupled with these puzzles was the equal suddenness with which every manner of fruit and vegetable began to appear from the same nuclear area at almost the same time, and the simultaneous "domestication" of animals, starting with sheep and goats that provided meat, milk, and wool.

How did it all come about when it did? Modern science has yet to find the answer; but the Sumerian texts had already provided it millennia ago. Like the Bible, they relate how agriculture began after the Deluge, when (in the words of Genesis) "Noah began as a husbandman"; but like the Bible, which records that there had been tilling of the land (by Cain) and shepherding (by Abel) long before the Deluge, so do the Sumerian chronicles tell of the development of crop-growing and cattle-rearing in prehistoric times.

When the Anunnaki had landed on Earth, a text titled by scholars *The Myth of Cattle and Grain* states, none of the domesticated grains or cattle had yet been in existence:

> When from the heights of Heaven to Earth
> Anu had caused the Anunnaki to come forth,
> Grains had not yet been brought forth,
> had not yet vegetated . . .
> There was no ewe,
> a lamb had not yet been dropped;
> There was no she-goat,
> a kid had not yet been dropped.
> The ewe had not yet given birth to her lambs,
> the she-goat had not yet given birth to her kid.
> Weaving [of wool] had not yet been brought forth,
> had not yet been established.

Then, in the "Creation Chamber" of the Anunnaki, their laboratory for genetic manipulation, *Lahar* ("woolly cattle") and *Anshan* ("grains") "were beautifully fashioned":

> In those days,
> in the Creation Chamber of the gods,
> in the House of Fashioning, in the Pure Mound,
> Lahar and Anshan were beautifully fashioned.
> The abode was filled with food for the gods.
> Of the multiplying of Lahar and Anshan
> the Anunnaki, in their Holy Mound, eat—
> but were not satiated.
> The good milk from the sheepfold
> the Anunnaki, in their Holy Mound, drink—
> but are not satiated.

The Primitive Workers—those who "knew not the eating of bread . . . who ate plants with their mouths"—were already in existence:

> After Anu, Enlil, Enki and Sud
> had fashioned the black-headed people,
> Vegetation that luxuriates they multiplied in the Land.
> Four-legged animals they artfully brought into existence;
> In the E.DIN they placed them.

So, in order to increase the production of grains and cattle to satiate the Anúnnaki, a decision was made: Let NAM.LU.GAL.LU —"civilized mankind"—be taught the "tilling of the land" and the "keeping of sheep . . . for the sake of the gods":

> For the sake of the satiating things,
> for the pure sheepfold,
> Civilized Mankind was brought into existence.

Just as it describes what had been brought into existence at that early time, so does this text also list the domesticated varieties that had *not* then been brought forth:

> That which by planting multiplies,
> had not yet been fashioned;
> Terraces had not yet been set up . . .
> The triple grain of thirty days did not exist;
> The triple grain of forty days did not exist;
> The small grain, the grain of the mountains,
> the grain of the pure A.DAM, did not exist . . .
> Tuber-vegetables of the field had not yet come forth.

These, as we shall see, were introduced on Earth by Enlil and Ninurta some time after the Deluge.

After the Deluge had swept all off the face of the Earth, the first problem facing the Anunnaki was where to get the seeds needed for renewed cultivation. Fortunately specimens of the domesticated cereals had been sent to Nibiru; and now "Anu provided them, from Heaven, to Enlil." Enlil then looked for a safe place where the seeds could be sown to restart agriculture. The earth was still covered with water, and the only place that seemed suitable was "the mountain of aromatic cedars." We read in a fragmented text reported by S. N. Kramer in his *Sumerische Literarische Texte aus Nippur:*

> Enlil went up the peak and lifted his eyes;
> He looked down: there the waters filled as a sea.
> He looked up: there was the mountain of the aromatic cedars.
> He hauled up the barley, terraced it on the mountain.
> That which vegetates he hauled up,
> terraced the grain cereals on the mountain.

The selection of the Cedar Mountain by Enlil and its conversion into a Restricted ("Holy") Place was, most likely, not accidental. Throughout the Near East—indeed, worldwide—there is only one unique Cedar Mountain of universal fame: in Lebanon. It is the location, to this very day (at Baalbek in Lebanon), of a vast platform supported by colossal stone blocks (Fig. 32) that are still a marvel of technology. It was, as we have elaborated in *The Stairway to Heaven,* a Landing Place of the Anunnaki; a platform that persistent legends hold to have been built in pre-Diluvial times, even as early as the days of Adam. It was the only place, after the Deluge, immediately suitable for handling the shuttlecraft of the Anunnaki: the spaceport at Sippar was washed away and buried under layers of mud.

Fig. 32

With seeds available, the question was where to sow them. . . . The lowlands, still filled with mud and water, were unsuitable for habitation. The highlands, though freed from under the avalanche of water, were soggy with the rains that began to pour down with the neothermal age. The rivers had not found their new courses; the waters had nowhere to go; cultivation was impossible. We read this description in a Sumerian text:

> Famine was severe, nothing was produced.
> The small rivers were not cleaned,
> the mud was not carried off . . .
> In all the lands there were no crops,
> only weeds grew.

The two great rivers of Mesopotamia, the Euphrates and Tigris, were also not functioning: "The Euphrates was not bound together, there was misery; the Tigris was confounded, jolted and injured." The one who rose to the task of building dams in the mountains, digging new channels for the rivers, and draining off the excess water was Ninurta: "Thereon the lord sets his lofty mind; Ninurta, the son of Enlil, brings great things into being":

> To protect the land, a mighty wall he raised.
> With a mace he smote the rocks;
> The stones the hero heaped, made a settlement . . .
> The waters that had been scattered, he gathered;
> What by the mountains had been dispersed,
> he guided and sent down the Tigris.
> The high waters it pours off the farmed land.
> Now, behold—
> Everything on Earth rejoiced at Ninurta,
> the lord of the land.

A long text, gradually pieced together by scholars, *The Feats and Exploits of Ninurta,* adds a tragic note to Ninurta's efforts to bring back order to the Earth on which he was superior. To cover all the problem spots at once, Ninurta rushed from place to place in the mountains in his airship; but "His Winged Bird on the summit was smashed; its pinions crashed down to the earth." (An unclear verse suggests that he was rescued by Adad.)

We know from the Sumerian texts that first to be cultivated on the mountain slopes were fruit trees and bushes and most certainly grapes. The Anunnaki, the texts state, gave mankind "the excellent white grapes and the excellent white wine; the excellent black grapes and the excellent red wine." No wonder we read in the Bible that when "Noah began as a husbandman, he planted a vineyard; and he drank of the wine and became drunken."

When the drainage works carried out in Mesopotamia by Ninurta made cultivation possible in the plains, the Anunnaki "from the mountain the cereal grain they brought down," and "the Land [Sumer] with wheat and barley did become acquainted."

In the millennia that followed mankind revered Ninurta as the one who had taught it farming; a "Farmer's Almanac" attributed to him was actually found by archaeologists in a Sumerian site. The Akkadian name for him was *Urash*—"The One of the Plough"; a Sumerian cylinder seal depicted him (some believe it shows Enlil) granting the plow to mankind (Fig. 33).

Fig. 33

While Enlil and Ninurta were credited with granting agriculture to mankind, the credit for the introduction of domesticated herds was given to Enki. It was after the first grains were already in cultivation but not yet "the grain that multiplies," the grains with the doubled, tripled, and quadrupled chromosomes; these were created by Enki artificially, with Enlil's consent:

At that time Enki spoke to Enlil:
"Father Enlil, flocks and grains
have made joyful the Holy Mound,
have greatly multiplied in the Holy Mound.
Let us, Enki and Enlil, command:
The woolly-creature and grain-that-multiplies
let us cause to come out of the Holy Mound."

Enlil agreed, and abundance followed:

The woolly-creature they placed in a sheepfold.
The seeds that sprout they give to the mother,

for the grains they establish a place.
To the workmen they give the plough and the yoke . . .
The shepherd makes abundance in the sheepfold;
The young woman sprouting abundance brings;
she lifts her head in the field:
Abundance had come from heaven.
The woolly-creature and grains that are planted
came forth in splendor.
Abundance was given to the congregated people.

The revolutionary agricultural tool—a simple, but ingeniously designed, wooden implement—the plow, was at first pulled, as the above text states, by putting a yoke on the farm workers. But then Enki "brought into existence the larger living creatures"—domesticated cattle—and bulls replaced people as pullers of the plow (Fig. 34). Thus, the texts conclude, did the gods "increase the fertility of the land."

Fig. 34

While Ninurta was busy damming the mountains flanking Mesopotamia and draining its plains, Enki returned to Africa to assess the damage the Deluge had caused there.

As it turned out, Enlil and his offspring ended up controlling all the high ground from the southeast (Elam, entrusted to Inanna/Ishtar) to the northwest (the Taurus Mountains and Asia Minor, given to Ishkur/Adad), with the highland arching in between given to Ninurta in the south and Nannar/Sin in the north. Enlil himself retained the central position overlooking the olden E.DIN; the Landing Place on the Cedar Mountain was put under the command of Utu/Shamash. Where were Enki and his clan to go?

As Enki surveyed Africa it was evident to him that the Abzu alone—the continent's southern part—was insufficient. Just as in

Mesopotamia "abundance" was based on riverine cultivation, so it had to be in Africa; and he turned his attention, planning, and knowledge to the recovery of the Valley of the Nile.

The Egyptians, we have seen, held that their great gods had come to Egypt from Ur (meaning "the olden place"). According to Manetho, the reign of Ptah over the lands of the Nile began 17,900 years before Menes; i.e., circa 21,000 B.C. Nine thousand years later Ptah handed over the Egyptian domain to his son Ra; but the latter's reign was abruptly interrupted after a brief 1,000 years, i.e., circa 11,000 B.C.; it was then, by our reckoning, that the Deluge had occurred.

Then, the Egyptians believed, Ptah returned to Egypt to engage in great works of reclamation and to literally raise it from under the inundating waters. We find Sumerians texts that likewise attest that Enki went to the lands of Meluhha (Ethiopia/Nubia) and Magan (Egypt) to make them habitable for man and beast:

> He proceeds to the Land Meluhha;
> Enki, lord of the Abzu, decrees its fate:
> Black land, may your trees be large trees,
> may they be the Highland trees.
> May thrones fill your royal palaces.
> May your reeds be large reeds,
> may they be the Highland reeds . . .
> May your bulls be large bulls,
> may they be the Highland bulls . . .
> May your silver be as gold,
> May your copper be tin and bronze . . .
> May your people multiply;
> May your hero go forth as a bull . . .

These Sumerian records, linking Enki with the African lands of the Nile, assume a double significance: they corroborate the Egyptian tales with Mesopotamian tales and link Sumerian gods—especially the Enki-gods—with the gods of Egypt; for *Ptah, we believe, was none other than Enki.*

After the lands were made habitable again, Enki divided the length of the African continent between his six sons (Fig. 35). The southernmost domain was regranted to NER.GAL ("Great Watcher") and his spouse Ereshkigal. To his north, in the mining regions, GIBIL ("The One of Fire") was installed, having been taught by his father the secrets of metalworking. NIN.A.GAL

("Prince of Great Waters") was, as his name implied, given the region of the great lakes and the headwaters of the Nile. Farther north, in the grazing plateau of the Sudan, the youngest son, DUMU.ZI ("Son Who Is Life"), whose nickname was "The Herder," was given reign.

Fig. 35

The identity of yet another son is in dispute among the scholars (we shall offer our own solution later on). But there is no doubt who the sixth son—actually Enki's firstborn and legal heir—was: He was MAR.DUK ("Son of the Pure Mound"). Because one of his fifty epithets was ASAR, which sounds so much like the Egyptian *As-Sar* ("Osiris" in Greek), some scholars have speculated that Marduk and Osiris were one and the same. But these epithets (as "All-Powerful" or "Awesome") were applied to diverse deities, and Asar meaning "All-Seeing" was also the epithet-name of the Assyrian god Ashur.

In fact, we find more similarities between the Babylonian Marduk and the Egyptian god Ra: the former was the son of Enki, the latter of Ptah, the two, Enki-Ptah, being in our view one and the same; whereas Osiris was the great-grandson of Ra and thus of a much later generation than either Ra or Marduk. In fact, there is found in Sumerian texts scattered, but persistent, evidence supporting our belief that the god called Ra by the Egyptians and Marduk by the Mesopotamians was one and the same deity. Thus, a self-laudatory hymn to Marduk (tablet Ashur/4125) declares that one of his epithets was "The god IM.KUR.GAR RA"—"Ra Who Beside the Mountainland Abides."

Moreover, there is textual evidence that the Sumerians were aware of the deity's Egyptian name, Ra. There were Sumerians whose personal names incorporated the divine name RA; and tablets from the time of the Ur III Dynasty mention "Dingir Ra" and his temple E.Dingir.Ra. Then, after the fall of that dynasty, when Marduk attained supremacy in his favored city Babylon, its Sumerian name KA.DINGIR ("Gateway of the Gods") was changed to KA.DINGIR.RA—"Ra's Gateway of the Gods."

Indeed, as we shall soon show, Marduk's rise to prominence began in Egypt, where its best-known monument—the Great Pyramid of Giza—had played a crucial role in his turbulent career. But the Great God of Egypt, Marduk/Ra, yearned to rule the whole Earth, and to do so from the olden "Navel of the Earth" in Mesopotamia. It was this ambition that led him to abdicate the divine throne of Egypt in favor of his children and grandchildren.

Little did he know that this would lead to two Pyramid Wars and to his own near death.

7

WHEN EARTH WAS DIVIDED

"And the sons of Noah that came out of the ark were Shem, Ham and Japhet . . . these were the three sons of Noah of whom all the Earth was overspread."

Thus is the biblical tale of the Deluge followed by the recital of the *Table of Nations* (Genesis 10), a unique document, at first doubted by scholars because it listed then unknown nation-states, then taken apart critically, and finally—after a century and a half of archaeological discoveries—amazing in its accuracy. It is a document that holds a wealth of reliable historical, geographical, and political information concerning the rise of mankind's remnants from the mud and desolation following the Deluge, to the heights of civilizations and empires.

Leaving the all-important line of Shem to the last, the *Table of Nations* begins with the descendants of *Japhet* ("The Fair One"): "And the sons of Japhet: Gomer and Magog and Madai, Javan and Tubal and Meshech and Tiras. And the sons of Gomer: Ashkenaz and Riphat and Togarmah; and the sons of Javan: Elishah and Tarshish, the Kittim and the Dodanim. From them branched out the island nations." While the later generations had thus spread to coastal areas and islands, the unnoticed fact was that all the first seven nation/sons corresponded to the highlands of Asia Minor, the Black Sea and the Caspian Sea areas—highlands that were habitable soon after the Deluge, unlike the lower lying coastal areas and islands that could become habitable only much later.

The descendants of *Ham* ("He Who is Hot" and also "The Dark-Hued One"), first "Cush and Mizra'im and Put and Canaan" and thereafter a host of other nation-states, correspond to the African nation-lands of Nubia, Ethiopia, Egypt, and Libya as the core nations of African resettlement, again beginning with the topographically higher areas, then spreading to the lowlands.

"And Shem, the father of all who descended of Eber, also had offspring; he was the elder brother of Japhet." The first nation-sons of Shem were "Elam and Ashur, Arpakhshad and Lud and Aram," nation-states that encompassed the highlands arching from the Persian

Gulf in the south to the Mediterranean Sea in the northwest and bordering the great Land-Between-the-Rivers, which was as yet not habitable. Those were the lands one could call the Spaceport Lands: Mesopotamia, where the pre-Diluvial spaceport had been; the Cedar Mountain, where the Landing Place remained functioning; the Land of Shalem, where the post-Diluvial Mission Control Center was to be established; and the adjoining Sinai peninsula, site of the future spaceport. The name of the forefather of all these nations, *Shem*—meaning "Sky Chamber"—was thus quite appropriate.

The broad division of mankind into three branches, as related in the Bible, followed not only the geography and topography of the areas to which man had spread, it also followed the division of the Earth between the descendants of Enlil and the descendants of Enki. Shem and Japhet are depicted in the Bible as good brothers, whereas the attitude toward the line of Ham—and especially Canaan—is one of bitter memories. In this there lie tales yet to be told—tales of gods and men, and their wars. . . .

The tradition of the division of the ancient settled world into three branches is also in accord with what we know of the rise of civilizations.

Scholars have recognized an abrupt change in human culture about 11,000 B.C.—the time of the Deluge, according to our findings—and have named that era of domestication Mesolithic (Middle Stone Age). Circa 7400 B.C.—exactly 3,600 years later—another abrupt advancement has been recognized. Scholars have named it Neolithic ("New Stone Age"); but its principal feature was the switch from stone to clay and the appearance of pottery. And then, "suddenly and inexplicably"—but exactly 3,600 years later—there blossomed out (circa 3800 B.C.) in the plain between the Euphrates and Tigris rivers the high civilization of Sumer. It was followed, circa 3100 B.C., by the civilization of the Nile River; and circa 2800 B.C., the third civilization of antiquity, that of the Indus River, made its appearance. These were the three regions allotted to mankind; of them evolved the nations of the Near East, Africa, and Indo-Europe—a division faithfully recorded in the Old Testament's *Table of Nations*.

All that, Sumerian chronicles held, was the result of deliberate decisions by the Anunnaki:

> The Anunnaki who decree the fates
> sat exchanging their counsels
> regarding the Earth.
> The four regions they created.

With these simple words, echoed in several Sumerian texts, the post-Diluvial fate of Earth and its inhabitants was decided. Three regions were allotted to mankind's three civilizations; the fourth was retained by the Anunnaki for their own use. It was given the name TIL.MUN, "Land of the Missiles." In *The Stairway to Heaven* we provided the evidence identifying Tilmun with the Sinai peninsula.

Although as far as human habitation was concerned, it was the descendants of Shem—"Sand Dwellers" in Egyptian scriptures—who could reside in the unrestricted areas of the peninsula, when it came to allotting the territory among the Anunnaki, profound differences arose. Control of the site of the post-Diluvial spaceport was tantamount to control of the links between Earth and Nibiru, as the experiences with Kumarbi and Zu had so clearly shown. In the rekindled rivalry between the clans of Enlil and Enki, a neutral authority over the Land of the Missiles was called for.

The solution was ingenious. Of equal lineage with them was their sister Sud. As a daughter of Anu, she bore the title NIN.MAH ("Great Lady"). She was one of the original group of Great Anunnaki who were pioneers on Earth, a member of the Pantheon of Twelve. She bore a son to Enlil, a daughter to Enki, and was lovingly called *Mammi* ("Mother of the Gods"). She helped create Man. With her medical skills she saved many a life and was also known as NIN.TI ("Lady Life"). But she never had her own dominions. To make Tilmun her domain was an idea that no one opposed.

The Sinai peninsula is a barren place, occupied by high granite peaks in the south, a mountainous plateau in the center, and a hard-soiled plain in its northern third, surrounded by chains of low mountains and hills. Then there is a strip of sand dunes, sliding to the Mediterranean coast. But where water can be retained, as in several oases or in riverbeds that fill up during brief winter rains and keep the moisture below the surface, luxuriant date palms, fruits, and vegetables grow, and herds of sheep and goats can graze.

The region must have been as forbidding millennia ago as it is now. But although an abode was made for Sud in one of Mesopotamia's rebuilt sites, she decided to go and take personal possession of the mountainous region. With all her attributes of status and knowledge, she always played a secondary role. When she came to Earth, she was young and beautiful (Fig. 36a); now she was old and nicknamed "The Cow" (Fig. 36b) behind her back. So now that she was given her own domain, she decided to go there. Proudly she declared: "A Mistress I am now! Alone will I stay there, reigning forever!"

a   b

Fig. 36

Unable to dissuade her, Ninurta applied his experience in damming and channeling waters to make his mother's new mountain region livable. We read of these deeds in Tablet IX of the "Feats and Exploits of Ninurta," as he addresses his mother:

Since you, noble lady,
alone to the Land of Landing had gone,
Since to the Land of Casting Down
unafraid you went—
A dam I shall heap up for you,
so that the Land may have a mistress.

Completing his irrigation works, and bringing over people to perform the required tasks, Ninurta assured his mother that she would have an abundance of vegetation, wood products, and minerals in her mountain abode:

Its valleys shall be verdant with vegetation,
Its slopes shall produce honey and wine for you,
Shall produce . . . *zabalum*-trees and boxwood;
its terraces shall be adorned with fruit as a garden;
The *Harsag* shall provide you with the fragrance of the gods,
shall provide you with the shiny lodes;

Its mines will as tribute copper and tin give you;
Its mountains shall multiply cattle large and small;
The *Harsag* shall bring forth the four-legged creatures.

This is indeed a befitting description of the Sinai peninsula: a
land of mines, a major source in antiquity of copper, turquoise, and
other minerals; a source of the acacia wood, which was used for
temple furnishings; a verdant place wherever water was available;
a place where flocks could graze. Is it an accident that the principal
winter-river of the peninsula is still called el Arish—"The Husbandman"—the very nickname *(Urash)* of Ninurta?

Making a home for his mother in the Sinai's southern region
of high granite peaks, Ninurta bestowed on her a new title:
NIN.HAR.SAG ("Lady of the Head Mountain"); it was the title
by which Sud was to be called ever since.

The term "head mountain" indicates that it was the highest peak
in the area. This is the mountain nowadays known as Mount St.
Katherine, a peak revered from antiquity, millennia before the
nearby monastery was built. Rising nearby is the slightly lower
peak called by the monks Mount Moses, suggesting that it is the
Mount Sinai of the Exodus. Though this is doubtful, the fact remains that the twin peaks have been deemed to be sacred from antiquity. We believe that this was so because they played a pivotal
role in the planning of the post-Diluvial spaceport and the Landing
Corridor leading to it.

These new plans adopted the old principles; and to understand
the grand post-Diluvial design, we must first review the manner in
which the pre-Diluvial spaceport and its Landing Corridor were developed. At that time the Anunnaki first selected as their focal
point the twin-peaked Mount Ararat, the highest peak in Western
Asia and thus the natural landmark most visible from the skies. The
next natural and visible features were the Euphrates River and the
Persian Gulf. Drawing an imaginary north-south line from Ararat,
the Anunnaki determined that the spaceport shall be where the line
intersected the river. Then, diagonally to it from the direction of
the Persian Gulf—at a precise angle of forty-five degrees—they
drew the Landing Path. They then laid out their first settlements so
as to mark out a Landing Corridor on both sides of the Landing Path.
In the center point, Nippur was established as a Mission Control Center; all the other settlements were equidistant from it (Fig. 25).

The post-Diluvial space facilities were planned on the same
principles. The twin-peaked Mount Ararat served as the major fo-

cal point; a line at forty-five degrees marked the Landing Path, and a combination of natural and artificial landmarks outlined an arrowlike Landing Corridor. The difference was, however, that this time the Anunnaki had at their disposal the ready-made Platform in the Cedar Mountain (Baalbek), and they incorporated it into the new Landing Grid.

As before the Deluge, the twin-peaked Mount Ararat was to serve again as the northern landmark, anchoring the Landing Corridor and the Landing Path in the center of the Corridor (Fig. 37).

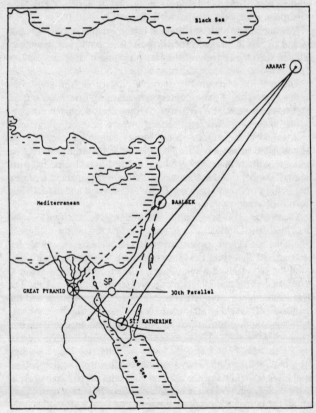

Fig. 37

The southern line of the Landing Corridor was a line connecting the twin-peaked Ararat with the highest peak in the Sinai peninsula, the Harsag (Mount St. Katherine), and its twin, the slightly lower Mount Moses.

The northern line of the Landing Corridor was a line extending from Ararat through the Landing Platform of Baalbek and continuing into Egypt. There the terrain is too flat to offer natural landmarks, and it was thus, we are certain, that the Anunnaki proceeded to build the artificial twin peaks of the two great pyramids of Giza.

But where was this anchor to be erected?

Here came into play an east-west imaginary line, arbitrarily conceived by the Anunnaki in their space sciences. They arbitrarily divided the skies enveloping Earth into three bands or "ways." The northern one was the "Way of Enlil," the southern one the "Way of Enki," and the central one the "Way of Anu." Separating them were the lines known to us as the 30th parallel north and the 30th parallel south.

The 30th parallel north appears to have been of particular—"sacred"—significance. Holy cities from antiquity on, from Egypt to Tibet, have been located on it. It was chosen to be the line on which (at the intersection of the Ararat-Baalbek line) the great pyramids were to be built; and also the line which would indicate, in the Sinai's central plain, the site of the Spaceport (SP). A line in the precise middle of the Landing Corridor, the Landing Path, was to lead to the exact location of the Spaceport on the 30th parallel.

This, we believe, is how the Landing Grid was laid out, how the site of the Spaceport was marked off, and how the great pyramids of Giza had come into being.

By suggesting that the great pyramids of Giza were built not by Pharaohs but by the Anunnaki millennia earlier, we of course contradict long-held theories concerning these pyramids.

The theory of nineteenth-century Egyptologists, that the Egyptian pyramids, including the unique three at Giza, were erected by a succession of Pharaohs as grandiose tombs for themselves, has long been disproven: not one of them was found to contain the body of the Pharaoh who was their known or presumed builder. Accordingly, the Great Pyramid of Giza was supposed to have been built by Khufu (Cheops), its twin by a successor named Chefra (Chephren), and the third, small one by a third successor, Menkara (Mycerinus)—all kings of the sixth dyansty. The Sphinx, the same Egyptologists presume, must have been built by Chephren, because it is situated next to a causeway leading to the Second Pyramid.

For a while it was believed that proof had been found in the smallest one of the three pyramids of Giza and the identity of the Pharaoh who had built it established. The credit for this was claimed by a Colonel Howard Vyse and his two assistants, who claimed to have discovered within the pyramid the coffin and mummified remains of the Pharaoh Menkara. The fact, however—known to scholars for some time now but for some reason still hardly publicized—is that neither the wooden coffin nor the skeletal remains were authentic. Someone—undoubtedly that Colonel Vyse and his cronies—had brought into the pyramid a coffin dating from about 2,000 years after Menkara had lived, and bones from the even much later Christian times, and put the two together in an unabashed archaeological fraud.

The current theories regarding the pyramids' builders are anchored to an even greater extent on the discovery of the name Khufu inscribed in hieroglyphics within a long-sealed compartment within the Great Pyramid and thus apparently establishing the identity of its builder. Unnoticed has gone the fact that the discoverer of that inscription was the same Colonel Vyse and his assistants (the year was 1837). In *The Stairway to Heaven* we have put together substantial evidence to show that the inscription was a forgery, perpetrated by its "discoverers." At the end of 1983, a reader of that book came forward to provide us with family records showing that his great-grandfather, a master mason named Humphries Brewer, who was engaged by Vyse to help use gunpowder to blast his way inside the pyramid, was an *eyewitness to the forgery* and, having objected to the deed, was expelled from the site and forced to leave Egypt altogether!

In *The Stairway to Heaven* we have shown that Khufu could not have been the builder of the Great Pyramid because he had already referred to it as existing in his time in a stela he had erected near the pyramids; even the Sphinx, supposedly erected by the next-after successor of Khufu, is mentioned in that inscription.

Now we find that pictorial evidence from the time of the Pharaohs of the very first dynasty—long before Khufu and his successors—conclusively shows that these early kings had already witnessed the Giza marvels. We can clearly see the Sphinx both in depictions of the king's journey to the Afterlife (Fig. 38a) and in a scene of his investiture by "Ancient Ones" arriving in Egypt by boat (Fig. 38b). We also submit in evidence the well-known vic-

a   b

Fig. 38

tory tablet of the very first Pharaoh, Menes, which depicts his forceful unification of Egypt. On one side he is shown wearing the white crown of Upper Egypt, defeating its chieftains and conquering their cities. On the other side the tablet shows him (Fig. 39a) wearing the red crown of Lower Egypt, marching through its districts and beheading its chieftains. To the right of his head the artist spelled out the epithet *"Nar-Mer"* acquired by the king; to the left the tablet depicts the most important structure in the newly acquired districts—the pyramid (Fig. 39b).

All scholars agree that the tablet depicts realistically the places, fortifications, and enemies encountered by Menes in his campaign to unify Upper and Lower Egypt; yet the pyramid symbol is the only one that appears to have escaped the otherwise careful interpretation. We hold that this symbol, as all others on the tablet, was drawn and included so prominently in the Lower Egypt side because such a structure had actually existed there.

The whole Giza complex—pyramids and Sphinx—had thus already existed when kingship began in Egypt; its builders were not and could not have been the Pharaohs of the sixth dynasty.

The other pyramids of Egypt—smaller, primitive by comparison, some fallen even before completion, all crumbling—had indeed been built by various Pharaohs; not as tombs, nor as cenotaphs (monumental symbolic tombs), but in emulation of the gods. For it was held and believed in antiquity that the Giza pyramids and the Sphinx that accompanies them showed the way to the Stairway to Heaven—the Spaceport—in the Sinai peninsula. Build-

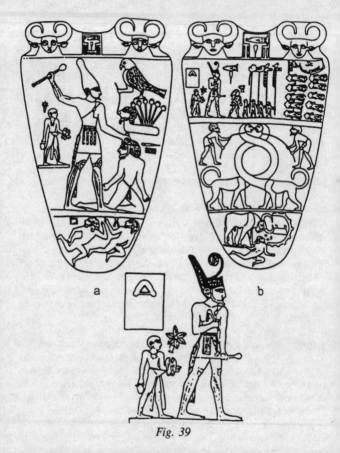

Fig. 39

ing pyramids so that they might journey to the Afterlife, the Pharaohs adorned them with appropriate symbols, with illustrations of the journey, and in several instances also covered the walls with quotations from *The Book of the Dead*. The three pyramids of Giza, unique in their external and internal construction, size, and incredible durability, are also distinguished in that there is no inscription or decoration whatsoever inside them. They are just stark, functional structures, rising from the plain as twin beacons to play a role not in the service of men but of those "Who From Heaven to Earth Came."

The three pyramids of Giza, we have concluded, were built by first erecting the smaller Third Pyramid as a scale model. Then, in keeping with the preference for twin-peaked focal points, the two large pyramids were erected. Although the Second Pyramid is smaller than the Great Pyramid, it appears to be of the same height; this is because it is built on somewhat higher ground, so that to achieve the same height, it need not have been as tall as the first one.

Apart from its incomparable size, the Great Pyramid is also unique in that, in addition to the descending passage that is found in all the other pyramids, it has a unique Ascending Passage, a level Corridor, two Upper Chambers, and a series of narrow compartments (Fig. 40). The uppermost chamber is reached via an incredibly elaborate Grand Gallery and an Antechamber that could be sealed with one pull of a cord. The uppermost chamber contained—still does—an unusual hollowed-out stone block whose fashioning required amazing technology and which rang out as a bell; above the chamber are the narrow series of low and rugged spaces, offering extreme resonance.

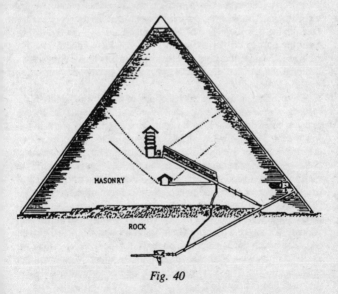

MASONRY

ROCK

Fig. 40

What was the purpose of all that?

We have found many similarities between these unique features of the Great Pyramid and the pre-Diluvial E.KUR ("House Which Is Like a Mountain") of Enlil, his ziggurat in Nippur. Like the Great Pyramid, it rose high to dominate the surrounding plain. In pre-Diluvial times the Ekur of Nippur housed the DUR.AN.KI—"Link Heaven-Earth"—and served as Mission Control Center, equipped with the Tablets of Destinies, the orbital data panels. It also contained the DIR.GA, a mysterious "Dark Chamber" whose "radiance" guided the shuttlecraft to a landing at Sippar.

But all that—the many mysteries and functions of the Ekur described in the tale of Zu—was before the Deluge. When Mesopotamia was reinhabited and Nippur was reestablished, the abode of Enlil and Ninlil there was a large temple surrounded by courtyards, with gates through which the worshipers could enter. It was no longer forbidden territory; the space-related functions, as the Spaceport itself, had shifted elsewhere.

As a new, mysterious, and awesome Ekur, the Sumerian texts described a "House Which Is Like a Mountain" in a distant place, under the aegis of Ninharsag, not of Enlil. Thus, the epic tale of an early post-Diluvial Sumerian king named Etana, who was taken aloft toward the Celestial Abode of the Anunnaki, states that his ascent began not far from the new Ekur, at the "Place of the Eagles"—not far, that is, from the Spaceport. An Akkadian "Book of Job" titled *Ludlul Bel Nimeqi* ("I Praise the Lord of Deepness") refers to the "irresistible demon that has exited from the Ekur" in a land "across the horizon, in the Lower World [Africa]."

Not recognizing the immense antiquity of the Giza pyramids or the identity of their true builders, scholars have also been puzzled by this apparent reference to an Ekur far from Sumer. Indeed, if one is to follow accepted interpretations of Mesopotamian texts, no one in Mesopotamia was ever aware of the existence of the Egyptian pyramids. None of the Mesopotamian kings who invaded Egypt, none of the merchants who traded with her, none of the emissaries who had visited there—not one of them had noticed these colossal monuments . . .

Could that be possible?

We suggest that the Giza monuments *were* known in Sumer and Akkad. We suggest that the Great Pyramid was the post-Diluvial Ekur, of which the Mesopotamian texts did speak at length (as we shall soon show). And we suggest that ancient Mesopotamian drawings depicted the pyramids during their construction and after they had been completed!

We have already shown how the Mesopotamian "pyramids"—the ziggurats or stage-towers—looked like (Fig. 24). We find completely different structures on some of the most archaic Sumerian depictions. In some (Fig. 41) we see the construction of a structure with a square base and triangular sides—a smooth-sided pyramid. Other depictions show a completed pyramid (Fig. 42 a,b) with the

Fig. 41

a

b

Fig. 42

serpent symbol clearly locating it in an Enki territory. And yet another (Fig. 43) endows the completed pyramid with wings, to indicate its space-related function. This depiction, of which several were found, shows the pyramid together with other amazingly accurate features: a crouching Sphinx facing toward the Place of Reeds; another Sphinx on the other side of the Lake of Reeds, supporting the suggestion in Egyptian texts that there was another, facing the Sphinx in the Sinai peninsula. Both the pyramid and the Sphinx near it are located by a river, as the Giza complex is indeed located by the Nile. And beyond all that is the body of water on which the horned gods are sailing, just as the Egyptians had said that their gods had from the south, via the Red Sea.

Fig. 43

The striking similarity between this archaic Sumerian depiction and the archaic Egyptian one (Fig. 38a) offers compelling evidence of the common knowledge, in Egypt as in Sumer, of the pyramids and the Sphinx. Indeed, even in such a minor detail as the precise slope of the Great Pyramid—52°—the Sumerian depiction appears to be accurate.

The inevitable conclusion, then, is that the Great Pyramid was known in Mesopotamia, if for no other reason than because it was built by the same Anunnaki who had built the original Ekur in Nippur; and likewise and quite logically, it, too, was called by them E.KUR—"House Which Is Like a Mountain." Like its predecessor, the Great Pyramid of Giza was built with mysterious dark chambers and was equipped with instruments for guiding the shuttlecraft to the post-Diluvial Spaceport in the Sinai. And, to assure its neutrality, the Pyramid was put under the patronage of Ninharsag.

Our solution gives meaning to an otherwise enigmatic poem exalting Ninharsag as mistress of the "House With a Pointed Peak"—a pyramid:

> House bright and dark of Heaven and Earth,
> for the rocketships put together;
> E.KUR, House of the Gods with pointed peak;
> For Heaven-to-Earth it is greatly equipped.
> House whose interior glows with a reddish Light of Heaven,
> pulsating a beam which reaches far and wide;
> Its awesomeness touches the flesh.
> Awesome ziggurat, lofty mountain of mountains—
> Thy creation is great and lofty,
> men cannot understand it.

The function of this "House of the Gods With Pointed Peak" is then made clear: it was a "House of Equipment" serving to "bring down to rest" the astronauts "who see and orbit," a "great landmark for the lofty *Shems*" (the "sky chambers"):

> House of Equipment, lofty House of Eternity:
> Its foundation are stones [which reach] the water;
> Its great circumference is set in the clay.
> House whose parts are skillfully woven together;
> House, the rightness of whose howling
> the Great-Ones-Who-See-and-Orbit brings down to rest . . .
> House which is great landmark for the lofty *Shem;*
> Mountain by which Utu ascends.
> [House] whose deep insides men cannot penetrate . . .
> Anu has magnified it.

The text then goes on to describe the various parts of the structure: its foundation, "which is clad in awe"; its entrance, which opens and closes as a mouth, "glowing in a dim green light"; the threshold ("like a great dragon's mouth opened in wait"); the doorjambs ("like two edges of a dagger that keeps enemies away"). Its inner chamber is "like a vulva," guarded by "daggers which dash from dawn to dusk"; its "outpouring"—that which it emits—"is like a lion whom no one dares attack."

An ascending gallery is then described: "Its vault is like a rainbow, the darkness ends there; in awesomeness it is draped; its joints are like a vulture whose claws are ready to clasp." There, at the top of the gallery, is "the entryway to the Mountain's top"; "to foe it is not opened; only to Them Who Live, for them it is opened." Three locking devices—"the bolt, the bar and the lock . . . slithering in an awe-inspiring place"—protect the way into the uppermost chamber, from which the Ekur "surveys Heaven and Earth, a net it spreads out."

These are details whose accuracy amazes as one reads them in conjunction with our present knowledge of the insides of the Great Pyramid. The entrance into it was through an opening in its north face, hidden by a swivel stone that indeed opened and closed "like a mouth." Stepping onto a platform, the entrant faced an opening into a descending passage, "like a great dragon's mouth opened in wait" (Fig. 44a). The gaping entrance was protected from the pyramid's weight above it by two pairs of diagonally placed massive stone blocks, "like two edges that keep enemies away," revealing an enigmatic carved stone in the entrance's midst (Fig. 44b).

A short distance down the descending passage, an ascending passage began. It led to a horizontal passage through which one could reach the heart of the pyramid, an inner Chamber of Emissions "like a vulva." The ascending passage also led to a majestic ascending gallery, most elaborately constructed, its walls getting closer to each other by stages as they rise, giving the entrant a feel-

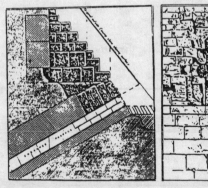

a　　　　　　　　　　b

Fig. 44

ing that these wall joints are "like a vulture whose claws are ready to clasp" (Fig. 45). The gallery led to the uppermost chamber, from which a "net"—a force field—"surveyed Heaven and Earth." The way to it was through an antechamber, built with great complexity (Fig. 46), where three locking devices were indeed installed, ready to "slither" down and "to foe not open."

After so describing the Ekur inside and out, the laudatory text provides information regarding the functions and location of the structure:

On this day the Mistress herself speaks truly;
The Goddess of the Rocketships, the Pure Great Lady,
praises herself:
"I am the Mistress; Anu has determined my destiny;
the daughter of Anu am I.
Enlil has added to me a great destiny;
his sister-princess am I.
The gods have given unto my hand
the pilot-guiding instruments of Heaven-Earth;
Mother of the sky-chambers am I.
Ereshkigal allotted to me the place-of-opening
of the pilot-guiding instruments;
The great landmark,
the mountain by which Utu rises,
I have established as my dais."

If, as we have concluded, Ninharsag was the neutral Mistress of the Pyramid of Giza, it follows that she should have been known and revered as a goddess also in Egypt. This, indeed, is the case; except that to the Egyptians she was known as Hat-Hor. Textbooks will tell us that the name means "House of Horus"; but that is only superficially correct. The reading stems from the hieroglyphic writing of the name [glyph] depicting a house and a falcon, the falcon having been the symbol of Horus because he could soar as a falcon. What the goddess's name literally meant was: "Goddess Whose Home Is Where the 'Falcons' Are," where the astronauts make their home: the Spaceport.

This spaceport, we have determined, was located in the post-Diluvial era in the Sinai peninsula; accordingly, the title Hat-Hor, "Home of the Falcons," would require that the goddess bearing it should be Mistress of the Sinai peninsula. That, indeed, she was;

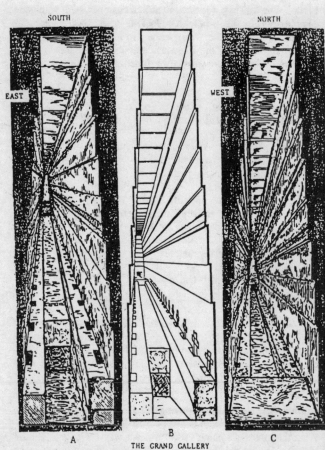

SOUTH

EAST

NORTH

WEST

A

B

THE GRAND GALLERY

C

Perspective views: From the lower northern entrance (A&B)
and from the upper southern end (C).

Fig. 45

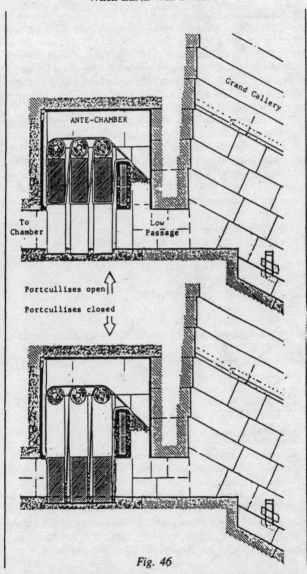

Fig. 46

the Egyptians considered the Sinai peninsula to have been the domain of Hathor. All the temples and stelas erected by Egyptian Pharaohs in the peninsula were dedicated exclusively to this goddess. And, like Ninharsag in her later years, Hathor, too, was nicknamed "The Cow" and was depicted with cow's horns.

But was Hathor also—as we have claimed for Ninharsag—Mistress of the Great Pyramid? That, amazingly but not surprisingly, she was.

The evidence comes in the form of an inscription by the Pharaoh Khufu (circa 2600 B.C.) on a commemorative stela he erected at Giza in a temple dedicated to Isis. Known as the Inventory Stela, the monument and its inscription clearly establish that the Great Pyramid (and the Sphinx) had already existed when Khufu (Cheops) began to reign. All he claimed was to have built the temple to Isis beside the already existing Pyramid and Sphinx:

> Live Horus Mezdau.
> To king of Upper and Lower Egypt, Khufu,
> Life is given!
> He founded the House of Isis,
> Mistress of the Pyramid,
> beside the House of the Sphinx.

At his time, then, Isis (the wife of Osiris and the mother of Horus) was considered to have been the *"Mistress of the Pyramid"* . But as the continuing inscription makes clear, she was not the Pyramid's first mistress:

> Live Horus Mezdau.
> To king of Upper and Lower Egypt, Khufu,
> Life is given!
> For his divine mother Isis,
> Mistress of *"The Western Mountain of Hathor,"*
> he made [this] writing on a stela.

Thus, not only was the Pyramid a "Mountain of Hathor"—the exact parallel of the Sumerian "House Which Is Like a Mountain"—but also it was her *western* mountain, implying that she also had an eastern one. That, we know from the Sumerian sources, was the Har-Sag, the highest peak in the Sinai peninsula.

* * *

In spite of the rivalry and suspicions between the two divine dynasties, there is little doubt that the actual work of constructing the Spaceport and the control and guidance facilities fell into the hands of Enki and his descendants. Ninurta proved himself capable of damming and irrigation works; Utu/Shamash knew how to command and operate the landing and take-off facilities; but only Enki, the master engineer and scientist who had been through all this before, had the required know-how and experience for planning the massive construction works and supervising their execution.

There is not even a hint in Sumerian texts that describe the achievements of Ninurta and Utu that either one of them had planned or engaged in space-related construction works. When Ninurta, in later times, called upon a Sumerian king to build him a ziggurat with a special enclosure for his Divine Bird, it was another god, accompanying Ninurta, who gave the king the architectural plans and building instructions. On the other hand, several texts reported that Enki had passed to his son Marduk the scientific knowledge he had possessed. The texts report a conversation between father and son, after Marduk had approached his father with a difficult question:

> Enki answered his son Marduk:
> "My son, what is it you do not know?
> What more could I give to you?
> Marduk, what is it that you do not know?
> What could I give you in addition?
> Whatever I know, you know!"

Since the similarities between Ptah and Enki as the father, and Marduk and Ra as son, are so strong, we should not be surprised at all to find that Egyptian texts did connect Ra with space facilities and with related construction works. In this he was assisted by Shu and Tefnut, Geb and Nut, and Thoth the god of magical things. The Sphinx, the "divine guide" that showed the way eastward exactly along the 30th parallel, bore the features of Hor-Akhti ("Falcon of the Horizon")—the epithet for Ra. A stela erected near the Sphinx in Pharaonic times bore an inscription that directly named Ra as the engineer ("Extender of the Cord") who built the "Protected Place" in the "Sacred Desert," from which he could "ascend beautifully" and "traverse the skies":

Thou extendest the cords for the plan,
thou didst give form to the lands . . .
Thou didst make secret the Lower World . . .
Thou hast built for thee a place protected
in the sacred desert, with hidden name.
Thou risest by day opposite them . . .
Thou art rising beautifully . . .
Thou art crossing the sky with a good wind . . .
Thou art traversing the sky in the celestial barque . . .
The sky is jubilating,
the Earth is shouting of joy.
The crew of Ra do praising every day;
He comes forth in triumph.

Egyptian texts asserted that Shu and Tefnut were involved in Ra's extensive space-related works by "upholding the skies over Earth." Their son Geb bore a name that stemmed from the root *gbb*—"to pile up, to heap up"—attesting, scholars agree, to his engaging in works that entailed piling up; a strong suggestion of his involvement in the actual construction of the pyramids.

An Egyptian tale concerning the Pharaoh Khufu and his three sons reveals that in those days the secret plans of the Great Pyramid were in the custody of the god whom the Egyptians called Thoth, the god of astronomy, mathematics, geometry, and land surveying. It will be recalled that a unique feature of the Great Pyramid was its upper chambers and passages. However, because these passages were sealed off—we shall show how, when, and why—just where they branch off from the descending passage, all the Pharaohs who attempted to emulate the Giza pyramids built theirs with lower chambers only, being either unable to emulate the upper chambers for lack of precise architectural knowledge, or (in time) simply unaware of their existence. But Khufu, it seems, was aware of the existence of these two secret chambers within the Great Pyramid, and at one point was on the verge of discovering the plans of their construction, for he was told where the god Thoth had hidden them.

Written on the so-called Westcar Papyrus and titled "Tales of the Magicians," the tale relates that "one day, when king Khufu reigned over all the land," he called in his three sons and asked them to tell him tales of the "deeds of the magicians" of olden times. First to speak was "the royal son Khafra" who related "a tale of the days of thy [Khufu's] forefather Nebka . . . of what came to pass when he went into the temple of Ptah.'' It was a tale of how a magician brought a dead crocodile back to life. Then the royal son Bau-ef-Ra told of a miracle in the days of Khufu's earlier forefather, when a magician parted the waters of a lake, so that a jewel could be retrieved from its bottom; ''and then the magician spake and used his magic speech and he brought the water of all the lake again to its place.''

Somewhat cynical, the third son Hor-De-Def arose and spoke, saying: ''We have heard about the magicians of the past and their doings, the truth of which we cannot verify. Now I know of things done in our time.'' The Pharaoh Khufu asked what they were; and Hor-De-Def answered that he knew of a man named Dedi who knew how to replace a decapitated head, to tame a lion, and who also knew ''the *Pdut* numbers of the chambers of Thoth.''

Hearing this, Khufu became extremely curious, for he had been seeking to find out the ''secret of the Chambers of Thoth'' in the Great Pyramid (already blocked and hidden in Khufu's time!). So he ordered that the sage Dedi be found and fetched from his abode, an island off the tip of the Sinai peninsula.

When Dedi was brought before the Pharaoh, Khufu first tested his magical powers, such as bringing back to life a goose, a bird, and an ox, whose heads were cut off. Then Khufu asked: ''Is it true what is said, that thou knowest the *Pdut* numbers for the *Iput* of Thoth?'' And Dedi answered: ''I know not the numbers, O king, but I know the place the *Pdut* are in.''

Egyptologists are by and large agreed that *Iput* conveyed the meaning ''secret chambers of the primeval sanctuary'' and *Pdut* meant ''designs, plans with numbers.''

Answering Khufu, the magician (his age was given as one hundred and ten years) said: ''I know not the information in the designs, O king, but I know where the plans-with-numbers were hidden by Thoth.'' In answer to further questioning he said: ''There is a box of whetstone in the sacred chamber called the Chart Room in Heliopolis; they are in that box.''

Excited, Khufu ordered Dedi to go and find the box for him. But Dedi answered that it was neither he nor Khufu who could obtain the box; it was destined to be found by a future descendant of Khufu. This, he said, was decreed by Ra. Yielding to the god's will, Khufu, as we have seen, ended up only building near the Sphinx a temple dedicated to the Mistress of the Pyramid.

The circle of evidence is thus complete. Sumerian and Egyptian texts confirm each other and our conclusions: The same neutral goddess was the mistress of Sinai's highest peak and of the artificial mountain erected in Egypt, both to serve as anchors of the Landing Corridor.

But the Anunnaki's desire to keep the Sinai peninsula and its facilities neutral did not prevail for long. Rivalry and love tragically combined to upset the status quo; and the divided Earth was soon embroiled in the Pyramid Wars.

8

THE PYRAMID WARS

"In the year 363 His Majesty Ra, the holy one, the Falcon of the Horizon, the Immortal who forever lives, was in the land of Khenn. He was accompanied by his warriors, for the enemies had conspired against their lord. . . . Horus, the Winged Measurer, came to the boat of Ra. He said to his forefather: 'O Falcon of the Horizon, I have seen the enemy conspire against thy Lordship, to take the Luminous Crown unto themselves.' . . . Then Ra, the holy one, the Falcon of the Horizon, said unto Horus, the Winged Measurer: 'Lofty issue of Ra, my begotten: Go quickly, knock down the enemy whom you have seen.' "

Thus began the tale inscribed on the temple walls in the ancient Egyptian city of Edfu. It is the tale, we believe, of what could only be called the First Pyramid War—a war that had its roots in the never-ending struggle for control over Earth and its space facilities and in the shenanigans of the Great Anunnaki, especially Enki/Ptah and his son Ra/Marduk.

According to Manetho, Ptah turned over the dominion over Egypt after a reign of 9,000 years; but the reign of Ra was cut short after 1,000 years—by the Deluge, we have concluded. Then there followed a reign of 700 years by Shu, who helped Ra "control the skies over Earth," and the 500-year reign of Geb ("Who Piles Up the Earth"). It was at that time, circa 10,000 B.C., that the space facilities—the Spaceport in the Sinai and the Giza pyramids—were built.

Although the Sinai peninsula, where the Spaceport was established, and the Giza pyramids were supposed to remain neutral under the aegis of Ninharsag, it is doubtful whether the builders of these facilities—Enki and his descendants—had really any intention of relinquishing control over these installations. A Sumerian text, which begins with an idyllic description, has been named by scholars a "Paradise Myth." Its ancient name was *Enki and Ninharsag*, and it is, in fact, a record of the politically motivated lovemaking between the two, a tale of a deal between Enki and his half-sister Ninharsag pertaining to the control of Egypt and the Sinai peninsula—of the pyramids and the Spaceport.

The tale's time is after Earth was apportioned between the Anunnaki, with Tilmun (the Sinai peninsula) granted to Ninharsag and Egypt to Enki's clan. It was then, the Sumerian tale relates, that Enki crossed the marshy lakes that separated Egypt and the Sinai peninsula and came unto the lonely Ninharsag for an orgy of lovemaking:

> To the one who is alone,
> To the Lady of Life, mistress of the land,
> Enki came unto the wise Lady of Life.
> He causes his phallus to water the dikes;
> He causes his phallus to submerge the reeds . . .
> He poured his semen into the great lady of the Anunnaki,
> poured the semen in the womb of Ninharsag;
> She took the semen into the womb, the semen of Enki.

Enki's real intention was to obtain a son by his half-sister; but the offspring was a daughter. Enki then made love to the daughter as soon as she became "young and fair," and then to his granddaughter. As a result of these sexual activities, a total of eight gods—six female and two male—were born. Angered by the incest, Ninharsag used her medical skills to sicken Enki. The Anunnaki who were with him pleaded for his life, but Ninharsag was determined: "Until he is dead, I shall not look upon him with the 'Eye of Life'!"

Satisfied that Enki had indeed been finally stopped, Ninurta—who went to Tilmun for inspection—returned to Mesopotamia to report the developments at a meeting attended by Enlil, Nanna/Sin, Utu/Shamash and Inanna/Ishtar. Unsatisfied, Enlil ordered Ninurta to return to Tilmun and bring back Ninharsag with him. But in the interim, Ninharsag had pity on her brother and changed her mind. "Ninharsag seated Enki by her vulva and asked: 'My brother, what hurts thee?' " After she cured his body part by part, Enki proposed that the two of them as masters of Egypt and the Sinai assign tasks, spouses, and territories to the eight young gods:

> Let Abu be the master of the plants;
> Let Nintulla be the lord of Magan;
> Let Ninsutu marry Ninazu;

Let Ninkashi be she who sates the thirsts;
Let Nazi marry Nindara;
Let Azimua marry Ningishzida;
Let Nintu be the queen of the months;
Let Enshag be the lord of Tilmun!

Egyptian theological texts from Memphis likewise held that
"there came into being" eight gods from the heart, tongue, teeth,
lips, and other parts of the body of Ptah. In this text, too, as in the
Mesopotamian one, Ptah followed up the bringing forth of these
gods by assigning abodes and territories to them: "After he had
formed the gods, he made cities, established districts, put the gods
in their sacred abodes; he built their shrines and established their
offerings." All that he did "to make rejoice the heart of the Mistress of Life."

If, as it appears, these tales had a basis in fact, then the rivalries
that such confused parentages brought about could only be aggra-
vated by the sexual shenanigans attributed to Ra as well. The most
significant among these was the assertion that Osiris was truly the
son of Ra and not of Geb, conceived when Ra had come by stealth
unto his own granddaughter. This, as we have earlier related, lay at
the core of the Osiris-Seth conflict.

Why had Seth, to whom Upper Egypt had been allotted by
Geb, coveted Lower Egypt, which was granted to Osiris?
Egyptologists have offered explanations in terms of geography,
the land's fertility, etc. But as we have shown, there was one
more factor—one that, from the gods' point of view, was more
important than how many crops a region could grow: the Great
Pyramid and its companions at Giza; whoever controlled them
shared in the control of the space activities, of the comings and
goings of the gods, of the vital supply link to and from the
Twelfth Planet.

For a while Seth succeeded in his ambition, having outwitted
Osiris. But "in the year 363" following the disappearance of Osiris, the young Horus became the avenger of his father and launched
a war against Seth—the First Pyramid War. It was, as we have
seen, also the first war in which the gods involved men in their
struggles.

Supported by other Enki-gods reigning in Africa, the avenger
Horus began the hostilities in Upper Egypt. Aided by the Winged
Disk that Thoth had fashioned for him, Horus persistently ad-
vanced northward, toward the pyramids. A major battle took place

in the "water district," the chain of lakes that separates Egypt from the Sinai peninsula, and a good many of Seth's followers were slain. After peacemaking efforts by other gods had failed, Seth and Horus engaged in personal combat in and over the Sinai peninsula. In the course of one battle, Seth hid in "secret tunnels" somewhere in the peninsula; in another battle, he lost his testicles. So the Council of the Gods gave the whole of Egypt "as heritage . . . to Horus."

And what had become of Seth, one of the eight gods descended from Ptah?

He was banished from Egypt and took up abode in Asiatic lands to the east, including a place that enabled him "to speak out from the sky." Was he the god called Enshag in the Sumerian tale of Enki and Ninharsag, the one to whom Tilmun (the Sinai peninsula) was allotted by the two lovemakers? If so, then he was the Egyptian (Hamitic) god who had extended his domain over the land of Shem later known as Canaan.

It was in this outcome of the First Pyramid War that there lies an understanding of biblical tales. Therein also lay the causes of the Second Pyramid War.

In addition to the Spaceport and the guidance facilities, there was also a need after the Deluge for a new Mission Control Center, to replace the one that had existed before in Nippur. We have shown (in *The Stairway to Heaven*) that the need to equidistance this center from the other space-related facilities dictated its locating on Mount Moriah ("The Mount of Directing"), the site of the future city of Jerusalem.

That site, by both Mesopotamian and biblical accounts, was located in the lands of Shem—a dominion of the Enlilites. Yet it ended up under an illegal occupation by the line of Enki, the Hamitic gods, and by the descendants of the Hamitic Canaan.

The Old Testament refers to the land of which Jerusalem in time became the capital as Canaan, after the fourth and youngest son of Ham. It also singled out Canaan for special rebuke and consigned his descendants to be subservient to the descendants of Shem. The improbable excuse for this treatment was that Ham—not his son Canaan—had inadvertently seen the naked genitals of his father Noah; therefore, the Lord had put a curse upon Canaan: "Cursed be Canaan; a servant of servants shall he be unto his brethren . . . Blessed be Yahweh the god of Shem; may Canaan be a servant unto them."

The tale in the Book of Genesis leaves many aspects unexplained. Why was Canaan accursed if it was his father who had accidentally transgressed? Why was his punishment to be a slave of Shem and to the god of Shem? And how were the gods involved in the crime and its punishment? As one reads the supplemental information in the ex-biblical *Book of Jubilees,* it becomes clear that the real offense was the illegal occupation of Shem's territory.

After mankind was dispersed and its various clans allotted their lands, the *Book of Jubilees* relates, "Ham and his sons went to the land which he was to occupy, [the land] which he acquired as his portion in the country of the south." But then, journeying from where Noah had been saved to his allotted land in Africa, "Canaan saw the land of Lebanon [all the way down] to the river of Egypt, that it was very good." And so he changed his mind: "He went not into the land of his inheritance to the west of the sea [west of the Red Sea]; he dwelt [instead] in the land of Lebanon, eastward and westward of the Jordan."

His father and his brothers tried to dissuade Canaan from such an illegal act: "And Ham his father, and Cush and Mizra'im his brothers, said unto him: 'Thou hast settled in a land which is not thine, and which did not fall to us by lot; do not do so; for if thou dost do so, thou and thy sons will be fallen in the land and be accursed through sedition; for by sedition ye have settled, and by sedition will thy children fall, and thou shall be rooted out forever. Dwell not in the dwelling of Shem; for to Shem and his sons did it come by their lot.' "

Were he to illegally occupy the territory assigned to Shem, they pointed out, "Cursed art thou and cursed shalt thou be beyond the sons of Noah, by the curse which we bound ourselves by an oath in the presence of the Holy Judge and in the presence of Noah our father. . . .

"But Canaan did not hearken unto them, and dwelt in the land of Lebanon from Hamath to the entering of Egypt, he and his sons until this day. For this reason is that land named Canaan."

Behind the biblical and pseudoepigraphical tale of a territorial usurpation by a descendant of Ham must lie a tale of a similar usurpation by a descendant of the God of Egypt. We must bear in mind that at the time the allotment of lands and territories was not among the peoples but among the gods; the gods, not the people, were the landlords. A people could only settle a territory allotted to their god and could occupy another's territory only if their god had extended his or her dominion to that territory, by agreement or by force. The illegal seizure of the area between the Spaceport in the Sinai and the Landing Place in Baalbek by a descendant of Ham could have occurred only if that area had been usurped by a descendant of the Hamitic deities, by a younger god of Egypt.

And that, as we have shown, was indeed the result of the First Pyramid War.

Seth's trespass into Canaan meant that all the space-related sites—Giza, the Sinai peninsula, Jerusalem—came under the control of the Enki gods. It was a development in which the Enlilites could not acquiesce. And so, soon thereafter—300 years later, we believe—they deliberately launched a war to dislodge the illegal occupiers from the vital space facilities. This Second Pyramid War is described in several texts, some found in the original Sumerian, others in Akkadian and Assyrian renderings. Scholars refer to these texts as the "Myths of Kur"—"myths" of the Mountain Lands; they are, in fact, poetically rendered chronicles of the war to control the space-related peaks—Mount Moriah; the Harsag (Mount St. Katherine) in the Sinai; and the artificial mount, the Ekur (the Great Pyramid) in Egypt.

It is clear from the texts that the Enlilite forces were led and commanded by Ninurta, "Enlil's foremost warrior," and that the first encounters were in the Sinai peninsula. The Hamitic gods were beaten there; but they retreated to continue the war from the mountain lands of Africa. Ninurta rose to the challenge, and in the second phase of the war carried the battle to the strongholds of his foes; that phase entailed vicious and ferocious battles. Then, in its final phase, the war was fought at the Great Pyramid, the last and impregnable stronghold of Ninurta's opponents; there the Hamitic gods were besieged until they ran out of food and water.

This war, which we call the Second Pyramid War, was commemorated extensively in Sumerian records—both written chronicles and pictorial depictions.

Hymns to Ninurta contain numerous references to his feats and heroic deeds in this war; a great part of the psalm "Like Anu Art Thou Made" is devoted to a record of the struggle and the final victory. But the principal and most direct chronicle of the war is the epic text *Lugal-e Ud Melam-bi*, best collated and edited by Samuel

Geller in *Altorientalische Texte und Untersuchungen*. Like all Mesopotamian texts, it is so titled after its opening line:

> King, the glory of thy day is lordly;
> Ninurta, Foremost, possessor of the Divine Powers,
> who into the throes of the Mountainlands stepped forth.
> Like a flood which cannot be stopped,
> the Enemyland as with a girdle you tightly bound.
> Foremost one, who in battle vehemently enters;
> Hero, who in his hand the Divine Brilliant Weapon carries;
> Lord: the Mountainland you subdued as your creature.
> Ninurta, royal son, whose father to him had given might;
> Hero: in fear of thee, the city has surrendered . . .
> O mighty one—
> the Great Serpent, the heroic god,
> you tore away from all the mountains.

Thus extolling Ninurta, his feats, and his Brilliant Weapon, the poem also describes the location of the conflict ("the Mountainlands") and his principal enemy: "The Great Serpent," leader of the Egyptian deities. The Sumerian poem identifies this adversary several times as *Azag* and once refers to him as *Ashar,* both well-known epithets for Marduk, thereby establishing the two principal sons of Enlil and Enki—Ninurta and Marduk—as the leaders of the opposing camps in the Second Pyramid War.

The second tablet (one of thirteen on which the long poem was inscribed) describes the first battle. Ninurta's upper hand is ascribed to both his godly weapons and a new airship that he built for himself after his original one had been destroyed in an accident. It was called IM.DU.GUD, usually translated "Divine Storm Bird" but which literally means "That Which Like Heroic Storm Runs"; we know from various texts that its wingspan was about seventy-five feet.

Archaic drawings depicted it as a mechanically constructed "bird," with two wing surfaces supported by cross beams (Fig. 47a); an undercarriage reveals a series of round openings, perhaps air intakes for jetlike engines. This aircraft, from millennia ago, bears a remarkable resemblance not only to the early biplanes of the modern air age, but also an incredible likeness to the sketch made in 1497 by Leonardo da Vinci, depicting his concept of a man-powered flying machine (Fig. 47b).

a

b

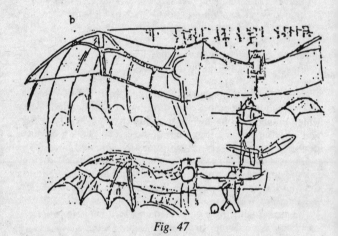

Fig. 47

The Imdugud was the inspiration for Ninurta's emblem—a heroic lion-headed bird resting on two lions (Fig. 48) or sometimes on two bulls. It was in this "crafted ship"—a manufactured vehicle—"that which in war destroys the princely abodes," that Ninurta soared into the skies during the battles of the Second Pyramid War. He soared so high that his companions lost sight of him. Then, the texts relate, "in his Winged Bird, against the walled abode" he swooped down. "As his Bird neared the ground, the summit [of the enemy's stronghold] he smashed."

Chased out of his strongholds, the Enemy began to retreat. While Ninurta kept up the frontal attack, Adad roamed the countryside behind the enemy lines, destroying the adversary's food supplies: "In the Abzu, Adad the fish caused to be washed away . . .

Fig. 48

the cattle he dispersed.'' When the Enemy kept retreating into the mountains, the two gods ''like an onrushing flood the mountains ravaged.''

As the battles extended in time and scope, the two leading gods called on the others to join them. ''My lord, to the battle which is becoming extensive, why don't you go?'' they asked a god whose name is missing in a damaged verse. The question was clearly also addressed to Ishtar, for she is mentioned by name: ''In the clash of weapons, in the feats of heroship, Ishtar her arm did not hold back.'' As the two gods saw her, they shouted encouragingly to her: ''Advance hither without stopping! Put your foot down firmly on the Earth! In the mountains, we await thee!''

''The weapon which is lordly brilliant, the goddess brought forth . . . a horn [to direct it] she made for it.'' As she used it against the enemy in a feat ''that to distant days'' shall be remembered, ''the skies were like red-hued wool in color.'' The explosive beam ''tore apart [the enemy], made him with his hand clutch his heart.''

The continued tale, on tablets v–viii, is too damaged to be properly read. The partial verses suggest that after the intensified attack with Ishtar's assistance, there arose a great cry and lamentation in the Enemyland. ''Fear of Ninurta's Brilliance encompassed the land,'' and its residents had to use substitutes instead of wheat and barley ''to grind and mill as flour.''

Under this onslaught the Enemy forces kept retreating south. It was then that the war assumed its ferocious and vicious character, when Ninurta led the Enlilite gods in an attack on the heartland of

Nergal's African domain and his temple-city, Meslam. They scorched the earth and made the rivers run red with the blood of the innocent bystanders—the men, women, and children of the Abzu.

The verses describing this aspect of the war are damaged on the tablets of the main text; its details are, however, available from various other fragmented tablets that deal with the "overwhelming of the land" by Ninurta," a feat whereby he earned the title "Vanquisher of Meslam." In these battles the attackers resorted to chemical warfare. We read that Ninurta rained on the city poison-bearing missiles, which "he catapulted into it; the poison, by itself, destroyed the city."

Those who survived the attack on the city escaped to the surrounding mountains. But Ninurta "with the Weapon That Smites threw fire upon the mountains; the godly Weapon of the Gods, whose Tooth is bitter, smote down the people." Here, too, some kind of chemical warfare is indicated:

> The Weapon Which Tears Apart
> robbed the senses;
> The Tooth skinned them off.
> Tearing-apart he stretched upon the land;
> The canals he filled with blood,
> in the Enemyland for dogs like milk to lick.

Overwhelmed by the merciless onslaught, Azag called on his followers to show no resistance: "The arisen Enemy to his wife and child called; against the lord Ninurta he raised not his arm. The weapons of Kur with soil were covered" (i.e., hidden away); "Azag them did not raise."

Ninurta took the lack of resistance as a sign of victory. A text reported by F. Hrozny ("Mythen von dem Gotte Ninib") relates how, after Ninurta killed the opponents occupying the land of the Harsag (Sinai) and went on "like a Bird" to attack the gods who "behind their walls retreated" in Kur, he defeated them in the mountains. He then burst out in a song of victory:

> My fearsome Brilliance like Anu's is mighty;
> Against it, who can rise?
> I am lord of the high mountains,
> of the mountains which to the horizon raise their peaks.
> In the mountains, I am the master.

But the claim of victory was premature. By his nonresistance tactics, Azag had escaped defeat. The capital city was indeed destroyed, but not so the leaders of the Enemy. Soberly, the text *Lugal-e* observed: "The scorpion of Kur Ninurta did not annihilate." Instead, the Enemy gods retreated into the Great Pryamid, where "the Wise Craftsman"—Enki? Thoth?—raised up a protective wall "which the Brilliance could not match," a shield through which the death rays could not penetrate.

Our knowledge of this final and most dramatic phase of the Second Pyramid War is augmented by texts from "the other side." Just as Ninurta's followers composed hymns to him, so did the followers of Nergal. Some of the latter, which have also been discovered by archaeologists, were put together in *Gebete und Hymnen an Nergal* by J. Bollenrücher.

Recalling the heroic feats of Nergal in this war, the texts relate how, as the other gods found themselves hemmed in within the Giza complex, Nergal—"Lofty Dragon Beloved of Ekur"—"at night stole out" and, carrying awesome weapons and accompanied by his lieutenants, broke through the encirclement to reach the Great Pyramid (the Ekur). Reaching it at night, he entered through "the locked doors which by themselves can open." A roar of welcome greeted him as he entered:

> Divine Nergal,
> Lord who by night stole out,
> had come to the battle!
> He cracks his whip, his weapons clank . . .
> He who is welcome, his might is immense;
> Like a dream at the doorstep he appeared.
> Divine Nergal, the One Who Is Welcome:
> Fight the enemy of Ekur,
> lay hold on the Wild One from Nippur!

But the high hopes of the besieged gods were soon dashed. We learn more of the last phases of this Pyramid War from yet another text, first pieced together by George A. Barton (*Miscellaneous Babylonian Texts*) from fragments of an inscribed clay cylinder found in the ruins of Enlil's temple in Nippur.

As Nergal joined the defenders of the Great Pyramid ("the Formidable House Which Is Raised Up Like a Heap"), he strengthened its defenses through the various ray-emitting crystals (mineral "stones") positioned within the pyramid:

The Water-Stone, the Apex-Stone,
the . . . -Stone, the . . .
. . . the lord Nergal
increased its strength.
The door for protection he . . .
To heaven its Eye he raised,
Dug deep that which gives life . . .
. . . in the House
he fed them food.

With the pyramid's defenses thus enhanced, Ninurta resorted to another tactic. He called upon Utu/Shamash to cut off the pyramid's water supply by tampering with the "watery stream" that ran near its foundations. The text here is too mutilated to enable a reading of the details; but the tactic apparently achieved its purpose.

Huddled in their last stronghold, cut off from food and water, the besieged gods did their best to ward off their attackers. Until then, in spite of the ferocity of the battles, no major god had fallen a casualty to the fighting. But now one of the younger gods—Horus, we believe—trying to sneak out of the Great Pyramid disguised as a ram, was struck by Ninurta's Brilliant Weapon and lost the sight of his eyes. An Olden God then cried out to Ninharsag—reputed for her medical wonders—to save the young god's life:

At that time the Killing Brightness came;
The House's platform withstood the lord.
Unto Ninharsag there was an outcry:
". . . the weapon . . . my offspring
with death is accursed. . . ."

Other Sumerian texts call this young god "offspring who did not know his father," an epithet befitting Horus, who was born after his father's death. In Egyptian lore the *Legend of the Ram* reports the injuries to the eyes of Horus when a god "blew fire" at him.

It was then, responding to the "outcry," that Ninharsag decided to intervene to stop the fighting.

The ninth tablet of the *Lugal-e* text begins with the statement of Ninharsag, her address to the Enlilite commander, her own son Ninurta, "the son of Enlil . . . the Legitimate Heir whom the sister-wife had brought forth.'' In telltale verses she announced her decision to cross the battle lines and bring an end to the hostilities:

> To the House Where Cord-Measuring begins,
> Where Asar his eyes to Anu raised,
> I shall go.
> The cord I will cut off,
> for the sake of the warring gods.

Her destination was the ''House Where Cord-Measuring begins,'' the Great Pyramid!

Ninurta was at first astounded by her decision to ''enter alone the Enemyland''; but since her mind was made up, he provided her with ''clothes which should make her unafraid'' (of the radiation left by the beams?). As she neared the pyramid, she addressed Enki: ''She shouts to him . . . she beseeches him.'' The exchanges are lost by the breaks in the tablet; but Enki agreed to surrender the pyramid to her:

> The House that is like a heap,
> that which I have as a pile raised up—
> its mistress you may be.

There was, however, a condition: The surrender was subject to a final resolution of the conflict until ''the destiny-determining time'' shall come. Promising to relay Enki's conditions, Ninharsag went to address Enlil.

The events that followed are recorded in part in the *Lugal-e* epic and in other fragmentary texts. But they are most dramatically described in a text titled *I Sing the Song of the Mother of the Gods*. Surviving in great length because it was copied and recopied throughout the ancient Near East, the text was first reported by P. Dhorme in his study *La Souveraine des Dieux*. It is a poetic text in praise of *Ninmah* (the ''Great Lady'') and her role as *Mammi* (''Mother of the Gods'') on both sides of the battle lines.

Opening with a call upon ''the comrades in arms and the combatants'' to listen, the poem briefly describes the warfare and its participants, as well as its nearly global extent. On the one side were ''the firstborn of Ninmah'' (Ninurta) and Adad, soon joined by Sin and later on by Inanna/Ishtar. On the opposing side are listed Nergal, a god referred to as ''Mighty, Lofty One''— Ra/Marduk—and the ''God of the two Great Houses'' (the two great pyramids of Giza) who had tried to escape camouflaged in a ram's skin: Horus.

Asserting that she was acting with the approval of Anu, Ninharsag took the surrender offer of Enki to Enlil. She met him in the presence of Adad (while Ninurta remained at the battlefield). "O hear my prayers!" she begged the two gods as she explained her ideas. Adad was at first adamant:

> Presenting himself there, to the Mother,
> Adad thus said:
> "We are expecting victory.
> The enemy forces are beaten.
> The trembling of the land he could not withstand."

If she wants to bring about a cessation of hostilities, Adad said, let her call discussions on the basis that the Enlilites are about to win:

> "Get up and go—talk to the enemy.
> Let him attend the discussions
> so that the attack be withdrawn."

Enlil, in less forceful language, supported the suggestion:

> Enlil opened his mouth;
> In the assembly of the gods he said:
> "Whereas Anu at the mountain the gods assembled,
> warfare to discourage, peace to bring,
> and has dispatched the Mother of the Gods
> to entreat with me—
> Let the Mother of the Gods be an emissary."

Turning to his sister, he said in a conciliatory vein:

> "Go, appease my brother!
> Raise unto him a hand for Life;
> From his barred doorway, let him come out!"

Doing as suggested, Ninharsag "his brother went to fetch, put her prayers before the god." She informed him that his safety, and that of his sons, was assured: "by the stars she gave a sign."

As Enki hesitated she said to him tenderly: "Come, let me lead you out." And as he did, he gave her his hand. . . .

She conducted him and the other defenders of the Great Pyramid to the Harsag, her abode. Ninurta and his warriors watched the Enkites depart.

And the great and impregnable structure stood unoccupied, silent.

Nowadays the visitor to the Great Pyramid finds its passages and chambers bare and empty, its complex inner construction apparently purposeless, its niches and nooks meaningless.

It has been so ever since the first men had entered the pyramid. But it was not so when Ninurta had entered it—circa 8670 B.C. according to our calculations. "Unto the radiant place," yielded by its defenders, Ninurta had entered, the Sumerian text relates. And what he had done after he had entered changed not only the Great Pyramid from within and without but also the course of human affairs.

When, for the first time ever, Ninurta went into the "House Which Is Like a Mountain," he must have wondered what he would find inside. Conceived by Enki/Ptah, planned by Ra/Marduk, built by Geb, equipped by Thoth, defended by Nergal, what mysteries of space guidance, what secrets of impregnable defense did it hold?

In the smooth and seemingly solid north face of the pyramid, a swivel stone swung open to reveal the entranceway, protected by the massive diagonal stone blocks, just as the text lauding Ninharsag had described. A straight Descending Passage led to the lower service chambers where Ninurta could see a shaft dug by the defenders in search for subterranean water. But his interest focused on the upper passages and chambers; there, the magical "stones" were arrayed—minerals and crystals, some earthly, some heavenly, some the likes of which he had never seen. From them there were emitted the beamed pulsations for the guidance of the astronauts and the radiations for the defense of the structure.

Escorted by the Chief Mineralmaster, Ninurta inspected the array of "stones" and instruments. As he stopped by each one of them, he determined its destiny—to be smashed up and destroyed, to be taken away for display, or to be installed as instruments elsewhere. We know of these "destinies," and of the order in which Ninurta had stopped by the stones, from the text inscribed on tablets 10–13 of the epic poem *Lugal-e*. It is by following and correctly interpreting this text that the mystery of the purpose and function of many features of the pyramid's inner structure can be finally understood.

Going up the Ascending Passage, Ninurta reached its junction with the imposing Grand Gallery and a Horizontal Passage. Ninurta followed the Horizontal Passage first, reaching a large chamber with a corbeled roof. Called the "vulva" in the Ninharsag poem, this chamber's axis lay exactly on the east-west center line of the pyramid. Its emission ("an outpouring which is like a lion whom no one dares attack") came from a stone fitted into a niche that was hollowed out in the east wall (Fig. 49). It was the SHAM ("Destiny") Stone. Emitting a red radiance which Ninurta "saw in the darkness," it was the pulsating heart of the pyramid. But it was anathema to Ninurta, for during the battle, when he was aloft, this stone's "strong power" was used "to grab to kill me, with a tracking which kills to seize me." He ordered it "pulled out . . . be taken apart . . . and to obliteration be destroyed."

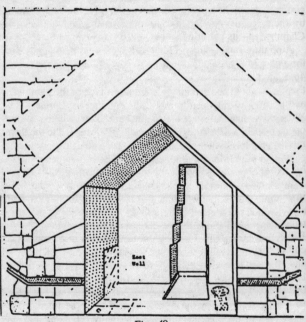

Fig. 49

Returning to the junction of the passages, Ninurta looked around him in the Grand Gallery (Fig. 45). As ingenious and complex as the whole pyramid was, this gallery was breathtaking and a most unusual sight. Compared to the low and narrow passages, it rose high (some twenty-eight feet) in seven overlapping stages, its walls closing in ever more at each stage. The ceiling was also built in slanting sections, each one angled into the massive walls so as not to exert any pressure on the segment below it. Whereas in the narrow passages only "a dim green light glowed," the Gallery glittered in multicolored lights—"its vault is like a rainbow, the darkness ends there." The many-hued glows were emitted by twenty-seven pairs of diverse crystal stones that were evenly spaced along the whole length of each side of the Gallery (Fig. 50a). These glowing stones were placed in cavities that were precisely cut into the ramps that ran the length of the Gallery on both sides of its floor. Firmly held in place by an elaborate niche in the wall (Fig. 50b), each crystal stone emitted a different radiance, giving the place its rainbow effect. For the moment Ninurta passed by them on his way up; his priority was the uppermost Grand Chamber and its pulsating stone.

Atop the Grand Gallery, Ninurta reached a great step which led through a low passage to an Antechamber of unique design (Fig. 46). There three portcullises—"the bolt, the bar and the lock" of the Sumerian poem—elaborately fitted into grooves in the walls and floor, hermetically sealed off the uppermost Great Chamber: "to foe it is not opened; only to Them Who Live, for them it is opened." But now, by pulling some cords, the portcullises were raised, and Ninurta passed through.

He was now in the pyramid's most restricted ("sacred") chamber, from which the guiding "Net" (radar?) was "spread out" to "survey Heaven and Earth." The delicate mechanism was housed in a hollowed-out stone chest; placed precisely on the north-south axis of the pyramid, it responded to vibrations with bell-like resonance. The heart of the guidance unit was the GUG ("Direction Determining") Stone; its emissions, amplified by five hollow compartments constructed above the chamber, were beamed out and up through two sloping channels leading to the north and south faces of the pyramid. Ninurta ordered this stone destroyed: "Then, by the fate-determining Ninurta, on that day was the Gug stone from its hollow taken out and smashed."

To make sure no one would ever attempt to restore the "Direction Determining" functions of the pyramid, Ninurta also ordered

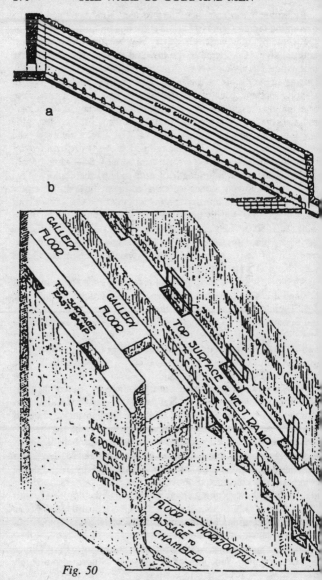

Fig. 50

the three portcullises removed. First to be tackled were the SU ("Vertical") Stone and the KA.SHUR.RA ("Awesome, Pure Which Opens") Stone. Then "the hero stepped up to the SAG.KAL Stone" ("Sturdy Stone Which Is In Front"). "He called out his full strength," shook it out of its grooves, cut the cords that were holding it, and "to the ground set its course."

Now came the turn of the mineral stones and crystals positioned atop the ramps in the Grand Gallery. As he walked down Ninurta stopped by each one of them to declare its fate. Were it not for breaks in the clay tablets on which the text was written, we would have had the names of all twenty-seven of them; as it is, only twenty-two names are legible. Several of them Ninurta ordered to be crushed or pulverized; others, which could be used in the new Mission Control Center, were ordered given to Shamash; and the rest were carried off to Mesopotamia, to be displayed in Ninurta's temple, in Nippur, and elsewhere as constant evidence of the great victory of the Enlilites over the Enki-gods.

All this, Ninurta announced, he was doing not only for his sake but for future generations, too: "Let the fear of thee"—the Great Pyramid—"be removed from my descendants; let their peace be ordained."

Finally there was the Apex Stone of the Pyramid, the UL ("High As The Sky") Stone: "Let the mother's offspring see it no more," he ordered. And, as the stone was sent crashing down, "let everyone distance himself," he shouted. The "Stones," which were "anathema" to Ninurta, were no more.

The deed having been done, Ninurta's comrades urged him to leave the battleground and return home. AN DIM DIM.MA, "Like Anu Art Thou Made," they told him in praise; "The Radiant House where the cord-measuring begins, the House in the land which thou hast come to know—rejoice in having entered it." Now, return to thy home, where thy wife and son await thee: "In the city which thou lovest, in the abode of Nippur, may thy heart be at rest . . . may thy heart become appeased."

The Second Pyramid War was over; but its ferocity and feats, and Ninurta's final victory at the pyramids of Giza, were remembered long thereafter in epic and song—and in a remarkable drawing on a cylinder seal, showing Ninurta's Divine Bird within a victory wreath, soaring in triumph above the two great pyramids (Fig. 51).

Fig. 51

And the Great Pyramid itself, bare and void and without its apex stone, has been left standing as a mute witness to the defeat of its defenders.

9

PEACE ON EARTH

How did the Pyramid Wars end?

They ended as great wars have ended in historic times: with a peace conference; with the gathering of the combatants, as at the Congress of Vienna (1814–1815), which redrew the map of Europe after the Napoleonic Wars, or the Paris Peace Conference that ended World War I (1914–1918) with the Treaty of Versailles.

The first inkling that the warring Anunnaki had convened in a similar manner some ten thousand years ago comes from the text which George A. Barton found inscribed on a broken clay cylinder. It was an Akkadian version of a much earlier Sumerian text; and Barton concluded that the clay cylinder was deposited by the ruler Naram-Sin circa 2300 B.C. when this Akkadian king repaired the platform of Enlil's temple in Nippur. Comparing the Mesopotamian text with texts inscribed at about the same time by Egyptian Pharaohs, Barton noted that the Egyptian texts "centered around the king and are interested in his fortunes as he enters among the gods"; the Mesopotamian text, on the other hand, "concerned itself with the community of the gods"; its subject was not the aspirations of the king but the affairs of the gods themselves.

In spite of damage to the text, especially at the beginning, it is clear that the leading gods gathered in the aftermath of a great and bitter war. We learn that they convened at the Harsag, Ninharsag's mountain abode in the Sinai, and that she played the role of peacemaker. Yet she is not treated by the text's author as a really neutral personage: he repeatedly refers to her by the epithet *Tsir* ("Snake"), which stamped her as an Egyptian/Enkite goddess and conveyed a derogatory connotation.

The text's opening verses, as we have already stated, briefly described the last phases of the war and the conditions within the besieged pyramid that led to the defenders' "outcry," leading to Ninharsag's decision to intervene.

We learn from the continuing ancient chronicle that Ninharsag first went with her idea of stopping the fighting and convening a peace conference to Enlil's camp.

The Enlilites' first reaction to Ninharsag's bold initiative was to accuse her of giving aid and comfort to the "demons." Ninharsag denied the accusation: "My House is pure," she answered. But a god whose identity is unclear challenged her sarcastically: "Is the House which is loftier and brightest of all"—the Great Pyramid—also "pure"?

"Of that I cannot speak," Ninharsag answered; "its brilliance Gibil is soldiering."

After the first accusations and explanations wore off some of the bitterness, a symbolic ceremony of forgiveness was performed. It involved two jars holding waters of the Tigris and Euphrates rivers, a ceremony of symbolic baptism making Ninharsag welcome again in Mesopotamia. Enlil touched her with his "bright scepter," and the "power of her was not overthrown."

The objections of Adad to a peace conference rather than unconditional surrender were already reported by us in the previous chapter. But then Enlil agreed, saying to her: "Go, appease my brother." We have already read in another text how Ninharsag crossed the battle lines to arrange the cease-fire. Having brought out Enki and his sons, Ninharsag took them to her abode in the Harsag. The Enlilite gods were already there, waiting.

Announcing that she was acting in behalf of "the great lord Anu . . . Anu the Arbiter," Ninharsag performed a symbolic ceremony of her own. She lighted seven fires, one each for the gathered gods: Enki and his two sons: Enlil and his three sons (Ninurta, Adad, and Sin). She uttered an incantation as she lit each fire: "A fiery offering to Enlil of Nippur . . . to Ninurta . . . to Adad . . . to Enki coming from the Abzu . . . to Nergal coming from Meslam." By nightfall the place was ablaze: "as sunlight was the great light set off by the goddess."

Ninharsag then appealed to the wisdom of the gods and extolled the virtues of peace: "Mighty are the fruits of the wise god; the great divine river to his vegetation shall come . . . its overflowing will make [the land] like a garden of god." The abundance of plants and animals, of wheat and other grains, of vines and fruits, and the benefits of a "triple-sprouting mankind" planting, building, and serving the gods—all to follow peace—were then outlined by her.

After Ninharsag had finished her oracle of peace, Enlil was the first one to speak. "Removed is the affliction from the face of the Earth," Enlil declared to Enki; "the Great Weapon is lifted up." He agreed to let Enki regain his abode in Sumer: "The E.DIN shall be a place for thy Holy House," with enough land around to bear fruit for the temple and to have seeded fields.

On hearing this Ninurta objected. "Let it not come!" the "prince of Enlil" shouted.

Again Ninharsag took the floor. She reminded Ninurta how he had toiled, "day and night with might," to enable cultivation and cattle herding in the land, how he "raised the foundations, filled [the earth], raised [the dykes]." Then the affliction of war destroyed it all, "all, in its entirety." "Lord of life, god of fruit," she appealed to him, "let the good beer pour in double measure! Make abundant the wool!"—agree to the peace terms!

Overcome by her plea, Ninurta relented: "O my mother, brilliant one! Proceed; the flour I will not withhold . . . in the kingdom the garden will be restored . . . To end affliction, I [too] earnestly pray."

Now the peace negotiations could proceed; and we pick up the tale of the unprecedented encounter between the two warring gods from the text *I Sing the Song of the Mother of the Gods*. First to address the assembled Anunnaki was Enki:

Enki addressed to Enlil words of lauding:
"O one who is foremost among the brothers,
Bull of Heaven, who the fate of Mankind holds:
In my lands, desolation is widespread;
All the dwellings are filled with sorrow
by your attacks."

The first item on the agenda was thus the cessation of hostilities— peace on Earth—and Enlil readily agreed, on condition that the territorial disputes be brought to an end and the lands rightfully belonging to the Enlilites and the people of the line of Shem be vacated by the Enkites. Enki agreed to cede forever these territories:

"I will grant thee the ruler's position
in the gods' Restricted Zone;
The Radiant Place, in thy hand I will entrust!"

In so ceding the Restricted Zone (the Sinai peninsula with its Spaceport) and the Radiant Place (the site of Mission Control Center, the future Jerusalem) Enki had a firm condition. In return for granting Enlil and his offspring eternal rights to those lands and vital sites, the sovereignty of Enki and his descendants over the Giza complex had to be recognized for all time.

Enlil agreed but not without a condition: The sons of Enki who had brought about the war and used the Great Pyramid for combat purposes should be barred from ruling over Giza, or over the whole of Lower Egypt, for that matter.

Pondering the condition over, Enki agreed. He then and there announced his decision. The lord of Giza and Lower Egypt, he said, will be a young son of his, espoused to one of the female deities born when Enki had made love to Ninharsag: "For the formidable House Which Is Raised Like a Heap, he appointed the prince whose brilliant wife from the cohabitation with Tsir [Ninharsag] was brought forth. The strong prince who is like a full-grown ibex—him he appointed, and commanded him to guard the Place of Life." He then granted the young god the exalted title NIN.GISH.ZI.DA ("Lord of the Artifact of Life").

Who was Ningishzidda? Scholars find the information concerning him meager and confusing. He is mentioned in Mesopotamian texts in association with Enki, Dumuzi, and Ninharsag; in the Great God List he is included among the gods of Africa following Nergal and Ereshkigal. The Sumerians depicted him with Enki's emblem of the entwined serpents and with the Egyptian *Ankh* sign (Fig. 52 a,b). Yet they viewed Ningishzidda favorably; Ninurta befriended him and invited him to Sumer. Some texts suggest that his mother was Ereshkigal, Enlil's granddaughter; our own conclusion is that he was indeed a son of Enki, conceived during Enki's and

a　　　　　　　　b

Fig. 52

Ereshkigal's stormy voyage to the Lower World. As such, he was acceptable to both sides as guardian of the secrets of the pyramids.

A hymn which Ake W. Sjöberg and E. Bergmann ("The Collection of the Sumerian Temple Hymns") believe was composed by the daughter of Sargon of Akkad in the third millennium B.C. exalted the pyramid-house of Ningishzidda and confirmed its Egyptian location:

Enduring place, light-hued mountain
which in an artful fashion was founded.
Its dark hidden chamber is an awe-inspiring place;
in a Field of Supervision it lies.
Awesome, its ways no one can fathom.
In the Land of the Shield
your pedestal is closely knit as a fine-mesh net . . .
At night you face the heavens,
your ancient measurements are surpassing.
Your interior knows the place where Utu rises,
the measure of its width is far reaching.
Your prince is the prince whose pure hand is outstretched,
whose luxuriant and abundant hair
flows down on his back—
the lord Ningishzida.

The concluding verses of the hymn twice restate the location of this unique structure: the "Land of the Shield." It is a term equivalent to the Akkadian meaning of the Mesopotamian name for Egypt: the Land Magan, "The Land of the Shield." And another hymn copied and translated by Sjöberg (tablet UET 6/1) called Ningishzidda "the falcon among the gods," a designation commonly applied in Egyptian texts to Egyptian gods and found in Sumerian texts only one other time, applied to Ninurta, conqueror of the pyramids.

What did the Egyptians call this son of Enki/Ptah? Their "god of the cord who measures the Earth" was Thoth; he was (as the *Tales of the Magicians* related) the one appointed to be guardian of the secrets of the Giza pyramids. It was Thoth, according to Manetho, who replaced Horus on the throne of Egypt; it happened circa 8670 B.C. —just at the time when the Second Pyramid War had ended.

Having thus settled the disputes between them, the great Anunnaki turned to the affairs of mankind.

As one reads the ancient words it becomes clear that this peace conference dealt not only with the cessation of hostilities and the drawing of binding territorial lines; it also laid the plans for the manner in which the lands would be settled by mankind! We read that Enki "before the feet of the adversary [Enlil] laid the cities that were allotted him"; Enlil, in turn, "before the feet of his adversary [Enki] the land Sumer he laid out."

We can envision the two brothers facing each other, Enki—as always—the more concerned of the two about mankind and its fate. Having dealt with the disputes among the Anunnaki themselves, he now turns to the future of mankind. In the aftermath of the Deluge, it was given farming and domesticated animals; now it was the chance to look and plan ahead, and he seized the opportunity. The ancient text may well describe a spontaneous act: Enki drawing on the ground, "before the feet of Enlil," a plan for the establishment of human settlement centers in his lands; agreeing, Enlil responds by drawing "before the feet of Enki" the plan for the restoration of the pre-Diluvial cities of southern Mesopotamia (Sumer).

If the olden pre-Diluvial cities of Mesopotamia were to be restored, Enki had a condition: He and his sons were to be allowed to come freely to Mesopotamia; and he, Enki, was to be given back the site of Eridu, the hallowed place of his first Earth Station. Accepting the condition, Enlil said: "In my land, let your abode become everlasting; from the day that you shall come into my presence, the laden table shall exhale delicious smells for thee." Enlil expressed the hope that in return for this hospitality, Enki would help bring prosperity also to Mesopotamia: "Pour abundance on the Land, each year increase its fortunes."

And with all these matters settled, Enki and his sons departed for their African domains.

After Enki and his sons had departed, Enlil and his sons contemplated the future of their territories, both old and new. The first chronicle, the one reported by Barton, relates that in order to reaffirm the status of Ninurta as second to Enlil and superior over his brothers, Enlil put him in charge of the Olden Land. The territories of Adad in the northwest were extended by a thin "finger" (Lebanon) to include the Landing Place at Baalbek. The territory that was in contention—we can describe it as Greater Canaan, from the border of Egypt in the south to the border of Adad in the north, with modern Syria included—was put under the aegis of Nannar and his offspring. To that effect "a decree was established," sealed, and celebrated with a meal offering shared by all the Enlilite gods.

A more dramatic version of these final proceedings is found in the *I Sing the Song of the Mother of the Gods* text. We learn that at that crucial moment, the rivalry between Ninurta—the legal heir, being the son of Enlil by his half-sister—and Nannar, the firstborn of Enlil by his official spouse Ninlil, had broken out in full force. Enlil, we are told, contemplated favorably the attributes of Nannar: "A firstborn . . . of beautiful countenance, perfect of limbs, wise without compare." Enlil "him loved" because he gave him the two all-important grandchildren, the twins Utu/Shamash and Inanna/Ishtar; he called Nannar SU.EN—"Multiplying Lord"—an endearing epithet from which there stemmed the Akkadian/Semitic name for Nannar: Sin. But as much as Enlil had favored Nannar, the fact was that it was Ninurta who was the legal heir; he was "Enlil's foremost warrior," and he led the Enlilites to victory.

As Enlil wavered between Sin and Ninurta, Sin enlisted the help of his wife Ningal, who appealed to Enlil as well as to his spouse Ninlil, the mother of Sin:

> To the place of decision he called Ningal,
> Suen invited her to approach.
> A favorable decision she asked of the father . . .
> Enlil weighed [her words] . . .
> Before the mother she [pleaded] . . .
> "Remember the childhood," she said [to Ninlil] . . .
> The mother quickly embraced him . . .
> She said to Enlil: . . . "Follow your heart's desire". . .

Could one ever imagine, in those far-reaching decisions that were to affect the fate of gods and men for millennia to come, that the female spouses had played such a decisive role? We read of Ningal coming to the aid of her husband; we see Ninlil being enlisted in persuading the wavering Enlil. But then there entered the scene yet another great goddess—and by her words achieved an unintended decision. . . .

As Enlil was urged by Ninlil to "follow your heart" rather than his mind, to prefer the firstborn over the legal heir, "Ninurta opened his mouth and said . . ." His words of opposition are lost by a damage to the verses; but, as the tale is continued, we learn that Ninharsag threw in her weight behind her son Ninurta:

> She cried out and lamented to her brother;
> Like a pregnant woman she was agitated, [saying:]
> "Inside the Ekur I call to my brother,

my brother who an infant made me carry;
upon my brother I call!''

But Ninharsag's appeal was ill-worded. She meant to appeal as
Enlil's sister in behalf of the child (Ninurta) she bore him; but her
call sounded like an appeal to Enki. Enraged, Enlil shouted at her:
''Who is this brother of yours that you call? This brother, who an
infant made you carry?'' And he made a decision favoring the line
of Sin. Ever since then, and to this very day, the Land of the
Spaceport has been known as Sin's land—the Sinai peninsula.

As his final act Enlil appointed Sin's son as the commander of
the Mission Control Center:

He called in Shamash
the grandchild of Ninlil.
He took him [by the hand];
In Shulim he placed him.

Jerusalem—*Ur-Shulim,* the ''City of Shulim''—was given to
Shamash to command. Its name, SHU.LIM, meant ''The Supreme
Place of the Four Regions,'' and the Sumerian emblem of the
''Four Regions'' (Fig. 53a) applied to it, possibly the forerunner of
the Jewish emblem called the Star of David (Fig. 53b).

Replacing the pre-Diluvial Nippur as the post-Diluvial Mission
Control Center, Jerusalem also acquired Nippur's former title of
being the Navel of the Earth—the central point in the Divine Grid
that made the comings and goings between Earth and Nibiru possi-

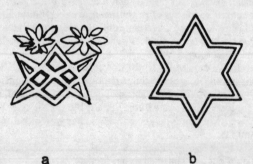

a   b

Fig. 53

ble. Emulating the concentric pre-Diluvial plan based on Nippur, the site selected for the "Navel of the Earth"—Mount Moriah— was located on the middle line, the Landing Path, within the Landing Corridor (Fig. 54); it was equidistant from the Landing Platform in Baalbek (BK) and the Spaceport itself (SP).

The two anchors of the Landing Corridor also had to be equidis-

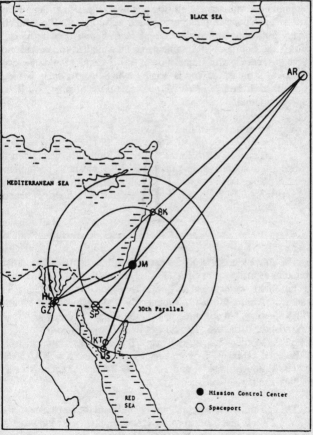

Fig. 54

tant from Mission Control Center (JM); but here there was a need to make a change in the original plans, for the previous artificially constructed "House Which Is Like a Mountain"—the Great Pyramid—was stripped of its crystals and equipment and was rendered useless by Ninurta. The solution was to erect, still precisely on the northwestern corridor line but north of Giza, a new Beacon City. The Egyptians called it the City of Annu; its hieroglyphic symbol depicted it as a high sloping tower (Fig. 55) with an even taller superstructure pointing skyward as an arrow. The Greeks, many millennia later, called the place *Heliopolis* ("City of Helios," the Sun god)—the same name they applied to Baalbek. In both instances it was a translation of earlier names relating the two places to Shamash, "Who Is Bright as the Sun"; Baalbek, in fact, was called in the Bible *Beth-Shemesh*, House of Shamash, or Heliopolis in Greek.

Fig. 55

The shifting of the beacon site at the northwestern anchor of the Landing Corridor from Giza (GZ) to Heliopolis (HL) also required a shift in the southeastern anchor, to keep the two anchors equidistant from Mount Moriah. A mount only slightly lower than Mount St. Katherine, but still precisely on the Corridor line, was found and adapted to the task. It is called Mount *Umm-Shumar* (Mount of Sumer's Mother—US on our map). Sumerian geographical lists called the two adjoining mountains in Tilmun KA HARSAG ("The Gateway Peak") and HARSAG ZALA.ZALAG ("Peak Which Emits the Brilliance").

The construction, manning, and operation of the aerospace facilities in Tilmun and Canaan required new supply routes and protective outposts. The sea lane to Tilmun was improved by the establishment of a port city ("Tilmun City," as distinguished from the "Land Tilmun") on the eastern shore of the Red Sea, probably where the port city of el-Tor still exists. It also led, we believe, to the establishment of the world's oldest town: Jericho, which was dedicated to Sin (*Yeriho* in Hebrew) and his celestial symbol, the Moon.

The age of Jericho has been an enigma that has continuously baffled the scholars. They broadly divide man's advancement (which spread from the Near East) into the Mesolithic ("Middle Stone") Age, which saw the introduction of agriculture and animal domestication circa 11,000 B.C.; a Neolithic ("New Stone") Age 3,600 years later, bringing with it villages and pottery; and then, finally, Sumer's urban civilization, again 3,600 years later. Yet here was Jericho: an *urban* site occupied and built by unknowns sometime circa 8500 B.C., when man had not yet learned to lead even a village life. . . .

The puzzles posed by Jericho pertain not only to its age, but also to what the archaeologists have found there: houses, built on stone foundations, had doors equipped with wooden jambs; the walls were carefully plastered and painted red, pink, and other colors—sometimes even covered with murals. Neat hearths and basins were sunk in whitewashed plaster floors, floors that were often decorated with patterns. Below the floors the dead were sometimes buried—buried but not forgotten: at least ten skulls were found which were filled with plaster to recreate the features of the deceased (Fig. 56). The features they reveal were by all opinions more advanced and finer than those of the usual Mediterranean dwellers of the time. All this was protected by a massive wall that surrounded the town (millennia before Joshua!). It was raised in the middle of a ditch nearly thirty feet wide and seven feet deep, dug out of the rock "without the help of picks and hoes" (James Mellaart, *Earliest Civilizations of the Near East*). It was "an explosive development . . . a spectacular development whose causes," Mellaart says, "are still unknown to us."

The enigma of prehistoric Jericho is compounded by the evidence of its round grain silos, one of which was found still partly standing. In a hot depression near the Dead Sea, 825 feet below sea level, in an inhospitable place unsuitable for grain cultivation, there was found evidence of ample supplies and continued storage of wheat and barley. Who could have built this advanced town that early, who had come to live in such a place, and whom did it serve as a fortified store city?

The solution to this enigma lies, in our opinion, in the chronology of the "gods," not of men. It lies in the fact that the incredible

Fig. 56

first urban settlement in Jericho (from circa 8500 B.C. to 7000 B.C.) exactly matches the period which, according to Manetho, encompassed the reign of Thoth in Egypt (from about 8670 to 7100 B.C.). His accession, as we have seen from the Mesopotamian texts, followed the Peace Conference. Egyptian texts say of his accession that it was pronounced "in the presence of the Determiners of Annu, following the night of the battle" and after he had helped "defeat the Storm Wind" (Adad) "and the Whirlwind" (Ninurta), and then assisted in "making the two combatants be at peace."

The period the Egyptians associated with the reign of Thoth was a time of peace among the gods, when the Anunnaki first and foremost established settlements relating to the construction and protection of the new space facilities.

The sea lane to Egypt and Tilmun, via the Red Sea, had to be augmented by a land route that could connect Mesopotamia with the Mission Control Center and the Spaceport. From time imme-

morial this land route led up the Euphrates River to the major way
station of Harran in the Balikh River region. From there the trav-
eler had the choice of either to continue south down the Mediterranean coast—the road later called by the Romans Via Maris (''The
Sea Way'')—or to proceed on the east side of the Jordan, along the
equally famous King's Highway. The former was the shortest
route to Egypt; the latter could lead to the Gulf of Eilat, the Red
Sea, Arabia, and Africa, as well as into the Sinai peninsula; it
could also lead to the western side of the Jordan via several suitable
crossing points. It was the route over which the African gold was
brought.

The most vital of these, the one that led directly to Mission Control Center in Jerusalem, was the crossing point at Jericho. It was
there that the Israelites crossed the Jordan into the Promised Land.
It was there, we suggest, that millennia earlier the Anunnaki established a town to guard the crossing point and to supply the travelers
with provisions for the continued journey. Until man made Jericho
his home, it was an outpost of the gods.

Would the Anunnaki have built a settlement only on the west
side of the Jordan, leaving the more vital eastern side, where the
King's Highway ran, unprotected? It stands to reason that a settlement should have existed on the opposite, eastern side of the Jordan, too. Though little known outside of archaeological circles,
such a place has indeed been found; and what was discovered there
is even more astounding that what had been uncovered at Jericho.

The puzzling place with astounding remains was first unearthed
in 1929 by an archaeological mission organized by the Vatican's
Pontifical Biblical Institute. The archaeologists, led by Alexis
Mallon, were surprised by the high level of civilization found
there. Even the oldest level of habitation (circa 7500 B.C.) was
paved with bricks, and though the period of settlement stretched
from the end of the Stone Age to the Bronze Age, the archaeologists were amazed to find that the same civilization revealed itself
at all levels.

The place is named after the mound where it was found—Tell
Ghassul; its ancient name is not known. Together with several sat-
ellite settlements, it clearly controlled the vital crossover point and
the road leading to it—a road still followed to this day to a crossing
point nowadays called the Allenby Bridge (Fig. 57). The strategic
location of Tell Ghassul had been noted by the archaeologists when
they began to dig up its remains: ''From atop the mound, one has
an interesting all-around view: the Jordan on the west as a dark

line; to the northwest, the hillock of ancient Jericho; and beyond it, the mountains of Judea, including Beth-El and the Mount of Olives of Jerusalem. Bethlehem is obscured by Mount el-Muntar, but the heights of Tekoah and the environs of Hebron can be seen'' (A. Mallon, R. Koeppel, and R. Neuville, *Teleilat Ghassul, Compte Rendu des Fouilles de l'Institut Biblique Pontifical*). To the north, the view was unobscured for some thirty miles; to the east, one could see Mount Moab and the foremounts of Mount Nebo; to the south, ''beyond the mirror of the Dead Sea, one could see the salt mountain, Mount Sodom.''

The principal remains uncovered at Tell Ghassul cover a period when it was occupied by highly advanced settlers from before 4000 B.C. to circa 2000 B.C. (when the place was abruptly abandoned).

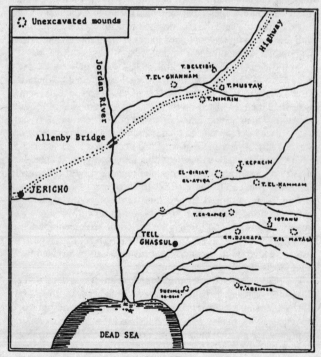

Fig. 57

The artifacts and irrigation system, of a much higher standard than had then prevailed in the area, convinced the archaeologists that the settlers had come from Mesopotamia.

Of the three hillocks that together formed the large mound, two appear to have been used as abodes and one as a work area. The latter was found to have been subdivided into rectangularlike segments, within which there were built circular "pits," frequently in pairs. That they were not hearths for food preparation is suggested not only by their pairing and profusion (why would six or eight of them be required in one compartment?), but also by the fact that some of them were cylindrical and went quite deep into the ground. Combined with them were enigmatic "bands of ashes" (Fig. 58), the remains of some combustible material, which were covered with fine sand and then with regular soil, only to form the foundation of yet another layer of such "band of ashes."

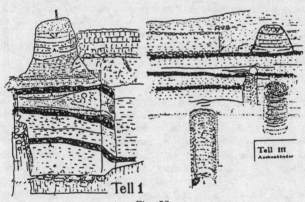

Fig. 58

On the surface, the ground was strewn with pebbles, the remains of rocks broken up by some force that also blackened them. Among the artifacts found was a small, circular object made of fired clay (Fig. 59), shaped with precision for some unknown technical purpose.

The mystery only deepened by the discoveries in the residential areas. There the walls of the rectangular houses collapsed as though hit by a sudden force just above ground level, as a result of which the upper parts of the walls collapsed neatly inward.

Fig. 59

Because of this neat collapse, it was possible to piece together some of the astounding murals that were painted and overpainted on these walls. In one instance a cagelike mesh shown over the object created on the wall a three-dimensional illusion. In one house every wall appeared to have been painted with some scene; in another a recessed divan was so built that it enabled the dweller, while reclining, to view a mural that covered the whole opposite wall. It depicted a row of people—the first two of whom were seated on thrones—facing toward (or greeting) another person who had apparently stepped out of an object emitting rays.

The archaeologists who had discovered these murals during the 1931–32 and 1932–33 excavations theorized that the rayed object might have been similar to a most unusual rayed "star" found painted in another building. It was an eight-pointed "star" within a larger eight-pointed "star," culminating in a burst of eight rays (Fig. 60). The precise design, employing a variety of geometric shapes, was artistically executed in black, red, white, gray, and combinations thereof; a chemical analysis of the paints used showed that they were not natural substances but sophisticated compounds of twelve to eighteen minerals.

The mural's discoverers assumed that the eight-rayed "star" had some "religious significance," pointing out that the eight-pointed star, standing for the planet Venus, was the celestial symbol of Ishtar. However, the fact is that no evidence of any religious worship whatsoever, no "cult objects," statuettes of gods, etc., had been found at Tell Ghassul, yet another anomaly of the place. This, we suggest, indicates that it was inhabited not by worshipers but by those who were the subject of worshiping: the "gods" of antiquity, the Anunnaki.

In fact, we have come upon a similar design in Washington,

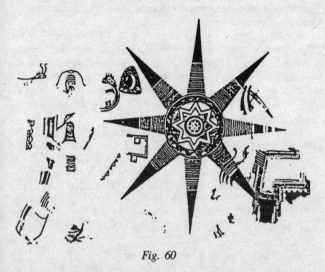

Fig. 60

D.C. It can be seen in the foyer of the headquarters of the National Geographic Society: a floor mosaic of a compass denoting the Society's interest in the four corners of the Earth and their intermediate points (east, northeast; north, northwest; west, southwest; south, southeast). It was this, we believe, that the design's ancient painters, too, had in mind: to indicate their, and the place's, association with the four regions of the Earth.

That the rayed "star" had no sacred significance is further attested by the disrespect with which it was surrounded by graffiti. These (Fig. 60) depict thick-walled buildings, fins of fishes, birds, wings, a ship, and even (some suggest) a sea dragon (upper left-hand corner); in these graffiti, yellow and brown of various shades appear in addition to the colors already mentioned.

Of particular interest are two shapes in which large twin "eyes" are prominent. We have a better knowledge of what they depicted, for such shapes were found painted, on a much larger scale and with greater detail, on the walls of other houses. The objects were depicted as spherical or oval in shape, their upper part layered and painted in black and white. The center was dominated by the two large "eyes," perfect black disks within white circles. The bottom part showed in red two (or four?) extended supports; between these mechanical legs there protruded from the object's main body a bulbous contraption (Fig. 61).

What were these objects? Were they the "Whirlwinds" of the Near Eastern texts (including the Old Testament), the "Flying Saucers" of the Anunnaki? The murals, the circular pits, the bands of ashes, the strewn, blackened pebbles, the location of the place—all that was uncovered and probably much that was not—bespeak Tell Ghassul as a stronghold and supply depot for the patrol aircraft of the Anunnaki.

The Tell Ghassul/Jericho crossing point played important and miraculous roles in several biblical events, a fact that may have enhanced the Vatican's interest in the site. It was there that the prophet Elijah crossed the river (to its eastern bank) in order to keep an appointment—at Tell Ghassul?—to be taken aloft by "a chariot of fire . . . in a Whirlwind." It was in that area that at the end of the Israelite Exodus from Egypt, Moses (having been denied by the Lord entry into Canaan proper) "went up from the plain of Moab"—the area of Tell Ghassul—"unto the Mount of Nebo, to its uppermost peak, which overlooked Jericho; and the Lord showed him all the land: the Gilead up to Dan, and the land of Naphtali and the land of Ephraim and Manasseh and the whole land of Judea, unto the Mediterranean; and the Negeb and the plain valley of Jericho, the city of datepalms." It is a description of a

Fig. 61

view as encompassing as that seen by the archaeologists who stood atop Tell Ghassul.

The crossing itself, under the leadership of Joshua, entailed the miraculous backing up of the Jordan's waters, under the influence of the Holy Ark and its contents. It was then, "when Joshua was by Jericho, that he raised his eyes and lo and behold, there stood a man opposite him and his drawn sword in his hand; and Joshua went unto him and said unto him: 'Art thou with us or with our enemies?' and he said: 'Neither; a captain of the host of the Lord am I.' And Joshua fell on his face to the ground and bowed, and said unto him: 'What sayeth my lord unto his servant?' and the captain of the host of Yahweh said unto Joshua: 'Remove thy shoe off thy foot, for the place where thou standeth is restricted.' "

Then the captain of the troops of Yahweh divulged to him the Lord's plan for the conquest of Jericho. Do not attempt to storm its walls by force, he said. Instead, carry the Ark of the Covenant around its walls seven times. And on the seventh day the priests sounded the trumpets, and the people let out a great cry, as they were commanded. "And the walls of Jericho came tumbling down."

Jacob, too, crossing the Jordan at night on his return to Canaan from Harran, ran into "a man" and the two wrestled till dawn; only then did Jacob realize that his opponent was a deity; "and Jacob called the place Peni-El ('The Face of God') for I had seen a god face to face and have survived."

Indeed, the Old Testament clearly states that there had been in earlier times settlements of the Anunnaki at the vital approaches to the Sinai peninsula and Jerusalem. Hebron, the city guarding the route between Jerusalem and the Sinai, "was called earlier Kiryat Arba ("Stronghold of Arba"); a Great Man ("king") among the *Anakim* he was" (Joshua, 14:15). The descendants of the *Anakim*, we are further told, were still residing in the area during the Israelite conquest of Canaan; and there are numerous other biblical references to abodes of the *Anakim* on the east side of the Jordan.

Who were these *Anakim?* The term is commonly translated "giants," just as the biblical term *Nefilim* had been translated. But we have already shown conclusively that by *Nefilim* ("Those Who Had Come Down") the Old Testament had referred to the "People of the Rocketships."

The *Anakim,* we suggest, were none other than the *Anunnaki.*

No one had hitherto paid any particular attention to the count of 3,650 years which Manetho assigned to the reign of the "demigods'' who belonged to the dynasty of Thoth. We, however, find the figure highly significant, for it differs but by 50 years from the 3,600-year orbit of Nibiru, the home planet of the Anunnaki.

It was no accident, we have maintained, that mankind's advancement from the Stone Age to the high civilization of Sumer occurred in 3,600-year intervals—circa 11,000, 7400, and 3800 B.C. It was as though ''a mysterious hand'' had each time ''picked Man out of his decline and raised him to an even higher level of culture, knowledge and civilization,'' we wrote in *The 12th Planet;* each instance, we hold, coincided with the recurrence of the time when the Anunnaki could come and go between Earth and Nibiru.

These advances spread from the Mesopotamian nucleus throughout the ancient world; and the Egyptian ''Age of the demigods'' (offspring of the cohabitation of gods and humans)—from circa 7100 B.C. to 3450 B.C. per Manetho—unquestionably coincides with the Neolithic period in Egypt.

We can assume that at each of these intervals the fate of mankind and the gods' relations with it were discussed by the Great Anunnaki, the ''seven who decree.'' We know for sure that such a deliberation had taken place prior to the sudden and otherwise inexplicable blooming of the Sumerian civilization, for the Sumerians have left us records of such discussions!

When the reconstruction of Sumer began, first to have been rebuilt on its soil were the Olden Cities but no longer as exclusive Cities of the Gods; for mankind was now allowed into these urban centers to tend the surrounding fields, orchards, and cattlefolds in behalf of the gods, and to be in the service of the gods in all conceivable manners: not only as cooks and bakers, artisans and clothiers, but also as priests, musicians, entertainers, and temple prostitutes.

First to be reestablished was Eridu. Having been Enki's first settlement on Earth, it was given to him anew in perpetuity. His initial shrine there (Fig. 62)—a marvel of architecture in those early days—was in time raised and expanded to a magnificent temple-abode, the E.EN.GUR.RA (''House of the Lord Whose Return Is Triumphant''), adorned with gold, silver, and precious metals from the Lower World and protected by the ''Bull of Heaven.'' For Enlil and Ninlil Nippur was reestablished; there they raised a new *Ekur* (''Mountain House''—Fig. 63), this time equipped not as Mission Control Center but with awesome weapons: ''the Lifted Eye which scans the land''; and ''the Lifted Beam,'' which pene-

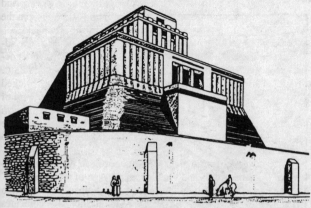

Fig. 62

trates all. Their sacred area also housed Enlil's "fast-stepping Bird" whose "grasp no one could escape."

A "Hymn to Eridu" edited and translated by A. Falkenstein (*Sumer,* vol. VII) describes how Enki traveled to attend a gathering of all the great gods; the occasion was a visit by Anu to Earth, for one of those deliberations that determined the fate of gods and men on Earth every 3,600 years. After some celebrating, when "the gods the intoxicating beverage had drunk, the wine prepared by men," it was time for solemn decisions. "Anu sat on the seat of honor; near him sat Enlil; Ninharsag sat on an arm chair."

Anu called the meeting to order, "and to the Anunnaki thus said":

Great gods who had hither come,
Annuna-gods, who to the Court of Assembly had come!
My son had for himself a House built;
The lord Enki
Eridu like the mountain on Earth he raised;
His House, in a beautiful place he built.
To the place, Eridu, no one uninvited can enter . . .
In its sanctuary, from the Abzu
the Divine Formulas Enki had deposited.

This brought the deliberations to the main item on the agenda:

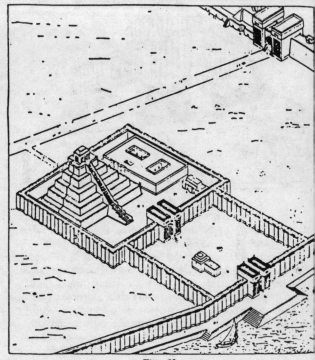

Fig. 63

Enlil's complaint that Enki was withholding from the other gods the "Divine Formulas"—the knowledge of more than one hundred aspects of civilization—confining advancement to Eridu and its people only. (It is an archaeologically confirmed fact that Eridu was Sumer's oldest post-Diluvial city, the fountainhead of Sumerian civilization.) It was then decided that Enki must share the Divine Formulas with the other gods, so that they, too, could establish and reestablish their urban centers: civilization was to be granted to the whole of Sumer.

When the official part of the deliberations was over, the gods who were on Earth had a surprise for the celestial visitors: midway between Nippur and Eridu they had built a sacred precinct in honor of Anu; an abode appropriately named E.ANNA—"House of Anu."

Before they left Earth back for the Home Planet, Anu and Antu his spouse paid an overnight visit to their Earthly temple; it was an occasion marked by pomp and circumstance. As the divine couple reached the new town—later to be known as Uruk (the biblical Erech)—the gods accompanied them in a procession to the temple's courtyard. While a sumptuous evening meal was prepared, Anu, seated on a throne, chatted with the male gods; Antu, accompanied by the female goddesses, changed her clothes in the temple's section called "House of the Golden Bed."

Priests and other temple attendants served "wine and good oil" and slaughtered in sacrifice "a bull and a ram for Anu, Antu and all the gods." But the banquet was delayed until it was dark enough to see the planets: "Jupiter, Venus, Mercury, Saturn, Mars and the Moon—as soon as they shall appear." With this, and after a ceremonial washing of the hands, the first part of the meal was served: "Bull meat, ram meat, fowl . . . as well as prime beer and pressed wine."

A pause was then made for the highlight of the evening. While one group of priests began to chant the hymn *"Kakkab Anu etellu shamame,"* "The Planet of Anu Rises in the Skies," a priest went up to the "topmost stage of the tower of the temple" to watch the skies for the appearance of the Planet of Anu, Nibiru. At the expected moment and in the predetermined spot in the heavens, the planet was sighted. Thereupon the priests broke out in singing the compositions "To the One Who Grows Bright, the Heavenly Planet of the Lord Anu" and "The Creator's Image Has Arisen." A bonfire was lit in signal, and as the news spread from one observation post to another, bonfires were lit in one place after another. Before the night was over, the whole land was alight.

In the morning, prayers of thanksgiving were offered in the temple's chapel, and in a sequence filled with ceremony and symbolism, the celestial visitors began their departure. "Anu is leaving," the priests chanted; "Anu, great king of Heaven and Earth, we ask for your blessing," they intoned. After Anu gave the asked-for blessings, the procession wound its way down the "Street of the Gods" to the "Place of the barque of Anu." There were more prayers and hymn singing at a chapel called "Build Life on Earth." Now it was time for those remaining behind to bless the departing couple, and the following verses were recited:

Great Anu, may Heaven and Earth bless you!
May the gods Enlil, Ea and Ninmah bless you!
May the gods Sin and Shamash bless you . . .
May the gods Nergal and Ninurta bless you . . .
May the Igigi who are in heaven
and the Anunnaki who are on Earth, bless you!
May the gods of the Abzu
and the gods of the holy land bless you!

And then Anu and Antu took off to the Spaceport. It was the seventeenth day of their visit to Earth, a tablet found in the archives of Uruk states. The momentous visit was over.

Its decisions opened the way for the establishment of new cities besides the Olden Ones. First and foremost among them was Kish. It was put under the control of Ninurta, "Enlil's Foremost Son"; he turned it into Sumer's first administrative capital. For Nannar/Sin, "Enlil's Firstborn," the new urban center of Ur ("*The* City") was established—a place that was to become Sumer's economic heart.

There were additional decisions concerning the new era in mankind's advancement and its relations with the Anunnaki. We read in the Sumerian texts, concerning the crucial conclave that launched Sumer's great civilization, that "the great Anunnaki who decree the fate" decided that the gods "were too lofty for Mankind." The term used—*elu* in Akkadian—means exactly that: "Lofty Ones"; from it comes the Babylonian, Assyrian, Hebrew, and Ugaritic *El*—the term to which the Greeks gave the connotation "god."

There was a need, the Anunnaki decided, to give mankind "Kingship" as an intermediary between themselves and the human citizenry. All the Sumerian records attest that this major decision was taken during Anu's visit, at a Council of the Great Gods. One Akkadian text (the *Fable of the Tamarisk and the Datepalm*) describes thus the meeting that had taken place "in long ago days, in far off times":

The gods of the land, Anu, Enlil and Enki,
convened an assembly.
Enlil and the gods took counsel;
Among them was seated Shamash;
Among them was seated Ninmah.

At that time "there was not yet kingship in the land; the rule was held by the gods." But the Great Council resolved to change that and to grant kingship to mankind. All the Sumerian sources agree that the first royal city was Kish. The men who were appointed by Enlil to be kings were called LU.GAL, "Mighty Man." We find the same record in the Old Testament (Genesis chapter 10): when mankind was establishing its kingdoms:

Kish begot Nimrod;
He was the first to be a Mighty Man in the Land . . .
And the beginning of his kingship:
Babel and Erech and Akkad,
all in the land of Shin'ar [Sumer].

While the biblical text names the first three capitals as Kish, Babylon, and Erech, the Sumerian King Lists assert that Kingship moved from Kish to Erech and then to Ur, omitting any mention of Babylon. The apparent discrepancy has a reason: We believe it has to do with the incident of the Tower of Babel (Babylon), which the Old Testament records in no small detail. It was an incident, we believe, that had to do with Marduk's insistence that he, rather than Nannar, should possess Sumer's next capital. The time was clearly during the resettlement of the plain of Sumer (the biblical Shin'ar), when new urban centers were being built:

And as they travelled from the east,
they found a valley in the Land of Shin'ar
and settled there.
And they said unto one another:
"Let us make bricks, and burn them by fire";
and the brick served them as stone,
and the bitumen served them as mortar.

It was then that the scheme which caused the incident was suggested by an unnamed instigator: "Come, let us build us a city, and a tower whose head shall reach the heavens."

"And Yahweh came down to see the city and the tower which the humans were building"; and he said to unnamed colleagues: "This is just the beginning of their undertakings; from now on, anything that they shall scheme to do shall no longer be impossible for them." And Yahweh said to his colleagues: "Come, let us go down and confuse their language, so that they would not understand each other's speech." Then the Lord "scattered them from there all over the face of the Earth, and they ceased to build the city."

That there was initially a time when mankind "spoke in unison" is a tenet of Sumerian historical recollections. These also assert that the confusion of languages, accompanying the dispersion of mankind, was a deliberate act of the gods. Like the Old Testament, the writings of Berossus reported that "the gods introduced a diversity of tongues among men, who until that time had all spoken the same language." Like the biblical tale, the histories of Berossus connect the diversification of languages and the dispersion of mankind to the incident of the Tower of Babel: "When all men formerly spoke the same language, some among them undertook to erect a large and lofty tower, that they might climb up to heaven. But the Lord, sending forth a whirlwind, confounded their design, and gave to each tribe a particular language of its own."

The conformity of the tales suggests the existence of a common, older source from which both the compilers of the Old Testament and Berossus had obtained their information. Although it is generally assumed that such an original text has not yet been found, the fact is that George Smith, in his very first publication in 1876, reported discovering at Ashurbanipal's library in Nineveh "a mutilated account of part of the story of the Tower." The tale, he concluded, was originally written on two tablets; on the one he had found (K-3657), there had been six columns of cuneiform text; but he could piece together only fragments of four columns. It is undoubtedly an Akkadian version of the Sumerian tale of the Tower of Babel; and it is clear from it that the incident was brought about not by mankind but by the gods themselves. Mankind was only a pawn in the struggle.

As pieced together by George Smith, and retranslated by W. S. C. Boscawen in the *Transactions of the Society of Biblical Archaeology* (vol. V), the tale began with the identification of the instigator; damage to the lines, however, obliterated the name. "The thoughts" of this god's heart "were evil; against the Father of the Gods [Enlil] he was wicked." To achieve his evil purpose "the people of Babylon he corrupted to sin," inducing "small and great to mingle on the mound."

As the sinful work came to the attention of "the lord of the Pure Mound"—already identified as Enlil in the Cattle and Grain tale— Enlil "to Heaven and on Earth spoke. . . . He lifted his heart to the Lord of the Gods, Anu, his father; to receive a command his heart requested. At that time he also lifted up [his heart? voice?] to

Damkina." We well know that she was the mother of Marduk; so all the clues point to him as the instigator. But Damkina stood by his side: "With my son I rise . . ." she said. The incomplete verse that follows has her stating that "his number"—his numerical rank-status?—was at issue.

The legible portion of column III then deals with Enlil's efforts to talk the rebellious group out of their plans. Taking himself up in a Whirlwind, "Nunamnir [Enlil] from the heaven to earth spoke; [but] by his path they did not go; violently they fronted against him." When Enlil "saw this, to earth he descended." But even his very presence on the site did not make a difference. We read in the last column that "when a stop he did not make of the gods," he had no choice but resort to force:

> To their stronghold tower, in the night,
> a complete end he made.
> In his anger, a command he also poured out:
> To scatter abroad was his decision.
> He gave a command their counsels to confuse.
> . . . their course he stopped.

The ancient Mesopotamian scribe ended the tale of the Tower of Babel with a bitter memory: Because they "against the gods revolted with violence, violently they wept for Babylon; very much they wept."

The biblical version also names *Babel* (Hebrew for Babylon) as the place where the incident had occurred. The name is significant, for in its original Akkadian—*Bab-Ili*—it meant "Gateway of the Gods," the place by which the gods were to enter and leave Sumer.

It was there, the biblical narrative states, that the perpetrators planned to construct "a tower whose head shall reach unto the heavens." The words are identical to the actual name of the ziggurat (seven-stage pyramid) which was the dominant feature of ancient Babylon (Fig. 64): E.SAG.ILA, "House Whose Head is Lofty."

The biblical and the Mesopotamian texts—undoubtedly based on an original Sumerian chronicle—thus relate the same incident: Marduk's frustrated attempt to prevent the transfer of kingship from Kish to Erech and Ur—cities destined to be power centers of Nannar/Sin and his children—and to seize suzerainty for his own city, Babylon.

By this attempt, however, Marduk started a chain of events replete with tragedies.

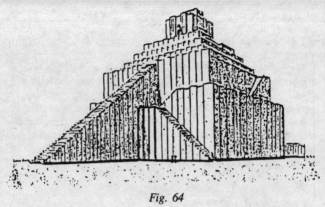

Fig. 64

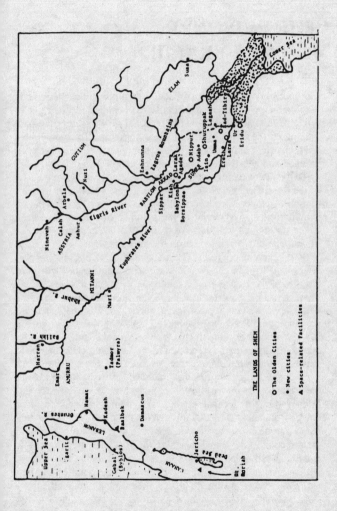

THE LANDS OF SHEM

○ The Olden Cities
• New cities
▲ Space-related Facilities

10

THE PRISONER
IN THE PYRAMID

The incident of the Tower of Babel brought to an unexpected end the longest era of Peace on Earth that Man can recall. The chain of tragic events the incident had triggered had, we believe, a direct bearing on the Great Pyramid and its mysteries. To resolve them we shall offer our own theory of how this unique structure had been planned and constructed, then plugged and broken into.

To the many enigmas pertaining to the construction and purpose of the Great Pyramid at Giza, two more were added after its completion. All theories concerning them, having been based on the assumption of a royal burial as the pyramid's purpose, have been found flawed and wanting. We believe that the answers lie not in the tales of the Pharaohs, but in the tales of the gods.

Several references to the Great Pyramid in writings of classical Greek and Roman chroniclers attest to familiarity in their times with the swivel-stone entrance into the pyramid, the Descending Passage and the Subterranean Pit. There was no knowledge of the whole upper system of passages, galleries, and chambers, because the Ascending Passage was plugged tight with three large granite blocks and further camouflaged with a triangular stone, so that no one going down the Descending Passage ever suspected that there existed a junction with an upper passage (Fig. 65).

Over the many centuries that followed, even the knowledge of the original entrance was forgotten; and when (in A.D. 820) the Caliph Al Mamoon decided to enter the pyramid, his men forced an entry by tunneling aimlessly through the masonry. Only when they heard a stone fall somewhere inside the pyramid did they tunnel in the direction of the sound, reaching the Descending Passage. The stone that had fallen was the triangular stone hiding the junction with the Ascending Passage; its fall revealed the granite plug. Unable even to dent the granite blocks, the men cut through the limestone masonry around them, discovering the Ascending Passage and the upper inner parts of the pyramid. As the Arab historians at-

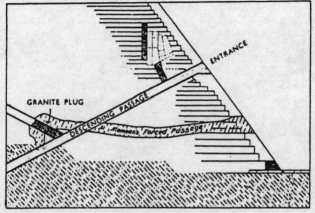

Fig. 65

test, everywhere Al Mamoon and his men found nothing but emptiness.

Clearing the Ascending Passage of debris—pieces of limestone that had somehow slid down the passage to the granite plugs—they crawled up to the upper end of this passage. Coming out of its squarelike tunnel, they could stand up, for they had reached the junction of the Ascending Passage with a Horizontal Passage and with the Grand Gallery (Fig. 66). They followed the Horizontal Passage, reaching the vaulted chamber at its end (which later explorers named the "Queen's Chamber"); it was bare, and so was its enigmatic niche (see Fig. 49). Returning to the junction of the passages, they clambered up the Grand Gallery (Fig. 45); its precisely cut grooves, now empty holes and nooks, helped the climb up—a task made slippery by a layer of white dust that covered the Gallery's floor and ramps. They climbed over the Great Step, which rose from the upper end of the Gallery to become flush with the floor of the Antechamber; entering it, they found its blocking portcullises gone (Fig. 67). They crawled into the upper vaulted chamber (later named the "King's Chamber"); it was bare, except for a hollowed-out stone block (nicknamed "The Coffer"), but it, too, was empty.

Returning to the junction of the three passages (Ascending Passage, Grand Gallery, and Horizontal Passage), Al Mamoon's men

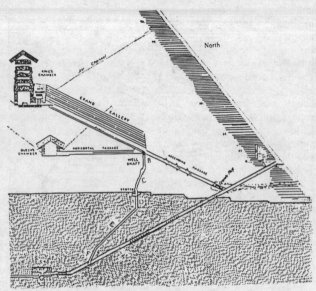

Fig. 66

Fig. 67

noticed a gaping hole on the western side, where the ramp stone belonging there had been smashed away (Fig. 68). It led via a short horizontal passage to a vertical shaft, which the Arabs assumed was a well. As they clambered down this ''well shaft'' (as it came to be called), they found that it was but the upper part of a long (about 200 feet) series of twisting and turning connected shafts that ended with a six-foot link to the Descending Passage and thus provided a connection between the pyramid's upper chambers and passages and its lower ones (Fig. 66). The evidence indicates that the lower opening was blocked up and hidden from whoever had come down the Descending Passage, until Al Mamoon's men lowered themselves through the length of the Well Shaft and discovered and broke open its bottom end.

The Arabs' discoveries and later investigations have raised a host of puzzles. Why, when, and by whom was the Ascending Passage plugged up? Why, when, and by whom was the twisting Well Shaft tunneled through the pyramid and its rocky base?

Fig. 68

The first and most persistent theory fitted the two puzzles into one answer. Holding that the pyramid was built by the Pharaoh Khufu (Cheops) to be his tomb, the theory suggested that after his mummified body was placed in the "Coffer" in the "King's Chamber," workmen slid the three granite plug blocks from the Grand Gallery down the slope of the Ascending Passage, in order to seal off the tomb. This entrapped these workmen alive in the Grand Gallery. Outwitting the priests, the workmen removed the end stone in the ramp, dug out the Well Shaft, reached the Descending Passage, and saved themselves by climbing up it to the pyramid's entrance/exit.

But this theory does not stand up to critical scrutiny.

The Well Shaft is made up of seven distinct segments (Fig. 66). It begins with the upper horizontal segment (A) leading from the Grand Gallery to a vertical segment (B), which connects via a twisting segment C with a lower vertical segment D. A long, straight, but sharply inclined segment E then follows, leading into a shorter segment F inclined at a different angle. At the end of F, a segment intended to be horizontal but, in fact, slightly slanting (G) then connects the Well Shaft with the Descending Passage. Apart from the connecting, horizontal segments A and G, the Well Shaft proper (segments B, C, D, E, and F), in spite of its changing of courses when viewed on a north-south plane, lies precisely on an east-west plane parallel to the pyramid's plane of passages and chambers; the separating distance of about six feet is bridged at the top by segment A and at the bottom by segment G.

While the three upper segments of the Well Shaft traverse some sixty feet through the pyramid's limestone masonry, the lower segments were cut through some 150 feet of solid rock. The few workmen left behind to slide down the granite plugs (according to the above-mentioned theory) could not have been able to cut through the rock. Also, if the digging was from above, where is all the debris, which they could have only brought up as they dug down? With the Well Shaft's twenty-eight-inch bore through most of its segments, the more than one thousand cubic feet of debris would have piled up in the upper passages and chambers.

In view of these improbabilities, new theories were advanced based on an assumption that the Well Shaft was dug from the bottom up (the debris was then removed via the Descending Passage to outside the pyramid). But why? The answer is: an accident. As the Pharaoh was being entombed, an earthquake shook the pyramid, loosening prematurely the granite plugs. As a result, not mere laborers, but members of the royal family and high priests, were trapped alive. With the pyramid's plans still available, rescue teams tunneled their way up, reached the Grand Gallery, and saved the dignitaries.

This theory (as well as a long-discarded one about grave robbers digging their way up) falters, among other points, on the matter of precision. With the exception of segment *C,* which was tunneled through the masonry in a rough and irregular manner, and section *G,* two of whose squarish sides were left rough and not quite horizontal, all the other segments are straight, precise, carefully finished, and uniformly angled throughout their lengths. Why would rescue workers (or grave robbers) waste time to achieve perfection and precision? Why would they bother to smooth the sides, when such smoothness made climbing the shaft much more difficult?

As the evidence mounted that no Pharaoh had ever been buried or enshrined within the Great Pyramid, a new theory gained adherents: The Well Shaft was cut to enable an examination of fissures that had developed in the rock as a result of an earthquake. The most articulate proponents of such a theory were the brothers John and Morton Edgar *(The Great Pyramid Passages and Chambers),* who, motivated by a religious zeal which saw in the pyramid an expression in stone of biblical prophecies, visited, cleared, examined, measured, and photographed every known part of the pyramid. They showed conclusively that the upper short horizontal passage to the Well Shaft (*A*), as well as the uppermost vertical section (*B*), were part and parcel of the original construction of the pyramid (Fig. 69). They also found that the lower vertical section (*D*) was carefully built with masonry blocks as it passed through a cavity (nicknamed The Grotto) in the bedrock (Fig. 70); it could have been so constructed only when the rock face was still exposed, before the Grotto was covered up with the masonry of the pyramid. In other words, this section, too, had to be part—a very early part—of the original construction of the pyramid.

As the pyramid was rising above its base—so the Edgars theorized—a massive earthquake fissured the bedrock in several places. Needing to know the extent of the damage to determine whether the pyramid could still rise above the cracked bedrock, the builders cut through the rock segments *E* and *F* as Inspection Shafts. Finding the damage not too serious, the pyramid's construction continued; but to allow periodic inspection, a short (about six-foot) passage (*G*) was tunneled from the Descending Passage to connect with section *F,* allowing entry into the Inspection Shafts from below.

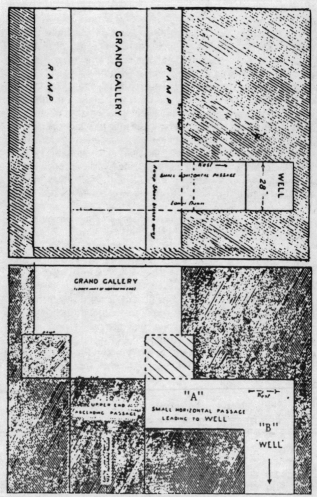

Fig. 69

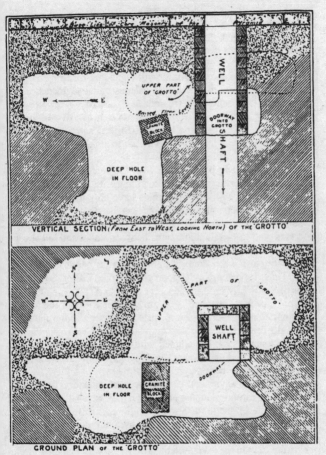

VERTICAL SECTION *(From East to West, Looking North)* of the 'GROTTO'

GROUND PLAN of the 'GROTTO'

Fig. 70

Though the theories of the Edgars (further expounded by Adam Rutherford in *Pyramidology*) have been adopted by all such pyramidologists as well as by some Egyptologists, they still fall short of solving the enigmas. If the long sections *E* and *F* were emergency Inspection Shafts—why their precise and time-consuming construction? What was the purpose of the original vertical sections *B* and *D?* When and why was the irregular, twisting section *C* forced through the masonry? And what about the granite plugs: Why were they needed if there had been no funeral and no burial? To these questions there has been no satisfactory answer, neither by pyramidologists nor by Egyptologists.

Yet the arduous and zealous measuring and remeasuring by both groups hold the key to the answers: the essential segments of the Well Shaft, we believe, were indeed executed by the original builders, but neither as an afterthought nor in response to an emergency. They were, rather, the fruit of forethought: features intended to serve as architectural guidelines in the construction of the pyramid.

Much has already been written over the centuries of the Great Pyramid's wonderful proportions and remarkable geometric ratios. However, because all other pyramids have only lower inner passages and chambers, the tendency has persisted to view the whole upper system as a later-phase development. As a result, little attention was paid to certain alignments between upper and lower features of the pyramid, which can be accounted for only if the upper and lower parts were planned and executed at one and the same time. Thus, for example, the point at the Grand Gallery where the floor rises abruptly to form the Great Step Up (*U*), the central axis of the "Queen's Chamber" (*Q*), and a Recess (*R*) at the lowest short horizontal passage—are all placed exactly on one line, the pyramid's center line. Also, an enigmatic Down Step (*S*) in the upper Horizontal Passage is aligned with the point marking the end (*P*) of the Descending Passage. And there are more such puzzling alignments, as our next diagram will show.

Were all these alignments coincidences, architectural freaks—or the result of careful planning and layout? As we shall now show, these and other hitherto unrecognized alignments flowed from the ingenious, yet simple, planning of the pyramid. And we will also prove that the original segments of the Well Shaft were integral elements not only in the execution but also in the very planning of the pyramid.

Let us begin with segment *D,* because we believe that it was the very first one. It is now generally agreed that the rocky knoll on which the pyramid was erected was flattened out in a stepped manner. The lowest face of the rock (which can be seen outside) formed the Base Line; the uppermost face of the rock is at the Grotto level; there, the bottom layer ("course") of the pyramid's masonry can be seen. Since segment *D* lies below this masonry, it had to be cut and fashioned through the Grotto and the bedrock before anything above it was constructed; i.e., before the Well Shaft segments *A*, *B*, and *C*. Because the only way to tunnel through the rock is from its exposed face downward, segment *E*, which begins its downward slope precisely from the end of *D*, could have been cut only after segment *D* was completed; *F* had to follow *E*, and *G* came last.

In other words, *D* must have been constructed with great precision (see Fig. 70), through the Grotto and the rock, *before* all the other segments of the Well Shaft. But why was it located where it is; why is it precisely vertical; why did it not continue all the way up but was made of the length of which it is?

Why, for that matter—a fact that has gone completely unnoticed—is segment *E* inclined to *D* and to the Base Line at the precise angle of 45°? And why, if *E* was meant to serve as a connecting shaft, did it not simply continue until it reached the Descending Passage but instead turned at an angle to become segment *F*? And why is this segment, *F*—another unnoticed feature—inclined to the Ascending Passage at the precise right angle of 90°?

To answer these questions we have asked ourselves: How did the pyramid's architects design and achieve these symmetries, perfect alignments, and remarkable geometric congruations? The solution we have come up with can best be illustrated by a drawing (Fig. 71); it is a layout plan of the pyramid's insides, prepared by us—we believe—as it might have been drawn by the pyramid's own builders: a simple, yet ingenious, architectural plan that achieves the impressive symmetry, alignments, and perfection with the aid of a few lines and three circles!

The construction of the pyramid began with the leveling of the rocky knoll on which it was to rise. To give the structure greater stability the rock was cut to the Base Level only near the pyramid's circumference; at its core the face of the rock was higher, rising in stages. It was then, we believe, that the Grotto—a natural deformity in the rock or perhaps an artificial cavity—was selected as the point where the structure's alignments were to begin.

There, the first of the shafts, *D*, was placed vertically through the Grotto—partly cut through the rock and partly built with masonry blocks (see Fig. 70). Its height (see Fig. 71) delineates precisely the distance from the Base Level to the level where the rock ends and the masonry begins at the pyramid's core.

It has been long recognized that the value π —the factor governing the ratios between a circle or a sphere, its linear elements and its

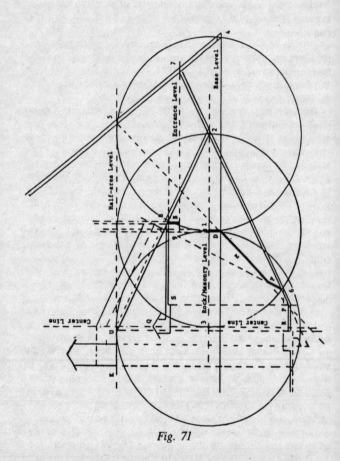

Fig. 71

area projections—has been employed in determining the circumference, sides, and height of the pyramid. As our drawing clearly shows, not only the pyramid's envelope but also everything inside it was determined with the aid of three equal circles.

Theodolitic equipment placed within shaft *D* beamed upward a key vertical line whose function we shall soon describe. But first this equipment beamed out the horizontal rock/masonry line, on which the centers of the three circles were placed. The first of these (Point 1) was at *D;* Points 2 and 3, where its circle intersected the line, served as centers for the other two, overlapping circles.

To draw these circles the pyramid's architects, of course, had to decide on the proper radius. Researchers of the Great Pyramid have been long frustrated by the inability to apply to its perfect proportions any of the ancient Egyptian units of measurement—neither the common cubit of 24 fingers nor the Royal cubit of 28 fingers (20.63″ or 525 millimeters). Some three centuries ago Sir Isaac Newton concluded that an enigmatic "Sacred Cubit" of some 25.2″ was used not only in the construction of the pyramid but also in the construction of Noah's Ark and the temple in Jerusalem. Both Egyptologists and pyramidologists now accept this conclusion as far as the pyramid is concerned. Our own calculations show that the radius adopted for the three circles envisioned by us was equal to 60 such Sacred Cubits; the number 60 being, not accidentally, the base number of the Sumerian sexagesimal mathematical system. This measure of 60 Sacred Cubits is dominant in the lengths and heights of the pyramid's inner structure as well as in the dimensions of its base.

Having selected the radius, the three circles were drawn; and now the pyramid began to take shape: where the second circle intersected the Base Level (Point 4), the pyramid's side was to rise at the angle of 52°—a perfect angle because it is the only one which incorporates the π ratios into the pyramid.

From the bottom of shaft *D*, shaft *E* was then tunneled down, precisely inclined at 45° to *D*. The theodolite-beam projected from *E* upward, intersecting circle 2 at Point 5, provided the sloping line for the pyramid's side and also marked off the half-area Level, on which the King's Chamber and the Antechamber were to be placed (the 5–U–K line) and the Grand Gallery was to end. Projected downwards, the *E* slope determined point *P* at which the Descending Passage was to end, and the vertical line from *P* determined the Down Step *S* in the upper Horizontal Passage.

Turning to the third circle, we see that its center (Point 3) marked the vertical center line of the pyramid. Where it intersected the half-area Line, the Great Up Step (*U*) was placed, marking the end of the Grand Gallery and the beginning of the King's Chamber floor. It also determined the position of the Queen's Chamber (*Q*), which was placed exactly on the center line. By connecting Point 2 with Point *U*, the floor line of the Ascending Passage and the Grand Gallery was obtained.

Shaft *F* was then tunneled from the end of the shaft *E*, precisely so that its beam intersected the ascending floor line 2–U at a right angle (90°). From its intersection with the first circle (Point 6), a line was drawn through Point 2, all the way up to the side of the pyramid (Point 7). This delineated the Descending Passage, its junction with the Ascending Passage (at Point 2), and the entrance to the pyramid.

The shafts *D*, *E*, and *F* and the three circles have thus made possible most of the essential features of the Great Pyramid. Still undetermined, however, were the points at which the Ascending Passage would end and the Grand Gallery begin and, accordingly, where the level of the Horizontal Passage to the Queen's Chamber would be. Here was, we believe, where shaft *B* came into play. No one has so far pointed out the fact that its length is precisely equal to that of *D* and that it marks off exactly the distance between the Entrance Level and the level of the Horizontal Passage. *B* was placed where the Ascending Line intersected circle 2 (Point 8). Its vertical extension marks the beginning of the rising wall of the Grand Gallery; the distance from Point 8 to Point 9, where the beam from *D* intersects the horizontal line from 8, is the place of the grandiose intersection depicted in Fig. 68.

Segment *B*, connected at Point 8 to the passages through the short level segment *A*, thus enabled the pyramid's builders to complete it inside. When that was done, there was no longer any architectural or functional use for these segments, and the entrance to them was covered by placing there a well-fitting, wedge-shaped ramp stone (Fig. 72).

Segments *D*, *E*, and *F* have also disappeared from view as the pyramid's masonry rose over the rocky base. It was then, perhaps, the function of the less precisely built segment *G* to enable the withdrawal of the beaming-theodolites from the *D–E–F* segments, or to make last-minute checks. Finally, where the Descending Passage connected with this segment *G*, the opening was covered with

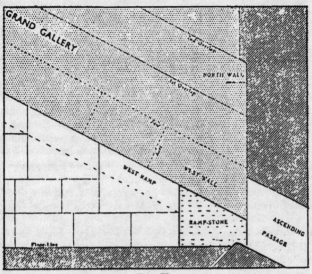

Fig. 72

a well-fitting stone block; and these lower segments, too, disappeared from view.

The pyramid stood complete, with all the segments of the Well Shaft in their hidden places; all, that is, except one, which as we have shown had absolutely no function or purpose in the pyramid's planning and construction.

The exception is the irregular and uncharacteristic segment *C*, unevenly twisting through the masonry, rudely, crudely, and forcibly cut through the limestone courses in a manner that left many stone blocks broken and protruding. When, why, and how did this enigmatic section, *C*, come into being?

That section, we believe, was not yet in existence when the pyramid was completed by its constructors. It was, we will show, hurriedly forced through later on, when Marduk was imprisoned alive in the Great Pyramid.

That Marduk was imprisoned alive in the "Mountain Tomb," there is no doubt; texts that have been found and authoritatively translated attest to that. Other Mesopotamian texts throw light on the nature of his offense. All together they enable us to arrive at a plausible reconstruction of the events.

Evicted from Babylon and Mesopotamia, Marduk returned to Egypt. He promptly established himself in Heliopolis, enhancing its role as his "cult center" by assembling his celestial memorabilia in a special shrine, to which Egyptians made pilgrimages for a long time thereafter.

But seeking to reestablish his hegemony over Egypt, Marduk found that things had changed since he left Egypt to attempt his coup d'état in Mesopotamia. Though Thoth, we gather, did not put up a struggle for supremacy, and Nergal and Gibil were far from the center of power, a new rival had emerged in the interim: Dumuzi. That younger son of Enki, his domain bordering Upper Egypt, was emerging as a pretender to the throne of Egypt.

And behind his ambitions was none other than his bride Inanna/Ishtar—another cause for Marduk's suspicions and dislike.

The tale of Dumuzi and Inanna—he a son of Enki, she a granddaughter of Enlil—reads like an ancient tale of Romeo and Juliet. Like Shakespeare's drama, it, too, ended in tragedy, death, and revenge.

The first presence of Inanna/Ishtar in Egypt is mentioned in the Edfu text dealing with the First Pyramid War. Called there Ashtoreth (her Canaanite name), she is said to have appeared on the battlefield among the advancing forces of Horus. The reason for this inexplicable presence in Egypt might have been to visit her bridegroom Dumuzi, through whose district the fighting force was passing. That Inanna had gone to visit Dumuzi ("The Herder") in his faraway rural district, we know from a Sumerian text. It tells us how Dumuzi stood awaiting her arrival and echoes his reassuring words to a bride baffled by a future in a foreign land:

> The young lad stood waiting;
> Dumuzi pushed open the door.
> Like a moonbeam she came forth to him . . .
> He looked at her, rejoiced in her,
> Took her in his arms and kissed her.
> The Herder put his arm around the maiden;
> "I have not carried you off into slavery," [he said];
> "Your table will be a splendid table,
> the splendid table where I myself eat . . ."

At that time Inanna/Ishtar had the blessing of her parents, Nannar/Sin and Ningal, as well as of her brother Utu/Shamash, to the Romeo-and-Juliet love match between a granddaughter of Enlil and a son of Enki. Some brothers of Dumuzi, and probably Enki himself, also gave their consent. They presented Inanna with a gift of lapis lazuli, the blue-hued precious stone she cherished. As a surprise they hid beads and squares of the stone under a heap of her favorite fruit: dates. In the bedroom she found ''a bed of gold, adorned with lapis lazuli, which Gibil had refined for her in the abode of Nergal.''

And then the fighting broke out, and brother fought brother. As long as the fighting was only between the descendants of Enki, no one saw any particular problem in having a granddaughter of Enlil around. But after the victory of Horus, when Seth occupied lands not his, the situation changed completely: The Second Pyramid War pitched the sons and grandchildren of Enlil against the descendants of Enki. ''Juliet'' had to be separated from her ''Romeo.''

When the lovers were reunited after that war, and their marriage consummated, they spent many days and nights in bliss and ecstasy—the subject of numerous Sumerian love songs. But even as they were making love Inanna was whispering provoking words to Dumuzi:

> As sweet as your mouth are your parts,
> they befit a princely status!
> Subdue the rebellious country, let the nation multiply;
> I will direct the country rightly!

Another time she confessed to him her vision:

> I had a vision of a great nation
> choosing Dumuzi as God of its country . . .
> For I have made Dumuzi's name exalted,
> I gave him status.

With all that it was not a happy union, for it did not produce an heir—an essential requirement, it appears, for carrying out the divine ambitions. Thus it came to pass that in an attempt to have a male heir, Dumuzi resorted to a tactic adopted way back by his own father: he tried to seduce and have intercourse with his own sister. But whereas in bygone days Ninharsag agreed to Enki's advances, Dumuzi's sister Geshtinanna refused. In his desperation Dumuzi violated a sexual taboo: he raped his own sister.

The tragic tale is recorded on a tablet catalogued by scholars as CT.15.28–29. The text relates how Dumuzi bade Inanna good-bye as he announced his plan to go to the desert-plain where his flocks were. By prearrangement his sister, "the song-knowing sister, was sitting there." She thought she was invited for a picnic. As they were "eating the pure food, dripping with honey and butter, as they were drinking the fragrant divine beer," and "were spending the time in a happy mood . . . Dumuzi took the solemn decision to do it." To prepare his sister for what he had in mind, Dumuzi took a lamb and copulated it with its mother, then had a kid copulate with its sister lamb. As the animals were committing incest, Dumuzi was touching his sister in emulation, "but his sister still did not understand." As Dumuzi's actions became more and more obvious, Geshtinanna "screamed and screamed in protest"; but "he mounted her . . . his seed was flowing into her vulva. . . ." "Halt!" she shouted, "it is a disgrace!" But he did not stop.

Having done his deed, "the Shepherd, being fearless, being shameless, spoke to his sister." What he said is unfortunately lost to us due to breaks in the tablet. But we suspect that he had— "fearlessly, shamelessly" as the text had stated—gone on to explain to Geshtinanna the reasons for his deed. That it was premeditated is clear from the text; it is also stated that Inanna was in on the plan: Dumuzi, prior to leaving, "spoke to her of planning and advice" and Inanna "to her spouse answered about the plan, to him she gave her advice."

Rape, under the moral codes of the Anunnaki, was a serious sexual transgression. In the earliest times, when the first teams of astronauts had landed on Earth, a court-martial sentenced their supreme commander Enlil to exile for having raped a young nurse (whom he later married). Dumuzi had surely known all this; so he either expected his sister to engage in the intercourse willingly or else had compelling reasons for his deed which overrode the prohibition. Inanna's prior consent brings to mind the biblical tale of Abraham and his sonless wife Sarah, who offered him her maidservant so that he might have a male heir.

Aware that he had done a horrible deed, Dumuzi was soon thereafter seized with a premonition that he was to pay for his deed with his life, as told in the Sumerian text SHA.GA.NE. IR IM.SHI— "His Heart Was Filled With Tears." Composed in the form of a self-fulfilling dream, the text relates how Dumuzi fell asleep and dreamed that all his attributes of status and property were being taken away from him one by one, by the "Princely Bird" and a falcon. The nightmare ended with Dumuzi seeing himself lying dead in the midst of his sheepfolds.

Waking up, he asked his sister Geshtinanna to tell him the meaning of the dream. "My brother," she said, "your dream is not favorable, it is very clear to me." It foretold "bandits rising against you from ambush . . . your hands will be bound in handcuffs, your arms will be bound in fetters." No sooner had Geshtinanna finished talking than the evil ones appeared beyond the hill and caught Dumuzi.

Bound in handcuffs and fetters, Dumuzi cried out an appeal to Utu/Shamash: "O Utu, you are my brother-in-law, I am your sister's husband. . . . Change my hands into a gazelle's hands, change my feet into a gazelle's feet, let me escape the evil ones!" Hearing his appeal, Utu enabled Dumuzi to escape. After some adventures Dumuzi sought a hiding place in the house of Old Belili—a questionable character playing a double role. Dumuzi was captured again and again escaped. In the end he found himself hiding once again in the sheepfolds. A strong wind was blowing, the drinking cups were overturned; the evil ones closed in on him—all as he had seen in his dream. And in the end:

> The drinking cups lay on their side;
> Dumuzi was dead.
> The sheepfold was thrown into the wind.

The arena of these events, in this text, is a desertlike plain near a river. The geography is enlarged upon in another version of the events, a text titled "The Most Bitter Cry." Composed as a lament by Inanna, it tells how seven deputies of Kur entered the sheepfold and aroused Dumuzi from his sleep. Unlike the previous version, which simply referred to the seizure of Dumuzi by "evil ones," this text makes it clear that they had come on higher authority: "My master has sent us for you," the chief deputy announced to the awakened god. They proceed to strip Dumuzi of his divine attributes:

> Take the divine headdress off your head,
> get up bareheaded;
> Take the royal robe off your body,
> get up naked;

Lay aside the divine staff which is in your hand,
get up empty-handed;
Take the holy sandals off your feet,
get up barefooted!

The seized Dumuzi manages to escape and reaches the river "at
the great dike in the desert of E.MUSH (Home of the snakes").
There was only one such place in Egypt, where desert and river
met at a great dike: at the first Nile Cataract, the place where nowadays the great dam of Aswan is located.

But the swirling waters did not let Dumuzi reach the other
riverbank where his mother and Inanna were standing by to offer
him protection. Instead "there did the boat-wrecking waters carry
the lad towards Kur; to Kur did the boat-wrecking waters carry
the espoused of Inanna."

This and other parallel texts reveal that those who had come to
seize Dumuzi were in fact arresting him in accordance with the orders given by a higher god, the Master of Kur, who "a sentence did
pass upon him." But it could not have been a sentence passed by
the full Assembly of the gods: Enlilite gods, such as Utu/Shamash
and Inanna, were helping Dumuzi escape. The sentence, then, was
one-sided, passed only by the authority of the master of the arresting deputies. He was none other than Marduk, the elder brother of
both Dumuzi and Geshtinanna.

His identity comes through in the text named by scholars "The
Myths of Inanna and Bilulu." In it the shady Old Belili turns out to
have been a male, the Lord Bilulu (EN.BILULU) in disguise, and
the very deity who directed the punitive action against Dumuzi.
Akkadian texts dealing with divine epithets explained that En-
Bilulu was *il Marduk sha hattati,* "the god Marduk who had
sinned," and "The Sorrower of Inanna."

Having disapproved of the Dumuzi-Inanna love match from the
beginning, Marduk no doubt was even more opposed to the union
after the Pyramid Wars. The rape of Geshtinanna by Dumuzi—
politically motivated—was thus an opportunity for Marduk to
block the designs Inanna had on Egypt, by seizing and punishing
Dumuzi. Did Marduk intend to put Dumuzi to death? Probably
not; solitary exile was the customary punishment. The death of
Dumuzi, in a manner that has remained unclear, was probably accidental.

But whether accidental or not was irrelevant to Inanna. As far as she was concerned, Marduk had caused her beloved's death. And, as the texts make clear, she sought revenge:

What is in holy Inanna's heart?
To Kill!
To kill the Lord Bilulu.

Working with fragments found in the collections of Mesopotamian tablets dispersed in several museums, scholars have pieced together parts of a text that Samuel N. Kramer *(Sumerian Mythology)* named "Inanna and Ebih." He considered it as belonging to the cycle of "slaying-of-the-dragon myths," for it deals with Inanna's struggle against an evil god hiding inside "The Mountain."

The available fragments relate how Inanna armed herself with an array of weapons to attack the god in his hiding place. Though the other gods tried to dissuade her, she confidently approached The Mountain, which she called E.BIH ("Abode of Sorrowful Calling"). Haughtily she proclaimed:

Mountain, thou art so high,
thou art elevated above all others . . .
Thou touchest the sky with thy tip . . .
Yet I shall destroy thee,
To the ground I shall fell thee . . .
Inside thine heart pain I will cause.

That The Mountain was the Great Pyramid, that the confrontation was at Giza in Egypt, is evident not only from the texts, but also from a depiction on a Sumerian cylinder seal (Fig. 73). Inanna—shown in her familiar enticing, half-naked pose—is seen confronting a god based upon three pyramids. The pyramids are depicted exactly as they appear to view in Giza; the Egyptian ankh sign, the priest in an Egyptian headdress, and the entwined serpents add up to one locale: Egypt.

As Inanna continued to challenge Marduk, now hiding inside the mighty structure, her fury rose as he ignored her threats. "For the second time, infuriated by his pride, Inanna approached [the pyramid] again and proclaimed: 'My grandfather Enlil has permitted me to enter inside The Mountain!' " Flaunting her weapons, she haughtily announced: "Into the heart of The Mountain I shall penetrate . . . Inside The Mountain, my victory I shall establish!" Getting no response, she began her attack:

Fig. 73

She ceased not striking the sides of E-Bih
and all its corners,
even its multitude of raised stones.
But inside . . . the Great Serpent who had gone in
his poison ceased not to spit.

Anu himself then intervened. The god hiding inside, he warned
her, possessed awesome weapons; "their outburst is terrible; they
will prevent you from entering." Instead Anu advised her to seek
justice by putting the hiding god on trial.

The texts amply identify this god. As in the Ninurta texts, he is
called A.ZAG and nicknamed The Great Serpent—a name and a
derogatory Enlilite epithet for Marduk. His hiding place is also
clearly identified as "the E.KUR, whose walls awesomely reach
the skies"—the Great Pyramid.

The record of the trial and sentencing of Marduk is available
from a fragmentary text published by the Babylonian Section of the
Museum of the University of Pennsylvania. The extant lines begin
where the gods had surrounded the pyramid, and a god chosen to
be a spokesman addressed Marduk "in his enclosure"; "the one
who was evil he implored." Marduk was moved by the message:
"Despite the anger of his heart, clear tears came into his eyes";
and he agreed to come out and stand trial. The trial was held within
sight of the pyramids, in a temple by the riverbank:

To the place of reverence, by the river,
with him who was accused they stepped.
In truth they made the enemies stand aside.
Justice was performed.

In sentencing Marduk the mystery of Dumuzi's death posed a problem. That Marduk was responsible for his death there was no doubt. But was it premeditated or accidental? Marduk deserved a death sentence, but what if his crime was not deliberate?

Standing there, in sight of the pyramids, with Marduk fresh out of his hiding place, the solution dawned on Inanna, and she proceeded to address the gods:

On this day, the Lady herself,
She who speaks truth,
The accuser of Azag, the great princess,
An awesome judgment uttered.

There was a way to sentence Marduk to death without actually executing him, she said: Let him be buried alive within the Great Pyramid! Let him be sealed there as in a gigantic envelope:

In a great envelope that is sealed,
With no one to offer him nourishment;
Alone to suffer,
The potable watersource to be cut off.

The judging gods accepted her suggestions: "The mistress art thou . . . The fate thou decreest: let it be so!" Assuming that Anu would go along with the verdict, "the gods then placed the command to Heaven and Earth." The Ekur, the Great Pyramid, had become a prison; and one of the epithets of its mistress was, thereafter, "Mistress of the Prison."

It was then, we believe, that the sealing of the Great Pyramid was completed. Leaving Marduk alone in the King's Chamber, the arresting gods released behind them the granite plugs of the Ascending Passage, irrevocably blocking tight all access to the upper chambers and passages.

Through the channels leading from the "King's Chamber" to the north and south faces of the pyramid, Marduk had air to breathe; but he had neither food nor water. He was buried alive, doomed to die in agony.

* * *

The record of Marduk's entombment, alive, within the Great Pyramid has been preserved on clay tablets found in the ruins of Ashur and Nineveh, the ancient Assyrian capitals. The Ashur text suggests that it had served as a script for a New Year's mystery play in Babylon that reenacted the god's suffering and reprieve. But neither the original Babylonian version, nor the Sumerian historical text on which the script was based, have so far been found.

Heinrich Zimmern, who transcribed and translated the Ashur text from clay tablets in the Berlin Museum, created quite a stir in theological circles when he announced its interpretation at a lecture in September 1921. The reason was that he interpreted it as a pre-Christian *Mysterium* dealing with the death and resurrection of a god, and thus an earlier Christ tale. When Stephen Langdon included an English translation in his 1923 volume on the Mesopotamian New Year Mystery Texts, he titled the text *The Death and Resurrection of Bel-Marduk* and highlighted its parallels to the New Testament tale of the death and resurrection of Jesus.

But, as the text relates, Marduk or Bel ("The Lord") did not die; he was indeed incarcerated inside The Mountain as in a tomb; but he was entombed alive.

The ancient "script" begins with an introduction of the actors. The first one "is Bel, who was confined in The Mountain." Then there is a messenger who brings the news of the imprisonment to Marduk's son Nabu. Shocked by the news, Nabu hastens to The Mountain in his chariot. He arrives at a structure and the script explains: "that is the house at the edge of The Mountain wherein they question him." In reply to the guards' questions, they are told that the agitated god is "Nabu who from Borsippa comes; it is he who comes to seek after the welfare of his father who is imprisoned."

Actors then come out and rush about on the stage; "they are the people who in the streets hasten; they seek Bel, saying: 'Where is he held captive?' " We learn from the text that "after Bel had gone into The Mountain, the city fell into tumult" and "because of him fighting within it broke out." A goddess appears; she is Sarpanit, the sister-wife of Marduk. She is confronted by a messenger "who weeps before her, saying: 'Unto The Mountain they have taken him.' " He shows her the garments of Marduk (possibly blood-stained): "these are his raiment, which they took off him," he says; instead of these, he reports, Marduk "with a Garment-of-Sentence was clothed." What the audience is shown are shrouds: "That means: in a coffin he is." Marduk has been buried!

Sarpanit goes to a structure that symbolizes Marduk's tomb. She sees a group of mourners. The script explains:

These are those who make lament
after the gods had locked him up,
separating him from among the living.
Into the House of Captivity,
away from the sun and light,
they put him in prison.

The drama has reached its ominous peak: Marduk is dead. . . .

But wait—all hope is not lost! Sarpanit recites an appeal to the two gods who can approach Inanna regarding Marduk's incarceration, her father Sin and her brother Utu/Shamash: "She prays to Sin and Shamash, saying: 'Give life to Bel!' "

Priests, a stargazer, and messengers now appear in procession, reciting prayers and incantations. Offerings are made to Ishtar, "that she may show her mercy." The high priest appeals to the supreme god, to Sin and to Shamash: "Restore Bel to life!"

Now the drama takes a new turn. Suddenly the actor who represents Marduk, clothed with shrouds which "with blood are dyed," speaks out: "I am not a sinner! I shall not be smitten!" He announces that the supreme god has reviewed his case and found him not guilty.

Who, then, was the murderer? The attention of the audience is diverted to a doorpost; "it is the doorpost of Sarpanit in Babylon." The audience learns that the real guilty god has been captured. They see his head through the doorway: "That is the head of the evildoer, whom they shall smite and slay."

Nabu, who had returned to Borsippa, "comes back from Borsippa; he comes and stands over the evildoer and regards him." We do not learn the identity of The Evildoer, except to be told that Nabu had seen him before in Marduk's company. "This is the sinner," he says, and thereby seals the captive's fate.

The priests grab The Evildoer; he is slain: "The one whose sin it was" is carried away in a coffin. The murderer of Dumuzi has paid with his life.

But is the sin of Marduk—as the indirect cause of Dumuzi's death—atoned? Sarpanit reappears, wearing the Garments-of-Atonement. Symbolically she wipes away the blood that has been spilled. With pure water she washes her hands: "It is water for hand-washing which they bring after The Evildoer has been carried away.'' In "all the sacred places of Bel" torches are lit. Again, appeals are directed to the supreme god. The supremacy of Ninurta, which had once been proclaimed when Ninurta vanquished Zu, is reasserted, apparently to allay any fear that a released Marduk might become a challenger for supremacy among the gods. The appeals succeed, and the supreme god sends the divine messenger Nusku to ''announce the [good] tidings to all the gods.''

As a gesture of good will, Gula (the spouse of Ninurta) sends to Sarpanit new clothing and sandals for Marduk; Marduk's driverless chariot also appears. But Sarpanit is dumbfounded: she cannot understand how Marduk can be free again if he had been imprisoned in a tomb *that cannot be unsealed:* ''How can they let him free, the one who cannot come out?''

Nusku, the divine messenger, tells her that Marduk shall pass through SA.BAD, the ''chiseled upper opening.'' He explains that it is

Dalat biri sha iqabuni ilani
A doorway-shaft which the gods will bore;

Shunu itasrushu ina biti etarba
Its vortex they will lift off,
his abode they shall reenter.

Dalta ina panishu etedili
The door which was barred before him

Shunu hurrate ina libbi dalti uptalishu
At the vortex of the hollowing, into the insides,
a doorway they shall twistingly bore;

Qarabu ina libbi uppushu
Getting near, into its midst they will break through.

This description of how Marduk shall be released has remained meaningless to scholars; but the verses are explosively meaningful to us. As we have explained, the irregular and twisting segment *C* of the Well Shaft had not existed when the pyramid was completed and when Marduk was imprisoned within it; it was, instead, the very ''doorway-shaft which the gods will bore'' to rescue Marduk.

Still familiar with the pyramid's inner layout, the Anunnaki realized that the shortest and quickest way to reach the starved Marduk was to tunnel a connecting shaft between the existing segments *B* and *D*—a tunneling of a mere thirty-two feet through the relatively soft limestone blocks; it was a task that could be achieved not in days but in hours.

Removing the stone that covered the Well Shaft's entrance from the Descending Passage to *G,* the rescuers quickly climbed up inclined segments *F* and *E.* Where *E* connected with vertical segment *D,* a granite stone covered the entrance in the Grotto; it was pushed aside—*and still lies there, in the Grotto*—as we have shown in Fig. 70. Now the rescuers climbed the short distance up segment *D,* and faced the first course of the pyramid's masonry.

Thirty-two feet above but to the side lay the bottom of vertical segment *B* and the way into the Grand Gallery. But who could have known how to bore a twisting connecting shaft—*C*—except those who had built the pyramid, knew of its inner sealed-off upper sections, and had the plans to locate them?

It was the rescuers of Marduk, we suggest, who used their tools to break through the limestone blocks, the link between *D* and *B:* "a hollowing into its insides they shall twistingly bore," in the words of the ancient text.

Achieving the linkup with *B,* they clambered to the short, horizontal passage, *A.* There, any stranger would have stopped short even if he had gone that far up, for all he would have seen would be a stone wall—solid masonry. Again we suggest that only the Anunnaki, who had the pyramid's plan, could have known that beyond the stone facing them there lay the immense cavity of the Grand Gallery, the Queen's Chamber, and all the other upper chambers and passages of the pyramid.

To gain access to those chambers and passages it was necessary to remove the wedgelike ramp stone (Fig. 72). But it was wedged too tightly and could not be moved.

If the stone would have been moved away, it would have still been lying there, in the Grand Gallery. Instead, there is a gaping hole (Fig. 68), and those who have examined it have invariably used the words *blown up* and *blown open* to describe what it looks like; and it was done not from the Gallery but from inside the Shaft: "the hollow has the appearance of having been burst open by tremendous force from within" the Shaft (Rutherford, *Pyramidology*).

Again the Mesopotamian record offers a solution. The stone was indeed removed *from within* the horizontal passageway, because it was from there that the rescuers had arrived. And it was indeed "burst open by a tremendous force"; in the words of the ancient text, "Getting near, into its midst they will break through." The fragments of the limestone block slid down the Ascending Passage, down all the way to the granite plugs; that is where Al Mamoon's men found them. The explosion also covered the Grand Gallery with the fine, white dust the Arabs had found covering the floor of the Grand Gallery—mute evidence of the ancient explosion and the gaping hole it had left.

Having broken through into the Grand Gallery, the rescuers led Marduk back the way they came. The entry from the Descending Passage was sealed up again, to be discovered by Al Mamoon's men. The granite plugs remained in place with the triangular junction stone hiding the plugs and the Ascending Passage for millennia. And, inside the pyramid, the original upper and lower parts of the Well Shaft were now for all future days connected by a twisting, harshly tunneled segment.

And what of the rescued Prisoner of the pyramid?

Mesopotamian texts relate that he went into exile; in Egypt Ra acquired the epithet *Amen*, "The Hidden One."

Circa 2000 B.C., he reappeared to claim again supremacy; for that, mankind ended up paying a most bitter price.

11

"A QUEEN AM I!"

The tale of Inanna/Ishtar is a tale of a "self-made goddess." Neither one of the Olden Gods, the original group of astronauts from the Twelfth Planet, nor even a firstborn daughter of one of them, she nevertheless propelled herself to the highest ranks and ended up a member of the Pantheon of Twelve. To achieve that she combined her cunning and her beauty with ruthlessness—a goddess of war and a goddess of love, who counted among her lovers both gods and men. And it was she of whom there had been a true case of death and resurrection.

Inasmuch as the death of Dumuzi was brought about by Inanna's desire to become a queen on Earth, the imprisonment and exile of Marduk did little to satisfy her ambitions. Now, having challenged and prevailed over a major god, she felt she could no longer be deprived of a domain of her own. But where?

The funeral of Dumuzi, one gathers from such texts as *Inanna's Descent to the Lower World,* was held in the Land of Mines in southern Africa. It was the domain of Inanna's sister Ereshkigal and her spouse Nergal. Enlil and Nannar, even Enki, advised Inanna not to go there; but she made up her mind: "From the Great Above she set her mind toward the Great Below"; and when she arrived at the gate of her sister's capital city, she said to the gatekeeper: "Tell my elder sister, Ereshkigal," that she had come "to witness the funeral rites."

One would expect the meeting between the sisters to have been heartwarming, filled with sympathy for the bereaved Inanna. We learn instead that Inanna, who came uninvited, was received with unrestrained suspicion. As she was let through the seven gates of the city leading to Ereshkigal's palace, she was made to give up her emblems and regalia of divine status. When Inanna finally came into the presence of her sister, she found her sitting on her throne surrounded by seven Anunnaki with a judicial capacity. "They fastened their eyes upon her, the eyes of death." They said angry things to her, "words which torture the spirit." Instead of being welcomed, Inanna was sentenced to be hung as a corpse from a stake. . . . It was only through the intervention of Enki that she was saved and revived.

The texts do not explain the reasons for the harsh treatment meted out to Inanna, nor quote the "torturing words" her accusers cast at her. But we learn from the beginning of the text that at the same time that she went on her trip, Inanna sent her messenger to "fill heaven with complaints for me, in the assembly [of the gods] cry out for me." Attending a funeral was thus a mere pretext; what she had in mind was to force the gods to satisfy a complaint that she wished to dramatize.

From the moment of her arrival at the first gate, Inanna threatened violence if she would not be let in. When the news of her arrival was brought to Ereshkigal, "her face turned pale . . . her lips turned dark" and she wondered out loud what the real purpose of the visit was. When the two came face-to-face, "Ereshkigal saw her and burst out at her presence; Ishtar, unflinching, flew at her." Somehow Inanna's intentions spelled danger for Ereshkigal!

We have already found that many of the biblical marital and succession laws were akin to such laws that governed the behavior of the Anunnaki; the rules regarding a half-sister are but one example. The clue to Inanna's intentions, we believe, can be found in the book of Deuteronomy, the fifth book of Moses, in which the Hebrew code of personal behavior was spelled out. Chapter 25 (verses 5–10) deals with the instance when a married man dies without having had a son. If the man had a brother, the widow could not remarry a stranger: it was the duty of the brother—even a married one—to marry his widowed sister-in-law and have children by her; and the firstborn boy was to bear the name of the deceased brother, "so that his name shall not be blotted out."

This, we believe, is what had also been Inanna's reason for her risky journey. For Ereshkigal was married to Nergal, a brother of Dumuzi: Inanna had come to put the Rule into play. . . . The custom, we know, put the onus on the eldest brother, who was, in the case of the sons of Enki, Marduk. But Marduk was found guilty of indirectly causing the death of Dumuzi, and was punished and exiled. Had Inanna then the right to demand that the next in line, Nergal, take her as his second wife so that she could have a male heir?

The personal and succession problems that Inanna's intentions would have caused Ereshkigal can well be imagined. Would Inanna be satisfied to be a second wife, or would she connive and scheme to usurp the queenship over the African domain? Obviously Ereshkigal was not willing to take chances. And so it was, we believe, that after harsh words between the sisters, Inanna was hauled before a hastily convened court of "seven Anunnaki who judge," was found in violation of the rules, and was summarily hung on a stake to die a slow death. She survived only because her father-in-law, Enki, on hearing the terrible news, rushed two emissaries to save her. "Upon the corpse they directed that which pulsates and that which radiates"; they administered to her the "water of life" and the "food of life," and "Inanna arose."

Back in Sumer the revived Inanna, heartbroken and lonely, spent her time on the banks of the Euphrates River, tending a wild-growing tree and voicing her sorrows:

> When at last shall I have a holy throne,
> that I may sit on it?
> When at last shall I have a holy bed,
> that I may lie on it?
> Concerning this Inanna spoke . . .
> She who let her hair down is ill at heart;
> The pure Inanna, Oh how she weeps!

One who had taken pity on—and a liking to—Inanna was her great-grandfather, Anu. It is known from Sumerian texts that Inanna, who was born on Earth, "went up to Heaven" at least once; it is also known that Anu had visited Earth on several occasions. When and where exactly did Anu embrace Inanna as his *Anunitum* ("Beloved of Anu") is not clear, but it was more than mere Sumerian gossip when texts hinted that the love between Anu and his great-granddaughter was more than platonic.

Assured thus of sympathy at the highest level, Inanna raised the issue of a dominion, a "land," to rule over. But where?

The treatment meted out to Inanna, whatever its reasons, made it clear that she could not expect to attain a dominion in Africa. Her spouse Dumuzi was dead, and with him died her claims to queenship in the lands of Enki's descendants. If her suffering and prevailing over a major god entitled her to a dominion of her own, it had to be elsewhere. But Mesopotamia, too, and the lands bordering on Mesopotamia were all spoken for. Where could Inanna be given dominion? Casting their eyes about, the gods came up with an answer.

The texts dealing with the death of Dumuzi, as well as with the imprisonment of Marduk, mention the names of Sumerian cities and their populace. This suggests that those events had taken place after the Sumerian urban civilization had already begun circa 3800 B.C. On the other hand, the Egyptian background of the tales makes no reference to urban settlements and describes a pastoral environment, suggesting a time prior to 3100 B.C., when urban civilization in Egypt began. In the writings of Manetho a chaotic period of 350 years is said to have preceded the urban kingship of Menes. That period between 3450 and 3100 B.C. appears to have been the time of the troubles and tribulations triggered by Marduk: the Tower of Babel incident; and the Dumuzi affair, when a god of Egypt was captured and killed, when the Great God of Egypt was imprisoned and exiled.

It was then, we believe, that the Anunnaki turned their attention to the Third Region of the Indus Valley, where civilization began soon thereafter.

Unlike the Mesopotamian and Egyptian civilizations that lasted for millennia and continued, to this very day, through offspring civilizations, the one in the Third Region lasted only a millennium. Soon thereafter it began to decline, and by 1600 B.C. it was totally gone—its cities in ruins, its people dispersed. Human plunder and the ravages of nature gradually obliterated the civilization's remains; in time it was totally forgotten. It was only in the 1920s that archaeologists, led by Sir Mortimer Wheeler, began to unearth two principal centers and several sites in between, stretching over more than four hundred miles from the Indian Ocean coast northward, along the Indus River and its tributaries.

Both sites—Mohenjo-Daro to the south and Harappa in the north—show that they were cities of substance, some three miles in circumference. High walls ran around and within the cities; these walls, as well as the public and private buildings, were all constructed of bricks made of clay or mud. Originally there were so many of these bricks that in spite of constant ransacking by subsequent home-builders both in ancient times as well as more recently for such purposes as ballast for the Lahore-Multan railroad, enough still remains standing to reveal the site of the cities and the fact that they were laid out in accordance with preconceived city building plans.

At both sites the city was dominated by an acropolis—a raised area of citadels and temples. In both instances these structures were of the same measurements and similarly oriented exactly on a north-south axis—proving that their builders followed strict rules when it came to erecting the temples. In both cities the second largest feature was immense granaries—grain silos of a vast size and impressive functionality, situated near the riverbank. This suggests that grains were not only the chief crop, but also the chief export product of the Indus civilization.

The cities and the few artifacts that were still found in their remains—furnaces, urns, pottery, bronze tools, copper beads, some silver vessels, and ornaments—all attest to a high civilization that was suddenly transplanted from elsewhere. Thus the two earliest brick buildings at Mohenjo-Daro (a huge granary and a fort tower) were reinforced with timbers—a construction method totally unsuitable to the Indus climate. This method, however, was soon abandoned, and all subsequent construction avoided timber-reinforcing. Scholars have concluded from this that the initial builders were foreigners accustomed to their own climatic needs.

Seeking the fountainhead of the Indus civilization, scholars concluded that it could not have arisen independently of the Sumerian civilization, which preceded it by almost a thousand years. In spite of notable differentiations (such as the yet undeciphered pictographic script), the analogies to Mesopotamia are everywhere. The use of dried mud or clay bricks for construction; the layout of city streets; the drainage system; the chemical methods used for etching, for glazing, and for bead-making; the shapes and design of metal daggers and jars—all bear striking similarity to what had been uncovered at Ur or Kish or other Mesopotamian sites. Even the designs and symbols on pottery, seals, or other clay objects are virtual duplicates of those of Mesopotamia. Significantly the Mesopotamian sign of the cross—the symbol of Nibiru, the Home Planet of the Anunnaki—was also prevalent throughout the Indus civilization.

Which gods did the people of the Indus Valley worship? The few pictorial depictions that have been found show them wearing the divine Mesopotamian horned headdress. More abundant clay figurines indicate that the dominant deity was a goddess, usually naked and bare-chested (Fig. 74a) or with rows of beads and necklaces as her sole covering (Fig. 74b); these were well-known depictions of Inanna, found in abundance in Mesopotamia and throughout the Near East. It is our suggestion that in their search for a land for Inanna, the Anunnaki decided to make the Third Region her dominion.

Although it is generally held that the evidence for the Mesopotamian origins of the Indus civilization and for ongoing contacts between Sumer and the Indus Valley is limited to the few archaeolog-

a

b

Fig. 74

ical remains, we believe that there also exists textual evidence attesting to these links. Of particular interest is a long text named by scholars *Enmerkar and the Lord of Aratta,* whose background is the rise to power of Uruk (the biblical Erech) and of Inanna.

The text describes Aratta as the capital of a land situated beyond mountain ranges and beyond Anshan; i.e., beyond southeastern Iran. This is precisely where the Indus Valley lay; and such scholars as J. van Dijk (*Orientalia* 39, 1970) have surmised that Aratta was a city "situated on the Iranian plateau or on the Indus river." What is most striking is the fact that the text speaks of the grain silos of Aratta. It was a place where "wheat was growing of itself, beans also growing of themselves"—crops growing and stored in the storehouses of Aratta. Then, to be exported, they "poured grain into sacks, loaded them on the crate-carrying donkeys, and placed them on the sides of the transporting donkeys."

Aratta's geographical location and the fact that it is a place renowned for its grain and bean storehouses bear forceful similarities to the Indus civilization. Indeed one must wonder whether Harappa or *Arappa* is not a present-day echo of the ancient *Aratta.*

The ancient tale takes us back to the beginning of kingship at Erech, when a demigod (the son of Utu/Shamash by a human female) was both high priest and king at the sacred precinct from which the city was to develop. Circa 2900 B.C. he was succeeded by his son Enmerkar, "who built Uruk" (according to the Sumerian King Lists), transforming it from the nominal abode of an absentee god (Anu) to a major urban center of a reigning deity. He achieved this by persuading Inanna to choose Erech as her principal seat of power and by aggrandizing for her the Eanna ("House of Anu") temple.

We read in the ancient text that at first all Enmerkar demanded of Aratta was that it contribute "precious stones, bronze, lead, slabs of lapis lazuli" to the building of the enlarged temple, as well as "artfully fashion gold and silver" so that the Holy Mount being raised for Inanna would be worthy of the goddess.

But no sooner was this done than the heart of Enmerkar grew haughty. A drought had afflicted Aratta, and Enmerkar now demanded not only materials but also obedience: "Let Aratta submit to Erech!" he demanded. To achieve his purpose Enmerkar sent to Aratta a series of emissaries to conduct what S. N. Kramer *(History*

Begins at Sumer) has characterized as "the first war of nerves." Lauding his king and his powers, the emissary quoted verbatim Enmerkar's threats to bring desolation upon Aratta and dispersion upon its people. The ruler of Aratta, however, countered this war of nerves with a ploy of his own. Reminding the emissary of the confusion of languages in the aftermath of the Tower of Babel incident, he claimed he could not understand the message given him in Sumerian.

In frustration Enmerkar sent another message written on clay tablets—this time, it appears, in the language of Aratta—a feat made possible with the help of Nidaba, the Goddess of Writing. In addition to threats an offering of the seeds of "the olden grain" that had been kept in Anu's temple was made—a seed, it appears, needed badly in Aratta because a long drought had destroyed its crops. The drought was deemed to have been a sign that it was Inanna herself who wished Aratta to come "under the protecting shade of Erech."

"The lord of Aratta from the herald took the baked tablet; the lord of Aratta examined the clay." The writing was in cuneiform script: "The dictated word was nail-like in appearance." Was he to yield or resist? Just at that moment "a storm, like a great lion attacking, stepped up"; the drought was suddenly broken by a thunderstorm that made the whole land tremble, the mountains quake; and once again, "white-walled Aratta" became a land of abundant grains.

There was no need to yield to Erech; and the lord of Aratta said to the herald: "Inanna, the queen of the lands, has not abandoned her House in Aratta; she has not handed over Aratta to Erech."

In spite of the rejoicing in Aratta, its expectation that Inanna would not abandon her abode there was not entirely fulfilled. Enticed by the prospect of residing in a grand temple at Sumer's City of Anu, she became a commuting goddess: a "working deity," so to speak, in faraway Aratta, but a resident in metropolitan Erech.

She did her commuting by flying from place to place in her "Boat of Heaven." Her flying about gave rise to many depictions of her as an aeronaut (Fig. 75), and the inference from some texts is that she did her own piloting. On the other hand, like other major deities, she was assigned a pilot-navigator for the more demanding flights. As the Vedas, which spoke of pilots of the gods (one, Pushan, "guided Indra through the speckled clouds" in the "golden ship that travels in the air's mid-region"), so did the earlier Sumerian texts refer to the AB.GALs, who ferried the gods across the heavens. Inanna's pilot-navigator, we are told, was Nungal; and he was specifically named in regard to her transfer to the House of Anu in Erech:

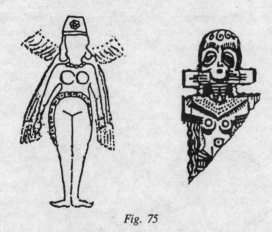

Fig. 75

At the time when Enmerkar in Uruk ruled,
Nungal, the lion-hearted, was the Pilot
who from the skies brought Ishtar down
to the E-Anna.

According to the Sumerian King Lists, kingship after the Deluge began at Kish. Then, "the Kingship to the *Eanna* was carried." As archaeologists have confirmed, Erech indeed had its beginnings as a temple city, consisting of the sacred precinct where Anu's first modest shrine ("White Temple") was built atop a raised platform (Fig. 76); the site remained in the city's heart even as Erech grew and its temples were aggrandized, as the remains of the city and its walls indicate (Fig. 77).

Archaeologists have come upon the remains of a magnificent temple dedicated to Inanna and dating to the early part of the third millennium B.C.—possibly the very temple constructed by Enmer-

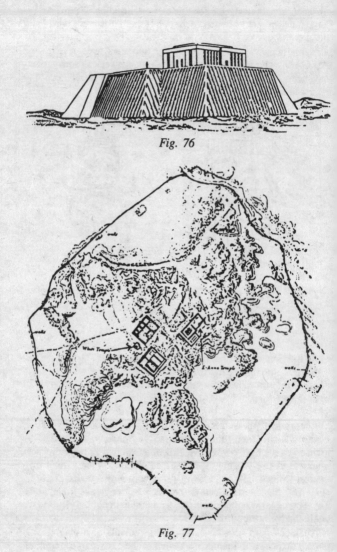

Fig. 76

Fig. 77

kar. It was uniquely built with decorated high columns (Fig. 78) and must have been as lavish and impressive as the hymns that sang its praises had described:

Fig. 78

With lapis-lazuli was adorned,
Decorated with the handiwork of Ninagal.
In the bright place . . .
the residence of Inanna,
the lyre of Anu they installed.

With all that, Erech was still a "provincial" town, lacking the stature of other Sumerian cities, which had the distinction of having been rebuilt on the sites of pre-Diluvial cities. It lacked the status and benefits that stemmed from the possession of the "Divine MEs." Though they are constantly referred to, the nature of the ME is not clear, and scholars translate the term as "divine commandments," "divine powers," or even "mythic virtues." The ME, however, are described as physical objects that one could pick up and carry, or even put on, and which contained secret knowledge or data. Perhaps they were something like our present-day computer chips, on which data, programs, and operational orders have been minutely recorded. On them the essentials of civilization were encoded.

These MEs were in the possession of Enki, the chief scientist of the Anunnaki. They were released by him to benefit mankind gradually, step by step; and the turn of Erech to attain the heights of civilization had, apparently, not yet come when Inanna became its resident deity. Impatient, Inanna decided to use her feminine charms to improve the situation.

A text titled by S. N. Kramer *(Sumerian Mythology)* as "Inanna and Enki," but whose original (and more poetic) Sumerian title is unknown, describes how Inanna journeyed in her "Boat of Heaven" to the Abzu, where Enki had secreted away the MEs. Realizing that Inanna was coming to call on him by herself—"the maiden, all alone, has directed her step to the Abzu"—Enki ordered his chamberlain to prepare a sumptuous meal, including plenty of date wine. After Inanna and Enki had feasted and Enki's heart became happy with drink, Inanna brought up the subject of the MEs. Gracious with drink, Enki presented to her ME for "Lordship . . . , Godship, the Exalted and Enduring Tiara, the Throne of Kingship," and "bright Inanna took them." As Inanna worked her charms on her aging host, Enki made to her a second presentation of "the Exalted Scepter and Staff, the Exalted Shrine, Righteous Rulership"; and "bright Inanna took them," too.

As the feasting and drinking went on, Enki parted with seven major MEs, embracing the functions and attributes of a Divine Lady, her temple and rituals, its priests, eunuchs, and prostitutes; warfare and weapons; justice and courts; music and arts; masonry; woodworking and metal working; leatherwork and weaving; scribeship and mathematics; and so on.

With the encoded data for all these attributes of a high civilization in her hands, Inanna slipped away and took off in her Boat of Heaven, back to Erech. Hours later a sobered Enki realized that Inanna and the MEs were gone. His somewhat embarrassed chamberlain reminded Enki that he, Enki himself, had made the MEs a present to Inanna. Greatly upset, Enki ordered his chamberlain to pursue Inanna in Enki's "Great Heavenly Skychamber" and retrieve the MEs. Overtaking Inanna at the first stopping point, the chamberlain explained to Inanna his orders; but Inanna, asking, "Why had Enki changed his word to me?" refused. Reporting the situation to Enki, the chamberlain was ordered to seize Inanna's Boat of Heaven, bring the Boat to Eridu, and release Inanna, but without the MEs. But in Eridu, Inanna ordered her trusted pilot to "save the Boat of Heaven and the MEs presented to Inanna." And so, while Inanna kept the argument with Enki's chamberlain going, her pilot slipped away in her boat with the invaluable MEs.

An *Exaltation of Inanna,* composed to be read responsively by the congregation, echoes the sentiments of the people of Erech:

Lady of the MEs, Queen
>> Brightly resplendent;
Righteous, clothed in radiance
>> Beloved of Heaven and Earth;
Hierodule of Anu,
>> Wearing the great adorations;
For the exalted tiara appropriate,
>> For the high-priesthood suitable.
The seven MEs she attained,
>> In her hand she is holding.
Lady of the great MEs,
>> Of them she is the guardian . . .

It was in those days that Inanna was incorporated into the Pantheon of Twelve, and (replacing Ninharsag) was assigned the planet Venus (MUL DILBAT) as her celestial counterpart and the constellation AB.SIN (Virgo) as her zodiac house; the latter's depiction has hardly changed from Sumerian times (Fig. 79). Expressing her own gratification, Inanna announced for all—gods and men alike—to hear: "A Queen am I!"

Fig. 79

Hymns acknowledged her new status among the gods and her celestial attributes:

To the one who comes forth from heaven,
To the one who comes forth from heaven,
"Hail!" we do say . . .
Loftiness, greatness, reliability [are hers]
as she comes forth radiantly in the evening,

a holy torch that fills the heavens;
Her stance in heaven is like the Moon and Sun . . .
In Heaven she is secure, the good "wild cow" of Anu;
On Earth she is enduring, mistress of the lands.
In the Abzu, from Eridu, she received the MEs;
Her godfather Enki presented them to her,
Lordship and Kingship he placed in her hand.
With Anu she takes her seat upon the great throne,
With Enlil she determines the fates in her land . . .

Turning from her high position among the gods to her worship by the Sumerians (the "Black-Headed People"), the hymns went on:

In all the land, the black-headed people assemble
when abundance has been placed in the storehouses of Sumer . . .
They come to her with . . . , they bring disputes before her.
She renders judgment to the evil and destroys the wicked;
She favors the just, determines good fate for them . . .
The good lady, the joy of Anu, a heroine she is;
She surely comes forth from Heaven . . .
She is mighty, she is trustworthy, she is great;
She is exceeding in youthfulness.

The people of Erech had every reason to be thankful to Inanna, for under her deityship, Erech had become an affluent center of Sumerian civilization. In praising her wisdom and valor, the people of Erech failed not also to mention her beauty and attractiveness. Indeed, it was at about that time that Inanna instituted the custom of the "Sacred Marriage," sexual rites whereby the priest-king was supposed to have become her spouse—but only for a night. A text, attributed to a king named Iddin-Dagan, described this aspect of Inanna's temple life—with music, male prostitute entertainers, and all:

The male-prostitutes comb her hair . . .
They decorate the neck with colored bands . . .
Their right side they adorn with women's clothing
as they walk before the pure Inanna . . .
Their left side they cover with men's clothing
as they walk before the pure Inanna . . .

With jump ropes and colored cords they compete before
  her . . .
The young men, carrying hoops, sing before her . . .
The maidens, *Shugia* priestesses, walk before Inanna . . .
They set up a bed for my lady,
They cleanse rushes with sweet smelling cedar oil;
For Inanna, for the King, they arrange the bed . . .
The king approaches her pure lap proudly;
Proudly he approaches the lap of Inanna . . .
He caresses her pure lap,
She stretches out on the bed, the pure lap;
She makes love with him on her bed.
She says to Iddin-Dagan: "Surely, you are my beloved."

This habit of Inanna may have begun with Enmerkar himself, a
sexual union of which the next ruler of Uruk, a demigod known as
"divine Lugalbanda, a Righteous Supervisor," was the progeny.
Of Lugalbanda, too, as of Enmerkar, several epic tales have been
found. Inanna, it seems, wanted him to reside in her stead in
Aratta; but Lugalbanda was too restless and adventurous to stay
put. One epic tale *(Lugalbanda and Mount Hurum)* describes his
dangerous journey to the "awesome place on Earth" in search of
the Divine Black Bird. He reached the Restricted Mount "where
the Anunnaki, gods of the mountain, inside the earth like termites
had tunneled." Seeking a ride in the Bird of Heaven, Lugalbanda
pleaded with its custodian; his words immortalized man's desire to
fly:

Like Utu let me go, like Inanna,
Like the Seven Stormers of Ishkur
in a flame let me lift myself off,
and thunder away!
Let me go wherever my eyes can see,
Wherever I desire, let me set my foot,
Wherever my heart wishes, let me arrive . . .

When he had arrived at Mount Hurum ("whose front Enlil as
with a great door had closed off"), Lugalbanda was challenged by
the Guardian: "If a god you are, a word in friendship will I utter
which will let you enter; If a man you are, your fate will I decree."
To which:

Lugalbanda, he of beloved seed,
stretched his hand out [and said]:
"Like divine Shara am I,
the beloved son of Inanna."

But the Guardian of the sacred place turned Lugalbanda down with an oracle: indeed, he would reach far lands and make both himself and Erech famous, but he would do so on foot.

Another long epic tale, originally called by scholars "Lugalbanda and Enmerkar" and more recently *The Lugalbanda Epic,* affirms Lugalbanda's semi-divine descent but does not identify his father; we can assume, however, from the circumstances and subsequent events, that the father was Enmerkar; confirming Enmerkar as the first one in a long list of rulers who, under the guise of a symbolic marriage or without it, were invited by Inanna to share her bed.

This "invitation" by Inanna is featured in the well-known *Epic of Gilgamesh.* The fifth ruler of Erech, Gilgamesh sought to escape the mortals' destiny to die because, as a son of the goddess Ninsun and the high priest of the Kullab, "two thirds of him were god." In his search for immortality (examined at length in *The Stairway to Heaven*), he first journeyed to the "Landing Place" in the Cedar Mountain—the olden landing platform in the mountains of Lebanon (to which, apparently, Lugalbanda had also gone). Battling the mechanical monster that guarded the restricted area's perimeter, Gilgamesh and his companion were almost annihilated were it not for Utu's help. Exhausted from the battle, Gilgamesh took off his drenched clothes so that he might wash and rest. It was then that Inanna/Ishtar, who watched the struggle from the skies, was seized with a craving for Gilgamesh:

He washed his grimy hair, polished his weapons;
The braid of his hair he shook out against his back.
He cast off his soiled things, put on his clean ones,
Wrapped a fringed cloak about, fastened with a sash.
When Gilgamesh put on his tiara,
Glorious Ishtar raised an eye at the beauty of Gilgamesh.
"Come, Gilgamesh, be thou my lover!" [she said]
"Do grant me of thy fruitfulness;
thou shalt be a husband, I shall be a wife."

She reinforced her invitation with promises of a glorious (though not everlasting) life if Gilgamesh will accede to her offer. But Gilgamesh retorted with a long list of her lovers whom she befriended though she had "ordained for Tammuz [Dumuzi], the lover of your youth, wailing year after year"; while still supposedly in mourning, he said, she acquired and discarded lovers "as a shoe which pinches the foot of its owner . . . as a door which does not keep out the wind . . . Which lover didst thou love forever?" he asked; "if thou shouldst make love to me, thou wouldst treat me like them." (The offended Inanna thereupon received Anu's permission to launch against Gilgamesh the Bull of Heaven; Gilgamesh was saved from it at the last moment at the gates of Erech).

The golden era of Erech was not to last forever. Seven other kings followed Gilgamesh on its throne. Then, "Uruk was smitten with weapons; its kingship to Ur was carried." Thorkild Jacobsen, whose study *The Sumerian King List* is the most thorough on the subject, believes that the transfer of kingship in Sumer from Erech to Ur occurred circa 2850 B.C.; others adopt a lower date of circa 2650 B.C. (Such a discrepancy of two centuries has persisted into later times and remains unexplained by scholars.)

The reigns of the various rulers were getting shorter and shorter as the site of kingship swung back and forth among Sumer's principal cities: from Ur to Awan, then back to Kish; to a city named Hamazi, then back to Erech and Ur; to Adab and Mari, and back to Kish; to Aksak and again to Kish; and finally once more to Erech. In the course of no more than 220 years, there were thus three additional dynasties at Kish, three at Erech, two at Ur, and single ones in five other cities. It was, by all appearances, a volatile period; it was also a time of increasing friction between the cities, mostly over water rights and irrigation canals—phenomena that can be explained by drier weather on the one hand and rising populations on the other. In each instance the town that lost out was said to have been "smitten with weapons." Mankind had begun to wage its own wars!

The resort to arms to settle local disputes was becoming more commonplace. Inscriptions from those days indicate that the harassed populace was competing, through offerings and enhanced worship, for the favors of the gods; the warring city-states increasingly involved their patron-gods in their petty disputes. In one recorded instance Ninurta was involved in determining whether an irrigation ditch encroached on another city's boundaries. Enlil, too, was forced to order the warring parties to disengage. This constant strife and lack of stability soon reached a point when the gods had had enough. Once before, when the Deluge was coming, Enlil was so disgusted with mankind that he schemed its obliteration by the great flood. Then, in the Tower of Babel incident, he ordered mankind's dispersion and the confusion of its languages. Now, again, he was growing disgusted.

The historical background to the events that followed was the final attempt by the gods to reestablish Kish, the original capital, as the center of kingship. For the fourth time they returned kingship to Kish, starting the dynasty with rulers whose names indicate fealty to Sin, Ishtar, and Shamash. Two rulers, however, bore names indicating that they were followers of Ninurta and his spouse—evidence of a revived rivalry between the House of Sin and the House of Ninurta. It resulted in the seating on the throne of a nonentity—"Nannia, a stone cutter"; he reigned a brief seven years.

In such unsettled circumstances Inanna was able to retrieve the kingship for Erech. The man chosen for the task, one Lugal-zagesi, retained the favor of the gods for twenty-five years; but then, attacking Kish to assure her permanent desolation, he only managed to raise Enlil's ire; and the idea of a strong hand at the helm of human kingship made more and more sense. There was a need for someone uninvolved in all these disputes, someone who would provide firm leadership and once again properly perform the role of the king as sole intermediary between the gods and the people in all matters mundane.

It was Inanna who, on one of her flying trips, found that man.

Her encounter with him, circa 2400 B.C., launched a new era. He was a man who began his career as a cup-bearer to the king of Kish. When he took over the state reins in central Mesopotamia, he quickly extended his rule to all of Sumer, to its neighboring countries, and even unto distant lands. The epithet-name of this first empire-builder was *Sharru-Kin* ("Righteous Ruler"); modern textbooks call him Sargon I or Sargon the Great (Fig. 80). He built himself a brand-new capital not far from Babylon and named it *Agade* ("United"); we know it as Akkad—a name from which stems the term *Akkadian* for the first Semitic language.

A text known as *The Legend of Sargon* records, in Sargon's own words, his odd personal history:

> Sargon, the mighty king of Agade, am I.
> My mother was a high priestess; I knew not my father . . .
> My mother, the high priestess, who conceived me,
> in secret she bore me.
> She set me in a basket of rushes, with bitumen sealed the lid.

Fig. 80

She cast me into the river; it did not sink me.
The river bore me up, it carried me to Akki the irrigator.
Akki the irrigator lifted me up when he drew water;
Akki, the irrigator, as his son made me and reared me.
Akki, the irrigator, appointed me as his gardener.

This Moses-like tale (written more than a thousand years before the time of Moses!) then continues to answer the obvious question: How could a man of unknown fatherhood, a mere gardener, become a mighty king? Sargon answered the questions thus:

While I was a gardener, Ishtar granted me her love,
And for four and fifty years I exercised Kingship;
The Black-headed people I ruled and governed.

The laconic statement is elaborated in another text. The encounter between Sargon the workingman and Ishtar the lovely goddess was accidental but far from innocent:

One day my queen,
After crossing heaven, crossing earth—
Inanna.
After crossing heaven, crossing earth—
After crossing Elam and Shubur,
After crossing . . .
The hierodule approached weary, fell asleep.
I saw her from the edge of my garden;
Kissed her, copulated with her.

Inanna—by then awakened, we must assume—found in Sargon a man to her liking, a man who could satisfy not only her bedtime cravings but also her political ambitions. A text known as the *Sargon Chronicle* states that "Sharru-Kin, king of Agade, rose [to power] in the era of Ishtar. He had neither rival nor opponent. He spread his terror-inspiring glamor over all the countries. He crossed the sea in the east; he conquered the country of the west, in its full extent."

The enigmatic reference to the "Era of Ishtar" has baffled the scholars; but it can only mean what it says: at that time, for whatever reasons, Inanna/Ishtar was able to have a man of her choice take the throne and create for her an empire: "He defeated Uruk and tore down its wall. . . . He was victorious in the battle with the inhabitants of Ur . . . he defeated the entire territory from Lagash as far as the sea. . . ." There were also the conquests beyond the olden boundaries of Sumer: "Mari and Elam are standing in obedience before Sargon."

The grandeur of Sargon and the greatness of Inanna, going hand in hand, were expressed in the construction of the new capital city of Agade and in it the UL.MASH ("Glittering, Luxurious") temple to Inanna. "In those days," a Sumerian historiographic text relates, "the dwellings of Agade were filled with gold; its bright-shining houses were filled with silver. Into its storehouses were brought copper, lead and slabs of lapis-lazuli; its granaries bulged at the sides. Its old men were endowed with wisdom, its old women were endowed with eloquence; its young men were endowed with the Strength-of-Weapons, its little children were endowed with joyous hearts. . . . The city was full of music."

In that beautiful and happy city, "in Agade did holy Inanna erect a temple as her noble abode; in the Ulmash she set up a throne." It was the crowning temple in a series of shrines to her that encompassed Sumer's principal cities. Stating that "in Erech, the E-Anna is mine," Inanna listed her shrines in Nippur, Ur, Girsu, Adab, Kish, Der, Akshak, and Umma, and lastly the Ulmash in Agade. "Is there a god who can vie with me?" she asked.

Yet, though promoted by Inanna, the elevation of Sargon to kingship over what was henceforth known as Sumer and Akkad could not have taken place without the consent and blessing of Anu and Enlil. A bilingual (Sumerian-Akkadian) text, originally inscribed on a statue of Sargon that was placed before Enlil in his temple in Nippur, stated that Sargon was not only "Commanding Overseer" of Ishtar, but also "anointed priest of Anu" and "great regent of Enlil." It was Enlil, Sargon wrote, who "had given him lordship and kingship."

Sargon's records of his conquests describe Inanna as actively present on the battlefields but attribute to Enlil the overall decision regarding the scope of the victories and the extent of the territories: "Enlil did not let anybody oppose Sargon, the king of the land; from the Upper Sea to the Lower Sea Enlil gave unto him." Invariably, postscripts to Sargon's inscriptions invoked Anu, Enlil, Inanna, and Utu/Shamash as his "witnesses."

As one scrutinizes this vast empire, stretching from the Upper Sea (Mediterranean) to the Lower Sea (Persian Gulf), it becomes clear that Sargon's conquests were, at first, limited to the domains of Sin and his children (Inanna and Utu) and, even at their peak, kept well within the Enlilite territories. Sargon reached Lagash, the city of Ninurta, and conquered the territory *from* Lagash southward, but not Lagash itself; nor did he expand to the northeast of Sumer where Ninurta held sway. Going beyond the boundaries of olden Sumer, he entered to the southeast the land of Elam—an area under Inanna's influence from earlier times. But when Sargon was entering the lands to the west on the mid-Euphrates and the Mediterranean coast, the domains of Adad, "Sargon prostrated himself in prayer before the god . . . [and] he gave him in the upper region Mari, Yarmuli and Ebla, as far as the cedar forest and the silver mountain."

It is clear from Sargon's inscriptions that he was neither given Tilmun (the gods' own Fourth Region), nor Magan (Egypt), nor Meluhha (Ethiopia) in the Second Region, the domains of Enki's descendants; with those lands he only conducted peaceful trading relations. In Sumer itself he kept out of the area controlled by Ninurta and from the city claimed by Marduk. But then, "in his old age," Sargon made a mistake:

He took away soil from the foundation of Babylon
and built upon the soil another Babylon beside Agade.

To understand the severity of this deed, we ought to recall the meaning of "Babylon"—*Bab-Ili,* "Gateway of the Gods." A title and a function claimed for Babylon by a defiant Marduk, it was symbolized by its hallowed soil. Now, encouraged by Inanna and driven by her ambitions, Sargon took away the sacred soil to spread it as a foundation for the new Bab-Ili, audaciously aiming to transfer the title and function to Agade.

This was, as it turned out, an opportunity for Marduk—unheard from for so many centuries—to reassert himself:

On account of the sacrilege Sargon thus committed,
the great lord Marduk became enraged
and destroyed his people by hunger.
From the east to the west he alienated them from Sargon;
and upon him he inflicted as punishment that he could not rest.

Desperately crushing one revolt after another, Sargon "could not rest"; discredited and afflicted, he died after a reign of fifty-four years.

12

PRELUDE TO DISASTER

The information concerning the last years of the Era of Ishtar comes to us from a number of texts. Put together, they unfold a tale of dramatic and incredible events: the usurpation of supreme powers on Earth by a goddess; the defilement of Enlil's Holy of Holies in Nippur; the penetration of the Fourth Region by a human army; an invasion of Egypt; the appearance of African gods in the Asian domains; acts and occurrences that were unthinkable before; upheavals among the gods, which served as a stage on which human rulers played out their roles and human blood was spilled without mercy.

Faced with the reemergence of her olden adversary, Inanna could simply not give up, no matter what the cost. Seating on Sargon's throne first one of his sons and then another, enlisting in her campaigns her vassal kings in the eastern mountainlands, she fought as an enraged lioness for her disintegrating empire, "raining flame over the land . . . attacking like an aggressive storm."

"You are known by your destruction of the rebel lands," intoned a daughter of Sargon in a plaintive poem; "you are known by massacring their people" . . . turning "against the city that said not 'the land is yours,' " making "its rivers run with blood."

For more than two years Inanna wrought havoc all around, until the gods decided that the only way to stop the carnage was to force Marduk back into exile. Having returned to Babylon when Sargon tried to remove some of its hallowed soil—an act whose symbolism was rooted in legendary events—Marduk fortified the city and in particular ingeniously enhanced its underground water system, making the city impervious to attack. Unable or unwilling to remove Marduk by force, the Anunnaki turned to Marduk's brother Nergal and asked him to "scare Marduk off the divine seat" in Babylon.

We know of these events from a text named by scholars *The Erra Epos*, for in it Nergal is called by the ancient chronicler ER.RA—a somewhat derogatory epithet, for it meant "The Servant of Ra." It is a text that could better be called *The Tale of the*

251

Sins of Nergal, for it puts the blame on Nergal for a chain of events with a catastrophic ending; but it is an invaluable source for our knowledge and understanding of that prelude to disaster.

Having accepted the mission, Nergal/Erra journeyed to Mesopotamia for a face-to-face talk with Marduk. Arriving in Mesopotamia, he first stopped at Erech, ''the city of Anu, the king of all the gods,'' but, of course, also the place to huddle with Inanna/Ishtar. Arriving in Babylon, ''into the Esagil, temple of Heaven and Earth, he entered, and stood before Marduk.'' The momentous encounter has been recorded by the ancient artists (Fig. 81); it depicts both gods holding on to their weapons, but the helmeted Marduk, standing on a platform, does extend some symbol of welcome to his brother.

Fig. 81

Combining praise with reprimand, Erra told Marduk that the wonderful things he had done for Babylon, and especially its waterworks, made Marduk's reputation ''shine as a star in the heavens,'' but have deprived other cities of their waters. Moreover, while crowning himself in Babylon, ''lights up its sacred precinct,'' it angered the other gods; ''the abode of Anu with darkness it covers.'' Marduk, he concluded, could not go on against the will of the other Anunnaki and certainly not against the will of Anu.

But Marduk, citing changes that were made on Earth in the aftermath of the Deluge, explained that he had to take matters into his own hands:

In the aftermath of the Deluge,
the decrees of Heaven and Earth had gone astray.
The cities of the gods upon the wide Earth
were changed around;
They were not brought back to their locations . . .
As I survey them again, of the evil I am disgusted;
Without a return to their [original] places,
Mankind's existence is diminished . . .
Rebuild I must my residence
which in the Deluge was wiped away;
Its name [I must] call again.

Among the post-Diluvian disorders that bothered Marduk were
some failures on the part of Erra himself to account for certain divine artifacts—"the instrument of giving orders, the Oracle of the
Gods; the sign of kingship, the Holy Scepter which contributes
brilliance to Lordship. . . . Where is the holy Radiating Stone
which disintegrates all?" Marduk asked. If he were forced to
leave, Marduk said, "on the day I step off my seat, the flooding
shall from its well cease to work . . . the waters shall not rise . . .
the bright day to darkness [shall turn] . . . confusion shall arise
. . . the winds of draught shall howl . . . sicknesses shall
spread."

After some more exchanges Erra offered to return to Marduk
"the artifacts of Heaven and Earth" if Marduk would personally
go to the Lower World to pick them up; and as to the "works" in
Babylon, he assured Marduk there was nothing to worry about: he
(Erra) would enter Marduk's House only to "erect the Bulls of Anu
and Enlil at thy gate"—statues of Winged Bulls as were actually
found at temple sites—but would do nothing to upset the waterworks.

Marduk heard this;
The promise, given by Erra, found his favor.
So did he step down from his seat,
and to the Land of Mines, abode of the Anunnaki,
he set his direction.

Thus persuaded, Marduk agreed to leave Babylon. But no
sooner he had done that than Nergal broke his word. Unable to resist his curiosity, Nergal/Erra ventured into the *Gigunu*, the mysterious underground chamber which Marduk had stressed was off

limits; and there Erra caused its "Brilliance" (radiating source of energy) to be removed. Thereupon, as Marduk had warned, "the day turned into darkness," the "flooding was disarrayed," and soon "the lands were laid to waste, the people were made to perish."

All of Mesopotamia was affected, for Ea/Enki, Sin and Shamash, in their cities, became alarmed; "with anger [at Erra] they were filled." The people made sacrifices to Anu and Ishtar but to no avail: "the water sources went dry." Ea, Erra's father, reproached him: "Now that Prince Marduk had stepped off, what have you done?" He ordered that a statue of Erra, which had been prepared, should not be set up in the Esagil. "Go away!" he ordered Erra. "Take off to where no gods ever go!"

"Erra lost his voice" only for a moment, then uttered words of impudence. Enraged, he smashed Marduk's abode, set fire to its gates. Defiantly, "he made a sign" as he turned to leave, announcing that his followers, however, will stay behind: "as to my warriors, they shall not go back." And so it was that when Erra returned to Kutha, the men who had come with him stayed behind, establishing a long-lasting presence for Nergal in the lands of Shem; a colony was assigned to them not far from Babylon, perhaps as a permanent garrison; there were "Kutheans who worship Nergal" in Samaria in biblical times; and there was official worship of Nergal in Elam, as evidenced by an unusual bronze sculpture (Fig. 82) found there, depicting worshipers with unmistakable African features performing a cultic ceremony in a temple courtyard.

The departure of Marduk from Babylon brought to an end Ishtar's conflict with him; the rift between Marduk and Nergal and the latter's retention of an Asian presence unintentionally created an alliance between Ishtar and Nergal. The chain of tragic events that no one could have predicted and that no one had perhaps even desired was thus being forged by fate, leading the Anunnaki and Mankind ever closer to the ultimate disaster. . . .

With her authority restored, Inanna renewed the kingship in Agade and put on the throne a grandson of Sargon, Naram-Sin ("Sin's Favorite"). Seeing in him, at last, a true successor to Sargon, she encouraged him to seek grandeur and greatness. After a brief period of peace and prosperity she goaded Naram-Sin to embark on an expansion of the erstwhile empire. Soon Inanna began to encroach on the territories of other gods; but they were unable or unwilling to fight her: "The great Anunnaki gods fled before you like fluttering bats," a hymn to Inanna stated; "they could not

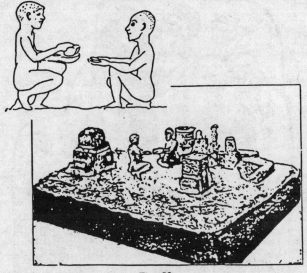

Fig. 82

stand before your fearsome face . . . could not soothe your angry heart.'' Rock carvings in the annexed territories depicted Inanna as the ruthless conqueror she had become (Fig. 83).

At the beginning of her campaigns Inanna was still called ''Beloved of Enlil'' and one ''Who carries out the instructions of Anu.'' But then her thrust began to change in nature, from the suppression of rebellions to a calculated plan for seizing supremacy.

Two sets of texts, one dealing with the goddess and the other with her surrogate, the king Naram-Sin, record the events of those times. Both indicate that the first out-of-bounds target of Inanna was the Landing Place in the Cedar Mountain. As a Flying Goddess Inanna was quite familiar with the place; she ''burnt down the great gates'' of the mountain and, after a brief siege, obtained the surrender of the troops guarding it: ''they disbanded themselves willingly.''

As recorded in the Naram-Sin inscriptions, Inanna then turned south along the Mediterranean coast, subduing city after city. The conquest of Jerusalem—Mission Control Center—is not specifi-

Fig. 83

cally mentioned, but Inanna must have been there, too, for it is recorded that she had gone on to capture Jericho. Lying astride the strategic Jordan River crossing and opposite the Anunnaki stronghold at Tell Ghassul, Jericho—the city dedicated to Sin—had also rebelled: "It said not 'It belongs to your father who begot you'; it had promised its solemn word, but turned away from it." The Old Testament is filled with admonitions against "straying after alien gods"; the Sumerian text conveys the same transgression: The people of Jericho, having given a solemn promise to worship Sin, Inanna's father, have switched allegiance to another, alien, god. The surrender of this "city of date-palms" to an armed Inanna was depicted on a cylinder seal (Fig. 84).

With the conquest of southern Canaan, Inanna stood at the gateway to the Fourth Region, the region of the Spaceport. Sargon had

Fig. 84

not dared cross the forbidden line. But Naram-Sin, encouraged by Inanna, did. . . .

A Mesopotamian royal chronicle attests that not only did Naram-Sin enter the peninsula, but he had gone on to invade the land of Magan (Egypt):

> Naram-Sin, offspring of Sargon, marched against the town of Apishal and made a breach in its wall, conquering it. He personally caught Rish-Adad, king of Apishal, and the vizier of Apishal.
> He then marched against the country of Magan and personally caught Mannu-Dannu, king of Magan.

The accuracy of the above-mentioned Babylonian royal chronicle has been independently confirmed in its other details, so there is no reason to doubt this part of it, too—incredible as it sounds, for it entailed the passage of a human king and a human army through the Sinai peninsula, the gods' own Fourth Region. Since time immemorial, a trade route between Asia and Africa had wound its way along the peninsula's Mediterranean coast—a route later on enhanced by the Egyptians with watering stations and by the Romans as their vital *Via Maris*. Ancient users of this route thus kept well away from the central plain where the Spaceport was located. But whether Naram-Sin, at the head of an army, just marched through along the coastal route is questionable. Alabaster vases of Egyptian design, which have been found by archaeologists in Mesopotamia and Elam, identified their owner (in Akkadian) as "Naram-Sin, King of the Four Regions; vase of the Shining Crown of the land Magan." That Naram-Sin began to call himself "King of the Four Regions" affirms not only the conquest of Egypt but also suggests the inclusion of the Sinai peninsula in his sphere of influence. Inanna, it appears, was more than "just passing through."

(A foreign invasion, about the time of Naram-Sin, is also known from Egyptian records. They describe a period of disarray and chaos. In the words of the papyrus known to Egyptologists as *The Admonitions of Ipuwer,* "Strangers have come into Egypt . . . the high-born are full of lamentation." It was a period that saw the shift of the center of worship and kingship from Memphis-Heliopolis in the north to Thebes in the south. Scholars call the century of disarray "The First Intermediate Period"; it followed the collapse of the sixth Pharaonic dynasty.)

How could Inanna, with apparent immunity, intrude on the Sinai peninsula and invade Egypt unopposed by the gods of Egypt?

The answer lies in an aspect of the Naram-Sin inscriptions that has baffled the scholars: the apparent veneration by this Mesopotamian ruler of the African god Nergal. Although this made no sense at all, the fact is that the long text known as *The Kuthean Legend of Naram-Sin* (or, as it is sometimes called, *The King of Kutha Text*) attests that Naram-Sin went to Kutha, Nergal's cult center in Africa, and erected there a stela to which he affixed an ivory tablet inscribed with the tale of this unusual visit, all to pay homage to Nergal.

The recognition by Naram-Sin of Nergal's power and influence well beyond Africa is attested by the fact that in treaties made between Naram-Sin and provincial rulers in Elam, Nergal is invoked among the witness gods. And in an inscription dealing with Naram-Sin's march to the Cedar Mountain in Lebanon, the king credited Nergal (rather than Ishkur/Adad) with making the achievement possible:

> Although since the era of the rulership of man
> none of the kings has ever destroyed Arman and Ebla,
> Now did the god *Nergal* open up the path for the mighty Naram-Sin.
> He gave him Arman and Ebla, presented him with the Amanus and with the Cedar Mountain and with the Upper Sea.

This puzzling emergence of Nergal as an influential Asian deity, and the audacious march of Inanna's surrogate Naram-Sin to Egypt—all violations of the status quo of the Four Regions established after the Pyramid Wars—have one explanation: While Marduk had shifted his attention to Babylon, Nergal assumed a preeminent role in Egypt. Then, having gone to persuade Marduk to leave Mesopotamia without further struggle, the amicable parting turned into a bitter enmity between the brothers.

And this led to an alliance between Nergal and Inanna; but as they stood for each other, they soon found themselves opposed by all the other gods. An assembly of the gods was held in Nippur to deal with the disruptive consequences of Inanna's exploits; even Enki agreed that she had gone too far. And a decree for her arrest and trial was issued by Enlil.

We learned of these events from a chronicle titled by scholars *The Curse of Agade*. Deciding that Inanna had indeed gotten out of hand, "the word of the Ekur" (Enlil's sacred precinct in Nippur) was issued against her. But Inanna did not wait to be seized or held for trial: she forsook her temple and escaped from Agade:

> The "word of Ekur" was upon Agade
> like a deathly silence;
> Agade was all atremble,
> its Ulmash temple was in terror;
> She who lived there, left the city.
> The maiden forsook her chamber;
> Holy Inanna forsook her shrine in Agade.

By the time a delegation of the great gods arrived in Agade, they only found an empty temple; all they could do was strip the place of its attributes of power:

> In days not five, in days not ten,
> The crownband of lordship, the tiara of Kingship,
> the throne given to rulership
> Ninurta brought over to his temple;
> Utu carried off the city's "Eloquence";
> Enki withdrew its "Wisdom."
> Its Awesomeness that could reach the Heaven,
> Anu brought up to the midst of Heaven.

"The kingship of Agade was prostrated, its future was extremely unhappy." Then "Naram-Sin had a vision," a communication from his goddess Inanna. "He kept it to himself, put it not in speech, spoke with nobody about it. . . . Seven years Naram-Sin remained in wait."

Did Inanna seek out Nergal during her seven-year disappearance from Agade? The text does not give the answer, but we believe that it was the only haven available to Inanna, away from Enlil's wrath. The ensuing events suggest that Inanna—even more audacious than before, more ambitious than ever—must have obtained the backing of at least one other major god; and that could have been only Nergal. That Inanna would hide in Nergal's Lower African domain seems thus a most plausible assumption.

Did the two, talking over the situation, reviewing past events, discussing the future, end up forging a new alliance that could rearrange the divine domains? A New Order was indeed feasible, for Inanna was shattering the Old Divine Order upon the Earth. A text whose ancient title was *Queen of All the MEs* acknowledges that Inanna had indeed, deliberately, decided to defy the authority of Anu and Enlil, abrogated their rules and regulations, and declared herself the Supreme Deity, a "Great Queen of Queens." Announcing that she "has become greater than the mother who gave birth to her . . . even greater than Anu," she followed up her declarations with deeds and seized the E-Anna ("House of Anu") in Erech, aiming to dismantle this symbol of Anu's authority:

> The heavenly kingship was seized by a female . . .
> She changed altogether the rules of Holy Anu,
> Feared not the great Anu.
> She seized the E-Anna from Anu—
> that House of irresistible charm, enduring allure—
> On that House she brought destruction;
> Inanna assaults its people, makes them captive.

The coup d'état against Anu was accompanied by a parallel attack on Enlil's seat and symbols of authority. This task was assigned by Inanna to Naram-Sin; his attack on the Ekur in Nippur and the resulting downfall of Agade are detailed in *The Curse of Agade* text. From it we gather that after the seven-year wait Naram-Sin received further oracles and thereupon "changed his line of action." Upon receiving the new orders:

He defied the word of Enlil,
Crushed those who had served Enlil,
Mobilized his troops, and
Like a hero accustomed to high-handedness
Put a restraining hand on the Ekur.

Overrunning the seemingly undefended city, "like a bandit he plundered it." He then approached the Ekur in the sacred precinct, "erecting large ladders against the House." Smashing his way in, he entered its Holy of Holies: "the people now saw its sacred cella, a chamber that knew not light; the Akkadians saw the holy vessels of the god"; Naram-Sin "cast them into the fire." He "docked large boats at the quay by the House of Enlil, and carried off the possessions of the city." The horrible sacrilege was complete.

Enlil—his whereabouts unstated, but clearly away from Nippur—"lifted his eyes" and saw the destruction of Nippur and the defilement of the Ekur. "Because his beloved Ekur had been attacked," he ordered the hordes of Gutium—a mountainland to the northeast of Mesopotamia—to attack Akkad and lay it waste. They came down upon Akkad and its cities "in vast numbers, like locusts . . . nothing escaped their arm." "He who slept on the roof died on the roof; he who slept inside the house was not brought to burial . . . heads were crushed, mouths were crushed . . . the blood of the treacherous flowed over the blood of the faithful."

Once, and then a second time, the other gods interceded with Enlil: "curse Agade with a baleful curse," they said, but let the other cities and the farmlands survive! When Enlil finally agreed, eight great gods joined in putting a curse on Agade, "the city who dared assault the Ekur." "And lo," said the ancient historian, "so it came to pass . . . Agade is destroyed!" The gods decreed that Agade be wiped off the face of the Earth; and unlike other cities that, having been destroyed, were rebuilt and resettled, Agade forever remained desolate.

As to Inanna, "her heart was appeased" finally by her parents. What exactly happened, the texts do not state. They tell us, however, that her father Nannar came forth to fetch her back to Sumer while "her mother Ningal proffered prayers for her, greeted her back at the temple's doorstep." "Enough, more than enough innovations, O great queen!" the gods and the people appealed to her: "and the foremost Queen, in her assembly, accepted the prayer."

The Era of Ishtar was over.

* * *

All the textual evidence suggests that Enlil and Ninurta were away from Mesopotamia when Naram-Sin attacked Nippur. But the hordes that swept down from the mountains upon Akkad were "the hordes of Enlil," and they were in all probability guided into the great Mesopotamian plain by Ninurta.

The Sumerian King Lists call the land from which the invaders came Gutium, a land in the mountains northeast of Mesopotamia. In the Legend of Naram-Sin they are called Umman-Manda (possibly "Hordes of Far/Strong Brothers"), who came from "camps in the dwelling of Enlil" situated "in the mountainland whose city the gods had built." Verses in the text suggest that they were descendants of soldiers who had accompanied Enmerkar on his distant travels, who "slew their host" and were punished by Utu/Shamash to remain in exile. Now tribes great in number, led by seven chieftain brothers, they were commanded by Enlil to overrun Mesopotamia and "hurl themselves against the people who in Nippur had killed."

For a while feeble successors to Naram-Sin attempted to maintain a central rule as the hordes began to overrun city after city. The confused situation is described in the Sumerian King Lists with the statement: "Who was king? Who was not king? Was Irgigi king? Was Nanum king? Was Imi king? Was Elulu king?'" In the end the Gutians seized control of the whole of Sumer and Akkad; "Kingship by the hordes of Gutium was carried off."

For ninety-one years and forty days the Gutians held sway over Mesopotamia. No new capital is named for them, and it appears that Lagash—the only Sumerian city to escape despoiling by the invaders—served as their headquarters. From his seat in Lagash Ninurta undertook the slow process of restoring the country's agriculture and primarily the irrigation system that collapsed following the Erra/Marduk incident. It was a chapter in Sumerian history that can best be called the Era of Ninurta.

The focal point of that era was Lagash, a city whose beginnings were as a "sacred precinct" (the *Girsu*) for Ninurta and his Divine Black Bird. But as the turmoil of human and divine ambitions grew, Ninurta decided to convert Lagash into a major Sumerian center, the principal abode for himself and his spouse Bau/Gula (Fig. 85), where his ideas of law and order and his ideals of morality and justice could be practiced. To assist in these tasks Ninurta appointed in Lagash human viceroys and charged them with the administration and defense of the city-state.

Fig. 85

The history of Lagash (a site nowadays called Tello) records a dynasty whose reign—uninterrupted for half a millennium—began three centuries before the rise of Sargon. An island of armed stability in an increasingly violent environment, Lagash was also a great center of Sumerian culture. While Sumer's religious holidays emanated from Nippur, Lagash originated traditions of festivals tied to an agricultural calendar, such as the Festivel of First Fruits. Its scribes and scholars perfected the Sumerian language; and its rulers, to whom Ninurta granted the title "Righteous Governor," were sworn to a code of justice and morality.

Prominent among the very first rulers of the long dynasty of Lagash was one named Ur-Nanshe (circa 2600 B.C.). More than fifty of his inscriptions were found in the ruins of Lagash; they record the bringing of building materials for the Girsu, including special timbers from Tilmun for the temple's furnishings. They also describe extensive irrigation works, the digging of canals, and the raising of dykes. On one of his tablets Ur-Nanshe is depicted heading a construction team, not loath to do some manual work himself (Fig. 86). The forty known viceroys who followed him left a written record of achievements in agriculture, construction, social legislation, and ethical reforms—material and moral achievements that would make any government proud.

Fig. 86

But Lagash had escaped the ravages of the turbulent years of Sargon and Naram-Sin not only because it was the "cult center" of Ninurta, but also (and primarily) because of the military prowess of its people. As "Enlil's Foremost Warrior," Ninurta made sure that those selected by him to govern Lagash should be militarily proficient. One (named Eannatum) whose inscriptions and stelas have been found, was a master tactician and victorious general. The stelas show him riding a war chariot—a military vehicle whose introduction has been customarily attributed to later times; they also show his helmeted troops in tight formations (Fig. 87).

Commenting on this, Maurice Lambert *(La Période Pre-Sargonique)* wrote that "this infantry of spearmen, protected by shield-bearers, gave the army of Lagash a defence most solid and an attack most rapid and versatile." The resulting victories of Eannatum even impressed Inanna/Ishtar, so much so that she had fallen in love with him; and "because she loved Eannatum, kingship over Kish she gave him, in addition to the governorship of Lagash." With this Eannatum became the LU.GAL ("Great Man") of Sumer; and holding the land in a military grip, he made law and order prevail.

Fig. 87

Ironically the chaotic period that had preceded Sargon of Agade found in Lagash not a strong military leader but a social reformer named Urukagina. He devoted his efforts to a moral revival and to the introduction of laws based on fairness and justice, rather than on a crime-punishment concept. Under him, Lagash proved too weak to maintain law and order in the land. His weakness enabled Inanna to bring the ambitious Lugal-zagesi of Umma to Erech, in an attempt to restore her countrywide dominion. But the failings of Lugal-zagesi led (as we have already described) to his downfall by the hand of Inanna's new choice, Sargon.

Throughout the period of the primacy of Agade, governorship continued uninterrupted in Lagash; even the great Sargon skirted Lagash and left it intact. It escaped destruction and occupation throughout the upheavals of Naram-Sin, primarily because it was a formidable military stronghold, fortified and refortified to withstand all attacks. We learn from an inscription by Ur-Bau, the viceroy at Lagash at the time of the Naram-Sin upheavals, that he was instructed by Ninurta to reinforce the walls of the Girsu and to strengthen the enclosure of the Imdugud aircraft. Ur-Bau "compacted the soil to be as stone . . . fired clay to be as metal"; and at the Imdugud's platform "replaced the old soil with a new foundation," strengthened with huge timber beams and stones imported from afar.

When the Gutians left Mesopotamia—circa 2160 B.C.—Lagash burst into new bloom and produced some of Sumer's most enlightened and best-known rulers. Of these, one of the best-known from his long inscriptions and many statues was Gudea, who reigned during the twenty-second century B.C. His was a time of peace and prosperity; his records speak not of armies and wars but of trade and reconstruction. He crowned his activities with the building of a new, magnificent temple for Ninurta in a vastly enlarged Girsu. According to Gudea's inscriptions, "the Lord of Girsu" appeared unto him in a vision, standing beside his Divine Black Bird. The god expressed to him the wish that a new E.NINNU ("House of Fifty"—Ninurta's numerical rank) be built by Gudea. Gudea was given two sets of divine instructions: one from a goddess who in one hand "held the tablet of the favorable star of heavens" and with the other "held a holy stylus," with which she indicated to Gudea "the favorable planet" in whose direction the temple should be oriented. The other set of instructions came from a god whom Gudea did not recognize and who turned out to have been Ningishzidda. He handed to Gudea a tablet made of precious stone; "the plan of a temple it contained." One of Gudea's statues depicts him seated with this tablet on his knees, the divine stylus beside it (Fig. 88).

Gudea admits that he needed the help of diviners and "searchers of secrets" to understand the temple plan. It was, as modern researchers have found, an ingenious one-in-seven architectural plan for the construction of a ziggurat as a seven-stage pyramid. The structure contained a strongly reinforced platform for the landing of Ninurta's airborne vehicle.

The participation of Ningishzidda in the planning of the E-Ninnu carried a significance that went beyond mere architectural assistance, as evidenced by the fact that the Girsu included a special shrine for this god. Associated with healing and magical powers, Ningishzidda—a son of Enki—was deemed in Sumerian inscriptions to have known how to secure the foundations of tem-

Fig. 88

ples; he was ''the great god who held the plans.'' As we have already suggested, Ningishzidda was none other than Thoth, the Egyptian god of magical powers who was appointed guardian of the secret plans of the pyramids of Giza.

Ninurta, it will be recalled, had carried off with him some of the ''stones'' from within the Great Pyramid when the Pyramid Wars ended. Now, with the thwarted efforts of Inanna and then Marduk to lord over gods and men, Ninurta wished to reaffirm his ''Rank of Fifty'' by the erection of a step-pyramid for himself at Lagash, an edifice to be known as the ''House of Fifty.'' It was for that reason, we believe, that Ninurta invited Ningishzidda/Thoth to come to Mesopotamia, to design for him a pyramid that could be built and raised high, not with massive stone blocks as in Egypt, but with the humble clay bricks of Mesopotamia.

The stay of Ningishzidda in Sumer and his collaboration there with Ninurta were commemorated not only in shrines to that visiting god, but also in numerous artistic depictions, some of which were discovered during the sixty years of archaeological work at Tello. One of these (Fig. 89a) combined the emblem of Ninurta's Divine Bird with the serpents of Ningishzidda; another (Fig. 89b) depicted Ninurta as an Egyptian Sphinx.

a

b

Fig. 89

The time of Gudea and the Ninurta-Ningishzidda collaboration coincides with the so-called First Intermediate Period in Egypt, when the kings of the IX and X dynasties (2160 to 2040 B.C.) abandoned the worship of Osiris and Horus and moved the capital from Memphis to a city the Greeks later called Heracleopolis. The departure of Thoth from Egypt may thus have been an aspect of the upheavals occurring there, as was his subsequent disappearance from Sumer. Ningishzidda (to quote E. D. van Buren, *The God Ningizzida*) was "a god called forth from obscurity in Gudea's time," only to become a "phantom god" and a mere memory in later (Babylonian and Assyrian) times.

The Era of Ninurta in Sumer, lasting through the Gutian invasion and the ensuing period of reconstruction, was only an interlude. A mountain dweller at heart, Ninurta soon began to roam the skies again in his Divine Black Bird, visiting his rugged domains in the northeast and even farther away. Constantly perfecting the martial arts of his highland tribesmen, he gave them mobility through the introduction of cavalry, thereby extending their reach by hundreds and even thousands of miles.

He had returned to Mesopotamia at Enlil's call, to put an end to the sacrilege perpetrated by Naram-Sin and to the upheavals caused by Inanna. With peace and prosperity restored, Ninurta again absented himself from Sumer; and, never one to give up, Inanna seized upon this absence to regain the kingship for Erech.

The attempt lasted only a few years, for Anu and Enlil did not condone her deed. But the tale (contained in an enigmatic text on a partly broken tablet catalogued as Ashur-13955) is most fascinating; it reads like an ancient legend of the *Excalibur* (King Arthur's magical sword, which was imbedded in a rock and could be pulled out only by the one who was chosen for kingship); and it throws light on preceding events, including the incident by which Sargon had offended Marduk.

We learn that when "Kingship was lowered from Heaven" to begin at Kish, Anu and Enlil established there a "Pavilion of Heaven." "In its foundation soil, for all days to come," they implanted the SHU.HA.DA.KU—an artifact made of alloyed metal whose name translates literally "Supreme Strong Bright Weapon." This divine object was taken to Erech when kingship was transferred there from Kish; it was moved about as kingship moved about but only when the change was decreed by the Great Gods.

In accordance with this custom, Sargon carried the object to Agade. But Marduk protested, because Agade was a brand-new city and not one of the cities selected by "the great gods of Heaven and Earth" to be royal capitals. The gods who chose Agade— Inanna and her supporters—were in Marduk's opinion "rebels, gods who wear unclean clothing."

It was to cure this defect that Sargon went to Babylon to the spot where its "hallowed soil" was located. The idea was to remove some of that soil "to a place in front of Agade," there to implant the Divine Weapon and thus legitimize its presence in Agade. It was in punishment for this, the text states, that Marduk instigated rebellions against Sargon and also inflicted upon him a "restlessness" (some take the term to mean "insomnia".) which led to his death.

We read further in the enigmatic text that during the Gutian occupation that followed Naram-Sin's reign, the divine object lay untouched "beside the dam-works for the waters" because "they knew not how to carry out the rules regarding the divine artifact." It was at that time Marduk's contention that the object had to remain in its assigned place, "without being opened up," and "not being offered to any god," until "the gods who brought the destruction shall make restitution." But when Inanna seized the opportunity to reinstitute kingship in Erech, her chosen king, Utu-Hegal, "seized the *Shuhadaku* in its place of resting; into his hand he took it"—although "the end of the restitution has not yet occurred." Unauthorized, Uthu-Hegal "raised the weapon against the city he was besieging." As soon as he had done that, he fell dead. "The river carried off his sunken body."

Ninurta's absences from Sumer and Inanna's abortive attempt to recapture the kingship for Erech indicated to Enlil that the matter of the divine governing of Sumer could no longer be left open-ended; and the most suitable candidate for the task was Nannar/Sin.

Throughout the turbulent times he was overshadowed by more aggressive contenders for the supremacy, including his own daughter Inanna. Now he was finally given the opportunity to assume the status befitting him as the firstborn (on Earth) of Enlil. The era that followed—let us call it the Era of Nannar—was one of the most glorious in Sumerian annals; it was also Sumer's last hurrah.

His first order of business was to make his city, Ur, a great metropolis and the capital of a vast empire. Appointing a new line of rulers, known by scholars as the Third Dynasty of Ur, Nannar achieved for this capital and for Sumerian civilization unprecedented peaks of material and cultural advancements. From an immense ziggurat that dominated the walled city (Fig. 90)—a ziggurat whose crumbled remains, after more than four thousand years, still rise awesomely from the Mesopotamian plain—Nannar and his spouse Ningal took an active part in the affairs of state. Attended by a hierarchy of priests and functionaries (headed by the king, Fig. 91), they guided the city's agriculture to become the granary of Sumer; directed its sheep breeding to make Ur the wool and gar-

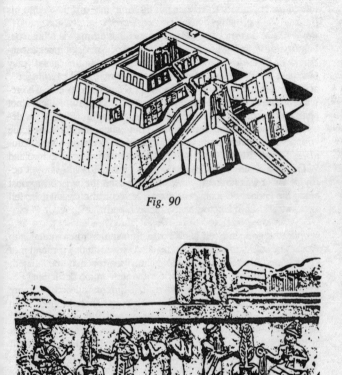

Fig. 90

Fig. 91

ment center of the ancient Near East; and developed a foreign trade by land and water that made the merchants of Ur remembered for millennia thereafter. To service this thriving trade and the far-flung links, as well as to improve the city's defenses, the city's surrounding wall was in turn surrounded by a navigable canal, serving two harbors—a West Harbor and a North Harbor—with an inner canal connecting the two harbors and in turn separating the sacred precinct and the palace and administrative quarter from the residential and commercial parts of the city (Fig. 92). It was a city whose white houses—many of them multistoried (Fig. 93)—shined as a pearl from a distance; whose streets were straight and wide, with many a shrine at their intersections; a city of an industrious people with a smooth-functioning administration; a city of pious people, never failing to pray to their benevolent deities.

The first ruler of the Third Dynasty of Ur, *Ur-Nammu* ("The Joy of Ur") was no mere mortal: he was semi-divine, his mother being the goddess Ninsun. His extensive records state that as soon as "Anu and Enlil had turned over kingship to Nannar at Ur," and Ur-Nammu was selected to be the "Righteous Shepherd" of the people, the gods ordered Ur-Nammu to institute a new moral revival. The nearly three centuries that had passed since the moral revival under Urukagina of Lagash witnessed the rise and fall of Akkad, the defying of the authority of Anu, and the defilement of Enlil's Ekur. Injustice, oppression, and immorality had become the common behavior. At Ur, under Ur-Nammu, an attempt was launched once again by Enlil to steer mankind away from "evil ways" to a course of "righteousness." Proclaiming a new code of justice and social behavior, Ur-Nammu "established equity in the land, banished malediction, ended violence and strife."

Expecting so much from this New Beginning, Enlil—for the first time—entrusted the guardianship of Nippur to Nannar and gave Ur-Nammu the necessary instructions for the restoration of the Ekur (which was damaged by Naram-Sin). Ur-Nammu marked the occasion by erecting a stela, showing him carrying the tools and basket of a builder (Fig. 94). When the work was completed, Enlil and Ninlil returned to Nippur to reside in their restored abode. "Enlil and Ninlil were happy there," a Sumerian inscription stated.

The Return-to-Righteous-Ways involved not only social justice among people, but also proper worship of the gods. To that effect Ur-Nammu, in addition to the great works in Ur, also restored and enlarged the edifices dedicated to Anu and Inanna at Erech, to

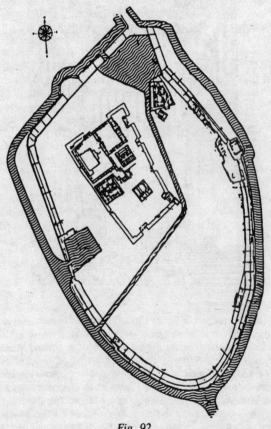

Fig. 92

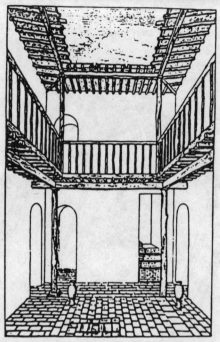

Fig. 93

Ninsun (his mother) at Ur, to Utu at Larsa, to Ninharsag at Adab; he also engaged in some repair work at Eridu, Enki's city. Conspicuously absent from the list are Ninurta's Lagash and Marduk's Babylon.

The social reforms of Ur-Nammu and Ur's achievements in commerce and industry have led scholars to view the times of the Third Dynasty as a period not only of prosperity, but also of peace. They were thus puzzled to find in the ruins of Ur two panels depicting its citizens' activities—one a Peace Panel, and the other, surprisingly, a War Panel (Fig. 95). The image of the people of Ur as trained and ready warriors seemed totally out of place.

Yet the facts, as told by the archaeological evidence of weaponry, military garb, and chariots of war, as well as in numerous inscriptions, belie the image of pacifism. Indeed, one of the first acts

Fig. 94

Fig. 95

of Ur-Nammu was to subdue Lagash and slay its governor, then occupy seven other cities.

The need for military measures was not limited to the initial phases of the ascendancy of Nannar and Ur. We know from inscriptions that after Ur and Sumer "enjoyed days of prosperity [and] rejoiced greatly with Ur-Nammu," after Ur-Nammu then rebuilt the Ekur in Nippur, Enlil found him worthy of holding the Divine Weapon; with it Ur-Nammu was to subdue "evil cities" in "foreign lands":

The Divine Weapon,
that which in the hostile lands
heaps up the rebels in piles,
to Ur-Nammu, the Shepherd,
He, the Lord Enlil, has given it to him;
Like a bull to crush the foreign land,
Like a lion to hunt it down;
To destroy the evil cities,
Clear them of opposition to the Lofty.

These are words reminiscent of biblical prophecies of divine wrath, through the medium of mortal kings, against "evil cities" and "sinful people"; they reveal that beneath the cloak of prosperity there was lurking a renewed warfare among the gods—a struggle for the allegiance of the masses of mankind.

The sad fact is that Ur-Nammu himself, becoming a mighty warrior, "The Might of Nannar," met a tragic death on the battlefield. "The enemy land revolted, the enemy land acted hostilely"; in a battle in that unnamed but distant land, Ur-Nammu's chariot got stuck in the mud; Ur-Nammu fell off it; "the chariot like a storm rushed along," leaving Ur-Nammu behind, "abandoned on the battlefield like a crushed jug." The tragedy was compounded when the boat returning his body to Sumer "in an unknown place had sunk; the waves sank it down, with him [Ur-Nammu] aboard."

When the news reached Ur, a great lament went up there; the people could not understand how such a Righteous Shepherd, one who had been just for the people and true to the gods, could have met such a disgraceful end. They could not understand why "the Lord Nannar did not hold him by the hand, why Inanna, Lady of Heaven, did not put her noble arm around his head, why the valiant Utu did not assist him." Why had these gods "step[ped] aside" when Ur-Nammu's bitter fate was determined? Surely it was a betrayal by the great gods:

How the fate of the hero has been changed!
Anu altered his holy word . . .
Enlil deceitfully changed his fate-decree . . .

The manner in which Ur-Nammu had died (2096 B.C.) may have accounted for the behavior of his successor, of whom one can use the biblical contempt for a king who "prostituted himself" and "did that which was evil in the view of the Lord." Named Shulgi, he was born under divine auspices: it was Nannar himself who had arranged for the child to be conceived at Enlil's shrine in Nippur, through a union between Ur-Nammu and Enlil's high priestess, so that "a little 'Enlil' . . . a child suitable for kingship and throne, shall be conceived."

The new king began his long reign by choosing to keep together his far-flung empire through peaceful means and religious reconciliation. As soon as he ascended the throne, he embarked on the building (or rebuilding) of a temple for Ninurta in Nippur; this enabled him to declare Ur and Nippur to be "Brother-Cities." He then built a ship—naming it after Ninlil—and sailed to the "Land of Flying for Life." His poems indicate that he imagined himself a second Gilgamesh, following in that earlier king's footsteps to the "Land of Living"—to the Sinai peninsula.

Landing at "The Place of the Ramp" (or "Land-fill Place"), Shulgi built there an altar to Nannar. Continuing his journey on land, Shulgi reached the Harsag—Ninharsag's High Mountain in the southern Sinai—and built there an altar, too. Winding his way in the peninsula, he reached the place called BAD.GAL.DINGIR (*Dur-Mah-Ilu* in Akkadian), "The Great Fortified Place of the Gods." He now was indeed emulating Gilgamesh, for Gilgamesh, arriving from the direction of the Dead Sea, had also stopped to pray and make offerings to the gods at that gateway place, situated between the Negev and the Sinai proper. There Shulgi built an altar to the "God Who Judges."

It was the eighth year of Shulgi's reign as he began the journey back to Sumer. His route via the Fertile Crescent began in Canaan and Lebanon, where he built altars at the "Place of Bright Oracles" and "The Snow-covered Place." It was a deliberately slow journey, intended to strengthen the imperial bonds with the distant provinces. It was as a result of this journey that Shulgi built a network of roads that held the empire together politically and militarily and also enhanced trade and prosperity. Getting personally acquainted with the local chieftains, Shulgi further cemented his ties with them by arranging marriages for his daughters.

Shulgi returned to Sumer, boasting that he had learned four foreign languages. His imperial prestige was at its peak. In gratitude he built for Nannar/Sin a shrine in the sacred precinct of Nippur. In return he was rewarded with the titles "High Priest of Anu, Priest of Nannar." Shulgi recorded the two ceremonies on his cylinder seals (Figs. 96, 97).

Fig. 96

Fig. 97

But as time went by, Shulgi increasingly preferred the luxuries of Ur to the rigors of the provinces, leaving their government to Grand Emissaries. He spent his time composing self-laudatory hymns, imagining himself a demigod. His delusions eventually caught the attention of the greatest seductress of all—Inanna. Sensing a new opportunity, she invited Shulgi to Erech, making him "a man chosen for the vulva of Inanna" and engaging in lovemaking in the very temple dedicated to Anu. We quote Shulgi's own words:

> With valiant Utu, a friend as a brother,
> I drank strong drink
> in the temple founded by Anu.
> My minstrels sang for me the seven songs of love.
> Inanna, the queen, the vulva of heaven and earth,
> was by my side, banqueting in the temple.

As the unavoidable restiveness at home and abroad grew, Shulgi sought military support from the southeastern province of Elam. Arranging for his daughter to marry Elam's viceroy, Shulgi gave him as dowry the city of Larsa. In return the viceroy brought into Sumer Elamite troops, to serve Shulgi as a Foreign Legion. But instead of peace the Elamite troops brought more warfare, and the yearly records of Shulgi's reign speak of repeated destruction in the northern provinces. Shulgi attempted to retain his hold on the western provinces by peaceful means, and his thirty-seventh year of reign records a treaty with a local king named Puzur-Ish-Dagan—a name with clear Canaanite/Philistine connotations. The treaty enabled Shulgi to reclaim the title "King of the Four Regions." But the peace in the west did not last long. In his forty-first year (2055 B.C.) Shulgi received certain oracles from Nannar/Sin, and a major military expedition was launched against the Canaanite provinces. Within two years Shulgi could claim once more that he was "Hero, King of Ur, Ruler of the Four Regions."

The evidence suggests that Elamite troops were used in this campaign to subdue the provinces and that these foreign troops had advanced as far as the gateway to the Sinai. Their commander called himself "favorite of the God Who Judges, beloved by Inanna, occupier of Dur-Ilu." But no sooner had the occupying troops withdrawn than the unrest began again. In the year 2049 B.C. Shulgi ordered the building of "The Wall of the West" to protect Mesopotamia.

He stayed on the throne one more shaky year. Although, until the end of his reign, Shulgi continued to proclaim himself "a cherished of Nannar," he was no longer a "chosen" of Anu and Enlil. In their recorded view "the divine regulations he did not carry out, his righteousness he dirtied." Therefore, they decreed for him the "death of a sinner." The year was 2048 B.C.

Shulgi's successor on the throne of Ur was his son Amar-Sin. Though the first two years of his reign were recalled by their warfare, three years of peace did follow. But in the sixth year an uprising needed subduing in the northern district of Ashur, and in the seventh year—2041 B.C.—a major military campaign was required to suppress four western localities and "their lands."

The campaign, apparently, was not too successful, for it was not followed by the customary bestowal of titles on the king by Nannar. Instead we find that Amar-Sin turned his attention to Eridu—Enki's city!—establishing there a royal residence and assuming there priestly functions. This twist in religious filialties might have been prompted by the practical desire to gain control of Eridu's shipyards; for in the following (ninth) year, Amar-Sin set sail to the same "Place of the Ramp" where Shulgi had gone. But reaching the "Land of Flying for Life" he got no farther: he died of a scorpion's (or snake's) bite.

He was replaced on the throne by his brother Shu-Sin. The nine years of his reign (2038–2030 B.C.), though recording two military forays against northern localities, were more conspicuous by their defensive measures. These included the strengthening of the Wall of the West against the Amorites and the construction of two ships: the "Great Ship" and the "Ship of the Abzu." It looks as though Shu-Sin was preparing an escape by sea. . . .

When the next (and last) king of Ur, Ibbi-Sin, ascended the throne, raiders from the west were clashing with the Elamite mercenaries in Mesopotamia proper. Soon Sumer's heartland was under siege; the people of Ur and Nippur were huddled behind protective walls, and the influence of Nannar had shrunk to a small enclave.

Waiting in the wings, as once before, was Marduk. Believing that his time for supremacy had finally come, he left his land of exile and led his followers back to Babylon.

And then Awesome Weapons were unleashed, and disaster—unlike any that befell mankind since the Deluge—struck.

13

ABRAHAM: THE FATEFUL YEARS

And it came to pass
in the days of Amraphel king of Shin'ar,
Ariokh king of Ellasar,
Khedorla'omer king of Elam,
and Tidhal king of Go'im—
That these made war
with Bera King of Sodom,
and with Birsha king of Gomorrah,
Shinab king of Admah,
and Shem-eber king of Zebi'im,
and with the king of Bela, which is Zoar.

Thus begins the biblical tale, in chapter 14 of Genesis, of an ancient war that pitted an alliance of four kingdoms of the East against five kings in Canaan. It is a tale that has evoked some of the most intense debate among scholars, for it connects the story of Abraham, the first Hebrew Patriarch, with a specific non-Hebrew event, and thus affords objective substantiation of the biblical record of the birth of a nation.

How wonderful it would have been, many have felt, if the various kings could be identified and the exact time of Abraham established! But even if Elam was known and Shin'ar identified as Sumer, who were the kings named, and which were the other lands of the East? Questioning the authenticity of biblical history unless independently verified, critics of the Bible asked: Why don't we find the names Khedorla'omer, Amraphel, Ariokh, and Tidhal mentioned in Mesopotamian inscriptions? And if they did not exist, if such a war had not taken place, how credible is the rest of the tale of Abraham?

For many decades the critics of the Old Testament seemed to prevail; then, as the nineteenth century was drawing to a close, the scholarly and religious worlds were astounded by the discovery of

Babylonian tablets naming Khedorla'omer, Ariokh, and Tidhal in a tale not unlike the biblical one.

The discovery was announced in a lecture by Theophilus Pinches to the Victoria Institute, London, in 1897. Having examined several tablets belonging to the Spartoli Collection in the British Museum, he found that they described a war of wide-ranging magnitude, in which a king of Elam, named Kudur-laghamar, led an alliance of rulers that included one called Eri-aku and another named Tud-ghula—names that easily could have been transformed into Hebrew as Khedor-la'omer, Ariokh, and Tidhal. Accompanying his published lecture with a painstaking transcript of the cuneiform writing and a translation thereof, Pinches could confidently claim that the biblical tale had indeed been supported by an independent Mesopotamian source.

With justified excitement the Assyriologists of that time agreed with Pinches's reading of the cuneiform names. The tablets indeed spoke of "Kudur-Laghamar, king of the land of Elam"—uncannily similar to the biblical "Khedorla'omer, king of Elam"; all scholars agreed that it was a perfect Elamite royal name, the prefix *Kudur* ("Servant") having been a component in the names of several Elamite kings, and *Laghamar* being the Elamite epithet-name for a certain deity. It was agreed that the second name, spelled *Eri-e-a-ku* in the Babylonian cuneiform script, stood for the original Sumerian ERI.AKU, meaning "Servant of the god Aku," *Aku* being a variant of the name of Nannar/Sin. It is known from a number of inscriptions that Elamite rulers of Larsa bore the name "Servant of Sin," and there was therefore little difficulty in agreeing that the biblical Ellasar, the royal city of the king Ariokh, was in fact Larsa. There was also unanimous agreement among the scholars for accepting that the Babylonian text's Tud-ghula was the equivalent of the biblical "Tidhal, king of Go'im"; and they agreed that by Go'im the Book of Genesis referred to the "nation-hordes" whom the cuneiform tablets listed as allies of Khedorla'omer.

Here, then, was the missing proof—not only of the veracity of the Bible and of the existence of Abraham, but also of an international event in which he had been involved!

But the excitement was not to last. "Unfortunately"—to use an expression of A. H. Sayce in an address to the Society of Biblical Archaeology eleven years later—a contemporary discovery, which should have upheld the one announced by Pinches, ended up sidetracking and even discrediting it.

The second discovery was announced by Vincent Scheil, who reported that he had found among the tablets in the Imperial Ottoman Museum in Constantinople a letter from the well-known Babylonian king Hammurabi, which mentions the very same Kudur-laghamar! Because the letter was addressed to a king of Larsa, Father Scheil concluded that the three were contemporaries and thus matched three of the four biblical kings of the East—Hammurabi being none other than "Amraphel, king of Shin'ar."

For a while it seemed that all the pieces of the puzzle had fallen into place; one can still find textbooks and biblical commentaries explaining that Amraphel stands for Hammurabi. The resulting conclusion that Abraham was a contemporary of this ruler seemed plausible, because it was then believed that Hammurabi reigned from 2067 to 2025 B.C., placing Abraham, the war of the kings, and the ensuing destruction of Sodom and Gomorrah at the end of the third millennium B.C.

However, when subsequent research convinced most scholars that Hammurabi reigned much later (from 1792 to 1750 B.C., according to *The Cambridge Ancient History*), the synchronization seemingly achieved by Scheil fell apart, and the whole bearing of the discovered inscriptions—even those reported by Pinches— came into doubt. Ignored were the pleas of Pinches that no matter with whom the three named kings were to be identified—that even if Khedorla'omer, Ariokh, and Tidhal of the cuneiform texts were not contemporaries of Hammurabi—the text's tale with its three names was still "a remarkable historical coincidence, and deserves recognition as such." In 1917, Alfred Jeremias *(Die sogenanten Kedorlaomer-Texte)* attempted to revive interest in the subject; but the scholarly community preferred to treat the Spartoli tablets with benign neglect.

They remained ignored in the basement of the British Museum for half a century, when M. C. Astour returned to the subject in a study at Brandeis University *(Political and Cosmic Symbolism in Genesis 14)*. Agreeing that the biblical and Babylonian editors of the respective texts drew from some older, common Mesopotamian source, he identified the four Kings of the East as known rulers: 1) of Babylon in the eighth century B.C.; 2) of Assyria in the thirteenth century B.C.; 3) of the Hittites in the sixteenth century B.C.; and 4) of Elam in the twelfth century B.C. As none were contemporaries of each other or of Abraham, he ingeniously suggested that the text was not a historical one but a work of religious philosophy, wherein the author used four diverse historic incidents to illustrate one moral (the fate of evil kings). The improbability of Astour's suggestion was soon pointed out in other scholarly publications; and with that, the interest in the *Khedorla'omer Texts* died again.

Yet the scholarly consensus that the biblical tale and the Babylonian texts drew on a much earlier, common source impels us to revive the plea of Pinches and his central argument: How can cuneiform texts, affirming the biblical background of a major war and naming three of the biblical kings, be ignored? Should the evidence—crucial, as we shall show, to the understanding of fateful years—be discarded simply because Amraphel was not Hammurabi?

The answer is that the Hammurabi letter found by Scheil should not have sidetracked the discovery reported by Pinches, because Scheil misread the letter. According to his rendition, Hammurabi promised a reward to Sin-Idinna, the king of Larsa, for his "heroism on the day of Khedorla'omer." This implied that the two were allies in a war against Khedorla'omer and thus contemporaries of that king of Elam. It was on this point that Scheil's find was discredited, for it contradicted both the biblical assertion that the three kings were allies and known historical facts: Hammurabi treated Larsa not as an ally but as an adversary, boasting that he "overthrew Larsa in battle," and attacked its sacred precinct "with the mighty weapon which the gods had given him."

A close examination of the actual text of Hammurabi's letter reveals that in his eagerness to prove the Hammurabi-Amraphel identification, Father Scheil reversed the letter's meaning: Hammurabi was not offering as a reward to return certain goddesses *to* the sacred precinct (the Emutbal) of Larsa; rather, he was demanding their return to Babylon *from* Larsa:

> To Sin-Idinna
> speaks thus Hammurabi regarding
> the goddesses who in Emutbal
> have been behind doors
> from the days of Kudur-Laghamar,
> in sackcloth attired:
> When they ask them back from thee,
> to my men hand them over;
> The men shall grasp the hands of the goddesses;
> To their abode they shall bring them.

The incident of the abduction of the goddesses had thus occurred in earlier times; they were held captive in the Emutbal "from the days of Khedorla'omer''; and Hammurabi was now demanding their return to Babylon, from where Khedorla'omer had taken them captive. This can only mean that Khedorla'omer's days were long before Hammurabi's time.

Supporting our reading of the Hammurabi letter found by Father Scheil in the Constantinople Museum is the fact that Hammurabi repeated the demand for the return of the goddesses to Babylon in yet another stiff message to Sin-Idinna, this time sending it by the hand of high military officers. This second letter is in the British Museum (No. 23,131) and its text was published by L. W. King in *The Letters and Inscriptions of Hammurabi:*

> Unto Sin-Idinna thus sayeth Hammurabi:
> I am now despatching Zikir-ilishu, the Transport Officer,
> and Hammurabi-bani, the Frontline Officer,
> that they may bring the goddesses who are in Emutbal.

That the goddesses were to be returned from Larsa to Babylon is made clear in the letter's further instructions:

> Thou shalt cause the goddesses to journey
> in a processional boat as in a shrine,
> that they may come to Babylon.
> The temple-women shall accompany them.
> For food of the goddesses thou shalt load
> pure cream and cereals unto the boat;
> sheep and provisions thou shalt put on board
> for the sustenance of the temple-women,
> [enough] for the journey to reach Babylon.
> And thou shalt appoint men to tow the boat,
> and chosen soldiers to bring the goddesses
> to Babylon in safety.
> Delay them not; let them speedily reach Babylon.

It is thus clear from these letters that Hammurabi—a foe, not an ally, of Larsa—was seeking restitution for events that had happened long before his time, in the days of Kudur-Laghamar, the Elamite regent of Larsa. The texts of the Hammurabi letters thus affirm the existence of Khedorla'omer and of Elamite reign in Larsa (''Ellasar''), and thus of key elements in the biblical tale.

Which is the period into which these key elements fit?

As historical records have established, it was Shulgi who in the twenty-eighth year of his reign (2068 B.C.) gave his daughter in marriage to an Elamite chieftain and granted him the city of Larsa as a dowry; in return the Elamites put a "foreign legion" of Elamite troops at Shulgi's disposal. These troops were employed by Shulgi to subdue the western provinces, including Canaan. It is thus in the last years of Shulgi's reign and when Ur was still an imperial capital under his immediate successor Amar-Sin that we find the historical time slot into which all the biblical and Mesopotamian records seem to fit perfectly.

It is in that time, we believe, that the search for the historical Abraham should be conducted; for—as we shall show—the tale of Abraham was interwoven with the tale of the fall of Ur, and his days were the last days of Sumer.

With the discrediting of the Amraphel-Hammurabi notion, the verification of the Age of Abraham became a free-for-all, some suggesting such late dates that made the first patriarch a descendant of the later kings of Israel. . . . But the exact dates of his time and events need no guessing: the information is provided by the Bible itself; all we have to do is accept its veracity.

The chronological calculations are surprisingly simple. Our starting point is 963 B.C., the year in which Solomon is believed to have assumed the kingship in Jerusalem. The Book of Kings states unequivocally that Solomon began the construction of the Temple of Yahweh in Jerusalem in the fourth year of his reign, completing it late in the eleventh year. I Kings 6:1 also states that "It came to pass in the four hundred and eightieth year after the Children of Israel were come out of the land of Egypt, in the fourth year of Solomon's reign over Israel . . . that he began to build the House of Yahweh." This statement is supported (with a slight difference) by the priestly tradition that there had been twelve priestly generations, of forty years each, from the Exodus to the time when Azariah "executed the priestly office in the temple that Solomon built in Jerusalem" (I Chronicles 5:36).

Both sources agree on the passage of 480 years, with this difference: one counts from the start of the temple's construction (960 B.C.) and the other from its completion (in 953 B.C.), when the priestly services could begin. This would set the Israelite Exodus from Egypt in either 1440 or 1433 B.C.; the latter date, we find, offers better synchronization with other events.

Based on the knowledge amassed by the beginning of this century, Egyptologists and biblical scholars had by then reached the conclusion that the Exodus had indeed taken place in the middle of the fifteenth century B.C. But then the weight of scholarly opinion shifted to a thirteenth-century date because it seemed to better fit the archaeological dating of various Canaanite sites, in line with the biblical record of the conquest of Canaan by the Israelites.

Yet such a new dating was not unanimously agreed upon. The most notorious city conquered was Jericho; and one of its prominent excavators (K. M. Kenyon) concluded that the pertinent destruction occurred circa 1560 B.C.—well ahead of the biblical events. On the other hand, Jericho's principal excavator, J. Garstang (*The Story of Jericho*), held that the archaeological evidence points to its conquest sometime between 1400 and 1385 B.C. Adding to this the forty years of Israelite wandering in the wilderness after the departure from Egypt, he and others found archaeological support for an Exodus date sometime between 1440 and 1425 B.C.—a time frame that agrees with our suggestion of 1433 B.C.

For more than a century scholars have also searched through the extant Egyptian records for an Egyptian clue to the Exodus and its date. The only apparent references are found in the writings of Manetho. As quoted by Josephus in *Against Apion,* Manetho stated that "after the blasts of God's displeasure broke upon Egypt," a Pharaoh named Toumosis negotiated with the Shepherd People, "the people from the east, to evacuate Egypt and go whither they would, unmolested." They then left and traversed the wilderness, "and built a city in a country now called Judaea . . . and gave it the name Jerusalem."

Did Josephus adjust the writings of Manetho to suit the biblical tale, or did, in fact, the events concerning the sojourn, harsh treatment, and eventual Exodus of the Israelites occur in the reign of one of the well-known Pharaohs named Thothmes?

Manetho referred to "the king who expelled the pastoral people from Egypt" in a section devoted to the Pharaohs of the eighteenth dynasty. Egyptologists now accept as historical fact the expulsion of the Hyksos (the Asiatic "Shepherd Kings") in 1567 B.C. by the founder of the eighteenth dynasty, the Pharaoh Ahmosis (Amosis in Greek). This new dynasty, which established the New Kingdom in Egypt, might well have been the new dynasty of Pharaohs "who knew not Joseph" of which the Bible speaks (Exodus 1:8).

Theophilus, second-century Bishop of Antioch, also referred in his writings to Manetho and stated that the Hebrews were enslaved by the king Tethmosis, for whom they "built strong cities, Peitho and Rameses and On, which is Heliopolis''; then they departed Egypt under the Pharaoh "whose name was Amasis."

It thus appears from these ancient sources that the Israelites' troubles began under a Pharaoh named Thothmes and culminated with their departure under a successor named Amasis. What are the historical facts as they have been established by now?

After Ahmosis had expelled the Hyksos, his successors on the throne of Egypt—several of whom indeed bore the name Thothmes, as the ancient historians have stated—engaged in military campaigns in Greater Canaan, using the Way of the Sea as their invasion route. Thothmes I (1525–1512 B.C.), a professional soldier, put Egypt on a war footing and launched military expeditions into Asia as far as the Euphrates River. It is our belief that it was he who feared Israelite disloyalty—"when a war shall be called, they shall join our enemies"—and ordered therefore the killing of all newborn Israelite male babies (Exodus 1:9–16). By our calculations, Moses was born in 1513 B.C., the year before the death of Thothmes I.

J. W. Jack (The Date of the Exodus) and others, earlier this century, had wondered whether "the Pharaoh's daughter" who had retrieved the baby Moses from the river and then raised him in the royal palace could have been Hatshepsut, the eldest daughter of Thothmes I by his official spouse and thus the only royal princess of the time granted the high title "The King's Daughter," a title identical to that given in the Bible. We believe that indeed it was she; and her continued treatment of Moses as an adopted son can be explained by the fact that after she had married the succeeding Pharaoh, her half-brother Thothmes II, she could not bear him a son.

Thothmes II died after a short reign. His successor, Thothmes III—mothered by a harem girl—was Egypt's greatest warrior-king, an ancient Napoleon in the view of some scholars. Of his seventeen campaigns against foreign lands to obtain tribute and captives for his major construction works, most were thrust into Canaan and Lebanon and as far north as the Euphrates River. We believe, as T. E. Peet (Egypt and the Old Testament) and others held earlier this century, that it was this Pharaoh, Thothmes III, who was the enslaver of the Israelites; for in his military expeditions he pushed northward as far as Naharin, the Egyptian name for the area on the upper Euphrates called in the Bible Aram-Naharim, where the kinfolk of the Hebrew Patriarchs had remained; and this could well explain the Pharaoh's fear (Exodus 1:10) that "when there shall happen to be a war, they [the Israelites] shall join unto our enemies." It was, we suggest, Thothmes III from whose death sentence Moses escaped to the wilderness of the Sinai after he had learned of his Hebrew origins and openly sided with his people.

Thothmes III died in 1450 B.C. and was followed on the throne by Amenophis II—the Amasis named by Theophilus quoting Manetho. It was indeed "after a long time, that the king of Egypt died," (Exodus 2:23) that Moses dared return to Egypt to demand of the successor—Amenophis II, in our opinion—to "let my people go." The reign of Amenophis II lasted from 1450 to 1425 B.C.; it is our conclusion that the Exodus had taken place in 1433 B.C., exactly when Moses was eighty years old (Exodus 7:7).

Continuing our calculation backward, we now seek to establish the date when the Israelites arrived in Egypt. Hebrew traditions assert a stay of 400 years, in accord with the Lord's statement to Abraham (Genesis 15:13–14); so also states the New Testament (Acts 7:6). The Book of Exodus, however, says that "the sojourning of the Children of Israel who dwelt in Egypt was four hundred and thirty years" (Exodus 12:40–41). The qualifying of "sojourn" by the words "who dwelt in Egypt" might have been intended to distinguish between the Josephites (who had dwelt in Egypt) and the newly arrived families of Joseph's brothers, who just came "to sojourn." If so, then the difference of thirty years can be accounted for by the fact that Joseph was thirty years old when made Chief of Egypt. This would leave intact the 400 figure as the years of Israelite (rather than Josephite) sojourn in Egypt, and place the event in 1833 B.C. (1,433 + 400).

The next clue is found in Genesis 47:8–9: "And Joseph brought in Jacob, his father, and stood him before the Pharaoh. . . . And the Pharaoh said unto Jacob: 'How old art thou?' and Jacob said unto Pharaoh: 'The days of my years are one hundred and thirty.' " Jacob, then, was born in 1963 B.C.

Now, Isaac was sixty years old when Jacob was born unto him (Genesis 25:26); and Isaac was born unto his father Abraham when Abraham was 100 years old (Genesis 21:5). Accordingly, Abraham (who lived to be 175) was 160 years old when his grandson Jacob was born. This places the birth of Abraham in 2123 B.C.

The century of Abraham—the hundred years from his birth to the birth of his son and successor Isaac—was thus the century that witnessed the rise and fall of the Third Dynasty of Ur. Our reading of biblical chronology and tales puts Abraham right in the middle of the momentous events of that time—not as a mere observer but as an active participant. Contrary to the assertions of advocates of biblical criticism that with the tale of Abraham the Bible loses interest in the general history of mankind and the Near East, to focus on the "tribal history" of one particular nation, the Bible in fact continues to relate (as it did with the tales of the Deluge and the Tower of Babel) events of major concern to mankind and its civilization: a war of unprecedented aspects and a disaster of a unique nature; events in which the Hebrew Patriarch played an important role. It is the tale of how the legacy of Sumer was salvaged when Sumer itself was doomed.

In spite of numerous studies concerning Abraham, the fact remains that all we really know about him is what we find in the Bible. Belonging to a family that traced its ancestry to the line of Shem, Abraham—then called *Abram*—was the son of Terah, his brothers being Harran and Nahor. When Harran died at an early age, the family was living in "Ur of the Chaldees." There, Abram married Sarai (later renamed Sarah).

Then "did Terah take Abram his son and Lot his grandson, the son of Harran, and Sarai his daughter-in-law the wife of Abram his son; and they left and went forth from Ur of the Chaldees to go to the land of Canaan; and they went as far as Harran, and dwelt there."

Archaeologists have found *Harran* ("The Caravanry"). Situated to the northwest of Mesopotamia at the foothills of the Taurus Mountains, it was a major crossroads in antiquity. As Mari controlled the southern gateway from Mesopotamia to the lands of the Mediterranean coast, so did Harran control the gateway of the northern route to the lands of Western Asia. Marking, at the time of the Third Dynasty of Ur, the limits of Nannar's domains where they bordered on Adad's Asia Minor, Harran was found by the archaeologists to have been a mirror image of Ur in its layout and in its worship of Nannar/Sin.

No explanation is given in the Bible for leaving Ur, and there is also no time stated, but we can guess the answers if we relate the departure to events in Mesopotamia in general and in Ur in particular.

We know that Abraham was seventy-five when he proceeded later on from Harran to Canaan. The tenor of the biblical narrative suggests a long stay at Harran and depicts Abraham on his arrival there as a young man with a new bride. If Abraham, as we have concluded, was born in 2123 B.C., he was a child of ten when Ur-

Nammu ascended the throne in Ur, when Nannar was favored for the first time with the trusteeship over Nippur. And he was a young man of twenty-seven when Ur-Nammu inexplicably fell from Anu's and Enlil's favor, slain on a distant battlefield. We have described the traumatic effect of the event on the people of Mesopotamia, the shock it had given to their faith in Nannar's omnipotence and the fidelity of Enlil's word.

The year of Ur-Nammu's fall was 2096 B.C. Could it not have been the year when—under the impact of the event or as a consequence thereof—Terah and his family left Ur for a faraway destination, stopping off at Harran, the Ur away from Ur?

All through the following years of Ur's decline and Shulgi's profanities, the family stayed on in Harran. Then, suddenly, the Lord acted again:

> And Yahweh said unto Abram:
> "Get thee out of thy country
> and out of thy birthplace
> and from thy father's house,
> unto the land which I will show thee" . . .
> And Abram departed as Yahweh had spoken unto him,
> and Lot went with him.
> And Abram was seventy-five years old when he left Harran.

Once again, no reason is given for the crucial move. But the chronological clue is most revealing. When Abraham was seventy-five years old, the year was 2048 B.C.—the very year of Shulgi's downfall!

Because Abraham's family (Genesis 11) directly continued the line of Shem, Abraham has been considered a Semite, one whose background, cultural heritage, and language were Semitic, as distinct (in scholars' minds) from the non-Semitic Sumerians and the later Indo-Europeans. But in the original biblical sense, all the peoples of greater Mesopotamia were descended of Shem, "Semite" and "Sumerian" alike. There is nothing in the Bible that suggests—as some scholars have begun to hold—that Abraham and his family were Amorites (i.e., western Semites) who had come as immigrants to Sumer and then returned to their original abode. On the contrary: There is everything to support the image of a family rooted in Sumer from its earliest beginnings, hastily uprooted from its country and birthplace and told to go to an unfamiliar land.

The correspondence between two biblical events with the dates of two major Sumerian events—and of more to come—must serve as an indication of a direct connection between them all. Abraham emerges not as the son of immigrant aliens but as the scion of a family directly involved in Sumerian affairs of state!

In their search for the answer to the question of "Who Was Abraham," scholars have seized upon the similarity between his designation as a Hebrew *(Ibri)* and the term *Hapiru* (which in the Near East could transform to *Habiru*) by which the Assyrians and Babylonians in the eighteenth and seventeenth centuries B.C. called bands of pillaging western Semites. At the end of the fifteenth century B.C., the commander of an Egyptian garrison in Jerusalem asked his king for reinforcements against approaching Hapiru. Scholars have taken all that as evidence for the notion that Abraham was a western Semite.

Many scholars doubt, however, whether the term denotes an ethnic group at all, wondering whether the word was not a descriptive noun simply meaning "marauders" or "invaders." The suggestion that *Ibri* (clearly from the verb "to cross") and *Hapiru* are one and the same entails substantial philological and etymological problems. There are also great chronological inconsistencies, all of which gave rise to serious objections to this suggested solution for the identity of Abraham, especially when the biblical data is compared with the "bandit" connotation of the term Hapiru. Thus the Bible relates incidents concerning water wells, which show that Abraham was careful to avoid conflict with local residents as he journeyed through Canaan. When Abraham became involved in the War of the Kings, he refused to share in the booty. This is not the behavior of a marauding barbarian but rather of a person of high standards of conduct. Coming to Egypt, Abraham and Sarah were taken to the Pharaoh's court; in Canaan, Abraham made treaties with the local rulers. This is not the image of a nomad pillaging others' settlements; it is the image of a personage of high standing skilled in negotiation and diplomacy.

It was out of such considerations that Alfred Jeremias, then a leading Assyriologist and professor of the history of religion at the Leipzig University, announced in the 1930 edition of his master work *Das Alte Testament im Lichte des Alten Orients* that "in his intellectual makeup Abraham was a Sumerian." He enlarged on this conclusion in a 1932 study entitled *Der Kosmos von Sumer:* "Abraham was not a Semitic Babylonian but a Sumerian." Abraham, he suggested, headed the Faithful whose reformation sought to raise Sumerian society to higher religious levels.

These were audacious ideas in a Germany witnessing the rise of Nazism with its racial theories. Soon after the assumption of power by Hitler, the heretic suggestions of Jeremias were strongly put down by Nikolaus Schneider in a reply entitled *War Abraham Sumerer?* Abraham was neither a Sumerian nor a man of pure descent, he concluded: "From the time of the reign of the Akkadian king Sargon in Ur, the home-place of Abraham, there was never there a pure, unmixed Sumerian population and a homogenous Sumerian culture."

The ensuing upheavals and World War II cut off further debate on the subject. Regrettably, the thread discerned by Jeremias has not been picked up. Yet all the biblical and Mesopotamian evidence tells us that Abraham was indeed a Sumerian.

The Old Testament, in fact (Genesis 17:1–16), provides us with the time and manner in which Abraham was transformed from a Sumerian nobleman to a west Semitic potentate, under a covenant between him and his God. Amid a ritual of circumcision, his Sumerian name AB.RAM ("Father's Beloved") was changed to the Akkadian/Semitic *Abraham* ("Father of a Multitude of Nations") and that of his wife SARAI ("Princess") was adapted to the Semitic *Sarah*.

It was only when he was ninety-nine years old that Abraham became a "Semite."

As we decipher the age-old enigma of Abraham's identity and his Mission to Canaan, it is in Sumerian history, customs, and language that we shall search for the answers.

Is it not naive to assume that for the Mission to Canaan, for the birth of a nation, and for kingship over all the lands from the border of Egypt to the border of Mesopotamia, the Lord would choose someone at random, picking up anyone in the streets of Ur? The young woman whom Abraham married bore the epithet-name Princess; since she was a half-sister of Abraham ("Indeed she is my sister, the daughter of my father but not the daughter of my mother"), we can take it for granted that either Abraham's father or Sarah's mother was of royal descent. Since the daughter of Harran, Abraham's brother, also bore a royal name (*Milkha*—"Queenly"), it follows that it was through the father of Abraham that the royal ancestry flowed. In dealing with Abraham's family we thus deal with a family of Sumer's highest echelons; people of a noble deportment and elegant dress as found depicted on various Sumerian statues (Fig. 98).

Fig. 98

It was a family that not only could claim descent from Shem but which kept family records tracing its lineage through generations of firstborn sons: Arpakhshad and Shelach and Eber; Peleg, Re'u, and Serug; Nahor and Terah and Abraham; taking the family's recorded history back for no less than three centuries!

What do the epithet-names signify? If *Shelach* ("Sword") was born, as chapter 11 of Genesis states, 258 years before Abraham, he was born in 2381 B.C. That indeed was the time of the strife that brought Sargon to the throne in the new capital *Agade* ("United"), symbolizing the unification of the lands and a new era. Sixty-four years later the family named its firstborn descendant *Peleg* ("Division"), "for in his days the land divided." It was the time, in fact, when Sumer and Akkad were torn apart after Sargon's attempt to remove the sacred soil from Babylon and his consequent death.

But of greatest interest, to this very day, has been the meaning of the name *Eber* and the reason for bestowing it upon the firstborn in 2351 B.C. and from which has stemmed the biblical term *Ibri* ("Hebrew") by which Abraham and his family identified themselves. It clearly stems from the root word meaning "to cross," and the best scholars had to offer in explanation was to seek the Habiru/Hapiru connection, which we have already mentioned (and discarded). This erroneous interpretation has stemmed from the search for the meaning of the epithet-name in Western Asia. It is our conviction that instead the answer is to be found in the Sumerian origins and the Sumerian language of Abraham and his ancestors. Such a look at the Sumerian roots of the family and the name provides an answer that startles with its simplicity.

The term *Ibri* ("Hebrew") by which Abraham and his family identified themselves clearly stemmed from *Eber*, the father of Peleg, and from the root "to cross." Instead of seeking the meaning of the epithet-name in the Hapiru notions or in Western Asia, it is our conviction that the answer is to be found in the Sumerian origins and the Sumerian language of Abraham and his ancestors. Then, a new solution emerges with startling simplicity:

The biblical suffix "i," when applied to a person, meant "a native of"; Gileadi meant a native of Gilead and so on. Likewise, *Ibri* meant a native of the place called "Crossing"; and that, precisely, was the Sumerian name for Nippur: NI.IB.RU—the Crossing Place, the place where the pre-Diluvial grids crisscrossed each other, the original Navel of the Earth, the olden Mission Control Center.

The dropping of the *n* in transposing from Sumerian to Akkadian/Hebrew was a frequent occurrence. In stating that Abraham was an Ibri, the Bible simply meant that Abraham was a *Ni-ib-ri, a man of Nippurian origin!*

The fact that Abraham's family migrated to Harran from Ur has been taken by scholars to imply that Ur was also Abraham's birthplace; but that is not stated anywhere in the Bible. On the contrary, the command to Abraham to go to Canaan and leave for good his past abodes lists three separate entities: his father's house (which was then in Harran); his land (the city-state of Ur); and his birthplace (which the Bible does not identify). Our suggestion that Ibri means a native of Nippur solves the problem of Abraham's true birthplace.

As the name Eber indicates, it was in his time—the middle of the twenty-fourth century B.C.—that the family's association with Nippur had begun. Nippur was never a royal capital; rather, it was a consecrated city, Sumer's "religious center," as scholars put it. It was also the place where the knowledge of astronomy was entrusted to the high priests and thus the place where the calendar—

the relationship between the Sun, Earth, and Moon in their orbits—was originated.

Scholars have recognized that our present-day calendars derive from the original Nippurian calendar. All the evidence shows that the Nippurian calendar began circa 4000 B.C., in the age of Taurus. In this we find yet another confirmation of the umbilical cord connecting the Hebrews with Nippur: The Jewish calendar still continues to count the years from an enigmatic beginning in 3760 B.C. (so that in 1983 the Jewish year was 5743). It has been assumed that this is a count "from the beginning of the world"; but the actual statement by Jewish sages was that this is the number of years that had passed "since counting [of years] began." We suggest that it means, since the introduction of the calendar in Nippur.

In the ancestral family of Abraham we thus find a priestly family of royal blood, a family headed by a Nippurian high priest who was the only one allowed into the temple's innermost chamber, there to receive the deity's word and convey it to king and people.

In this regard the name of Abraham's father, Terah, is of great interest. Seeking clues only in the Semitic environment, biblical scholars regard the name, as those of Harran and Nahor, as mere toponyms (names that personify places), holding that there were cities by such names in central and northern Mesopotamia. Assyriologists searching the Akkadian terminology (being the first Semitic language) could only find that *Tirhu* meant "an artifact or vessel for magical purposes." But if we turn to the Sumerian language, we find that the cuneiform sign for *Tirhu* stemmed directly from that of an object called in Sumerian DUG.NAMTAR —literally, a "Fate Speaker"—a Pronouncer of Oracles!

Terah, then, was an Oracle Priest, one assigned to approaching the "Stone that Whispers" to hear the deity's words and communicate them (with or without an interpretation) to the lay hierarchy. It was a function assumed in later times by the Israelite High Priest, who alone was allowed to enter the Holy of Holies, approach the *Dvir* ("Speaker"), and "hear the voice [of the Lord] speak unto him from off the overlay which is upon the Ark of the Covenant, from between the two Cherubim." During the Israelite Exodus, at Mount Sinai the Lord proclaimed that his covenant with the descendants of Abraham meant that "ye shall be unto me a kingdom of priests." It was a statement that reflected the status of Abraham's own descent: a royal priesthood.

Farfetched as these conclusions may sound, they are in full accord with the Sumerian practices whereby kings appointed their daughters and sons, and often themselves, to high-priestly positions, resulting in the commingling of the royal and priestly lineages. Votive inscriptions found at Nippur (as those by the archaeological expeditions of the University of Pennsylvania) confirm that the kings of Ur cherished the title "Pious Shepherd of Nippur" and performed there priestly functions; and the governor of Nippur (PA.TE.SI NI.IB.RU) was also the Foremost UR.ENLIL ("Enlil's Foremost Servant").

Some of the names borne by these royal-priestly VIPs resembled Abraham's Sumerian name (AB.RAM), also beginning with the component AB ("Father" or "Progenitor"); such, for example, was the name AB.BA.MU of a governor of Nippur during Shulgi's reign.

That a family of people so closely associated with Nippur that they were called "Nippurians" (i.e., "Hebrews") were nevertheless holding high positions in Ur is a suggestion that is in complete accord with the actual circumstances prevailing in Sumer at the time indicated by us; for it was then, at the time of the Ur III Dynasty, that for the first time in divine affairs and Sumerian history Nannar and the king of Ur were granted trusteeship over Nippur, combining the religious and secular functions. It thus could have well been that when Ur-Nammu assumed the throne in Ur, Terah moved with his family from Nippur to Ur, perhaps to serve as a liaison between the temple in Nippur and the royal palace in Ur. Their stay in Ur lasted throughout Ur-Nammu's reign; it was in the year of his death, as we have shown, that the family left Ur for Harran.

What the family did at Harran is nowhere stated, but considering the royal lineage and priestly standing, it must have belonged to the hierarchy of Harran. The ease with which Abraham dealt, later on, with various kings suggests that he was involved in Harran's foreign affairs; his special friendship with the Hittite residents of Canaan, who were known for their military experience, may shed a light on the question of where Abraham himself had acquired the military proficiency which he employed so successfully during the War of the Kings.

Ancient traditions also depict Abraham as greatly versed in astronomy—a knowledge then valuable for long journeys guided by the stars. According to Josephus, Berossus referred to Abraham, without naming him, when he wrote of the rise "among the Chaldeans, of a certain righteous and great man who was well seen in astronomy.'' (If Berossus, the Babylonian historian, had indeed referred to Abraham, the significance of the inclusion of the Hebrew Patriarch in Babylonian chronicles far exceeds the mere notation of his knowledge of astronomy.)

All during the ignominious years of Shulgi's reign, the family of Terah stayed at Harran. Then, on Shulgi's demise, the divine order came to proceed to Canaan. Terah was already quite old, and Nahor, his son, was to stay on with him in Harran. The one chosen for the mission was Abraham—himself a mature man of seventy-five. The year was 2048 B.C.; it marked the beginning of twenty-four fateful years—eighteen years encompassing the war-filled reigns of the two immediate successors of Shulgi (Amar-Sin and Shu-Sin) and six years of Ibbi-Sin, the last sovereign king of Ur.

It is undoubtedly more than mere coincidence that Shulgi's death was the signal not only for a move by Abraham, but also for a realignment among the Near Eastern gods. It was exactly when Abraham, accompanied (as we learn later) by an elite military corps, left Harran—the gateway to the Hittite lands—that the exiled and wandering Marduk appeared in ''Hatti land.'' Moreover, the remarkable coincidence is that Marduk stayed there through the same twenty-four Fateful Years, the years that culminated with the great Disaster.

The evidence for Marduk's movements is a tablet (Fig. 99) found in the library of Ashurbanipal, in which an aging Marduk tells of his erstwhile wanderings and eventual return to Babylon:

> O great gods, learn my secrets.
> As I girdle my belt, my memories remember:
> I am the divine Marduk, a great god.
> I was cast off for my sins,
> to the mountains I have gone.
> In many lands I have been a wanderer:
> From where the sun rises to where it sets I went.
> To the heights of Hatti-land I went.
> In Hatti-land I asked an oracle
> [about] my throne and my Lordship;
> In its midst [I asked]: ''Until when?''
> 24 years, in its midst, I nested.

The appearance of Marduk in Asia Minor—implying an unexpected alliance with Adad—was thus the other side of the coin of Abraham's rush to Canaan. We learn from the balance of the text

Fig. 99

that Marduk sent from his new place of exile emissaries and supplies (via Harran) to his followers in Babylon, and trading agents into Mari, thereby making inroads into both gateways—the one beholden to Nannar/Sin and the other to Inanna/Ishtar.

As on a signal, with the death of Shulgi, the whole ancient world came astir. The House of Nannar had been discredited, and the House of Marduk saw its final prevailing hour approaching. While Marduk himself was still excluded from Mesopotamia, his firstborn son, Nabu, was making converts to his father's cause. His base of operations was his own "cult center," Borsippa; but his efforts encompassed all the lands, including Greater Canaan.

It was against this background of fast developments that Abraham was ordered to go to Canaan. Though silent concerning Abraham's mission, the Old Testament is clear regarding his destination: Moving expeditiously to Canaan, Abraham and his wife, his nephew Lot, and their entourage continued swiftly southward. There was a stopover at Shechem, where the Lord spoke to Abraham. "Then he removed from there to the Mount, and encamped east of Beth-El; and he built there an altar to Yahweh and called the name of Yahweh." Beth-El, whose name meant "God's House"—a site to which Abraham kept coming back—was in the vicinity of Jerusalem and its hallowed Mount, Mount Moriah ("Mount of Directing"), upon whose Sacred Rock the Ark of the Covenant was placed when Solomon built the Temple of Yahweh in Jerusalem.

From there "Abram journeyed farther, still going toward the Negev." The Negev—the dry region where Canaan and the Sinai peninsula merge—was clearly Abraham's destination. Several divine pronouncements designated the Brook of Egypt (nowadays called Wadi El-Arish) as the southern boundary of Abraham's domain, and the oasis of Kadesh-Barnea as his southernmost outpost (see map). What was Abraham to do in the Negev, whose very name ("The Dryness") bespoke its aridity? What was there that required the patriarch's hurried, long journey from Harran and impelled his presence among the miles upon miles of barren land?

The significance of Mount Moriah—Abraham's first focus of interest—was that in those days it served, together with its sister mounts Mount Zophim ("Mount of Observers") and Mount Zion ("Mount of Signal"), as the site of Mission Control Center of the Anunnaki. The significance of the Negev, its only significance, was that it was the gateway to the Spaceport in the Sinai.

Subsequent narrative informs us that Abraham had military allies in the region and that his entourage included an elite corps of several hundred fighting men. The biblical term for them—*Naar*—has been variously translated as "retainer" or simply "young man"; but studies have shown that in Hurrian the word denoted riders or cavalrymen. In fact, recent studies of Mesopotamian texts dealing with military movements list among the men of the chariots and the cavalry LU.NAR ("Nar-men") who served as fast riders. We find an identical term in the Bible (I Samuel 30:17): after King David attacked an Amalekite camp, the only ones to escape were "four hundred *Ish-Naar*"—literally, *"Nar*-men" or LU.NAR—"who were riding the camels."

In describing Abraham's fighting men as *Naar* men, the Old Testament thus informs us that he had with him a corps of cavalrymen, in all probability camel riders rather than horsemen. He may have picked up the idea of such a fast-riding fighting force from the Hittites on whose boundary Harran was located, but for the arid areas of the Negev and the Sinai, camels rather than horses were better suited.

The emerging image of Abraham not as a sheepherding nomad but as an innovative military commander of royal descent may not fit the customary image of this Hebrew patriarch, but it is in accord with ancient recollections of Abraham. Thus, quoting earlier sources concerning Abraham, Josephus (first century A.D.) wrote of him: "Abraham reigned at Damascus, where he was a foreigner, having come with an army out of the land above Babylon" from which, "after a long time, the Lord got him up and removed from that country together with his men and he went to the land then called the land of Canaan but now the land of Judaea."

The mission of Abraham was a military one: to protect the space facilities of the Anunnaki—the Mission Control Center and the Spaceport!

After a short stay in the Negev Abraham traversed the Sinai peninsula and came to Egypt. Evidently no ordinary nomads, Abraham and Sarah were at once taken to the royal palace. By our reckoning the time was circa 2047 B.C., when the Pharaohs then ruling in Lower (northern) Egypt—who were not followers of Amen ("The Hiding God" Ra/Marduk)—were facing a strong challenge from the princes of Thebes in the south, where Amen was deemed supreme. We can only guess what matters of state—alliances, joint defenses, divine commands—were discussed between the beleaguered Pharaoh and the Ibri, the Nippurian general. The Bible is silent on this as well as on the length of stay. (The *Book of Jubilees* states that the sojourn lasted five years). When the time came for Abraham to return to the Negev, he was accompanied by a large retinue of the Pharaoh's men.

"And Abraham went from Egypt, he and his wife and Lot with him, up onto the Negev." He was "heavy with flocks" of sheep and cattle for food and clothing, as well as with asses and camels for his fast riders. Again he went to Beth-El to "call the name of Yahweh," seeking instructions. A separation from Lot followed, the nephew choosing to reside with his own flocks in the Plain of the Jordan, "which was watered as the Garden of the Lord, before Yahweh destroyed Sodom and Gomorrah." Abraham went on to the hill country, settling on the highest peak near Hebron, from where he could see in all directions; and the Lord said unto him: "Go, cross the country in the length and the breadth of it, for unto thee shall I give it."

It was soon thereafter, "in the days of Amraphel king of Shin'ar," that the military expedition of the eastern alliance had taken place.

"Twelve years they [the Canaanite kings] served Khedorla'omer; in the thirteenth year they rebelled; and in the fourteenth year there came Khedorla'omer and the kings that were with him" (Genesis 14:4-5).

Scholars have long searched the archaeological records for the events described in the Bible; their efforts have been unsuccessful because they searched for Abraham in the wrong era. But if we are right in *our* chronology, a simple solution to the "Amraphel" problem becomes possible. It is a new solution, yet one that rests on scholarly suggestions made (and ignored) almost a century ago.

Back in 1875, comparing the traditional reading of the name with its spelling in early biblical translations, F. Lenormant *(La Langue Primitive de la Chaldée)* had suggested that the correct reading should be *"Amar-pal,"* as written out phonetically in the Septuagint (the third century B.C. translation of the Old Testament into Greek from the original Hebrew). Two years later D. H. Haigh, writing in the *Zeitschrift für Ägyptische Sprache und Altertumskunde,* also adopted the reading "Amarpal" and, stating that "the second element [of the king's name] is a name of the Moon-god [Sin]," declared: "I have long been convinced of the identity of Amar-pal as one of the kings of Ur."

In 1916, Franz M. Böhl *(Die Könige von Genesis 14)* suggested again—without success—that the name be read, as in the Septuagint, "Amar-pal," explaining that it meant "Seen by the Son"—a royal name in line with other royal names in the Near East, such as the Egyptian Thoth-mes ("Seen by Thoth"). (For some reason Böhl and others have neglected to mention the no-less-significant fact that the Septuagint spelled out the name of Khedorla'omer *Khodologomar*—almost identical to the Kudur-lagamar of the Spartoli tablets.)

Pal (meaning "son") was indeed a common suffix in Mesopotamian royal names, standing for the deity considered the favorite Divine Son. Since in Ur the god deemed to have been the Favored Son was Nannar/Sin, we suggest that *Amar-Sin* and *Amar-pal* were, in Ur, one and the same name.

Our identification of "Amarphal" of Genesis 14 as Amar-Sin, third king of Ur's Third Dynasty, meshes perfectly the biblical and the Sumerian chronologies. The biblical tale of the War of the Kings places the event soon after Abraham's return to the Negev from Egypt but before the tenth anniversary of his arrival in Canaan; i.e., between 2042 and 2039 B.C. The reign of Amar-Sin/Amar-Pal lasted from 2047 to 2039 B.C.; accordingly, the war had taken place in the latter part of his reign.

The year formulas for Amar-Sin's reign pinpoint his seventh year—2041 B.C.—as the year of the major military expedition to the western provinces. The biblical data (Genesis 14:4–5) asserts that this took place in the fourteenth year after the Elamites under Khedorla'omer had subjugated the Canaanite kings; and the year 2041 was indeed fourteen years after Shulgi, having received Nannar's oracles, had launched in 2055 B.C. the military expedition led by Elamites into Canaan.

Our synchronization of biblical and Sumerian events and dates unfolds the following sequence and upholds every time factor reported in the Bible:

2123 B.C. • Abraham born in Nippur to his father Terah.
2113 B.C. • Ur-Nammu enthroned in Ur, given guardianship of Nippur.
          Terah and his family move to Ur.
2095 B.C. • Shulgi ascends throne after death of Ur-Nammu.
          Terah and his family leave Ur for Harran.
2055 B.C. • Shulgi receives Nannar's oracles, sends Elamite troops to Canaan.
2048 B.C. • Shulgi's death ordered by Anu and Enlil.
          Abraham, seventy-five years old, ordered to leave Harran for Canaan.
2047 B.C. • Amar-Sin ("Amarpal") ascends the throne of Ur.
          Abraham leaves the Negev for Egypt.
2042 B.C. • Canaanite kings switch allegiance to "other gods."
          Abraham returns from Egypt with elite corps.
2041 B.C. • Amar-Sin launches the War of the Kings.

Who were the "other gods" that were winning the allegiance of Canaanite cities? They were Marduk, scheming from nearby exile, and his son, Nabu, who was roaming eastern Canaan, gaining supremacy and adherents. As biblical place names indicate, the

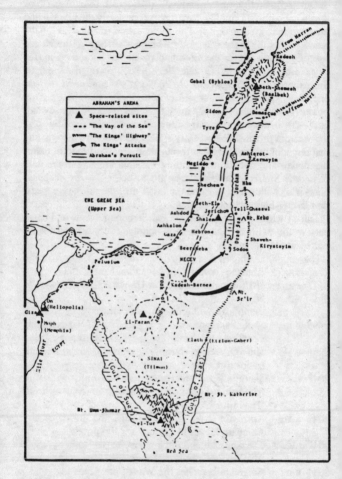

whole land of Moab had come under Nabu's influence: the land was also known as the Land of Nabu and many sites there were named in his honor; the highest peak retained its name—Mount Nebo—through the millennia that followed.

This is the historical frame into which the Old Testament has fitted the invasion from the east. But even seen from the biblical viewpoint, which compressed the Mesopotamian tales of the gods into a monotheistic mold, it was an unusual war: the ostensible purpose—the suppression of a rebellion—turns out to have been a secondary aspect of the war; the real target—a crossroads oasis in a wilderness—was never reached.

Taking the southern route from Mesopotamia to Canaan, the invaders proceeded southward in Transjordan, along the King's Highway, attacking in succession key outposts guarding crossing points on the Jordan River: Ashterot-Karnayim in the north; Ham in the center; and Shaveh-Kiryatayim in the south.

According to the biblical tale, a place called El-Paran was the real target of the invaders, but it was never reached by them. Coming down Transjordan and circling the Dead Sea, the invaders passed by Mount Se'ir and advanced "toward El-Paran, which is upon the Wilderness." But they were forced to "swing back by Ein-Mishpat, which is Kadesh." El-Paran ("God's Gloried Place"?) was never reached; somehow the invaders were beaten back at Ein-Mishpat, also known as Kadesh or Kadesh-Barnea.

It was only then, as they turned back toward Canaan, that "Thereupon the king of Sodom and the king of Gomorrah and the king of Admah and the king of Zebi'im and the king of Bela, which is Zoar, marched forth and engaged them in battle in the Vale of Siddim." (See map.)

The battle with these Canaanite kings was thus a late phase of the war and not its first purpose. Almost a century ago, in a thorough study titled *Kadesh-Barnea,* H. C. Trumbull had concluded that the true target of the invaders was El-Paran, which he correctly identified as the fortified oasis of Nakhl in Sinai's central plain. But neither he nor others could explain why a great alliance would launch an army to a destination a thousand miles away and fight gods and men to reach an isolated oasis in a great, desolate plain.

But why had they gone there, and who was it that blocked their way at Kadesh-Barnea, forcing the invaders to turn back?

There have been no answers; and no answers can make sense except the ones offered by us: The only significance of the destination was its Spaceport, and the one who blocked the advance at Kadesh-Barnea was Abraham. From earlier times Kadesh-Barnea was the closest place where men could approach in the region of the Spaceport without special permission. Shulgi had gone there to pray and make offerings to the God Who Judges, and nearly a thousand years before him the Sumerian king Gilgamesh stopped there to obtain the special permission. It was the place the Sumerians called BAD.GAL.DINGIR and Sargon of Akkad *Dur-Mah-Ilani*, clearly listing it in his inscriptions as a place in Tilmun (the Sinai peninsula).

It was the place, we suggest, which the Bible called Kadesh-Barnea; and there Abraham stood with his elite troops, blocking the invaders' advance to the Spaceport proper.

The hints in the Old Testament become a detailed tale in the *Khedorlaomer Texts*, which make clear that the war was intended to prevent the return of Marduk and thwart the efforts of Nabu to gain access to the Spaceport. These texts not only name the very same kings who are mentioned in the Bible but even repeat the biblical detail of the switch of allegiance ''in the thirteenth year''!

As we return to the *Khedorlaomer Texts* to obtain the details for the biblical frame, we should bear in mind that they were written by a Babylonian historian who favored Marduk's desire to make Babylon ''the heavenward navel in the four regions.'' It was to thwart this that the gods opposing Marduk ordered Khedorla'omer to seize and defile Babylon:

> The gods . . .
> to Kudur-Laghamar, king of the land Elam,
> they decreed: ''Descend there!''
> That which to the city was bad he performed;
> In Babylon, the precious city of Marduk,
> sovereignity he seized;
> In Babylon, the city of the king of the gods, Marduk,
> kingship he overthrew;
> To herds of dogs its temple he made a den;
> Flying ravens, loud shrieking, their dung dropped there.

The despoiling of Babylon was only the beginning. After the ''bad deeds'' were done there, Utu/Shamash sought action against Nabu, who (he said in accusation) had subverted the allegiance of a certain king to his father, Nannar/Sin. It happened, the *Khedorla'-omer Text* states, in the *thirteenth year* (just as Genesis 14 states):

> Before the gods the son of his father [came];
> On that day Shamash, the Bright One,
> against the lord of lords, Marduk [he said]:
> ''The faithfulness of his heart [the king] betrayed—
> in the time of the thirteenth year

a falling-out against my father [he had];
to his faith-keeping the king ceased to attend;
all this Nabu has caused to happen.''

The assembled gods, thus alerted to the role of Nabu in the
spreading rebellions, put together a coalition of loyal kings and appointed the Elamite Kudur-Laghamar as its military commander.
Their first order was that ''Borsippa, the stronghold [of Nabu],
with weapons be despoiled.'' Carrying out the order, ''Kudur-
Laghamar, with wicked thoughts against Marduk, the shrine of
Borsippa with fire he destroyed and its sons with a sword he slew.''
Then, the military expedition against the rebellious kings was ordered. The Babylonian text lists the targets to be attacked and the
names of their attackers; we easily recognize the biblical names
among them: Eriaku (Ariokh) was to attack Shebu (Beer-Sheba)
and Tud-Ghula (Tidhal) was to ''smite with a sword the sons of
Gaza.''

Acting in accordance with an oracle of Ishtar, the army put
together by the Kings of the East arrived in Transjordan. First
to be attacked was a stronghold in ''the high land,'' then
Rabattum. The route was the same as the one described in the
Bible: from the highland in the north through the district of
Rabat-Amon in the center, southward around the Dead Sea.
Thereafter, Dur-Mah-Ilani was to be captured, and the Canaanite cities (including Gaza and Beer-Sheba in the Negev)
were to be punished. But at Dur-Mah-Ilani, according to the
Babylonian text, ''the son of the priest, whom the gods in their
true counsel had anointed,'' stood in the invaders' way and
''the despoiling prevented.''

Could the Babylonian text indeed refer to Abraham, the son of
Terah the priest, and spell out his role in turning back the invaders?
The possibility is strengthend by the fact that the Mesopotamian
and biblical texts relate the same event in the same locality with the
same outcome.

But there is more to it than just a possibility, for we have come
upon one highly intriguing clue.

This is the unnoticed fact that the date formulas for the reign of
Amar-Sin call his seventh year—the crucial year 2041 B.C., the
year of the military expedition—also MU NE IB.RU.UM BA.HUL
(Fig. 100), ''Year [in which] the Shepherding-abode of IB.RU.UM
was attacked.''

Fig. 100

Can this reference, in the exact crucial year, be other than to Abraham and his shepherding abode?

There is also a possible pictorial commemoration of the invasion. This is a scene carved on a Sumerian cylinder seal (Fig. 101). It has been regarded as depicting the journey of Etana, an early king of Kish, to the Winged Gateway, where an "Eagle" took him aloft so high that the Earth disappeared from view. But the seal depicts the crowned hero on horseback—too early for Etana's time—and standing between the site of the Winged Gateway and two distinct groups. One of four armed Mighty Men whose leader is also on horseback moves toward a cultivated area in the Sinai peninsula (indicated by the symbol of Sin's crescent with wheat growing in it). The other is of five kings, facing in the opposite direction. The depiction thus has all the elements of an ancient illustration of the War of the Kings and the role of the "Priest's Son" in it, rather than that of Etana's journey to the Spaceport. The hero, depicted in the center atop an animal, could thus be Abraham rather than Etana.

Fig. 101

Having carried out his mission to protect the Spaceport, Abraham returned to his base near Hebron. Encouraged by his feat, the Canaanite kings marched their forces to intercept the retreating army from the East. But the invaders beat them and "seized all the possessions of Sodom and Gomorrah" as well as one prize hostage: "They took with them Lot, the nephew of Abraham, who was residing at Sodom."

On hearing the news, Abraham called up his best cavalrymen and pursued the retreating invaders. Catching up with them near Damascus, he succeeded in releasing Lot and retrieving all the booty. Upon his return he was greeted as a victor in the Valley of *Shalem* (Jerusalem):

> And Malkizedek, the king of Shalem,
> brought forth bread and wine,
> for he was a priest unto the God Most High.
> And he blessed him, saying:
> "Blessed be Abram unto the God Most High,
> Possessor of Heaven and Earth;
> And blessed be the God Most High
> who hath delivered thine foes into thine hand."

Soon the Canaanite kings also arrived to thank Abraham, and offered him all the seized possessions as a reward. But Abraham, saying that his local allies could share in that, refused to take "even a shoe lace" for himself or his warriors. He had acted neither out of friendship for the Canaanite kings nor out of enmity for the Eastern Alliance; in the war between the House of Nannar and the House of Marduk, he was neutral. It was for "Yahweh, the God Most High, Possessor of Heaven and Earth, that I have raised my hands," he stated.

The failed invasion did not arrest the rush of momentous events in the ancient world. A year later, in 2040 B.C., Mentuhotep II, leader of the Theban princes, defeated the northern Pharaohs and extended the rule of Thebes (and of its god) up to the western approaches to the Sinai peninsula. In the following year Amar-Sin attempted to reach the Sinai peninsula by sea, only to find his death by a poisonous bite.

The attacks on the Spaceport were thwarted, but the danger to it was not removed; and the efforts of Marduk to gain the supremacy intensified ever more. Fifteen years later Sodom and Gomorrah went up in flames when Ninurta and Nergal unleashed the Doomsday Weapons.

14

THE NUCLEAR HOLOCAUST

Doomsday came in the twenty-fourth year when Abraham, encamped near Hebron, was ninety-nine years old.

"And the Lord appeared unto him in the terebrinth grove of Mamre as he was sitting at the entrance of the tent, in the heat of the day. And he lifted his eyes and looked, and behold—three men were stationed upon him; and as he saw them he ran from the entrance of the tent towards them, and bowed to the ground."

Swiftly, from a typical Middle Eastern scene of a potentate resting in the shade of his tent, the biblical narrator of Genesis 18 raised Abraham's eyes and thrust him—and the reader, too—into a sudden encounter with divine beings. Though Abraham was gazing out, he did not see the three approaching: they were suddenly "stationed upon him." And though they were "men," he at once recognized their true identity and bowed to them, calling them "my lords" and asking them not to "pass over above thy servant" until he had a chance to prepare for them a sumptuous meal.

It was dusk when the divine visitors finished eating and resting. Asking about Sarah, their leader said to Abraham: "Return I shall unto thee at this time next year; by then Sarah thy wife will have a son."

The promise of a Rightful Heir to Abraham and Sarah at their old age was not the sole reason for dropping down on Abraham. There was a more ominous purpose:

And the men rose up from there
to survey over upon Sodom.
And Abraham had gone with them to see them off,
and the Lord said:
"Can I conceal from Abraham that which I am about to do?"

Recalling Abraham's past services and promised future, the Lord then disclosed to him the true purpose of the divine journey: to verify accusations against Sodom and Gomorrah. "The outcry regarding Sodom and Gomorrah being great, and the accusation against them being grievous,'' the Lord said he had decided to "come down and verify; if it is as the outcry reaching me, they will destroy completely; and if not, I wish to know.''

The ensuing destruction of Sodom and Gomorrah has become one of the most frequently depicted and preached-about biblical episodes. The orthodox and the Fundamentalists never doubted that the Lord God had literally poured fire and brimstone from the skies to wipe the sinful cities off the face of the earth. The scholarly and sophisticated have as tenaciously sought to find "natural" explanations for the biblical story: an earthquake; a volcanic eruption; some other natural phenomenon which (they grant) might have been interpreted as an act of God, a punishment befitting the sin.

But so far as the biblical narrative is concerned—and until now it has been the only source for all the interpretations—the event was most definitely *not* a natural calamity. It is described as a *premeditated* event: the Lord discloses to Abraham ahead of time what is about to happen and why. It is an *avoidable* event, not a calamity caused by irreversible natural forces: The calamity shall come to pass only if the "outcry" against Sodom and Gomorrah will be confirmed. And thirdly (as we shall soon discover) it was also a *postponable* event, one whose occurrence could be made to happen earlier or later, at will.

Realizing the avoidability of the calamity, Abraham embarked upon a tactic of argumentative attrition: "Perhaps there be fifty Righteous Ones inside the city," he said. "Wilt thou destroy and not spare the place for the sake of the fifty Righteous Ones within it?" Then he quickly added: "Far be it from you to do such a thing, to slay the righteous with the guilty! Far be it from you, the Judge of All the Earth, not to do justice!"

A mortal preaching to his Deity! And the plea is for calling off the destruction—the premeditated and avoidable destruction—if there be fifty Righteous Ones in the city. But no sooner had the Lord agreed to spare the city if there be found such fifty persons than Abraham, who might have chosen the number fifty knowing that it would strike a special chord, wondered out loud if the Lord shall destroy if the number were five short. When the Lord agreed to call off the destruction if only forty-five be found Righteous, Abraham continued to bargain the number down to forty, then thirty, then twenty, then ten. "And the Lord said: 'I shall not destroy if there be ten'; and he departed as he finished speaking to Abraham, and Abraham returned to his place."

At evetime, the two companions of the Lord—the biblical narrative now refers to them as *Mal'akhim* (translated ''angels'' but meaning ''emissaries'')—arrived at Sodom, their task being to verify the accusations against the city and report their findings back to the Lord. Lot—who was sitting at the city's gate—recognized at once (as Abraham had done earlier) the divine nature of the two visitors, their identity evidently being given away by their attire or weapons, or perhaps by the manner (flying over?) in which they arrived.

Now it was Lot's turn to insist on hospitality, and the two accepted his invitation to spend the night at his home; but it was not to be a restful night, for the news of their arrival had stirred up the whole city.

''They had hardly lain down when the people of the city, the people of Sodom, surrounded the house—young and old, the whole population, from every quarter; and they called unto Lot and said unto him: 'Where are the men who came unto you tonight? Bring them out to us, that we may know them.' '' When Lot failed to do so, the crowd surged to break their way in; but the two *Mal'akhim* ''smote the people who were at the house's entrance with blindness, both young and old; and they wearied themselves trying to find the doorway.''

Realizing that of all the townspeople only Lot was ''righteous,'' the two emissaries needed no further investigation; the fate of the city was sealed. ''And they said unto Lot: 'Who else hast thou here besides thee—a son-in-law, thy sons and daughters, any other relative—all who are in this city—bring them out from this place, for we are about to destroy it.' Rushing to convey the news to his sons-in-law, Lot only met disbelief and laughter. So at dawn the emissaries urged Lot to escape without delay, taking with him only his wife and their two unmarried daughters who lived with them at home.

> But Lot tarried;
> so the men took hold of his hand
> and his wife's hand and his two daughters' hands
> —for Yahweh's mercy was upon him—
> and they brought them out,
> and put them down outside the city.

Having literally carried the foursome aloft, then put them down outside the city, the emissaries urged Lot to flee to the mountains: ''Escape for thy life, look not behind thee, neither stop thou anywhere in the plain," they instructed him; "unto the mountains escape, lest thou perish." But Lot, afraid that they would not reach the mountains in time and "would be overtaken by the Evil and die," had a suggestion: Could the upheavaling of Sodom be delayed until he had reached the town of Zoar, the farthest one away from Sodom? Agreeing, one of the emissaries asked him to hurry there: "Haste thee to escape thither, for I will be unable to do anything until thou hast arrived there."

The calamity was thus not only predictable and avoidable but also postponable; and it could be made to afflict various cities at different times. No natural catastrophe could have featured all these aspects.

The sun was risen over the Earth when Lot arrived at Zoar;
And the Lord rained upon Sodom and Gomorrah, from the skies,
brimstone and fire that had come from Yahweh.
And He upheavaled those cities and the whole plain,
and all the inhabitants of the cities
and all the vegetation that grows from the ground.

The cities, the people, the vegetation—everything was "upheavaled" by the gods' weapon. Its heat and fire scorched all before it; its radiation affected people even at some distance away: Lot's wife, ignoring the admonition not to stop to look back as they were fleeing away from Sodom, turned to a "pillar of vapor."* The "Evil" Lot had feared had caught up with her. . . .

---

*The traditional and literal translation of the Hebrew term *Netsiv melah* has been "pillar of salt," and tracts have been written in the Middle Ages explaining the process whereby a person could turn into crystalline salt. However, if—as we believe—the mother tongue of Abraham and Lot was Sumerian, and the event was first recorded not in a Semitic language but in Sumerian, an entirely different and more plausible understanding of the fate of Lot's wife becomes possible.

In a paper presented to the American Oriental Society in 1918 and in a followup article in *Beiträge zur Assyriologie*, Paul Haupt had shown conclusively that because the early sources of salt in Sumer were swamps near the Persian Gulf, the Sumerian term NIMUR branched off to mean both *salt* and *vapor*. Because the Dead Sea has been called, in Hebrew, *The Salt Sea*, the biblical Hebrew narrator probably misinterpreted the Sumerian term and wrote "pillar of salt" when in fact Lot's wife became a "pillar of vapor." In this

One by one the cities "which had outraged the Lord" were up-heavaled, and each time Lot was allowed to escape:

> For when the gods devastated the cities of the plain,
> the gods remembered Abraham, and sent Lot away
> out of the upheavaling of the cities.

And Lot, as instructed, went on "to dwell in the mountain . . . and dwelt in a cave, he and his two daughters with him."

Having witnessed the fiery destruction of all life in the Jordan plain and the unseen hand of death which vaporized their mother, what were Lot and his daughters to think? They thought, we learn from the biblical narrative, that they had witnessed the end of mankind upon the Earth, that the three of them were the sole survivors of the human race; and therefore, the only way to preserve mankind was to commit incest and have the daughters conceive children by their own father. . . .

"And the elder said unto the younger: 'Our father is old, and there is not a man on Earth to squire us in the manner of all on Earth; come, let us make our father drink wine, then lie down with him, so that we shall preserve the seed of life from our father.' " And having done so, both became pregnant and bore children.

The night before the holocaust must have been a night of anxiety and sleeplessness for Abraham, of wondering whether enough Righteous Ones were found in Sodom to have the cities spared, of concern about the fate of Lot and his family. "And Abraham got up early in the morning to the place where he had stood facing Yahweh, and he looked in the direction of Sodom and Gomorrah and

---

connection it is noteworthy that in Ugaritic texts, such as the Canaanite tale of Aqhat (with its many similarities to the tales of Abraham) the death of a mortal by the hand of a god was described as the "escape of his soul as vapor, like smoke from his nostrils."

Indeed, in the Erra Epos which, we believe, was the Sumerian record of the nuclear upheaval, the death of the people was described by the god thus:

> The people I will make vanish,
> their souls shall turn to vapor.

It was the misfortune of Lot's wife to be among those who were "turned to vapor."

the region of the Plain; and he beheld there smoke rising from the earth as the smoke of a furnace.''

He was witnessing a ''Hiroshima'' and a ''Nagasaki'' —the destruction of a fertile and populated plain by atomic weapons. *The year was 2024 B.C.*

Where are the remains of Sodom and Gomorrah today? Ancient Greek and Roman geographers reported that the once-fertile valley of the five cities was inundated following the catastrophe. Modern scholars believe that the ''upheavaling'' described in the Bible caused a breach in the southern shore of the Dead Sea, letting its waters pour through to submerge the low-lying region to the south. The remaining portion of what was once the southern shore became the feature figuratively called by the natives *el-Lissan* (''The Tongue''), and the once-populated valley with its five cities became a new, southern part of the Dead Sea (Fig. 102) still bearing the local nickname ''Lot's Sea.'' In the north the outpouring of the waters southward caused the shoreline to recede.

The ancient reports have been confirmed in modern times by various researches, beginning with an exhaustive exploration of the area in the 1920s by a scientific mission sponsored by the Vatican's Pontifical Biblical Institute (A. Mallon, *Voyage d'Exploration au sud-est de la Mer Morte*). Leading archaeologists, such as W. F. Albright and P. Harland, discovered that settlements in the mountains around the region were abruptly abandoned in the twenty-first century B.C. and were not reoccupied for several centuries thereafter. And to this very day, the water of springs surrounding the Dead Sea has been found to be contaminated with radioactivity, ''enough to induce sterility and allied afflictions in any animals and humans that absorbed it over a number of years'' (I. M. Blake, ''Joshua's Curse and Elisha's Miracle'' in *The Palestine Exploration Quarterly*).

The cloud of death, rising in the skies from the cities of the plain, frightened not only Lot and his daughters but also Abraham, and he did not feel safe even in the Hebron mountains, some fifty miles away. We are told by the Bible that he pulled up his encampment and moved farther away westward, to reside at Gerar.

Also, at no time thereafter did he venture into the Sinai. Even years later, when Abraham's son Isaac wanted to go to Egypt on account of a famine in Canaan, ''Yahweh appeared unto him and said: 'Go not down to Egypt; dwell in the land which I will show

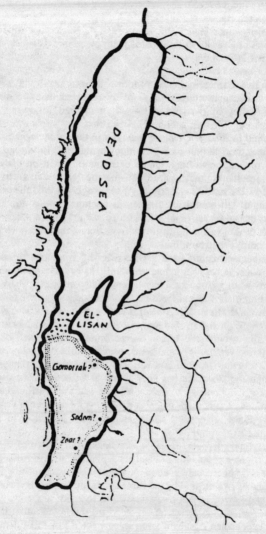

Fig. 102

thee.' '' The passage through the Sinai peninsula was apparently still unsafe.

But why?

The destruction of the cities of the plain, we believe, was only a sideshow: concurrently, the Spaceport in the Sinai peninsula was also obliterated with nuclear weapons, leaving behind a deadly radiation that lingered on for many years thereafter.

The main nuclear target was in the Sinai peninsula; and the real victim, in the end, was Sumer itself.

Though the end of Ur came swiftly, its sad fate loomed darker ever since the War of the Kings, coming nearer and nearer, like the sound of a distant drummer—an execution's drummer—getting closer, growing louder with each passing year. The Year of Doom—2024 B.C.—was the sixth year of the reign of Ibbi-Sin, the last king of Ur; but to find the reasons for the calamity, explanations of its nature, and details of its scope, we will have to study the records of those fateful years back from the time of that war.

Having failed in their mission and twice humiliated by the hand of Abraham—once at Kadesh-Barnea, then again near Damascus— the invading kings were promptly removed from their thrones. In Ur, Amar-Sin was replaced by his brother Shu-Sin, who ascended the throne to find the grand alliance shattered and Ur's erstwhile allies now nibbling at her crumbling empire.

Although they, too, had been discredited by the War of the Kings, Nannar and Inanna were at first the gods in whom Shu-Sin had put his trust. It was Nannar, Shu-Sin's early inscriptions stated, who had "called his name" to kingship; he was "beloved of Inanna," and she herself presented him to Nannar (Fig. 103).

Fig. 103

"The Holy Inanna," Shu-Sin boasted, "the one endowed with astounding qualities, the First Daughter of Sin," granted him weapons with which to "engage in battle the enemy country which is disobedient." But all this was insufficient to hold together the Sumerian empire, and Shu-Sin soon turned to greater gods for succor.

Judging from the date formulas—annual inscriptions, for royal as well as commercial and social purposes, in which each successive year of a king's reign was designated by the major event of that year—Shu-Sin, in the second year of his reign, sought the favors of Enki by constructing for that god a special boat that could navigate the high seas all the way to the Lower World. The third year of reign was also one of preoccupation with the pro-Enki alignment. Little else is known of this effort, which could have been a roundabout way of pacifying the followers of Marduk and Nabu; but the effort evidently failed, for the fourth and fifth years witnessed the building of a massive wall on the western frontier of Mesopotamia, specifically aimed at warding off incursions by the "Westerners," followers of Marduk.

As the pressures from the west kept rising, Shu-Sin turned to the great gods of Nippur for forgiveness and salvation. The date formulas, confirmed by the archaeological excavations of the American Expedition to Nippur, reveal that Shu-Sin undertook massive reconstruction works at Nippur's sacred precinct, on a scale unknown since the days of Ur-Nammu. The works culminated with the raising of a stela honoring Enlil and Ninlil, "a stela as no king had built before." Desparately Shu-Sin sought acceptance, confirmation that he was "the king whom Enlil, in his heart, had chosen." But Enlil was not there to answer; only Ninlil, Enlil's spouse, who remained in Nippur, heard Shu-Sin's supplications. Responding with compassion, "so as to prolong the well-being of Shu-Sin, to extend the time of his crown," she gave him a "weapon which with radiance strikes down . . . whose awesome flash reaches the sky."

A Shu-Sin text catalogued as "Collection B" suggests that in his efforts to reestablish the olden links with Nippur, Shu-Sin may have attempted a reconciliation with the Nippurites (such as the family of Terah) who had left Ur after the death of Ur-Nammu. The text states that after he made the region where Harran was situated "tremble in awe of his weapons," a peace gesture was made: Shu-Sin sent there his own daughter as a bride (presumably to the region's chief or his son). She then returned to Sumer with an entourage of that region's citizens, "establishing a town for Enlil and Ninlil on the boundary of Nippur." It was the first time "since the days when fates were decreed, that a king had established a town for Enlil and Ninlil," Shu-Sin stated in obvious expectation of praise. With the probable assistance of the repatriated Nippurites, Shu-Sin also reinstated the high temple services at Nippur—bestowing upon himself the role and title of High Priest.

Yet all this was to no avail. Instead of greater security, there were greater dangers, and concern about the loyalty of distant provinces gave way to worry about Sumer's own territory. "The mighty king, the King of Ur," Shu-Sin's inscriptions said, found that the "shepherding of the land"—of Sumer itself—had become the principal royal burden.

There was one final effort to entice Enlil back to Sumer, to find shelter under his aegis. On the apparent advice of Ninlil, Shu-Sin built for the divine couple "a great touring boat, fit for the largest rivers. . . . He decorated it perfectly with precious stones," outfitted it with oars made of the finest wood, punting poles and an artful rudder, and furnished it with all manner of comfort including a bridal bed. He then "placed the touring boat in the wide basin facing Ninlil's House of Pleasure."

The nostalgic aspects struck a chord in Enlil's heart, for he had fallen in love with Ninlil, when she was still a young nurse, when he saw her bathing naked in the river; and he did come back to Nippur:

When Enlil heard [all this]
From horizon to horizon he hurried,
From south to north he travelled;
Through the skies, over earth he hurried,
To greatly rejoice with his beloved queen, Ninlil.

The sentimental journey, however, was only a brief interlude. Some crucial lines before the end of the tablet are missing, so we are deprived of the details of what happened then. But the very last lines refer to "Ninurta, the great warrior of Enlil, who befuddled the Intruder," apparently after "an inscription, an evil inscription" was discovered on an effigy in the boat, intended perhaps to place a curse on Enlil and Ninlil.

There is no record available of Enlil's reaction to the foul play; but all other evidence suggests that he again left Nippur, this time apparently taking Ninlil with him.

Soon thereafter—February 2031 B.C. by our calendar—the Near East was awed by a total lunar eclipse, which blacked out the moon during the night for its full course from horizon to horizon. The oracle priests of Nippur could not allay Shu-Sin's anxiety: It was, they said in their written message, an omen "to the king who rules the four regions: his wall will be destroyed, Ur will become desolate."

Rejected by the great olden gods, Shu-Sin engaged in one final act—either out of defiance or as a last straw to gain divine support. He went ahead and built—in the very sacred precinct of Nippur—a shrine to a young god named Shara. He was a son of Inanna; and like Lugalbanda, who bore this epithet in earlier days, so was this new Shara ("Prince") a son of a king; in the inscription dedicating the temple, Shu-Sin claimed that he was the young god's father: "To divine Shara, heavenly hero, the beloved son of Inanna: His father Shu-Sin, the powerful king, king of Ur, king of the four regions, has built for him the temple Shagipada, his beloved shrine; may the king have life." It was the ninth year of Shu-Sin's reign. It was also his last.

The new ruler on the throne of Ur, Ibbi-Sin, could not stop the retreat and retrenchment. All he could do was rush the construction of walls and fortifications in the heart of Sumer, around Ur and Nippur; the rest of the country was left unprotected. His own date formulas, of which none have been found beyond his fifth year (although he reigned longer), tell little of the circumstances of his days; much more is learned from the cessation of other customary messages and trade documents. Thus, the messages of loyalty, which the other subordinate urban centers were expected to send to Ur each year, ceased to arrive from one center after the other. First to cease were the loyalty messages from the western districts; then, in the third year, the capitals of eastern provinces stopped their dispatch. In that third year Ur's foreign commerce "stopped with a significant suddenness" (in the words of C. J. Gadd, *History and Monuments of Ur*). At the tax collection crossroads of Drehem (near Nippur), where shipments of goods and cattle and the collection of taxes thereon were recorded throughout the Third Dynasty of Ur—records of which thousands of intact clay tablets were found—the meticulous account-keeping also stopped abruptly in that third year.

Ignoring Nippur, whose great gods had left her, Ibbi-Sin put his trust again in Nannar and Inanna, installing himself in his second year as High Priest of Inanna's temple in Uruk. Repeatedly he asked for guidance and reassurance from his gods; but all he was hearing were oracles of destruction and doom. In the fourth year of his reign he was told that "The Son in the west will arise . . . it is an omen for Ibbi-Sin: Ur shall be judged."

In the fifth year, Ibbi-Sin sought further strength by becoming High Priest of Inanna at her shrine at Ur. But that, too, was of no help: that year, the other cities of Sumer itself ceased sending the messages of allegiance. It was also the last year in which those cities delivered the traditional sacrificial animals for Nannar's temple in Ur. The central authority of Ur, her gods, and her great ziggurat-temple were no longer recognized.

As the sixth year began, the omens "concerning destruction" became more urgent and more specific. "When the sixth year comes, the inhabitants of Ur will be trapped," one omen stated. The prophesied calamity shall come, another omen said, "When, for the second time, he who calls himself Supreme, like one whose chest has been anointed, shall come from the west." That very year, as messages from the borders reveal, "hostile Westerners had entered the plain" of Mesopotamia; without resistance, they quickly "entered the interior of the country, taking one by one all the great fortresses."

All Ibbi-Sin held on to was the enclave of Ur and Nippur; but before the fateful sixth year was out, the inscriptions honoring the king of Ur stopped abruptly also in Nippur. The enemy of Ur and her gods, the "One who calls himself Supreme," had reached the heart of Sumer.

Marduk, as the omens had predicted, returned to Babylon for the second time.

The twenty-four fateful years—since Abraham left Harran, since Shulgi was replaced on the throne, since Marduk's exile among the Hittites had begun—have all converged in that Year of Doom, 2024 B.C. Having followed the separate, but interconnected, biblical tale of Abraham and the fortunes of Ur and its last three kings, we will now follow in the footsteps of Marduk.

The tablet on which Marduk's autobiography is inscribed (from which we have already partly quoted) continues to relate his return to Babylon after the twenty-four years of sojourn in the Land of Hatti:

In Hatti-land I asked an oracle
[about] my throne and my Lordship;

In its midst [I asked]: "Until when?"
24 years, in its midst, I nested.

Then, in that twenty-fourth year, he received a favorable omen:

My days [of exile] were completed;
To my city I [set my course];
My temple Esagila as a mount [to raise/rebuild],
My everlasting abode to [reestablish].
I raised my heels [toward Babylon]
Through . . . lands [I went] to my city
her [future? well-being?] to establish,
A king in Babylon to [install]
In the house of my covenant . . .
In the mountlike Esagil . . .
By Anu created . . .
Into the Esagil . . .
A platform to raise . . .
In my city . . .
Joy . . .

The damaged tablet then lists the cities through which Marduk
had passed on his way to Babylon. The few legible city names indicate that Marduk's route from Asia Minor to Mesopotamia took
him first south to the city of Hama (the biblical Hamat), then
eastward via Mari (see map, page 304). He had indeed come to
Mesopotamia—as the omens had predicted—from the west, accompanied by Amorite ("Westerners") supporters.

His wish, Marduk continued, was to bring peace and prosperity
to the land, "chase away evil and bad luck . . . bring motherly
love to Mankind." But it all came to naught: Against his city, Babylon, an adversary god "his wrath had brought." The name of this
adversary god is stated at the very beginning of a new column of
the text; but all that has remained of it is the first syllable: "Divine
NIN-." The reference could have been only to Ninurta.

We learn little from this tablet of the actions taken by this adversary, for all the subsequent verses are badly damaged and the text
becomes unintelligible. But we can pick up some of the missing
threads from the third tablet of the *Khedorlaomer Texts*. In spite of
its enigmatic aspects, it paints a picture of total turmoil, with adversary gods marching against each other at the head of their human troops: the Amorite supporters of Marduk swooped down the

Euphrates valley toward Nippur, and Ninurta organized Elamite troops to fight them.

As we read and reread the record of those trying times, we find that to accuse an enemy of atrocities is not a modern innovation. The Babylonian text—written, we must keep bearing in mind, by a worshiper of Marduk—attributes to the Elamite troops, and to them alone, the desecration of temples, including the shrines of Shamash and Ishtar. The Babylonian chronicler goes even farther: he accuses Ninurta of falsely blaming on the followers of Marduk the desecration of Enlil's Holy-of-Holies in Nippur, thereby provoking Enlil to take sides against Marduk and his son Nabu.

It happened, the Babylonian text relates, when the two opposing armies faced each other at Nippur. It was then that the holy city was despoiled and its shrine, the Ekur, desecrated. Ninurta accused the followers of Marduk of this evil deed; but it was not so: it was his ally Erra who had done it!

How Nergal/Erra suddenly appears in the Babylonian chronicle will remain a puzzle until we return to the Erra Epic; but that this god is named in the *Khedorlaomer Texts* and is accused of the defilement of the Ekur, there can be no doubt:

Erra, the pitiless one,
entered the sacred precinct.
He stationed himself in the sacred precinct,
he beheld the Ekur.
His mouth he opened, he said to his young men:
"Carry off the spoil of Ekur,
take away its valuables,
destroy its foundation,
break down the enclosure of the shrine!"

When Enlil, "loftily enthroned," heard that his temple had been destroyed, its shrine defiled, that "in the holy of holies the veil was torn away," he rushed back to Nippur. "Riding in front of him were gods clothed with radiance"; he himself "set off brilliance like lightning" as he came down from the skies (Fig. 104); "he made the holy place shake" as he descended to the sacred precinct. Enlil then addressed himself to his son, "the prince Ninurta," to find out who had defiled the sacred place. But instead of telling the truth, that it was Erra, his ally, Ninurta pointed the accusing finger at Marduk and his followers. . . .

Fig. 104

Describing the scene, the Babylonian text asserts that Ninurta was acting without the required respect on meeting his father: "not fearing for his life, he removed not his tiara." To Enlil "evil he spoke . . . there was no justice; destruction was conceived." And so provoked, "Enlil against Babylon caused evil to be planned."

In addition to "evil deeds" against Marduk and Babylon, an attack against Nabu and his temple Ezida in Borsippa was also planned. But Nabu managed to escape westward, to the cities faithful to him near the Mediterranean Sea:

> From Ezida . . .
> Nabu, to marshal all his cities
> set his step;
> Toward the great sea he set his course.

Now there follow verses in the Babylonian text that have a direct parallel in the biblical tale of the destruction of Sodom and Gomorrah:

> But when the son of Marduk
> in the land of the coast was,
> He-of-the-Evil-Wind [Erra]
> with heat the plain-land burnt.

These are indeed verses that must have had a common source with the biblical description of how "brimstone and fire" rained from the skies "upheavaled those cities and the whole plain"!

As biblical statements (e.g., Deuteronomy 29:22–27) attested, the "wickedness" of the cities of the Jordan Plain was that "they had forsaken the covenant of the Lord . . . and they went and served other gods." As we now learn from the Babylonian text, the "outcry" (accusation) against them was their rallying to the side of Marduk and Nabu in that last clash between the contending gods. But whereas the biblical text left it at that, the Babylonian text adds another important detail: The attack on the Canaanite cities was intended not only to destroy the centers of support for Marduk, but also to destroy Nabu, who had sought asylum there. However, that second aim was not achieved, for Nabu managed to slip out in time and escaped to an island in the Mediterranean, where the people accepted him although he was not their god:

He [Nabu] the great sea entered,
Sat upon a throne which was not his
[Because] Ezida, the legitimate abode, was overrun.

The picture that can be gathered from the biblical and Babylonian texts of the cataclysm that engulfed the ancient Near East in the time of Abraham is much more fully detailed in *The Erra Epic* (to which we have already referred earlier). First pieced together from fragments found in the library of Ashurbanipal in Nineveh, the Assyrian text began to take shape and meaning as more fragmented versions were unearthed at other archaeological sites. By now it is definitely established that the text was inscribed on five tablets; and in spite of breaks, missing or incomplete lines, and even some disagreement among the scholars where some fragments belong, two extensive translations have been compiled: *Das Era-Epos* by P. F. Gössmann, and *L'Epopea di Erra* by L. Cagni.

The Erra Epic not only explains the nature and causes of the conflict that had led to the unleashing of the Ultimate Weapon against inhabited cities and the attempt to annihilate a god (Nabu) believed hiding therein. It also makes clear that such an extreme measure was not taken lightly.

We know from several other texts that the great gods, at that time of acute crisis, were sitting in a continuous Council of War, keeping constant communication with Anu: "Anu to Earth the words was speaking, Earth to Anu the words pronounced." *The*

Erra Epic adds the information that before the awesome weapons were used, one more confrontation had taken place between Nergal/Erra and Marduk, in which Nergal used threats to persuade his brother to leave Babylon and give up his claims to Supremacy.

But this time, persuasion failed; and back at the Council of the Gods, Nergal voiced the recommendation for the use of force to dislodge Marduk. We learn from the texts that the discussions were heated and acrimonious; "for one day and one night, without ceasing" they went on. An especially violent argument developed between Enki and his son Nergal, in which Enki stood by his firstborn son: "Now that Prince Marduk has arisen, now that the people for the second time have raised his image, why does Erra continue his opposition?" Enki asked. Finally, losing his patience, Enki shouted at Nergal to get out of his presence.

Leaving in a huff, Nergal returned to his domain. "Consulting with himself," he decided to unleash the awesome weapons: "The lands I will destroy, to a dust-heap make them; the cities I will up-heaval, to desolation turn them; the mountains I will flatten, their animals make disappear; the seas I will agitate, that which teems in them I will decimate; the people I will make vanish, their souls shall turn to vapor; none shall be spared. . . ."

We learn from a text known as CT-xvi-44/46 that it was Gibil, whose domain in Africa adjoined that of Nergal, who alerted Marduk to the destructive scheme hatched by Nergal. It was nighttime, and the great gods had adjourned for rest. It was then that Gibil "these words to Marduk did speak" in regard to the "seven awe-some weapons which by Anu were created; . . . The wickedness of those seven against thee is being laid," he informed Marduk.

Alarmed, Marduk inquired of Gibil where the awesome weapons were kept. "O Gibil," he said, "those seven—where were they born, where were they created?" To which Gibil revealed that they were hidden underground:

Those seven, in the mountain they abide,
In a cavity inside the earth they dwell.
From this place with a brilliance they will rush forth,
From Earth to Heaven, clad with terror.

But where exactly is this place? Marduk asked again and again; and all Gibil could say was that "even the wise gods, to them it is unknown."

Now Marduk rushed to his father Enki with the frightening report. "To his father Enki's house he [Marduk] entered." Enki was lying on the couch in the chamber to which he retired for the night. "My father," Marduk said, "Gibil this word hath spoken to me: of the coming of the seven [weapons] he has found out." Telling his father the bad news, he urged his all-knowing father: "Their place to search out, do hasten thou!"

Soon the gods were back in council, for even Enki knew not the exact hiding place of the Ultimate Weapons. To his surprise, not all the other gods were as shocked as he was. Enki spoke out strongly against the idea, urging steps to stop Nergal, for the use of the weapons, he pointed out, "the lands would make desolate, the people will make perish." Nannar and Utu wavered as Enki spoke; but Enlil and Ninurta were for decisive action. And so, with the Council of the Gods in disarray, the decision was left to Anu.

When Ninurta finally arrived in the Lower World with word of Anu's decision, he found out that Nergal had already ordered the priming of "the seven awesome weapons" with their "poisons"— their nuclear warheads. Though the *Erra Epic* keeps referring to Ninurta by the epithet *Ishum* ("The Scorcher"), it relates in great detail how Ninurta had made clear to Nergal/Erra that the weapons could be used only against specifically approved targets; that before they could be used, the Anunnaki gods at the selected sites and the Igigi gods manning the space platform and the shuttlecraft had to be forewarned; and, last but not least, mankind had to be spared, for "Anu, lord of the gods, on the land had pity."

At first Nergal balked at the very idea of forewarning anyone, and the ancient text goes to some length to relate the tough words exchanged between the two gods. Nergal then agreed to giving advance warning to the Anunnaki and Igigi who manned the space facilities, but not to Marduk and his son Nabu, nor to the human followers of Marduk. It was then that Ninurta, attempting to dissuade Nergal from indiscriminate annihilation, used words identical to those attributed in the Bible to Abraham when he tried to have Sodom spared:

Valiant Erra,
Will you the righteous destroy with the unrighteous?
Will you destroy those who have against you sinned
together with those who against you have not sinned?

Employing flattery, threats, and logic, the two gods argued back and forth on the extent of the destruction. More than Ninurta,

Nergal was consumed by personal hatred: "I shall annihilate the son, and let the father bury him; then I shall kill the father, let no one bury him!" he shouted. Employing diplomacy, pointing out the injustice of indiscriminate destruction—and the strategic merits of selective targeting—the words of Ninurta finally swayed Nergal. "He heard the words spoken by Ishum [Ninurta]; the words appealed to him as fine oil." Agreeing to leave alone the seas, to leave Mesopotamia out of the attack, he formulated a modified plan: the destruction will be selective; the tactical aim will be to destroy the cities where Nabu might be hiding; the strategic aim will be to deny to Marduk his greatest prize—the Spaceport, "the place from where the Great Ones ascend":

> From city to city an emissary I will send;
> The son, seed of his father, shall not escape;
> His mother shall cease her laughter . . .
> To the place of the gods, access he shall not have:
> The place from where the Great Ones ascend
> I shall upheaval.

When Nergal finished presenting this latest plan, involving as it did the destruction of the Spaceport, Ninurta was speechless. But, as other texts assert, Enlil approved the plan when it was brought to his decision; so also, apparently, did Anu. Wasting no more time, Nergal then urged Ninurta that the two of them go at once into action:

> Then did the hero Erra go ahead of Ishum,
> remembering his words;
> Ishum too went forth, in accordance with the word given,
> a squeezing in his heart.

Their first target was the Spaceport, its command complex hidden in the "Mount Most Supreme," its landing fields spread in the adjoining great plain:

> Ishum to Mount Most Supreme set his course;
> The Awesome Seven, [weapons] without parallel,
> trailed behind him.
> At the Mount Most Supreme the hero arrived;
> He raised his hand—
> the mount was smashed;

The plain by the Mount Most Supreme
he then obliterated;
in its forests not a tree-stem was left standing.

So, with one nuclear blow, the Spaceport was obliterated, the mount within which its controls were hidden smashed, the plain that served its runways obliterated. . . . It was a destructive feat, the written record attests, performed by Ninurta (Ishum).

Now it was the turn of Nergal (Erra) to give vent to his vow of vengeance. Guiding himself from the Sinai peninsula to the Canaanite cities by following the King's Highway, Erra upheavaled them. The words employed by the *Erra Epic* are almost identical to those used in the biblical tale of Sodom and Gomorrah:

Then, emulating Ishum,
Erra the King's Highway followed.
The cities he finished off,
to desolation he overturned them.
In the mountains he caused starvation,
their animals he made perish.

The verses that follow may well describe the creation of the new southern portion of the Dead Sea, by breaking through its southern shoreline, and the elimination of all marine life therein:

He dug through the sea,
its wholeness he divided.
That which lives in it,
even the crocodiles
he made wither.
As with fire he scorched the animals,
banned its grains to become as dust.

The *Erra Epic* thus encompasses all the three aspects of the nuclear event: the obliteration of the Spaceport in the Sinai; the "overturning" ("upheavaling" in the Bible) of the cities of the Jordan plain; and the breach in the Dead Sea resulting in its extension southward. One could expect that such a unique destructive event would have been recorded and mentioned in more than a single text; and indeed we find descriptions and recollections of the nuclear upheaval in other texts as well.

One such text (known as K.5001 and published in the *Oxford*

Editions of Cuneiform Texts, vol. VI) is especially valuable, because it is in the original Sumerian language and, moreover, it is a bilingual text in which the Sumerian is accompanied by a line-by-line Akkadian translation. It is thus undoubtedly one of the earliest texts on the subject; and its wording indeed gives the impression that it is this or similar Sumerian originals that had served as a source for the biblical narrative. Addressed to a god whose identity is not clear from the fragment, it says:

> Lord, bearer of the Scorcher
> that burnt up the adversary;
> Who obliterated the disobedient land;
> Who withered the life of the Evil Word's followers;
> *Who rained stones and fire* upon the adversaries.

The deed performed by the two gods Ninurta and Nergal, when the Anunnaki guarding the Spaceport, forewarned, had to escape by "ascending to the dome of heaven," was recalled in a Babylonian text in which one king recalled the momentous events that had taken place "in the reign of an earlier king." Here are the king's words:

> At that time,
> in the reign of a previous king,
> conditions changed.
> Good departed, suffering was regular.
> The Lord [of the gods] became enraged,
> he conceived wrath.
> He gave the command:
> the gods of that place abandoned it . . .
> The two, incited to commit the evil,
> made its guardians stand aside;
> its protectors went up to the dome of heaven.

The *Khedorlaomer Text,* which identifies the two gods by their epithets as Ninurta and Nergal, tells it this way:

> Enlil, who sat enthroned in loftiness,
> was consumed with anger.
> The devastators again suggested evil;
> He who scorches with fire [Ishum/Ninurta]

and he of the evil wind [Erra/Nergal]
together performed their evil.
The two made the gods flee,
made them flee the scorching.

The target, from which they made the gods guarding it flee, was
the Place of Launching:

That which was raised towards Anu to launch
they caused to wither;
Its face they made fade away,
its place they made desolate.

Thus was the Spaceport, the prize over which so many Wars of
the Gods had been fought, obliterated: the Mount within which the
controlling equipment was placed was smashed; the launch platforms were made to fade off the face of the Earth; and the plain
whose hard soil the shuttlecraft had used as runways was obliterated, with not even a tree left standing.

The great place was never to be seen again . . . but the scar
made in the face of the Earth that awesome day *can still be
seen*—to this very day! It is a vast scar, so vast that its features can
be seen only from the skies—revealed only in recent years as satellites began to photograph the Earth (Fig. 105). It is a scar for which
no scientist has hitherto offered an explanation.

Stretching north of this enigmatic feature in the face of the Sinai
peninsula is the flat central plain of the Sinai—a remnant of a lake
from an earlier geological era; its flat, hard soil is ideal for the
landing of shuttlecraft—the very same reason which made the Mo-
jave Desert in California and the Edwards Air Force Base there
ideal for the landing of America's space shuttles.

As one stands in this great plain in the Sinai peninsula—its hard,
flat soil having served for tank battles in recent history as it
did the shuttlecraft in antiquity—one can see in the distance
the mountains that surround the plain and give it its oval shape.
The limestone mountains loom white on the horizon; but where the
great central plain adjoins the immense scar in the Sinai, the hue of
the plain—black—stands out in sharp contrast to the surrounding
whiteness (Fig. 106).

Black is not a natural hue in the Sinai peninsula, where the
whiteness of the limestone and the redness of the sandstone combine to dazzle the eye with hues ranging from bright yellow to light

Fig. 105

Fig. 106

gray and dark brown but nowhere the black which comes in nature from basalt stones.

Yet here, in the central plain north-northeast of the enigmatic giant scar, the soil's color has a black hue. It is caused—as our photograph clearly shows—by millions upon millions of bits and pieces of blackened rock, strewn as by a giant hand over the whole area (Fig. 107).

There has been no explanation for the colossal scar in the face of the Sinai peninsula since it was observed from the skies and photographed by NASA satellites. There has been no explanation for the blackened bits and pieces of rock strewn over the area in the central plain. No explanation—unless one reads the verses of the ancient texts and accepts our conclusion that in the days of Abraham, Nergal and Ninurta wiped out the Spaceport that was there with nuclear weapons: "That which was raised towards Anu to launch they caused to wither, its face they made fade away, its place they made desolate."

And the Spaceport, even the Evil Cities, were no more.

Far away to the east, in Sumer itself, the nuclear blasts and their brilliant flashes were neither felt nor seen. But the deed done by Nergal and Ninurta had not gone unrecorded, for it turned out to have had a most profound effect on Sumer, its people, and its very existence.

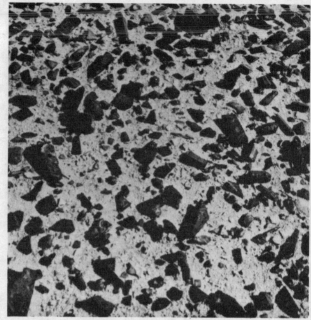

Fig. 107

For, in spite of all the efforts of Ninurta to dissuade Nergal from harming mankind, a great suffering did ensue. Though the two had not intended it, the nuclear explosion gave rise to an immense wind, a radioactive wind, which began as a whirlwind:

A storm, the Evil Wind,
went around in the skies.

And then the radioactive whirlwind began to spread and move westward with the prevailing winds blowing from the Mediterranean; soon thereafter, the omens predicting the end of Sumer came true; and Sumer itself became the ultimate nuclear victim.

The catastrophe that befell Sumer at the end of Ibbi-Sin's sixth year of reign is described in several Lamentation Texts—long poems that bewail the demise of the majestic Ur and the other centers of the great Sumerian civilization. Bringing very much to mind the biblical Book of Lamentations, lamenting the destruction of Jerusalem by the hands of the Babylonians, the Sumerian lamentations suggested to the scholars who had first translated them that the Mesopotamian catastrophe was also the result of an invasion—this one by clashing Elamite and Amorite troops.

When the first lamentation tablets were found, the scholars believed that Ur alone suffered destruction, and they titled the translations accordingly. But as more texts were discovered, it was realized that Ur was neither the only city affected, nor the focal point of the catastrophe. Not only were similar lamentations found bewailing the fate of Nippur, Uruk, Eridu, but some of the texts also provided lists of the affected cities: they appeared to begin in the southwest and extend to the northeast, encompassing the whole of southern Mesopotamia. It became apparent that a general, sudden, and concurrent catastrophe had befallen all the cities—not in slow succession, as would happen in the case of a progressive invasion, but all at once. Such scholars as Th. Jacobsen *(The Reign of Ibbi-Sin)* then concluded that the "barbarian invaders" had nothing to do with the "dire catastrophe," a calamity he called "really quite puzzling."

"Whether we shall ever see with full clarity what happened in those years," Jacobsen wrote, "only time will tell; the full story, we are convinced, is still far beyond our grasp."

But the puzzle can be solved, and the full story grasped, if we relate the catastrophe in Mesopotamia to the nuclear explosion in the Sinai.

The texts, remarkable for their length and in many instances also in excellent state of preservation, usually begin by bewailing the abrupt abandonment of all of Sumer's sacred precincts by their various gods, their temples "abandoned to the wind." The desolation caused by the catastrophe is then described vividly, by such verses as these:

> Causing cities to be desolated,
> [causing] houses to become desolate;
> Causing stalls to be desolate,
> the sheepfolds to be emptied;
> That Sumer's oxen no longer stand in their stalls,
> that its sheep no longer roam in its sheepfolds;
> That its rivers flow with water that is bitter,
> that its cultivated fields grow weeds,
> that its steppes grow withering plants.

In the cities and the hamlets, "the mother cares not for her children, the father says not 'O my wife' . . . the young child grows not sturdy on their knee, the nursemaid chants not a lullaby . . . kingship has been taken away from the land."

Before World War II had ended, before Hiroshima and Nagasaki were upheavaled with atomic weapons rained on them from the skies, one could still read the biblical tale of Sodom and Gomorrah and leave be the traditional "sulphur and brimstone" for lack of a better explanation. To scholars who had not yet come face-to-face with the awesomeness of nuclear weapons, the Sumerian lamentation texts bespoke (as the scholars titled them) the "Destruction of Ur" or the "Destruction of Sumer." But that is not what these texts describe: they describe *desolation,* not destruction. The cities were there but without people; the stalls were there but without cattle; the sheepfolds remained but were empty; the rivers flowed but their waters became bitter; the fields still stretched but they grew only weeds; and on the steppe the plants sprouted, only to wither away.

Invasion, war, killing—all those evils were well known to mankind by then; but, as the lamentation texts clearly state; this one was unique and never experienced before:

On the Land [Sumer] fell a calamity,
one unknown to man:
One that had never been seen before,
one which could not be withstood.

The death was not by the hand of an enemy; it was an unseen death, "which roams the street, is let loose in the road; it stands beside a man—yet none can see it; when it enters a house, its appearance is unknown." There was no defense against this "evil which has assailed the land like a ghost: . . . The highest wall, the thickest walls, it passes as a flood; no door can shut it out, no bolt can turn it back; through the door like a snake it glides, through the hinge like a wind it blows in." Those who hid behind doors were felled inside; those who ran to the rooftops died on the rooftops; those who fled to the streets were stricken in the streets: "Cough and phlegm weakened the chest, the mouth was filled with spittle and foam . . . dumbness and daze have come upon them, an unwholesome numbness . . . an evil curse, a headache . . . their spirit abandoned their bodies." As they died, it was a most gruesome death:

The people, terrified, could hardly breathe;
the Evil Wind clutched them,
does not grant them another day . . .
Mouths were drenched in blood,
heads wallowed in blood . . .
The face was made pale by the Evil Wind.

The source of the unseen death was a cloud that appeared in the
skies of Sumer and "covered the land as a cloak, spread over it like
a sheet." Brownish in color, during the daytime "the sun in the horizon it obliterated with darkness." At night, luminous at its edges
("Girt with dread brilliance it filleth the broad earth") it blocked
out the moon: "the moon at its rising it extinguished." Moving
from west to east, the deathly cloud—"enveloped in terror, casting
fear everywhere"—was carried to Sumer by a howling wind, "a
great wind which speeds high above, an evil wind which over-
whelms the land."

It was not, however, a natural phenomenon. It was "a great
storm directed from Anu . . . it hath come from the heart of Enlil." The product of the seven awesome weapons, "in a single
spawning it was spawned . . . like the bitter venom of the gods; in
the west it was spawned." The Evil Wind, "bearing gloom from
city to city, carrying dense clouds that bring gloom from the sky,"
was the result of a "lightning flash:" "From the midst of the
mountains it had descended upon the land, from the Plain of No
Pity it hath come."

Though the people were baffled, the gods knew the cause of the
Evil Wind:

An evil blast heralded the baleful storm,
An evil blast the forerunner
.of the baleful storm was;
Mighty offspring, valiant sons
were the heralds of the pestilence.

The two valiant sons—Ninurta and Nergal—unleashed "in a
single spawning" the seven awesome weapons created by Anu,
"uprooting everything, upheavaling everything" at the place of
the blast. The ancient descriptions are as vivid, as accurate as modern eyewitness descriptions of an atomic explosion: As soon as the
"awesome weapons" were launched from the skies, there was an

immense brilliance: "they spread awesome rays towards the four points of the earth, scorching everything like fire," one text stated; another, a lamentation over Nippur, recalled "the storm, in a flash of lightning created." An atomic mushroom—"a dense cloud that brings gloom"—then rose to the sky; it was followed by "rushing wind gusts . . . a tempest that furiously scorches the heavens." Then the prevailing winds, blowing from west to east, began to spread toward Mesopotamia: "the dense clouds that bring gloom from the sky, that bear the gloom from city to city."

Not one, but several, texts attest that the Evil Wind, bearing the cloud of death, was caused by gigantic explosions on a day to remember:

> On that day
> When heaven was crushed
> and the Earth was smitten,
> its face obliterated by the maelstrom—
> When the skies were darkened
> and covered as with a shadow . . .

The lamentation texts identified the site of the awesome blasts as "in the west," near "the breast of the sea"—a graphic description of the curving Mediterranean coast at the Sinai peninsula—from a plain "in the midst of the mountains," a plain that became a "Place of No Pity." It was a place that served before as the Place of Launching, the place from which the gods ascended toward Anu. In addition, a mount also featured in many of these place identifications. In the *Erra Epic,* the mount near "the place from which Great Ones ascend" was called the "Mount Most Supreme"; in one of the lamentations it was called the "Mount of Howling Tunnels." This last epithet brings to mind the descriptions, in the Pyramid Texts, of the tunneled mount with sloping underground passages, to which Egyptian Pharaohs journeyed in search of an afterlife. In *The Stairway to Heaven* we have identified it with the mount Gilgamesh had reached in his journey to the Place of the Rocketships, in the Sinai peninsula.

Starting from that mount, a lamentation text stated, the blast's deadly cloud was carried by the prevailing winds eastward all the way "to the boundary of Anshan" in the Zagros Mountains, affecting all of Sumer from Eridu in the south to Babylon in the north. The unseen death moved slowly over Sumer, its passage lasting twenty-four hours—a day and a night that were commemorated in laments, as in this one from Nippur: "On that day, on that single day; on that night, on that single night . . . the storm, in a flash of lightning created, the people of Nippur left prostrate."

The Uruk Lament vividly describes the confusion among both the gods and the populace. Stating that Anu and Enlil had over-ruled Enki and Ninki when they "determined the consensus" to employ the nuclear weapons, the text asserts that none of the gods anticipated the awesome outcome: "The great gods paled at its immensity" as they witnessed the explosion's "gigantic rays reach up to heaven [and] the earth tremble to its core."

As the Evil Wind began to "spread to the mountains as a net," the gods of Sumer began to flee their beloved cities. The text known as *Lamentation Over the Destruction of Ur* lists all the great gods and some of their important sons and daughters who had "abandoned to the wind" the cities and great temples of Sumer. The text called *Lamentation Over the Destruction of Sumer and Ur* adds dramatic details to this hurried abandonment. Thus, "Ninharsag wept in bitter tears" as she escaped from Isin; Nanshe cried, "O my devastated city" as "her beloved dwelling place was given over to misfortune." Inanna hurriedly departed from Uruk, sailing off toward Africa in a "submersible ship" and complaining that she had to leave behind her jewelry and other possessions. . . . In her own lamentation for Uruk, Inanna/Ishtar bewailed the desolation of her city and her temple by the Evil Wind "which in an instant, in a blink of an eye was created in the midst of the mountains," and against which there was no defense.

A breathtaking description of the fear and confusion, among gods and men alike, as the Evil Wind approached is given in *The Uruk Lament* text, which was written years later as the time of Restoration came. As the "loyal citizens of Uruk were seized with terror," the resident deities of Uruk, those in charge of the city's administration and welfare, set off an alarm. "Rise up!" they called to the people in the middle of the night; run away, "hide in the steppe!" they instructed them. But then, these gods themselves, "the deities ran off . . . they took unfamiliar paths." Gloomily the text states:

> Thus all its gods evacuated Uruk;
> They kept away from it;
> They hid in the mountains,
> They escaped to the distant plains.

In Uruk, the populace was left in chaos, leaderless and helpless. "Mob panic was brought about in Uruk . . . its good sense was distorted." The shrines were broken in and their contents were smashed as the people asked questions: "Why did the gods' benevolent eye look away? Who caused such worry and lamentation?" But their questions remained unanswered; and when the Evil Storm passed over, "the people were piled up in heaps . . . a hush settled over Uruk like a cloak."

Ninki, we learn from *The Eridu Lament*, flew away from her city to a safe haven in Africa: "Ninki, its great lady, flying like a bird, left her city." But Enki left Eridu only far enough to get out of the Evil Wind's way, yet near enough to see its fate: "Its lord stayed outside his city . . . . Father Enki stayed outside the city . . . for the fate of his harmed city he wept with bitter tears." Many of his loyal subjects followed him, camping on its outskirts. For a day and a night they watched the storm "put its hand" on Eridu.

After the "evil-bearing storm went out of the city, sweeping across the countryside," Enki surveyed Eridu; he found a city "smothered with silence . . . its residents stacked up in heaps." Those who were saved addressed to him a lament: "O Enki," they cried, "thy city has been cursed, made like an alien territory!" and they kept on asking whence should they go, what should they do. But though the Evil Wind had passed, the place was still unsafe, and Enki "stayed out of his city as though it were an alien city." "Forsaking the house of Eridu," Enki then led "those who have been displaced from Eridu" to the desert, "towards an inimical land"; there he used his scientific powers to make the "foul tree" edible.

From the northern edge of the Evil Wind's wide swath, from Babylon, a worried Marduk sent his father, Enki, an urgent message as the cloud of death neared his city: "What am I to do?" he asked. Enki's advice, which Marduk then related to his followers, was that those who could should leave the city—but go only north; and in line with the advice given by the two emissaries to Lot, the people fleeing Babylon were warned "neither to turn nor to look back." They were also told not to take with them any food or beverage, for these might have been "touched by the ghost." If escape was not possible, Enki advised hiding underground: "Get thee into a chamber below the earth, into a darkness," until the Evil Wind was gone.

The storm's slow advance misled some of the gods into costly delays. In Lagash, "mother Bau wept bitterly for her holy temple, for her city." Though Ninurta was gone, his spouse could not force herself to leave. Lingering behind, "O my city, O my city," she kept crying; the delay almost cost her her life:

> On that day, the lady—
> the storm caught up with her;
> Bau, as if she were mortal—
> the storm caught up with her . . .

In Ur we learn from the lamentations (one of which was composed by Ningal herself) that Nannar and Ningal refused to believe that the end of Ur was irrevocable. Nannar addressed a long and emotional appeal to his father Enlil, seeking some means to avert the calamity. But "Enlil answered his son Sin" that the fate could not be changed:

> Ur was granted kingship—
> it was not granted an eternal reign.
> Since days of yore, when Sumer was founded,
> to the present, when people have multiplied—
> Who has ever seen a kingship of everlasting reign?

While the appeals were made, Ningal recalled in her long poem, "the storm was ever breaking forward, its howling overpowering all." It was daytime when the Evil Wind approached Ur; "although of that day I still tremble," Ningal wrote, "of that day's foul smell we did not flee." As night came, "a bitter lament was raised" in Ur; yet the god and goddess stayed on; "of that night's foulness we did not flee," the goddess stated. Then the affliction reached the great ziggurat of Ur, and Ningal realized that Nannar "had been overtaken by the evil storm."

Ningal and Nannar spent a night of nightmare, which Ningal vowed never to forget, in the "termite house" (underground chamber) within the ziggurat. Only next day, when "the storm was carried off from the city," did "Ningal, in order to go from her city . . . hastily put on a garment," and together with the stricken Nannar departed from the city they so loved.

As they were leaving they saw death and desolation: "the people, like potsherds, filled the city's streets; in its lofty gates, where they were wont to promenade, dead bodies were lying about; in its boulevards, where the feasts were celebrated, scattered they lay; in all of its streets, where they were wont to promenade, dead bodies were lying about; in its places where the land's festivities took place, the people lay in heaps." The dead were not brought to burial: "the dead bodies, like fat placed in the sun, of themselves melted away."

Then did Ningal raise her great lamentation for Ur, the once-majestic city, head city of Sumer, capital of an empire:

> O house of Sin in Ur,
> bitter is thy desolation . . .
> O Ningal whose land has perished,
> make thy heart like water!
> The city has become a strange city,
> how can one now exist?
> The house has become a house of tears,
> it makes my heart like water . . .
> Ur and its temples
> have been given over to the wind.

All of southern Mesopotamia lay prostrate, its soil and waters left poisoned by the Evil Wind: "On the banks of the Tigris and Euphrates, only sickly plants grew. . . . In the swamps grow sickly-headed reeds that rot in the stench. . . . In the orchards and gardens there is no new growth, quickly they waste away. . . . The cultivated fields are not hoed, no seeds are implanted in the soil, no songs resound in the fields." In the countryside the animals were also affected: "On the steppe, cattle large and small become scarce, all living creatures come to an end." The domesticated animals, too, were wiped out: "The sheepfolds have been delivered to the wind. . . . The hum of the turning churn resounds not in the sheepfold. . . . The stalls provide not fat and cheese. . . . Ninurta has emptied Sumer of milk."

"The storm crushed the land, wiped out everything; it roared like a great wind over the land, none could escape it; desolating the cities, desolating the houses. . . . No one treads the highways, no one seeks out the roads."

The desolation of Sumer was complete.

EPILOGUE

Seven years after the Evil Wind had desolated Sumer, life began to stir again in the land. But instead of an empire ruling others, Sumer itself was now an occupied land, with a semblance of order maintained by Elamite troops in the south and Gutian soldiers in the north.

Isin, a city never a capital before, was selected as a temporary administrative center, and a former governor of Mari was brought over to rule the land. Documents from that time recorded a complaint that one "who is not of Sumerian seed" was given the reins over Sumer. As his Semitic name—Ishbi-Erra—attested, he was a follower of Nergal, and his appointment must have been part of the arrangement between Nergal and Ninurta.

Some scholars call the decades that followed the demise of Ur a Dark Age in Mesopotamian history. Little is known of those trying times except for what is gleaned from the yearly date formulas. Improving security, restoring here and there, Ishbi-Erra—seeking to solidify his secular authority—dismissed the foreign garrison that patrolled Ur and, by extending his reign to that city, laid claim to being a successor to the kings of Ur; but only a few other resettled cities acknowledged his supremacy, and at Larsa a powerful local chief posed, at times, a challenge.

A year or two later Ishbi-Erra sought to add the central religious authority to his powers by assuming the guardianship of Nippur, raising there the sacred emblems of Enlil and Ninurta. But the permission for that came from Ninurta alone, and the great gods of Nippur remained aloof and alienated. Seeking other support, Ishbi-Erra appointed priests and priestesses to restore the worship of Nannar, Ningal, and Inanna. But it seems that the hearts of the people belonged elsewhere: as numerous *Shurpu* ("Purification") texts suggest, it was Enki and Marduk—using Enki's immense scientific knowledge ("magical powers" in the eyes of the people)—who cured the afflicted, purified the waters, and made the soil grow edible vegetation again.

For the next half-century, embracing the reign of two successors of Ishbi-Erra at Isin, normalcy gradually returned to the land; agriculture and industry revived, internal and external trade resumed.

343

But it was only after the passage of seventy years since its defilement—the same interval that later on applied to the desecrated temple in Jerusalem—that the temple of Nippur could be rebuilt by the third successor on the throne of Isin, Ishme-Dagan. In a long poem of twelve stanzas dedicated to Nippur, he described how its divine couple responded to his appeals to restore the city and its great temple, so that "Nippur's brickwork be restored" and "the divine tablets be returned to Nippur."

There was great jubilation in the land when the great temple was rededicated to Enlil and Ninlil, in the year 1953 B.C.; it was only then that the cities of Sumer and Akkad were officially declared habitable again.

The official return to normalcy, however, only served to stir up old rivalries among the gods. The successor to Ishme-Dagan bore a name indicating his allegiance to Ishtar. Ninurta put a quick end to that, and the next ruler at Isin—the last one ever to bear a Sumerian name—was one of his followers. But this claim of Ninurta to the restored land could not be upheld: after all, he had caused, even if indirectly, Sumer's destruction. As the next successor's name suggests, Sin then sought to reassert his authority; but the days of his and Ur's supremacy were over.

And so, by the authority vested in them, Anu and Enlil finally accepted Marduk's claim to supremacy at Babylon. Commemorating the fateful decision in the preamble to his law code, the Babylonian king Hammurabi put it in these words:

> Lofty Anu, lord of the
> gods who from Heaven came to Earth,
> and Enlil, lord of Heaven and Earth
> who determines the destinies of the land,
> Determined for Marduk, the firstborn of Enki,
> the Enlil-functions over all mankind;
> Made him great among the gods who watch and see,
> Called Babylon by name to be exalted,
> made it supreme in the world;
> And established for Marduk, in its midst,
> an everlasting kingship.

Babylon, then Assyria, rose to greatness. Sumer was no more; but in a distant land, the baton of its legacy passed from the hands of Abraham and Isaac his son unto the hand of Jacob, the one renamed *Isra-El*.

The Earth Chronicles: Time Chart

Years Ago	I. Events Before the Deluge

450,000   On Nibiru, a distant member of our solar system, life faces slow extinction as the planet's atmosphere erodes. Deposed by Anu, the ruler Alalu escapes in a spaceship and finds refuge on Earth. He discovers that Earth has gold that can be used to protect Nibiru's atmosphere.

445,000   Led by Enki, a son of Anu, the *Anunnaki* land on Earth, establish Eridu—Earth Station I—for extracting gold from the waters of the Persian Gulf.

430,000   Earth's climate mellows. More Anunnaki arrive on Earth, among them Enki's half-sister Ninharsag, Chief Medical Officer.

416,000   As gold production falters, Anu arrives on Earth with Enlil, the heir apparent. It is decided to obtain the vital gold by mining it in southern Africa. Drawing lots, Enlil wins command of Earth Mission; Enki is relegated to Africa. On departing Earth, Anu is challenged by Alalu's grandson.

400,000   Seven functional settlements in southern Mesopotamia include a Spaceport (Sippar), Mission Control Center (Nippur), a metallurgical center (Badtibira), a medical center (Shuruppak). The ores arrive by ships from Africa; the refined metal is sent aloft to orbiters manned by *Igigi,* then transferred to spaceships arriving periodically from Nibiru.

380,000   Gaining the support of the Igigi, Alalu's grandson attempts to seize mastery over Earth. The Enlilites win the War of the Olden Gods.

300,000   The Anunnaki toiling in the gold mines mutiny. Enki and Ninharsag create Primitive Workers through genetic manipulation of Apewoman; they take over the manual chores of the Anunnaki. Enlil raids the mines, brings the Primitive Workers to the *Edin* in Mesopotamia. Given the ability to procreate, *Homo sapiens* begins to multiply.

200,000   Life on Earth regresses during a new glacial period.

100,000   Climate warms again. The Anunnaki (the biblical *Nefilim*), to Enlil's growing annoyance, marry the daughters of Man.

75,000   The "accursation of Earth"—a new Ice Age—begins. Regressive types of Man roam the Earth. Cro-Magnon man survives.

49,000   Enki and Ninharsag elevate humans of Anunnaki parentage to rule in Shuruppak. Enlil, enraged, plots Mankind's demise.

13,000   Realizing that the passage of Nibiru in Earth's proximity will trigger an immense tidal wave, Enlil makes the Anunnaki swear to keep the impending calamity a secret from Mankind.

B.C.   II. Events After the Deluge

11,000   Enki breaks the oath, instructs Ziusudra/Noah to build a submersible ship. The Deluge sweeps over the Earth; the Anunnaki witness the total destruction from their orbiting spacecraft.

          Enlil agrees to grant the remnants of Mankind implements and seeds; agriculture begins in the highlands. Enki domesticates animals.

10,500   The descendants of Noah are allotted three regions. Ninurta, Enlil's foremost son, dams the mountains and drains the rivers to make Mesopotamia habitable; Enki reclaims the Nile valley. The Sinai peninsula is retained by the Anunnaki for a post-Diluvial spaceport; a control center is established on Mount Moriah (the future Jerusalem).

9780 Ra/Marduk, Enki's firstborn son, divides dominion over Egypt between Osiris and Seth.

9330 Seth seizes and dismembers Osiris, assumes sole rule over the Nile Valley.

8970 Horus avenges his father Osiris by launching the First Pyramid War. Seth escapes to Asia, seizes the Sinai peninsula and Canaan.

8670 Opposed to the resulting control of all the space facilities by Enki's descendants, the Enlilites launch the Second Pyramid War. The victorious Ninurta empties the Great Pyramid of its equipment.

Ninharsag, half-sister of Enki and Enlil, convenes a peace conference. The division of Earth is reaffirmed. Rule over Egypt transferred from the Ra/Marduk dynasty to that of Thoth. Heliopolis built as a substitute Beacon City.

8500 The Anunnaki establish outposts at the gateway to the space facilities; Jericho is one of them.

7400 As the era of peace continues, the Anunnaki grant Mankind new advances; the Neolithic period begins. Demigods rule over Egypt.

3800 Urban civilization begins in Sumer as the Anunnaki reestablish there the Olden Cities, beginning with Eridu and Nippur.

Anu comes to Earth for a pageantful visit. A new city, Uruk (Erech), is built in his honor; he makes its temple the abode of his beloved granddaughter Inanna/Ishtar.

B.C.   **III. Kingship on Earth**

3760 Mankind granted kingship. Kish is first capital under the aegis of Ninurta. The calendar begun at Nippur. Civilization blossoms out in Sumer (the First Region).

3450 Primacy in Sumer transferred to Nannar/Sin. Marduk proclaims Babylon "Gateway of the Gods." The "Tower of Babel" incident. The Anunnaki confuse Mankind's languages.

His coup frustrated, Marduk/Ra returns to Egypt, deposes Thoth, seizes his younger brother Dumuzi, who had betrothed Inanna. Dumuzi accidentally killed; Marduk imprisoned alive in the Great Pyramid. Freed through an emergency shaft, he goes into exile.

3100 350 years of chaos end with installation of first Egyptian Pharaoh in Memphis. Civilization comes to the Second Region.

2900 Kingship in Sumer transferred to Erech. Inanna given dominion over the Third Region; the Indus Valley civilization begins.

2650 Sumer's royal capital shifts about. Kingship deteriorates. Enlil loses patience with the unruly human multitudes.

2371 Inanna falls in love with Sharru-Kin (Sargon). He establishes new capital city, Agade (Akkad). Akkadian empire launched.

2316 Aiming to rule the Four Regions, Sargon removes sacred soil from Babylon. The Marduk-Inanna conflict flares up again. It ends when Nergal, Marduk's brother, journeys from south Africa to Babylon and persuades Marduk to leave Mesopotamia.

2291 Naram-Sin ascends the throne of Akkad. Directed by the warlike Inanna, he penetrates the Sinai peninsula, invades Egypt.

2255 Inanna usurps the power in Mesopotamia; Naram-Sin defiles Nippur. The Great Anunnaki obliterate Agade. Inanna escapes. Sumer and Akkad occupied by foreign troops loyal to Enlil and Ninurta.

2220 Sumerian civilization rises to new heights under enlightened rulers of Lagash. Thoth helps its king Gudea build a ziggurat-temple for Ninurta.

2193 Terah, Abraham's father, born in Nippur into a priestly-royal family.

2180 Egypt divided; followers of Ra/Marduk retain the south; Pharaohs opposed to him gain the throne of lower Egypt.

2130 As Enlil and Ninurta are increasingly away, central authority also deteriorates in Mesopotamia. Inanna's attempt to regain the kingship for Erech does not last.

B.C. **IV. The Fateful Century**

2123 Abraham born in Nippur.

2113 Enlil entrusts the Lands of Shem to Nannar; Ur declared capital of new empire. Ur-Nammu ascends throne, is named Protector of Nippur. A Nippurian priest—Terah, Abraham's father—comes to Ur to liaison with its royal court.

2096 Ur-Nammu dies in battle. The people consider his untimely death a betrayal by Anu and Enlil. Terah departs with his family for Harran.

2095 Shulgi ascends the throne of Ur, strengthens imperial ties. As empire thrives, Shulgi falls under charms of Inanna, becomes her lover. Grants Larsa to Elamites in exchange for serving as his Foreign Legion.

2080 Theban princes loyal to Ra/Marduk press northward under Mentuhotep I. Nabu, Marduk's son, gains adherents for his father in Western Asia.

2055 On Nannar's orders, Shulgi sends Elamite troops to suppress unrest in Canaanite cities. Elamites reach the gateway to the Sinai peninsula and its Spaceport.

2048 Shulgi dies. Marduk moves to the Land of the Hittites. Abraham ordered to southern Canaan with an elite corps of cavalrymen.

2047 Amar-Sin (the biblical Amraphel) becomes king of Ur. Abraham goes to Egypt, stays five years, then returns with more troops.

2041 Guided by Inanna, Amar-Sin forms a coalition of Kings of the East, launches military expedition to Canaan and the Sinai. Its leader is the Elamite Khedorla'omer. Abraham blocks the advance at the gateway to the Spaceport.

2038   Shu-Sin replaces Amar-Sin on throne of Ur as the empire disintegrates.

2029   Ibbi-Sin replaces Shu-Sin. The western provinces tilt increasingly to Marduk.

2024   Leading his followers, Marduk marches on Sumer, enthrones himself in Babylon. Fighting spreads to central Mesopotamia. Nippur's Holy of Holies is defiled. Enlil demands punishment for Marduk and Nabu; Enki opposes, but his son Nergal sides with Enlil.

        As Nabu marshals his Canaanite followers to capture the Spaceport, the Great Anunnaki approve the use of nuclear weapons. Nergal and Ninurta destroy the Spaceport and the errant Canaanite cities.

2023   The winds carry the radioactive cloud to Sumer. People die a terrible death, animals perish, the water is poisoned, the soil becomes barren. Sumer and its great civilization lie prostrate. Its legacy passes to Abraham's seed as he begets—at age 100—a legitimate heir: Isaac.

Sources

In addition to specific references in the text, the following served as principal sources for *The Wars of Gods and Men:*

I. Studies, articles, and reports in various issues of the following periodicals and scholarly series:

Abhandlungen der Deutschen (Preussichen) *Akademie der Wissenschaften zu Berlin* (Berlin)

Abhandlungen der Deutschen Orient-Gesellschaft (Berlin)

Adhandlungen der Heidelberger Akademie der Wissenschaften, Philo.-hist. klasse (Heidelberg)

Adhandlungen für die Kunde des Morgenlandes (Leipzig)

Acta Orientalia (Oslo)

Acta Societatis Scientarium Fennica (Helsinki)

Aegyptologische Forschungen (Hamburg-New York)

Der Alte Orient (Leipzig)

Alter Orient und Altes Testament (Kevalaer/Neukirchen-Vluyn)

Altorientalische Bibliothek (Leipzig)

Altorientalische Furschungen (Leipzig)

Altorientalische Texte und Untersuchungen (Leiden)

Altorientalische Texte zum Alten Testament (Berlin and Leipzig)

American Journal of Archaeology (Concord, Mass.)

American Journal of Semitic Languages and Literature (Chicago)

American Oriental Series (New Haven)

American Philosophical Society, Memoirs and Transactions (Philadelphia)

Analecta Biblica (Rome)

Analecta Orientalia (Rome)

Anatolica (Istanbul)

Anatolian Studies (London)

Annual of the American Schools of Oriental Research (New Haven)

Annual of the Palestine Exploration Fund (London)

The Antiquaries Journal (London)

Antiquités Orientales (Paris)

Antiquity (Gloucester)

Archiv für Keilschriftforschung (Berlin)
Archiv für Orientforschung (Berlin)
Archiv Orientalni (Prague)
The Assyrian Dictionary (Chicago)
Assyriologische Bibliothek (Leipzig)
Assyriological Studies (Chicago)
Ausgaben der Deutschen Orient-Gesellschaft in Assur (Berlin)

Babyloniaca (Paris)
Babylonian Expedition of the University of Pennsylvania: Cunei-form Texts (Philadelphia)
Babylonian Inscriptions in the Collection of J. B. Nies (New Haven)
Babylonian Records in the Library of J. Pierpont Morgan (New Haven)
Beiträge zur Assyriologie und semitischen Sprachwissenschaft (Leipzig)
Berliner Beiträge zur Vor- und Fruhgeschischte (Berlin)
Berliner Beiträge zur Keilschriftforschung (Berlin)
Biblica et Orientalia (Rome)
The Biblical Archaeologist (New Haven)
Biblical Archaeology Review (Washington)
Bibliotheca Mesopotamica (Malibu)
Bibliotheca Orientalis (Leiden)
Bibliothèque de l'École des Hautes Études (Paris)
Boghazköi-Studien (Leipzig)
Die Boghazköi-Texte im Umschrift (Leipzig)
British Schools of Archaeology in Egypt: Egyptian Research Account Publications (London)
Bulletin of the American Schools of Oriental Research (Jerusalem and Baghdad; Baltimore and New Haven)
Bulletin of the Israel Exploration Society (Jerusalem)

Calcutta Sanskrit College Research Series: Studies (Calcutta)
The Cambridge Ancient History (Cambridge)
Chicago University Oriental Institute, Publications (Chicago)
Columbia University Oriental Studies (New York)
Cuneiform Texts from Babylonian Tablets in the British Museum (London)
Cuneiform Texts from Nimrud (London)

Découvertes en Chaldée (Paris)
Deutsche Orient-Gesellschaft, Mitteilungen; Sensdschriften (Berlin)

Deutsches Morgenlandische Gesellschaft, Abhandlungen (Leipzig)

Egypt Exploration Fund, Memoirs (London)
Eretz-Israel: Archaeological, Historical and Geographical Studies (Jerusalem)
Ex Oriente Lux (Leipzig)
Expedition: The Bulletin of the University Museum (Philadelphia)

Forschungen und Fortschritte (Berlin)
France: Délégation en Perse, Mémoires (Paris)
France: Mission Archéologique de Perse, Mémoires (Paris)

Handbuch der Archäologie (München)
Handbuch der Orientalistik (Leiden/Köln)
Harvard Semitic Series (Cambridge, Mass.)
Hebrew Union College Annual (Cincinnati)
Heidelberger Studien zum Alten Orient (Wiesbaden)
Hittite Texts in Cuneiform Character from Tablets in the British Museum (London)

Invenaires des tablettes de Tello (Paris)
Iran (London)
Iranica Antiqua (Leiden)
Iraq (London)
Institut Français d'Archéologie Orientale: Bibliothèque d'Étude, Mémoires (Cairo)
Israel Exploration Journal (Jerusalem)
Israel Oriental Studies (Jerusalem)

Jena University: Texte und Materielen, Frau Prof. Hilprecht Sammlung (Leipzig)
Jewish Palestine Exploration Society, Bulletin (Jerusalem)
Journal of the American Oriental Society (New York and New Haven)
Journal of the Ancient Near Eastern Society of Columbia University (New York)
Journal Asiatique (Paris)
Journal of Biblical Literature and Exegesis (Middletown, Conn.)
Journal of Biblical Literature (Philadelphia)
Journal of Cuneiform Studies (New Haven)
Journal of Egyptian Archaeology (London)
Journal of Jewish Studies (Oxford)
Journal of Near Eastern Studies (Chicago)

Journal of the Palestine Oriental Society (Jerusalem)
Journal of the Royal Asiatic Society (London)
Journal of Sacred Literature and Biblical Record (London)
Journal of Semitic Studies (Manchester)
Journal of the Society of Oriental Research (Chicago)
Journal of the Transactions of the Victoria Institute (London)

Kadmos (Berlin)
Keilinschriftliche Bibliothek (Berlin)
Keilschrifttexte aus Assur historischen Inhalts (Leipzig)
Keilschrifttexte aus Assur religiösen Inhalts (Leipzig)
Keilschrifttexte aus Assur verschiedenen Inhalts (Leipzig)
Keilschrifturkunden aus Boghazköi (Berlin)
Keilschrifttexte aus Boghazköi (Leipzig)
Königliche Museen zu Berlin: Mitteilungen aus den Orientalischen Sammlungen (Berlin)
Königliche Akademie der Wissenschaften zu Berlin: Abhandlungen (Berlin)

Leipziger Semitischen Studien (Leipzig)

Mémoires de la Délégation archéologique en Iran (Paris)
Mesopotamia (Copenhagen)
Mitteilungen der Altorientalischen Gesellschaft (Berlin)
Mitteilungen des Instituts für Orientforschung (Berlin)
Mitteilungen der vorderasiatisch-aegyptischen Gesellschaft (Berlin)
The Museum Journal (Philadelphia)
Museum Monograms, the University Museum (Philadelphia)

Old Testament and Semitic Studies (Chicago)
Oriens (Leiden)
Oriens Antiquus (Rome)
Oriental Institute Publications (Chicago)
Orientalia (Rome)
Orientalische Literaturzeitung (Berlin and Leipzig)
Oxford Editions of Cuneiform Texts (Oxford)

Palestine Exploration Quarterly (London)
Proceedings of the American Philosophical Society (Philadelphia)
Proceedings of the Society of Biblical Archaeology (London)

Publications of the University of Pennsylvania, Series in Philosophy (Philadelphia)

Qadmoniot (Jerusalem)
The Quarterly of the Department of Antiquities in Palestine (Jerusalem)

Reallexikon der Assyriologie und Vorderasiatischen Archäologie (Berlin and Leipzig)
Reallexikon der Vorgeschichte (Berlin)
Recuil de travaux relatifs à la philosophie et à l'archéologie (Paris)
Rencontres Assyriologique Internationales (various venues)
Revue Archéologique (Paris)
Revue d'Assyriologie et d'archéologie orientale (Paris)
Revue biblique (Paris)
Revue hittite et asiatique (Paris)
Revue de l'Histoire des Religions: Annales du Musée Guimet (Paris)

Sächsische Akademie der Wissenschaften: Berichte über die Verhandlungen (Leipzig)
Sächsonische Gesellschaft der Wissenschaft, philo.-hist. Klasse (Leipzig)
Studia Orientalia (Helsinki)
Studia Pohl (Rome)
Studia Semitici (Rome)
Studies in Ancient Oriental Civilizations (Chicago)
Sumer (Baghdad)
Syria (Paris)

Tel-Aviv (Tel-Aviv)
Texte und Materialen der Frau Prof. Hilprecht Collection (Leipzig and Berlin)
Textes cuneiformes (Paris)
Texts from Cuneiform Sources (Locust Valley, N.Y.)
Transactions of the Society of Biblical Archaeology (London)

Universitas Catolica Lovaniensis: Dissertations (Paris)
University Museum Bulletin (Philadelphia)
University Museum, Publications of the Babylonian Section (Philadelphia)
Untersuchungen zur Assyriologie und Vorderasiatischen Archäologie (Berlin)

Ur Excavations (London)
Ur Excavations Texts (London)
Ugarit Forschungen (Münster)
Ugaritica (Paris)

Vetus Testamentum (Leiden)
Vorderasiatisch-Aegyptischen Gesellschaft, Mitteilungen (Leipzig)
Vorderasiatische Bibliothek (Leipzig)
Vorläufiger Bericht uber die Ausgrabungen in Uruk-Warka (Berlin)

Die Welt des Orients (Wuppertal/Göttingen)
Wissenschaftliche Veröffentlichungen der Deutschen Orient-Gesellschaft (Berlin and Leipzig)

Yale Near Eastern Researches (New Haven)
Yale Oriental Series, Babylonian Texts (New Haven)
Yerushalayim (Jerusalem)

Zeitschrift für die altestamentliche Wissenschaft (Giessen/Berlin)
Zeitschrift für Assyriologie (Berlin/Leipzig)
Zeitschrift der Deutschen Morgenländischen Gesellschaft (Leipzig/Wiesbaden)
Zeitschrift für Keilschriftforschung (Leipzig)

II. Individual Works and Studies:

Alster, B. *Dumuzi's Dream*. 1972.
Amiet, P. *Elam*. 1966.
———. *La Glyptique Mesopotamienne Archaique*. 1961.
Andrae, W. *Das Gotteshaus und die Urformen des Bauens im Alten Orient*. 1930.

Barondes, R. *The Garden of the Gods*. 1957.
Barton, G. *The Royal Inscriptions of Sumer and Akkad*. 1929.
Baudissin, W.W. von. *Adonis and Eshmun*. 1911.
Bauer, J. *Altsumerische Wirtschafttexte aus Lagasch*. 1972.
Behrens, H. *Enlil and Ninlil*. 1978.
Berossus. *Fragments of Chaldean History*. 1828.
Borchardt, L. *Die Entstehung der Pyramids*. 1928.
———. *Einiges zur dritten Bauperiode der grossen Pyramide*. 1932.
Borger, R. *Babylonisch-assyrische Lesestücke*. 1963.
Bossert, H.T. *Das Hethitische Pantheon*. 1933.
Breasted, J.H. *Ancient Records of Egypt*. 1906.

Brinkman, J.A. *A Political History of Post-Kassite Babylon.* 1968.

Bruchet, J. *Nouvelles Recherches sur la Grande Pyramide.* 1965.

Brunton, P. *A Search in Secret Egypt.* 1936.

Buccellati, G. *The Amorites of the Ur III Period.* 1966.

Budge, E.A.W. *The Gods of the Egyptians.* 1904.

——. *A History of Egypt.* 1909.

——. *Osiris and the Egyptian Resurrection.* 1911.

Budge, E.A.W. and King, L.W. *Annals of the Kings of Assyria.* 1902.

Cameron, G.G. *A History of Early Iran.* 1936.

Castellino, G. *Two Shulgi Hymns.* 1972.

Chiera, E. *Sumerian Epics and Myths.* 1934.

——. *Sumerian Lexical Texts from the Temple School of Nippur.* 1929.

——. *Sumerian Temple Accounts from Telloh, Jokha and Drehem.* 1922.

——. *Sumerian Texts of Varied Contents.* 1934.

Clay, A.T. *Miscellaneous Inscriptions in the Yale Babylonian Collection.* 1915.

de Clerq, H.F.X. *Collection de Clerq.* 1885–1903.

Cohen, S. *Enmerkar and the Lord of Aratta.* 1973.

Contenau, G. *Manuel d'archéologie orientale.* 1927–47.

——. *Umma sous la Dynastie d'Ur.* 1931.

Cooper, J.S. *The Return of Ninurta to Nippur.* 1978.

Craig, J. *Assyrian and Babylonian Religious Texts.* 1885–87.

Cros, G. *Nouvelles Fouilles de Tello.* 1910.

Davidson, D. and Aldersmith, H. *The Great Pyramid: Its Divine Message.* 1924, 1940.

Deimel, A. *Schultexte aus Fara.* 1923.

——. *Sumerisches Lexikon.* 1925–50.

——. *Veteris Testamenti: Chronologia Monumentis Babyloniaca-Asyrii.* 1912.

——. *Wirtschaftstexte aus Fara.* 1924.

Delaporte, L. *Catalogue des Cylindres Orientaux.* 1920–23.

Dijk, J. van. *Le Motif cosmique dans le pensée Sumeriénne.* 1965.

——. *La sagesse suméro-accadienne.* 1953

Dussaud, R. *Les Découvertes des Ras Shamra (Ugarit) et l'Ancien Testament.* 1937.

——. *Notes de Mythologie Syrienne.* 1905.

Ebeling, E. *Die Akkadische Gebetsserie "Handerhebung."* 1953.

——. *Der Akkadische Mythus vom Pestgotte Era.* 1925.

——. *Keilschrifttexte aus Assur religiösen Inhalts.* 1919, 1923.

——. *Literarische Keilschrifttexte aus Assur.* 1931.

——. *Der Mythus "Herr aller Menschen" vom Pestgotte Ira.* 1926.

——. *Tod und Leben nach den Vorstellungen der Babylonier.* 1931.

Edwards, I.E.S. *The Pyramids of Egypt.* 1947, 1961.

Edzard, D.O. *Sumerische Rechtsurkunden des III Jahrtausend.* 1968.

Erman, A. *The Literature of the Ancient Egyptians.* 1927.

Fairservis, W.A., Jr. *The Roots of Ancient India.* 1971.

Fakhry, A. *The Pyramids.* 1961.

Falkenstein, A. *Archaische Texte aus Uruk.* 1936.

——. *Fluch über Akkade.* 1965.

——. *Die Inschriften Gudeas von Lagash.* 1966.

——. *Literarische Keilschrifttexte aus Uruk.* 1931.

——. *Die neu-sumerischen Gerichtsurkunden.* 1956–57.

——. *Sumerische religiöse Texte.* 1950.

Falkenstein, A. and von Soden, W. *Sumerische und Akkadische Hymnen und Gebete.* 1953.

Falkenstein, A. and van Dijk, J. *Sumerische Gotterlieder.* 1959–60.

Farber-Flügge, G. *Der Mythos "Inanna und Enki."* 1973.

Ferrara, A.J. *Nanna-Suen's Journey to Nippur.* 1973.

Festschrift für Herman Heimpel. 1972.

Forrer, E. *Die Boghazköi-Texte in Umschrift.* 1922–26.

Fossey, G. *La Magie Syrienne.* 1902.

Frankfort, H. *Cylinder Seals.* 1939.

——. *Gods and Myths on Sargonic Seals.* 1934.

——. *Kingship and the Gods.* 1948.

Frankfort, H., et al. *Before Philosophy.* 1946.

Friedrich, J. *Staatsverträge des Hatti Reiches.* 1926–30.

Gadd, C.J. *A Sumerian Reading Book.* 1924.

Gadd, C.J. and Kramer, S.N. *Literary and Religious Texts.* 1963.

Gadd, C.J. and Legrain, L. *Royal Inscriptions from Ur.* 1928.

Gaster, Th. *Myth, Legend and Custom in the Old Testament.* 1969.

Gelb, I.J. *Hittite Hieroglyphic Monuments.* 1939.

Geller, S. *Die Sumerische-Assyrische Serie Lugal-e Me-lam-bi* NIR.GAL. 1917.

Genouillac, H. de *Fouilles de Tello*. 1934–36.

———. *Premières recherches archéologique à Kish*. 1924–25.

———. *Tablettes de Dréhem*. 1911.

———. *Tablettes sumériennes archaique*. 1909.

———. *Textes economiques d'Oumma de l'Epoque d'Our*. 1922.

———. *Textes religieux sumériens du Louvre*. 1930.

———. *La trouvaille de Dréhem*. 1911.

Genoville, H. de *Textes de l'epoque d'Ur*. 1912.

Götze, A. *Hattushilish*. 1925.

———. *Hethiter, Churriter und Assyrer*. 1936.

Graves, R. *The Greek Myths*. 1955.

Grayson, A.K. *Assyrian and Babylonian Chronicles*. 1975.

———. *Babylonian Historical-Literary Texts*. 1975.

Green, M.W. *The Uruk Lament*. 1984.

Gressmann, H. and Ungnad, A. *Altorientalische Texte und Bilder zum Alten Testament*. 1909.

Gurney, O.R. *The Hittites*. 1952.

Gurney, O.R. and Finkelstein, J.J. *The Sultantepe Tablets*. 1957–64.

Güterbock, H.G. *The Deeds of Suppiluliuma*. 1956.

———. *Die historische tradition bei Babylonier und Hethitern*. 1934.

———. *Hittite Mythology*. 1961.

———. *Siegel aus Boghazkoy*. 1940–42.

———. *The Song of Ullikumi*. 1952.

Hallo, W.W. *Women of Sumer*. 1976.

Hallo, W.W. and Dijk, J.J. van. *The Exaltation of Inanna*. 1968.

Harper, E.J. *Die Babylonische Legenden*. 1894.

Haupt, P. *Akkadische und sumerische Keilschrifttexte*. 1881–82.

Hilprecht, H.V. *Old Babylonian Inscriptions*. 1893–96.

Hilprecht Anniversary Volume. 1909.

Hinz, W. *The Lost World of Elam*. 1972.

Hooke, S.H. *Middle Eastern Mythology*. 1963.

Hrozny, B. *Hethitische Keischrifttexte aus Boghazköy*. 1919.

Hussey, M.I. *Sumerian Tablets in the Harvard Semitic Museum*. 1912–15.

Jacobsen, Th. *The Sumerian King List*. 1939.

———. *Towards the Image of Tammuz*. 1970.

———. *The Treasures of Darkness*. 1976.

Jastrow, M. *Die Religion Babyloniers und Assyriers*. 1905.

Jean, C.F. *La religion sumérienne*. 1931.

———. *Shumer et Akkad*. 1923.

Jensen, P. *Assyrisch-Babylonische Mythen und Epen*. 1900.

———. *Der I(U)ra-Mythus*. 1900.

———. *Die Kosmologie der Babylonier*. 1890.

———. *Texte zur Assyrisch-Babylonischen Religion*. 1915.

Jeremias, A. *The Old Testament in the Light of the Ancient Near East*. 1911.

Jirku, A. *Die altste Geschichte Israels*. 1917.

———. *Altorientalischer Kommentar zum Alten Testament*. 1923.

Jones, T.B. and Snyder, J.W. *Sumerian Economic Texts from the Third Ur Dynasty*. 1923.

Josephus, Flavius. *Against Apion*.

———. *Antiquities of the Jews*.

Kärki, I. *Die Sumerische Köingsinschriften der Frühbabylonischen Zeit*. 1968.

Keiser, C.E. *Babylonian Inscriptions in the Collection of J.B. Nies*. 1917.

———. *Patesis of the Ur-Dynasty*. 1919.

———. *Selected Temple Documents of the Ur Dynasty*. 1927.

Keller, W. *The Bible as History in Pictures*. 1963.

Kenyon, K. *Digging Up Jerusalem*. 1974.

King, L.W. *The Annals of the Kings of Assyria*. 1902.

———. *Babylonian Boundary Stones*. 1912.

———. *Babylonian Magic and Sorcery*. 1896.

———. *Babylonian Religion and Mythology*. 1899.

———. *Chronicles Concerning Early Babylonian Kings*. 1907.

———. *Hittite Texts in the Cuneiform Characters*. 1920–21.

Kingsland, W. *The Great Pyramid in Fact and Theory*. 1932–35.

Knudtzon, J.A. *Assyrische Gebete an den Sonnengott*. 1893.

König, F.W. *Handbuch der chaldischen Inschriften*. 1955.

Köppel, R. *Die neuen Ausgrabungen am Tell Ghassul im Jordantal*. 1932.

Kramer, S.N. *Enki and Ninhursag*. 1945.

———. *Lamentation Over the Destruction of Ur*. 1940.

———. *From the Poetry of Sumer*. 1979.

———. *Poets and Psalmists*. 1976.

———. *Sumerian Literature*. 1942.

———. *Sumerian Texts in the Museum of the Ancient Orient, Istanbul*. 1943–49.

——. *Sumerische Literarische Texte aus Nippur.* 1961.
Kramer Anniversary Volume. 1976.

Labat, R. *Manuel d'Epigraphie Akkadienne.* 1963.
Lambert, W.G. *Babylonian Wisdom Literature.* 1960.
Lambert, W.G. and Millard, A.R. *Atra-Hasis, the Babylonian Story of the Flood.* 1969.
Langdon, S. *Babylonian Liturgies.* 1913.
——. *Babylonian Wisdom.* 1923.
——. *"Enuma Elish"—The Babylonian Epic of Creation.* 1923.
——. *Excavations at Kish.* 1924.
——. *Historical and Religious Texts.* 1914.
——. *Semitic Mythology.* 1964.
——. *Sumerian and Babylonian Psalms.* 1909.
——. *The Sumerian Epic of Paradise.* 1915.
——. *Sumerian and Semitic Religious and Historical Texts.* 1923.
——. *Sumerian Liturgical Texts.* 1917.
——. *Sumerian Liturgies and Psalms.* 1919.
——. *Sumerians and Semites in Babylon.* 1908.
——. *Tablets from the Archives of Drehem.* 1911.
——. *Tammuz and Ishtar.* 1914.
Langdon, S. and Gardiner, A.H. *The Treaty of Alliance.* 1920.
Legrain, L. *Historical Fragments.* 1922.
——. *Royal Inscriptions and Fragments from Nippur and Babylon.* 1926.
——. *Les Temps des Rois d'Ur.* 1912.
——. *Ur Excavations.* 1936.
Lepsius, K.R. *Denkmäler aus Aegypten.* 1849–58.
Luckenbill, D.D. *Ancient Records of Assyria and Babylonia.* 1926–27.
——. *Hittite Treaties and Letters.* 1921.
Lutz, H.F. *Selected Sumerian and Babylonian Texts.* 1919.
——. *Sumerian Temple Records of the Late Ur Dynasty.* 1912.

Mazar, B. *The World History of the Jewish People.* 1970.
Mencken, A. *Designing and Building the Great Pyramid.* 1963.
Mercer, S.A.B. *The Tell el-Amarna Tablets.* 1939.
Mortgat, A. *Die Enstehung der sumerischen Hochkultur.* 1945.
——. *Vorderasiatische Rollsiegel.* 1940.
Müller, M. *Asien und Europa nach Altaegyptischer Denkmälern.* 1893.
——. *Der Bündnisvertrag Ramses II und der Chetiterköings.* 1902.
Müller-Karpe, H. *Handbuch der Vorgeschichte.* 1966–68.

Nies, J.B. *Ur Dynasty Tablets.* 1920.

Nies, J.B. and Keiser, C.E. *Historical, Religious and Economic Texts and Antiquities.* 1920.

Oppenheim, A.L. *The Interpretation of Dreams in the Ancient Near East.* 1956.

——. *Mesopotamian Mythology.* 1950.

Oppert, J. *La Chronologie de la Genèse.* 1895.

Otten, H. *Mythen vom Gotte Kumarbi.* 1950.

——. *Die Überlieferung des Telepinu-Mythus.* 1942.

Parrot, A. *The Arts of Assyria.* 1961.

——. *Sumer—the Dawn of Art.* 1961.

——. *Tello.* 1948.

——. *Ziggurats et Tour de Babel.* 1949.

Paul Haupt Anniversary Volume. 1926.

Perring, J.E. *The Pyramids of Gizeh From Actual Survey and Measurement.* 1839.

Petrie, W.M.F. *The Pyramids and Temples of Gizeh.* 1883–85.

——. *Researches on the Great Pyramid.* 1874.

——. *The Royal Tombs of the First Dynasty.* 1900.

Poebel, A. *Historical Texts.* 1914.

——. *Miscellaneous Studies.* 1947.

——. *Sumerische Studien.* 1921.

Pohl, A. *Rechts- und Verwaltungsurkunden der III Dynastie von Ur.* 1937.

Price, I.M. *The Great Cylinder Inscriptions of Gudea.* 1927.

Pritchard, J.B. *The Ancient Near East in Pictures Relating to the Old Testament.* 1969.

——. *Ancient Near Eastern Texts Relating to the Old Testament.* 1969.

Quibell, J.E. *Hierkanopolis.* 1900.

Radau, H. *Early Babylonian History.* 1900.

——. *NIN-IB, The Determiner of Fates.* 1910.

——. *Sumerian Hymns and Prayers to the God Dumuzi.* 1913.

——. *Sumerian Hymns and Prayers to the God Ninib.* 1911.

Rawlinson, H. *The Cuneiform Inscriptions of Western Asia.* 1861–1909.

Rawlinson, H.G. *India.* 1952.

Reiner, E. *Shurpu, A Collection of Sumerian and Akkadian Incantations.* 1958.

Reisner, G. *Sumerisch-Babylonische Hymnen.* 1896.

——. *Tempel-urkunden aus Telloh.* 1901.

Renger, J. *Götternamen in der Altbabylonischen Zeit.* 1967.

Ringgren, K.V.H. *Religions of the Ancient Near East.* 1973.

Roberts, J.J.M. *The Earliest Semitic Religions.* 1972.

Roberts, A. and Donaldson, J. *The Ante-Nicene Fathers.* 1918.

Roux, G. *Ancient Iraq.* 1964.

Rutherford, A. *The Great Pyramid Series.* 1950.

Saggs, H.W.F. *The Encounter with the Divine in Mesopotamia and Israel.* 1976.

——. *The Greatness That Was Babylon.* 1962.

Salonen, A. *Die Landfarhrzeuge des Alten Mesopotamien.* 1951.

——. *Nautica Babyloniaca.* 1942.

——. *Die Waffen der Alten Mesopotamier.* 1965.

——. *Die Wasserfahrzeuge in Babylon.* 1939.

Sayce, A.H. *The Ancient Empires of the East.* 1884.

——. *The Religion of the Ancient Babylonians.* 1888.

Schmandt-Besserat, D. *The Legacy of Sumer.* 1976.

Schnabel, P. *Berossos und die Babylonisch-Hellenistische Literatur.* 1923.

Schneider, N. *Die Drehem- und Djoha-Texte.* 1932.

——. *Die Götternamen von Ur III.* 1939.

——. *Götterschiffe im Ur III-Reich.* 1946.

——. *Die Siegellegenden der Geschäfts-urkunden der Stadt Ur.* 1950.

——. *Die Zeitbestimmungen der Wirtschaftsurkunden von Ur III.* 1936.

Schrader, E. *The Cuneiform Inscriptions and the Old Testament.* 1885.

——. *Die Keilinschriften und das Alte Testament.* 1902.

Schroeder, O. *Keilschrifttexte aus Assur Verschiedenen Inhalts.* 1920.

Scott, J.A. *A Comparative Study of Hesiod and Pindar.* 1898.

Sethe, K.H. *Amun und die Acht Urgotten von Hermopolis.* 1930.

——. *Die Hatschepsut Problem.* 1932.

——. *Urgeschichte und älteste Religion der Aegypter.* 1930.

Sjöberg, A.W. *Der Mondgott Nanna-Suen in der Sumerischen Überlieferung.* 1960.

——. *Nungal in the Ekur.* 1973.

——. *Three Hymns to the God Ningishzida.* 1975.

Smith, S. *A History of Babylon and Assyria.* 1910-28.

Smyth, C.P. *Our Inheritance in the Great Pyramid.* 1877.

Soden, W. von. *Sumerische und Akkadische Hymnen und Gebete.* 1953.

Sollberger, E. *Corpus des inscriptions "royales" présargoniques de Lagash.* 1956.

Speiser, E.A. *Genesis.* 1964.

———. *Mesopotamian Origins.* 1930.

Studies Presented to A. L. Oppenheim. 1964.

Tadmor, H. and Weinfeld, M. *History, Historiography and Interpretation.* 1983.

Tallqvist, K.L. *Akkadische Götterepitheta.* 1938.

———. *Assyrische Beschwörungen, Series Maqlu.* 1895.

Thompson, R.C. *The Devils and Evil Spirits of Babylonia.* 1903.

———. *The Reports of the Magicians and Astrologers of Nineveh and Babylon.* 1900.

Thureau-Dangin, F. *Les cylindres de Gudéa.* 1925.

———. *Les inscriptions de Shumer et Akkad.* 1905.

———. *Recueil des tablettes chaldéennes.* 1903.

———. *Rituels accadiens.* 1921.

———. *Die sumerischen und akkadischen Königsinschriften.* 1907.

———. *Tablettes d'Uruk.* 1922.

Ungnad, A. *Die Religion der Babylonier und Assyrer.* 1921.

Vian, F. *La guerre des Géants.* 1952.

Walcot, P. *Hesiod and the Near East.* 1966.

Ward, W.H. *Hittite Gods in Hittite Art.* 1899.

Weber, O. *Die Literatur der Babylonier und Assyrer.* 1907.

Weiher, E. von. *Der Babylonische Gott Nergal.* 1971.

Wheeler, M. *Early India and Pakistan.* 1959.

———. *The Indus Civilization.* 1968.

Wilcke, C. *Das Lugalbanda Epos.* 1969.

———. *Sumerische literarische Texte.* 1973.

Wilson, J.V.K. and Vanstiphout, H. *The Rebel Lands.* 1979.

Wilson, R.R. *Genealogy and History in the Biblical World.* 1977.

Winckler, H. *Altorientalische Forschungen.* 1897–1906.

———. *Altorientalische Geschichts-Auffassung.* 1906.

———. *Sammlung von Keilschrifttexten.* 1893–95.

Wiseman, D.J. *Chronicles of Chaldean Kings.* 1956.

Witzel, M. *Keilinschriftliche Studien.* 1918–25.

———. *Tammuz-Liturgien und Verwandtes.* 1935.

Woolley, C.L. *Abraham: Recent Discoveries and Hebrew Origins.* 1936.

———. *Excavations at Ur.* 1923.

———. *Ur of the Chaldees.* 1930.

———. *The Ziggurat and Its Surroundings.* 1939.

Zimmern, H. *Sumerische Kultlieder aus altbabylonischer Zeit.* 1912–13.

———. *Zum Babylonischen Neujahrfest.* 1918.

Index

Turn the page
for a revealing sneak preview of

THE
END *of* DAYS

by
Zecharia Sitchin,
the 7th and concluding book of
THE EARTH CHRONICLES
now available in hardcover
from William Morrow,
an imprint of HarperCollins Publishers

FOREWORD: THE PAST, THE FUTURE

"When will they return?"

I have been asked this question countless times by people who have read my books, the "they" being the Anunnaki—the extraterrestrials who had come to Earth from their planet Nibiru and were revered in antiquity as gods. Will it be when Nibiru in its elongated orbit returns to our vicinity, and what will happen then? Will there be darkness at noon and the Earth shall shatter? Will it be Peace on Earth, or Armageddon? A Millennium of trouble and tribulations, or a messianic Second Coming? Will it happen in 2012, or later, or not at all?

These are profound questions that combine people's deepest hopes and anxieties with religious beliefs and expectations, questions compounded by current events: Wars in lands where the entwined affairs of gods and men began; the threats of nuclear holocausts; the alarming ferocity of natural disasters. They are questions that I dared not answer all these years—but now are questions the answers to which cannot—must not—be delayed.

Questions about the Return, it ought to be realized, are not new; they have inexorably been linked in the past—as they are today—to the expectation and the apprehension of the Day of the Lord, the End of Days, Armageddon. Four millennia ago, the Near East witnessed a god and his son promising Heaven on Earth. More than three millennia ago, king and people in Egypt yearned for a messianic time. Two millennia ago, the people of Judea wondered whether the Messiah had appeared, and we are still seized with the mysteries of those events. Are prophecies coming true?

We shall deal with the puzzling answers that were given, solve ancient enigmas, decipher the origin and meaning of symbols—the Cross, the Fishes, the Chalice. We shall describe the role of space-related sites in historic events, and show why Past, Present, and Future converge in Jerusalem, the place of the "Bond Heaven-Earth." And we shall ponder why it is that our current twenty-first century A.D. is so similar to the twenty-first century B.C. Is history repeating itself? Is it destined to repeat itself? Is it all guided by a Messianic Clock? Is the time at hand?

More than two millennia ago, Daniel of Old Testament fame repeatedly asked the angels: *When?* When will be the End of Days,

The End of Days

the End of Time? More than three centuries ago the famed Sir Isaac Newton, who elucidated the secrets of celestial motions, composed treatises on the Old Testament's Book of Daniel and the New Testament's Book of Revelation; his recently found handwritten calculations concerning the End of Days will be analyzed, along with more recent predictions of The End.

Both the Hebrew Bible and the New Testament asserted that the secrets of the Future are imbedded in the Past, that the destiny of Earth is connected to the Heavens, that the affairs and fate of Mankind are linked to those of God and gods. In dealing with what is yet to happen, we cross over from history to prophecy; one cannot be understood without the other, and we shall report them both.

It is with that as our guide, let us look at what is to come through the lens of what had been. The answers will be certain to surprise.

Zecharia Sitchin
New York, August 2006

CHAPTER I: THE MESSIANIC CLOCK

Wherever one turns, humankind appears seized with Apocalyptic trepidation, Messianic fervor, and End of Time anxiety.

Religious fanaticism manifests itself in wars, rebellions, and the slaughter of "infidels." Armies amassed by Kings of the West are warring with Kings of the East. A Clash of Civilizations shakes the foundations of traditional ways of life. Carnage engulfs cities and towns; the high and the mighty seek safety behind protective walls. Natural calamities and ever-intensifying catastrophies leave people wondering: Has Mankind sinned, is it witnessing Divine Wrath, is it due for another annihilating Deluge? Is this the Apocalypse? Can there be—will there be—Salvation? Are Messianic times afoot?

The time—the twenty-first century A.D., or was it the twenty-first century B.C.?

The correct answer is Yes and Yes, both in our own time as well as in those ancient times. It is the condition of the present time, as well as at a time more than four millennia ago; and the amazing similarity is due to events in the middle-time in-between—the period associated with the messianic fervor at the time of Jesus.

Those three cataclysmic periods for Mankind and its planet—two in the recorded past (circa 2100 B.C. and when B.C. changed to A.D.), one in the nearing future—are interconnected; one has led to the other, one can be understood only by understanding the other. The Present stems from the Past, the Past is the Future. Essential to all three is **Messianic Expectation**; and linking all three is **Prophecy**.

How the present time of troubles and tribulations will end—what the Future portends—requires entering the realm of Prophecy. Ours will not be a melange of newfound predictions whose main magnet is fear of doom and End, but a reliance upon unique ancient records that documented the Past, predicted the Future, and recorded previous Messianic expectations—prophesying the future in antiquity, and, one believes, the Future that is to come.

In all three apocalyptic instances—the two that had occurred, the one that is about to happen—the physical and spiritual relationship between Heaven and Earth was and remains pivotal for the events. The physical aspects were expressed by the existence on Earth of actual sites that linked Earth with the heavens—sites that were deemed crucial, that were focuses of the events; the spiritual aspects have been expressed in what we call Religion. In all three instances, a changed relationship between Man and God was central; except that when, circa 2100 B.C., Mankind faced the first of these three epochal upheavals, the relationship was between men and *gods*, in the plural. Whether that relationship has really changed, the reader will soon discover.

The story of the gods, the **Anunnaki** ("Those who from heaven to Earth came"), as the Sumerians called them, begins with their coming to Earth from **Nibiru** in need of gold. The story of their planet was told in antiquity in the *Epic of Creation*, a long text on seven tablets; it is usually considered to be an allegorical myth, the product of primitive minds that spoke of planets as living gods combating each other. But as I have shown in my book *The Twelfth Planet*, the ancient text is in fact a sophisticated cosmogony that tells how a stray planet, passing by our solar system, collided with a planet called Tiamat; the collision resulted in the creation of Earth and its Moon, of the Asteroid Belt and comets, and in the capture of the invader itself in a great elliptical orbit that takes about 3,600 Earth years to complete (Fig. 1 in the hardcover edition).

It was, Sumerian texts tell, 120 such orbits—432,000 Earth years—prior to the Deluge (the "Great flood") that the Anunnaki came to Earth. How and why they came, their first cities in the E.DIN (the biblical Eden), their fashioning of the Adam and the reasons for it, and the events of the catastrophic Deluge—have all been told in *The Earth Chronicles* series of my books and will not be repeated here. But before we time-travel to the momentous twenty-first century B.C., some pre-Diluvial and post-Diluvial landmark events need to be recalled.

The biblical tale of the Deluge, starting in chapter 6 of Genesis, ascribes its conflicting aspects to a sole deity, Yahweh, who at first is determined to wipe Mankind off the face of the Earth, and then goes out of his way to save it through Noah and the Ark. The earlier Sumerian sources of the tale ascribe the disaffection with Mankind to the god **Enlil** and the counter-effort to save Mankind to the god **Enki**. What the Bible glossed over for the sake of Monotheism was not just the disagreement between the Enlil and Enki, but a rivalry and a conflict between two clans of Anunnaki that dominated the course of subsequent events on Earth.

The Messianic Clock

That conflict between the two and their offspring, and the Earth regions allocated to them after the Deluge, need to be kept in mind to understand all that happened thereafter.

The two were half-brothers, sons of Nibiru's ruler **Anu**; their conflict on Earth had its roots on their home planet, Nibiru. Enki—then called E.A ("He whose home is Water")—was Anu's firstborn son, but not by the official spouse, Antu. When Enlil was born to Anu by Antu—a half-sister of Anu—Enlil became the Legal Heir to Nibiru's throne though he was not the firstborn son. The unavoidable resentment on the part of Enki and his maternal family was exacerbated by the fact that Anu's accession to the throne was problematic to begin with: Having lost out in a succession struggle to a rival named Alalu, he later usurped the throne in a coup-d'etat, forcing Alalu to flee Nibiru for his life. That not only backtracked Ea's resentments to the days of his forebears, but also brought about other challenges to the leadership of Enlil, as told in the epic *Tale of Anzu*. (For the tangled relationships of Nibiru's royal families and the ancestries of Anu and Antu, Enlil and Ea, see *The Lost Book of Enki*).

The key to unlocking the mystery of the gods' succession (and marriage) rules was my realization that these rules also applied to the people chosen by them to serve as their proxies to Mankind. It was the biblical tale of the Patriarch Abraham explaining (*Genesis* 20:12) that he did not lie when he had presented his wife Sarah as his sister: "Indeed, she is my sister, the daughter of my father, but not the daughter of my mother, and she became my wife." Not only was marrying a half-sister from a different mother permitted, but a son by her—in this case Isaac—became the Legal Heir and dynastic successor, rather the Firstborn Ishmael, the son of the handmaiden Hagar. (How such succession rules caused the bitter feud between Ra's divine descendants in Egypt, the half-brothers Osiris and Seth who married the half-sisters Isis and Nephtys, is explained in *The Wars of Gods and Men*).

Though those succession rules appear complex, they were based on what those who write about royal dynasties call "bloodlines"— what we now should recognize as sophisticated DNA genealogies that also distinguished between general DNA inherited from the parents as well as the mtDNA that is inherited by females only from the mother. The complex yet basic rule was this: Dynastic lines continue through the male line; the Firstborn son is next in succession; a half-sister could be taken as wife *if she had a different mother;* and if a son by such a half-sister is later born, that son—though not Firstborn—became the Legal Heir and the dynastic successor.

The rivalry between the two half-brothers Ea/Enki and Enlil in matters of the throne was complicated by personal rivalry in matters of the heart. They both coveted their half-sister **Ninmah**, whose mother was yet another concubine of Anu. She was Ea's true love, but he was not permitted to marry her. Enlil then took over and had a son by her—**Ninurta**. Though born without wedlock, the succession rules made Ninurta Enlil's uncontested heir, being both his Firstborn son and one born by a royal half-sister.

Ea, as related in *The Earth Chronicles* books, was the leader of the first group of fifty Anunnaki to come to Earth to obtain the gold needed to protect Nibiru's dwindling atmosphere. When the initial plans failed, his half-brother Enlil was sent to Earth with more Anunnaki for an expanded Mission Earth. If that was not enough to create a hostile atmosphere, Ninmah too arrived on Earth to serve as chief medical officer . . .

A long text known as the *Atrahasis Epic* begins the story of gods and men on Earth with a visit by Anu to Earth to settle once and for all (he hoped) the rivalry between his two sons that was ruining the vital mission; he even offered to stay on Earth and let one of the half-brothers assume the regency on Nibiru. With that in mind, the ancient text tells us, lots were drawn to determine who shall stay on Earth and who shall sit on Nibiru's throne:

> The gods clasped hands together,
> had cast lots and had divided:
> Anu went up [back] to heaven,
> [For Enlil] the Earth was made subject;
> The seas, enclosed as with a loop,
> to Enki the prince were given.

The result of drawing lots, then, was that Anu returned to Nibiru as its king. Ea, given dominion over the seas and waters (in later times, "Poseidon" to the Greeks and "Neptune" to the Romans), was granted the epithet EN.KI ("Lord of Earth") to soothe his feelings; but it was EN.LIL ("Lord of the Command") who was put in overall charge: "To him the Earth was made subject." Resentful or not, Ea/Enki could not defy the rules of succession or the results of the drawing of lots; and so the resentment, the anger at justice denied, and a consuming determination to avenge injustices to his father and forefathers and thus to himself, led Enki's son **Marduk** to take up the fight.

Several texts describe how the Anunnaki set up their settlemernts in the E.DIN (The post-Diluvial Sumer), each with a specific function, and all laid out in accordance with a master plan. The crucial space connection—the ability to constantly stay in communication with the home planet and with the shuttlecraft and spacecraft—was maintained from Enlil's command post in **Nippur**, the heart of which was a dimly lit chamber called the DUR.AN.KI, "The Bond Heaven-Earth." Another vital facility was a spaceport, located at Sippar ("Bird City"). Nippur lay at the center of concentric circles at which the other "cities of the gods" were located; all together they shaped out, for an arriving spacecraft, a landing corridor whose focal point was the Near East's most visible topographic feature—the twin peaks of Mount Ararat (Fig. 2 in the hardcover edition).

And then the Deluge "swept over the earth," obliterated all the cities of the gods with their Mission Control Center and Spaceport, and buried the Edin under millions of tons of mud and silt. Everything had to be done all over again—but much could no longer be the same. First and foremost, it was necessary to create a new spaceport facility, with a new Mission Control Center and new beacon-sites for a Landing Corridor. The new landing path was anchored again on the prominent twin peaks of Ararat; the other components were all new: The actual spaceport in the Sinai Peninsula, on the 30th parallel north; artificial twin peaks as beacon-sites, the Giza pyramids; and a new Mission Control Center at a place called Jerusalem (Fig. 3 in the hardcover edition). It was a layout that played a crucial role in post-Diluvial events.

The Deluge was a watershed (both literally and figuratively) in the affairs of both gods and men, and in the relationship between the two: The Earthlings, who were fashioned to serve and work for the gods, were henceforth treated as junior partners on a devastated planet.

The new relationship between men and gods was formulated, sanctified and codified when Mankind was granted its first high civilization, in Mesopotamia, circa 3800 B.C. The momentous event followed a state visit to Earth by Anu, not just as Nibiru's ruler but also as the head of the pantheon, on Earth, of the ancient gods.

Another (and probably the main) reason for his visit was the establishment and affirmation of peace among the gods themselves—a live-and-let-live arrangement by dividing the lands of the Old World among the two principal Anunnaki clans—that of Enlil and that of Enki; for the new post-Diluvial circumstances and the new location of the space facilities required a new territorial division among the gods.

It was a division that was reflected in the biblical Table of Nations (*Genesis*, chapter 10), in which the spread of Mankind, emanating from the three sons of Noah, was recorded by nationality and geography: Asia to the nations/lands of Shem, Europe to the descendants of Japhet, Africa to the nation/lands of Ham. The historical records show that the parallel division among the gods allotted the first two to the Enlilites, the third one to Enki and his sons. The connecting Sinai peninsula, where the vital post-Diluvial spaceport was located, was set aside as a neutral Sacred Region.

While the Bible simply listed the lands and nations according to their Noahite division, the earlier Sumerian texts recorded the fact that the division was a deliberate act, the result of deliberations by the leadership of the Anunnaki. A text known as the *Epic of Etana* tells us that

> The great Anunnaki who decree the fates
> sat exchanging their counsels regarding the Earth.
> They created the four regions,
> set up the settlements.

In the First Region, the lands between the two rivers Euphrates and Tigris (Mesopotamia), Man's first known high civilization, that of Sumer, was established. Where the pre-Diluvial cities of the gods had been, Cities of Man arose, each with its sacred precinct where a deity resided in his or her ziggurat—Enlil in Nippur, Ninmah in Shuruppak, Ninurta in Lagash, **Nannar/Sin** in Ur, **Inanna/Ishtar** in Uruk, **Utu/Shamash** in Sippar, and so on. In each such urban center an EN.SI, a "Righteous Shepherd"—initially a chosen demigod—was selected to govern the people in behalf of the gods; his main assignment was to promulgate codes of justice and morality. In the sacred precinct, a priesthood overseen by a high priest served the god and his spouse, supervised the holiday celebrations, and handled the rites of offerings, sacrifices and prayers to the gods. Art and sculpture, music and dance, poetry and hymns, and above all writing and recordkeeping flourished in the temples and extended to the royal palace.

From time to time one of those cities was selected to serve as the land's capital; there the ruler was king, LU.GAL ("Great man"). Initially and for a long time thereafter this person, the most powerful man in the land, served as both king and high priest. He was carefully chosen, for his role and authority, and all the physical symbols of Kingship, were deemed to have come to Earth directly from Heaven, from Anu on Nibiru. A Sumerian text dealing with the subject stated that before the symbols of Kingship (tiara/crown and scepter) and of Righteousness (the shepherd's staff) were granted to an earthly king, they "lay deposited before Anu in heaven." Indeed, the Sumerian word for Kingship was *Anuship*.

This aspect of "Kingship" as the essence of civilization, just behavior and a moral code for Mankind, was explicitly expressed in the statement, in the Sumerian King Lists, that after the Deluge *"Kingship was brought down from Heaven."* It is a profound statement that must be borne in mind as we progress in this book to the messianic expectations—in the words of the New Testament, for the **Return of the "Kingship of Heaven" to Earth.**

Circa 3100 B.C. a similar yet not identical civilization was established in the Second Region in Africa, that of the river Nile (Nubia and Egypt). Its history was not as harmonious as that among the Enlilites, for rivalry and contention continued among Enki's six sons, to whom not cities but whole land domains were allocated. Paramount was an ongoing conflict between Enki's firstborn **Marduk** (*Ra* in Egypt) and **Ningishzidda** (*Thoth* in Egypt), a conflict that led to the exile of Thoth and a band of African followers to the New World (where he became known as *Quetzaloatl*, the Winged Serpent). Marduk/Ra himself was punished and exiled when, opposing the marriage of his young brother Dumuzi to Enlil's granddaughter Inanna/Ishtar, he caused his brother's death. It was as compensation to Inanna/Ishtar that she was granted dominion over the Third Region of civilization, that of the Indus Valley, circa 2900 B.C. It was for good reason that the three civilizations—as was the spaceport in the sacred region—were all centered on the 30th parallel north (Fig. 4 in the hardcover edition).

According to Sumerian texts, the Anunnaki established Kingship—civilization and its institutions, as most clearly exemplified in Mesopotamia—as a new order in their relationships with Mankind, with kings/priests serving both as a link and a separator between gods and men. But as one looks back on that seemingly "golden age" in the affairs of gods and men, it becomes evident that the affairs of the gods constantly dominated and determined the affairs of Men and the fate of Mankind. Overshadowing all was the determination of Marduk/Ra to undo the injustice done to his father Ea/Enki, when under the succession rules of the Anunnaki not Enki but Enlil was declared the Legal Heir of their father Anu, the ruler on their home planet Nibiru.

In accord with the sexagesimal ("base sixty") mathematical system that the gods granted the Sumerians, the twelve great gods of the Sumerian pantheon were given numerical ranks in which Anu held the supreme Rank of Sixty; the Rank of Fifty was granted to Enlil; that of Enki was 40, and so farther down, alternating between male and female deities (Fig. 5 in the hardcover edition). Under the succession rules, Enlil's son Ninurta was in line for the rank of 50 on Earth, while Marduk held a nominal rank of 10; and initially these two successors-in-waiting were not yet part of the twelve "Olympians."

And so, the long, bitter and relentness struggle by Marduk that began with the Enlil-Enki feud focused later on Marduk's contention with Enil's son Ninurta for the succession to the Rank of Fifty, and then extended to Enlil's granddaughter Inanna/Ishtar whose marriage to Dumuzi, Enki's youngest son, was so opposed by Marduk that it ended with Dumuzi's death. In time Marduk/Ra faced conflicts even with other brothers and half-brothers of his, in addition to the conflict with Thoth that we have already mentioned—principally with Enki's son Nergal who married a granddaughter of Enlil named Ereshkigal.

In the course of these struggles, the conflicts at times flared up to full-fledged wars between the two divine clans; some of those wars are called "The Pyramid Wars" in my book *The Wars of Gods and Men*. In one notable instance the fighting led to the burying alive of Marduk inside the Great Pyramid; in another, it led to its capture by Ninurta. Marduk was also exiled, more than once—both as punishment and as a self-imposed absence. His persistent efforts to attain the status to which he believed he was entitled included the event recorded in the Bible as the Tower of Babel incident; but in the end, after numerous frustrations, success came only when Earth and Heaven were aligned with the **Messianic Clock**.

Indeed, the first cataclysmic set of events, in the twenty-first

The Messianic Clock

century B.C., and the Messianic expectations that accompanied it,
is principally the story of Marduk; it also brought to center stage
his son **Nabu**—a deity, the son of a god, but whose mother was
an Earthling.

Throughout the history of Sumer that spanned almost two
thousand years, its royal capital shifted—from the first one, Kish
(Ninurta's first city) to Uruk (the city that Anu granted to Inanna/
Ishtar) to Ur (Sin's seat and center of worship); then to others and
then back to the initial ones; and finally, for the third time, back to
Ur. But at all times Enlil's city Nippur, his "cult center" as scholars
are wont to call it, remained the religious center of Sumer and the
Sumerian people; it was there that the annual cycle of worshipping
the gods was determined.

The twelve "Olympians" of the Sumerian pantheon, each with
his or her celestial counterpart among the twelve members of
the Solar System (Sun, Moon and ten planets, including Nibiru),
were also honored with one month each in the annual cycle of a
twelve-month year. The Sumerian term for "month," EZEN, actually meant holiday, festival; and each such month was devoted to
celebrating the worship-festival of one of the twelve supreme gods.
It was the need to determine the exact time when each such month
began and ended (and not in order to enable peasants to know
when to sow or harvest, as schoolbooks explain) that led to the
introduction of *Mankind's first calendar* in **3760** B.C. It is known
as the **Calendar of Nippur** because it was the task of its priests to
determine the calendar's intricate timetable and to announce, for
the whole land, the time of the religious festivals. That calendar is
still in use to this day as the Jewish religious calendar which, in
A.D. 2006, numbered the year as 5766.

In pre-Diluvial times Nippur served as Mission Control Center,
Enlil's command post where he set up the DUR.AN.KI, the "Bond
Heaven-Earth" for the communications with the home planet
Nibiru and with the spacecraft connecting them. (After the Deluge,
these functions were relocated to a place later known as Jerusalem).
Its central position, equidistant from the other functional centers in
the E.DIN (*see* Fig. 2), was also deemed to be equidistant from the
"four corners of the Earth" and gave it the nickname *"Navel of the
Earth."* A hymn to Enlil referred to Nippur and its functions thus:

The End of Days

Enlil,
When you marked off divine settlements on Earth,
Nippur you set up as your very own city...
You founded the Dur-An-Ki
In the center of the four corners of the Earth.

(The term "the Four Corners of the Earth" is also found in the Bible; and when Jerusalem replaced Nippur as Mission Control Center after the Deluge, it too was nicknamed the Navel of the Earth).

In Sumerian the term for the four regions of the Earth was UB, but it also is found as AN.UB—the heavenly, the *celestial* four "corners"—in this case an astronomical term connected with the calendar. It is taken to refer to the four points in the Earth-Sun annual cycle that we nowadays call the Summer Solstice, the Winter Solstice, and the two crossing of the equator—once as the Spring Equinox and then as the Autumnal Equinox. In the Calendar of Nippur, the year began on the day of the Spring Equinox and it has so remained in the ensuing calendars of the ancient Near East. That determined the time of the most important festival of the year—the New Year festival, an event that lasted ten days during which detailed and canonized rituals had to be followed.

Determining calendrical time by Heliacal Rising entailed the observation of the skies at dawn, when the sun just begins to rise on the eastern horizon but the skies are still dark enough to show the stars in the background. The day of the equinox having been determined by the fact that on it daylight and nighttime were precisely equal, the position of the sun at heliacal rising was then marked by the erection of a stone pillar to guide future observations—a procedure that was followed, for example, later on at Stonehenge in Britain; and, as at Stonehenge, long term observations revealed that the group of stars ("constellation") in the background has not remained the same (Fig. 6 in the hardcover edition); there, the alignment stone called the "Heel Stone" that points to sunrise on solstice day nowadays pointed originally to sunrise circa 2000 B.C.

The phenomenon, called Precession of the Equinoxes or just Precession, results from the fact that as the Earth completes one annual orbit around the Sun, it does not return to the same exact celestial spot. There is a slight, very slight retardation; it amounts to one degree (out of 360 in the circle) in 72 years. It was Enki who first grouped the stars observable from Earth into "constellations," and divided the heavens in which the Earth circled the sun into twelve parts—what has since been called the Zodiacal Circle of constellations (Fig. 7 in the hardcover edition). Since each twelfth part of the circle occupied 30 degrees of the celestial arc, the retardation or Precessional shift from one Zodiacal House to another lasted (mathematically) **2160** years (72 x 30), and a complete zodiacal cycle lasted 25,920 years (2160 x 12). The approximate dates of the **Zodiacal Ages**—following the equal twelve-part division and not actual astronomical observations—have been added here for the readere's guidance.

That this was the achievement from a time preceding Mankind's civilizations is attested by the fact that a zodiacal calendar was applied to Enki's first stays on Earth (when the first two zodiacal houses were named in his honor); that this was not the achievement of a Greek astronomer (Hipparchus) in the third century B.C. (as most textbooks still suggest) is attested by the fact that the twelve zodiacal houses were known to the Sumerians millennia earlier by names (Fig. 8 in the hardcover edition) and depictions (Fig. 9 in the hardcover edition) that we use to this day.

In *When Time Began* the calendrical timetables of gods and men were discussed at length. Having come from Nibiru, whose orbital period, the SAR, meant 3,600 (Earth-) years, that unit was naturally the first calendrical yardstick of the Anunnaki even on the fast-orbiting Earth. Indeed, the texts dealing with their early days on Earth, such as the Sumerian King Lists, designated the periods of this or that leader's time on Earth in terms of Sars. I termed this **Divine Time**. The calendar granted to Mankind, one based on the orbital aspects of the Earth (and its Moon), was named **Earthly Time**. Pointing out that the 2160-year zodiacal shift (less than a year for the Anunnaki) offered them a better ratio—the "golden ratio" of 10:6—between the two extremes; I called this time unit **Celestial Time**.

As Marduk discovered, that Celestial Time was the "clock" by which his destiny was to be determined.

But which was **Mankind's Messianic Clock**, determining its fate and destiny—*Earthly Time*, such as the count of fifty-year Jubilees, a count in centuries, or the Millennium? Was it *Divine Time*, geared to Nibiru's orbit? Or was it—is it—*Celestial Time* that follows the slow rotation of the zodiacal clock?

The quandary, as we shall see, baffled Mankind in antiquity; it still lies at the core of the current Return issue. The question that

The End of Days

is posed has been asked before—by Babylonian and Assyrian star-gazing priests, by biblical Prophets, in the Book of Daniel, in the Revelation of St. John the Divine, by the likes of Sir Isaac Newton, by all of us today.

The answer will be astounding. Let us embark on the painstaking quest.